Yet More Adventures with Britannia

YET MORE ADVENTURES WITH

*B*RITANNIA

Personalities, Politics and Culture in Britain

Edited by Wm. Roger Louis

I.B. TAURIS

LONDON · NEW YORK

HRC HARRY RANSOM CENTER

Published in 2005 by I.B.Tauris & Co Ltd
6 Salem Road, London W2 4BU
In the United States of America and Canada distributed by
Palgrave Macmillan a division of St. Martin's Press
175 Fifth Avenue, New York NY 10010
www.ibtauris.com

Harry Ransom Humanities Research Center
The University of Texas at Austin
P.O. Drawer 7219
Austin, Texas 78713-7219

The paper used in this publication meets the minimum requirements of
American National Standard for Information Sciences—Permanence of
Paper for Printed Library Materials

ISBN 1-84511-082-X hardcover
ISBN 1-84511-092-7 paperback

Library of Congress Control Number 2005921640

Typeset, printed, and bound by Capital Spectrum and CSI, Inc.
Austin, Texas

Table of Contents

List of Authors

Antony Best is Senior Lecturer in International History at the London School of Economics. His books include *Britain, Japan and Pearl Harbor: Avoiding War in East Asia 1936–41* (1995) and *British Intelligence and the Japanese Challenge in Asia, 1914–1941* (2002). He is also co-author (with Jussi Hanhimaki, Joseph Maiolo, and Kirsten Schulze) of *International History of the Twentieth Century* (2004).

Brian Bond of King's College, London, is President of the British Commission for Military History. His books include *Liddell Hart: A Study of his Military Thought* (1977) and *The Unquiet Western Front: Britain's Role in Literature and History* (2002). His most recent publication, as editor and contributor, is *British and Japanese Military Leadership in the Far Eastern War, 1941–1945* (2004).

David Cannadine is the Queen Elizabeth the Queen Mother Professor of British History at the Institute of Historical Research, University of London. His books include *The Decline and Fall of the British Aristocracy* (1990); *G. M. Trevelyan: A Life in History* (1992); *Class in Britain* (1998); *Ornamentalism: How the British Saw their Empire* (2001); and *In Churchill's Shadow: Confronting the Past in Modern Britain* (2002).

Anne Chisholm is a biographer and reviewer who has worked in journalism and publishing. Her books include *Philosophers of the Earth: Conversations with Ecologists* (1972); *Nancy Cunard* (1979), *Beaverbrook* (written with her husband, Michael Davie, 1992) and *Rumer Godden: A Storyteller's Life* (1998). She is at work on Frances Partridge's biography. She is a Fellow of the Royal Society of Literature.

James Currey began his career in publishing with Oxford University Press in Cape Town in the early 1960s. He became Editorial Director of Heinemann's Africa series in 1967; with African colleagues he published some 250 volumes. In 1985 he started the African publishing house James Currey Publishers. In 2000 the African Studies Association of the United States gave him a special award—the first ever bestowed on a publisher.

Alex Danchev is Professor of International Relations at the University of Nottingham. His biographical studies include *Very Special*

Relationship: Field Marshal Sir John Dill and the Anglo-American Alliance, 1941–44 (1986) and *Oliver Franks: Founding Father* (1993). He is the editor (with Daniel Todman) of the unexpurgated *Alanbrooke Diaries*. His latest books are *The Iraq War and Democratic Politics* (2004) and *Georges Braque: A Life* (2005).

John Darwin is Beit Lecturer in the History of the British Commonwealth at Oxford and a Fellow of Nuffield College. His books include *Britain, Egypt, and the Middle East: Imperial Policy in the Aftermath of War, 1918–1922*; and *Britain and Decolonisation: The Retreat from Empire in the Post-War World.* He was a student of Jack Gallagher.

Richard Drayton is Senior University Lecturer in Imperial and Extra-European History since 1500 at Cambridge University and a Fellow of Corpus Christi College. His books include *Nature's Government: Science, Imperial Britain and the 'Improvement' of the World* (2000), which won the Forkosch Prize of the American Historical Association. He is currently writing a history of the Caribbean.

Niall Ferguson is Professor of History at Harvard University. His books include *The World's Banker: The History of the House of Rothschild* (1998); *The Pity of War: Explaining World War One* (1998); *Virtual History: Alternatives and Counterfactuals* (1999); *Empire: The Rise and Demise of the British World Order and the Lessons for Global Power* (2003); and *Colossus: The Price of America's Empire* (2004).

S. J. D. Green is a Fellow of All Souls College, Oxford. His books include *Religion in The Age of Decline* (1996) and, edited with R. C. Whiting, *The Boundaries of The State in Modern Britain* (1996). He is also the author of numerous essays on modern Church history and the history of political thought. His study, *The Secularization of Protestant England, 1920–1960*, is forthcoming from Cambridge University Press.

Gertrude Himmelfarb, formerly of the Graduate School of the City University of New York, has a long-standing interest in Victorian history and culture. Her most recent book is *The Roads to Modernity: The British, French, and American Enlightenments* (2004). Among her other books are *The New History and the Old* (rev. edn., 2004), *One Nation, Two Cultures* (1999), and *The De-Moralization of Society: From Victorian Virtues to Modern Values* (1995).

Dan Jacobson of University College, London, is a novelist and critic. Born and brought up in South Africa, he holds an Honorary D.Litt.

from Witwatersrand University. His autobiography *Time and Time* (1985) won the J. R. Ackerley Prize. His novels include *The Confessions of Josef Baisz* (1977) and his criticism, *Adult Pleasures* (1988). His memoir *Heshel's Kingdom* was published in 1998. His most recent novel *All for Love* has just been published in London by Hamish Hamilton.

Scott Lucas is Professor of American Studies at the University of Birmingham. His books include *Divided We Stand: Britain, the US, and the Suez War* (1991); *Freedom's War: The US Crusade against the Soviet Union* (1999); *George Orwell: Life and Times* (2003); and *The Betrayal of Dissent: Beyond Orwell, Hitchens, and the New American Century* (2004). He is now working on a study of the conflict between power and liberation in US foreign policy since 1945.

Deirdre McMahon studied at University College Dublin and Churchill College, Cambridge. Her main areas of research are Anglo-Irish relations, Ireland and the Commonwealth, and Irish-Indian relations. Her books include *Republicans and Imperialists: Anglo-Irish Relations in the 1930s* (1984), and the edited letters of *The Moynihan Brothers in Peace and War* (2004). She is a Lecturer in History at Mary Immaculate College, University of Limerick.

Erez Manela studied as an undergraduate at the Hebrew University and then pursued his Ph.D. at Yale University, where he worked under John Gaddis and Paul Kennedy. He is now Assistant Professor of History at Harvard University. His book, *The Wilsonian Moment*, which utilizes sources in Arabic and Chinese as well as French, will be published in 2006 by Oxford University Press.

Ferdinand Mount was editor of the *Times Literary Supplement* 1991–2002. Before his editorship at the *TLS*, he worked for the *Sunday Telegraph*, *The Times*, the *Spectator*, the *Daily Telegraph*, and the *Sunday Times*. His books include *Of Love and Asthma* (1991), winner of the Hawthornden Prize, and *The British Constitution Now* (1992). His essay, "Mind the Gap: The New Class Divide in Britain," and his new novel, *Heads You Win*, were both published in 2004.

Patrick O'Brien, F.B.A., is Centennial Professor of Economic History at the London School of Economics and Convenor of the Global Economic History Network in the LSE Department of Economic History. He is the author of *The Economic Effects of the American Civil*

War (1988) and editor of *The Industrial Revolution in Europe* (vols. 4 and 5). He is a past President of the Economic History Society.

Bernard Porter of Newcastle University has also taught at Yale. Among his books are *Critics of Empire* (1968); *Plots and Paranoia: A History of Political Espionage in Britain* (1989); *The Lion's Share: A Short History of British Imperialism* (4th edn., 2004); and *The Absent-Minded Imperialists: Empire, Society, and Culture in Britain* (2004). He has published works on the British secret services and the history of Britain and Europe.

Avi Shlaim is Professor of International Relations at Oxford University and a Fellow of St. Antony's College. His books include *Collusion across the Jordan: King Abdullah, the Zionist Movement, and the Partition of Palestine* (1988); *The Iron Wall: Israel and the Arab World* (2000); and *The War for Palestine: Rewriting the History of 1948* (2001).

Geoffrey Wheatcroft is a former literary editor of the *Spectator* and still a frequent contributor to it as well as the *Guardian*, the *TLS*, the *New York Times*, and *Atlantic Monthly*. His books include *The Randlords* (1985), and *The Controversy of Zion: Jewish Nationalism, the Jewish State and the Unresolved Jewish Dilemma*, which won a National Jewish Book Award in 1996. He has just published *The Strange Death of Tory England.*

Katharine Whitehorn was a columnist for the *Observer*, 1960–96. She was the first woman Rector of St. Andrews University, 1983–85. Her books include *Cooking in a Bedsitter* (1960). Since 1997 she has been "agony aunt" for *Saga Magazine*. When she was voted Woman Who Makes a Difference for Britain by the International Women's Forum, she summed up her achievement: "I have helped to give intelligent women a voice."

The Editor Wm. Roger Louis is Kerr Professor of English History and Culture and Distinguished Teaching Professor at the University of Texas at Austin. He is an Honorary Fellow of St. Antony's College, Oxford. His books include *Imperialism at Bay* (1976) and *The British Empire in the Middle East* (1984). He is the Editor-in-Chief of the *Oxford History of the British Empire*. In 2001 he was President of the American Historical Association.

Introduction

WM. ROGER LOUIS

In introducing another volume of adventures—*Yet More Adventures with Britannia*—I am reminded once more of the wisdom of the Cambridge mathematician G. H. Hardy, who wrote that the pain of having to repeat himself was so excruciating that he decided to end the agony by offering no apology for doing so. In the spirit of the adventurous refrain—more, still more, and yet more—I again follow his example. I begin by stating that this book consists of a representative selection of lectures given to the British Studies seminar at the University of Texas at Austin. Most of these lectures were delivered in the years 2003–05.

Lectures are different from essays or scholarly articles. A lecture presumes an audience rather than a reader and usually has a more conversational tone. It allows greater freedom in the expression of personal or subjective views. It permits and invites greater candor. It is sometimes informally entertaining as well as anecdotally instructive. In this volume, the lecture often takes the form of intellectual autobiography—the relating of how the speaker has come to grips with a significant topic in the field of British Studies, which broadly defined means "things British" throughout the world as well as things that happen to be English, Irish, Scottish, or Welsh. The scope of British Studies includes all disciplines in the social sciences and humanities as well as music and architecture. Most of the lectures in this collection fall within the fields of history, politics, and literature, though the dominant theme, here as previously, is historical. The full sweep of the lectures given before the seminar

will be apparent from the list at the end of the book, which is reproduced in its entirety to give a comprehensive idea of the seminar's substance.

In the year 2005 the British Studies seminar at the University of
Texas celebrates its thirtieth anniversary. It is thus a remarkable institution, if only for longevity. It may be of general interest to retrace
briefly its history. For those at other universities or colleges who feel
trapped within the narrow confines of a single field or discipline, the
experience here may offer inspiration. What makes a seminar successful is the willingness of its participants to meet on a regular basis for discussion of work-in-progress, whether their own or that of
visiting scholars. The circumstances for the founding of the seminar
at the University of Texas were exceptionally favorable because of
the existence of the Humanities Research Center, now known as the
Harry Ransom Humanities Research Center. Harry Ransom was the
founder of the HRC, a Professor of English and later Chancellor of
the University, a collector of rare books and a man of humane vision.
Through his administrative and financial genius, the HRC has developed into a great literary archive with substantial collections, especially in English literature. Ransom thought a weekly seminar
might provide the opportunity to learn of the original research being conducted at the HRC and coincidentally to create common
bonds of intellectual interest in a congenial setting of overstuffed
armchairs, Persian carpets, and generous libations of sherry. This
was an ingenious idea. The seminar was launched in the fall semester 1975. It had the dual purpose of providing a forum for visiting
scholars engaged in research at the HRC and of enabling the members of the seminar to discuss their own work.

The sherry at the Friday seminar sessions symbolizes the attitude.
The seminar meets to examine in a civilized way whatever happens
to be on the agenda, Scottish or Indian, Canadian or Jamaican, English or Australian. When Oscar Wilde said that England and America were two great countries divided by a common language, he un-
derstated the case by several countries. The interaction of British
and other societies is an endlessly fascinating subject on which points
of view do not often converge. The discussion is civil, but diverse
preconceptions, which are tempered by different disciplines, help
to initiate and then sustain controversy, not to end it. What makes
the ongoing debate in British Studies engaging is the clash of different perspectives as well as the nuance of cultural interpretation.
Though the printed page cannot capture the atmosphere of engaged discussion, the following lectures do offer the opportunity to
savor the result of wide-ranging research and reflection.

In the life of any institution, especially one based on voluntary participation, there comes a time for renewal of effort and regeneration of purpose. The test for the British Studies seminar came at the end of two decades, when the participants congratulated themselves on, in their view, the heroic achievement of twenty years of intellectual adventure. But, with a collective sense of shock, they saw that the faces around the seminar table were essentially the same ones—only twenty years older. Might not the seminar grow old and stale? Where were the younger faces, the fresh blood needed to keep this or any comparable institution alive and well, generating new ideas and prospering from the intellects of young and brash junior faculty members?

The seminar now has some fifty Junior Fellows, appointed over the last ten years as assistant professors or instructors of comparable status. Some of them have advanced in rank, some even are now full professors, but they remain Junior Fellows. They are concentrated in English and History, but departments as diverse as Art History, Theater, Music, Architecture, Middle Eastern Studies, Asian Studies, Library Science, Radio-Television-Film, and even Finance are represented. Junior Fellows are not restricted to the University of Texas. They come from Southwestern University at Georgetown, Texas State University at San Marcos, Trinity University at San Antonio—even as far distant as Wichita Falls on the Oklahoma border. The intellectual vitality and range of interests of the Junior Fellows, individually and collectively, continues to be the saving grace of the seminar.

The British Studies seminar has two University sponsors, the College of Liberal Arts and the Humanities Research Center. We are immensely grateful to Richard Lariviere, the Dean of Liberal Arts, for the financial resources and unwavering support that help to sustain the program. We are equally grateful to Thomas F. Staley, the Director of the HRC, for providing a home for the seminar and for his irrepressible enthusiasm and unfailing assistance in many other ways. I wish also to thank Frances Terry, who has handled the week-by-week administrative detail from early on in the seminar's history. Above all I am indebted to Maeve Cooney for the many ways in which she has heroically assisted in the production of the Britannia volumes with precision and all-round competence.

The seminar has been the beneficiary of generous gifts by Creekmore and Adele Fath of Austin, Baine and Mildred Kerr of Houston, John and Susan Kerr of San Antonio, Becky Gale and the late Edwin Gale of Beaumont, Custis Wright and the late Charles Alan Wright of Austin, Lowell Lebermann of Austin, and the twelve or so stout-hearted senior members of the seminar who have recently generously contributed to its endowment. We are indebted to Dean Robert D. King for his help over many years. I again extend warmest and special thanks to Sam Jamot Brown and Sherry Brown of Durango, Colorado, for enabling the seminar to offer undergraduate and graduate scholarships and generally to advance the cause of the liberal arts.

THE CHAPTERS—MORE PRECISELY, THE LECTURES—are presented in approximate chronological sequence but are clustered together around certain themes. The lecture on terrorism in Britain in the nineteenth century places present-day terrorism in a curious perspective. The anarchists were to the 1880s and 1890s what the suicide bombers are to our own post-September 11 era. Do we live in times less or more ominous than the Victorians did? The other introductory historical essay is also built around a comparison. The subject is the myth of the British Empire as a precedent for the American global presence today, but it deals as well with economic decline. By implication the similarity of the plight of the British pound in the twentieth century and the now precarious position of the American dollar provokes an irony that earlier generations of Americans would probably not have appreciated. In the subsequent literary sequence, the lectures on Waugh, Powell, and Larkin all suggest an analogous theme of how things change over time, how three writers cannot but represent slightly different things to different generations of readers. Bloomsbury—for better or worse one of the standing interests of the seminar—is illustrated by a lecture on Frances Partridge and what might be called late Bloomsbury. Intellectual biography or autobiography, represented by lectures on Herbert Butterfield and John Gallagher, is another topic of recurrent interest to the seminar. Woodrow Wilson may seem a slightly odd choice for a collection of lectures on Britain, but the Wilsonian principle of self-determination exerted a profound influence on the evolving fate of the British Empire. Occasionally the seminar strays into contemporary matters, as in the last chapter touching on the different American and British responses to the war in Iraq and thus distilling, in one lecture at least, an interpretation reminiscent of what is to be found in the *London Review of Books*. The connections between other subjects and themes will be more obvious.

The reader's immediate reaction to the drawings of the imaginary bombings of New York and London will probably be *plus ça change, plus c'est la même chose*. Perhaps we should take heart. The danger of the anarchist and Fenian bombers did not generally make life for the Victorians nastier, more brutish, or shorter than it had been, nor did it prevent the growth of trade and industry. On the other hand, as **Bernard Porter** argues, developments in science and technology have tilted the odds in favor of those who can cause damage entirely disproportionate to their numbers. The invention of dynamite portended further and even more deadly innovations. The nightmares in science fiction a hundred years ago have become reality in the form of nerve agents, computer viruses, and nuclear weapons. In the early twentieth century, destructive threats to British society often seemed to originate with newly arrived immigrants—hence the indignant question "'Oo Let 'Em In?"—but measures aimed to exclude dangerous or undesirable ethnic groups were not enacted. A century ago the British were still supremely confident that their society could withstand the strains of violence. Terrorism was accepted as a fact of life. The British learned to live with it—an enduring theme through the Irish troubles of recent decades and perhaps a lesson for our own time.

Patrick O'Brien aims to blow out of the water the theory that the British Empire provides a precedent for understanding the position of the United States in the world today. His theme is Britain's supposed economic decline and the reasons for American ascendancy. In unique historical circumstances Britain's economy as well as empire prospered in the century following the French Revolution. The Royal Navy protected Britain's colonies and trade in Asia, Africa, and the Americas. But by the late nineteenth century, certainly by the beginning of the twentieth, the British themselves speculated whether they could sustain a global economic system and a worldwide empire. "Decline" in a relative sense can better be understood as adjustments or changes leading to a more realistic position in the world economy, though O'Brien is not arguing that there were not plenty of missed opportunities, nor that the British could not have been more effective or efficient in managing their economy. Nor does he suggest that the recurrent economic crises of the post-Second World War era did not resemble something of a national disaster. His point is that Britain's economy and the resources of the British Isles were simply too small to bear comparison with the immense economic power of the United States, which even by the time of the American Civil War exceeded the combined economic strength of Britain, France, and Germany. As an offshore island with a far smaller and more modest economy, Britain could not match America and its vast natural resources and industry. In short, the basis for the comparison between the British Empire, as representing the singular circumstances of an economic and political configuration at a particular time, and the United States, as a military and economic global power today, simply does not exist. The American economic system, whatever its present degree of crisis because of spiraling debt and other afflictions, is on a different order of magnitude. The British Empire as a precedent for the global reach of the United States is thus a myth.

Evelyn Waugh would certainly have borne testimony to the inefficient yet rapacious quality of the British Inland Revenue in the post-Second World War era. One of the striking features of the examination of the writer by **Geoffrey Wheatcroft** is the extent to which Waugh managed to manipulate the tax laws to make charitable gifts. This is a lecture that reassesses Waugh's character as well as his writing. In the centennial year of his birth, 2003, various writers concluded that he was, as convention has it, a monster as well as a stylist. But he could be a loyal and affectionate friend, and despite the ferocity of his bad moods he could be kind. In the context of *Yet More Adventures*, it is his political insight that is of especial interest. Wheatcroft points out that before the outbreak of the Second World War he wrote that human capacity for barbarism could never be subdued—"men and women who seem quite orderly will commit every conceivable atrocity." There was a certain social realist side of Waugh's intellect that occasionally revealed ruthless insight. Perhaps his shrewdest political comment was on the Suez crisis of 1956, which, as Wheatcroft points out, has a chilling relevance to today's war in Iraq: the Suez expedition could not "be justified on moral or legal grounds." Waugh emerges as something much more complicated than a reactionary blimp, and certainly as a more human being than the usual portrayal of him suggests.

The lecture on Anthony Powell by **Ferdinand Mount**—Powell was Mount's uncle—can be regarded as a study in public mood as well as idiosyncratic personalities. The four dancers to Powell's music of time are not, as is commonly believed, a group of the four seasons, but Poverty, Industry, Wealth, and Luxury—though, in the four decades after 1914, the dance seemed to turn into one of poverty and stoic despair. "No nonsense about economics or world disarmament with him," one of Powell's characters with an inimitable name comments about another with an equally inimitable name. Yet there are glimpses in his work of a lingering bright Bohemia, a gaiety of spirit, and a subdued but unquenchable idealism, as if some of Powell's protagonists exist uncomfortably yet simultaneously in different eras. The theme of national exhaustion finds a parallel with the argument by Patrick O'Brien on economic decline. In many of Powell's characters there is an almost ingrained shabbiness bordering on genteel squalor and little or no hope for national regeneration. Endurance and fortitude as well as melancholy nevertheless characterize one of the most forceful of Powell's fictional creations, the Chief of the General Staff, easily recognizable as General Alan Brooke (who is the subject of Alex Danchev's lecture). The depiction of military life in *Dance to the Music of Time* makes an engaging contrast to Waugh's in *Sword of Honor*. Waugh was a disillusioned amateur soldier who had only gone to war for a cause, while Powell was fascinated by military life and accepted its ups and downs. There is also an interesting comparison to be made with Powell's curiosity—"no human life is uninteresting"—and Philip Larkin's more restricted outlook.

Larkin once commented that he would not mind going to China if he could return the same day. His sole comment on the end of the Second World War was a complaint about the noise some revelers were making. The lecture by **Dan Jacobson** is chiefly an analysis of the merits of Larkin's poetry, but the reader is reminded of the posthumous buffeting his reputation received after the publication of his letters and the official biography had revealed his misogyny, foul language, fondness for pornography, and fascination with young girls. Before these revelations Larkin had been regarded as an exemplary figure because of his plain and comprehensible language, his humor, and his sorrow for a country that had lost the sense of its national and imperial past. But if he had become a sort of national monument, his private thoughts seemed to reveal, in the words of one overheated critic, the sewer that ran under it. Dan Jacobson draws up the balance sheet. Readers will want to make their own judgment about Larkin's moral worth, but it is clear that he himself was poignantly aware of his failures as a human being. His poetry is another matter. It may be a long time before Larkin finds a place in Poet's Corner in Westminster Abbey, but Jacobson attests to the power, clarity, and inventiveness of his poetry.

Public opinion has been even less kind to C. P. Snow, who was at the peak of his popular acclaim in the mid-1960s. Snow seemed to represent the bridge between the sciences and the arts, interpreting the one to the other. He delivered his Rede Lecture in Cambridge on "The Two Cultures" in 1959. No topic has more consistently roused the interest of members of the British Studies seminar, partly no doubt because Snow was a founding member of the seminar in the late 1970s (while arranging the transfer of his papers to the Humanities Research Center). He is now largely unread and the concept of the two cultures for the most part derided. **David Cannadine** traces the rise and fall of his reputation and the nature of his national renown and international fame. Snow dealt with issues of science and technology on the basis of his own scientific background. He commanded attention on issues of higher education, and he appeared to hold one of the keys to the future by arguing that science and technology could reduce the gap between richer and poorer countries, perhaps even eliminating world poverty. Harold Macmillan, one of the most intelligent Prime Ministers of the twentieth century and certainly the best read, held him in high esteem. Snow's sequence of novels, "Strangers and Brothers," not only revealed the troubled lives of Oxford and Cambridge dons but also—perhaps his strongest suit—the internecine warfare (or, to pitch it no higher, in Maurice Cowling's phrase, the "placid malice") of the common room. Yet by the 1970s he already seemed to be a figure from a different age. In a time of economic crisis, militant trade unions, and the changing national mood in the aftermath of retreat from empire, his ideas met with an increasingly hostile reception, even scorn. Nevertheless no one studying British politics and culture of the 1950s and 1960s—especially on the themes of science, education, and government—can fail to take Snow into account as, in David Cannadine's phrase, a person who once mattered.

Frances Partridge, who died in 2004 at the age of 103, was the last survivor of Bloomsbury. She was an unusually independent-minded observer of her times as well as a gifted diarist and memoir writer. The lecture by **Anne Chisholm** discusses the way in which her writings resemble a mirror in which one can observe the personalities and work not only of Lytton Strachey and Dora Carrington but her own husband, Ralph Partridge—all of whom bring to mind a certain circularity in the study of Bloomsbury: "Frances loved Ralph, who loved Dora, who loved Lytton, who loved Ralph." These tangled relationships continue to intrigue, and a study of them from the perspective of Frances Partridge reveals something of the legacy of Bloomsbury to successive generations. The question of how reputations change over time is a theme here as elsewhere in this volume. By the time of the Second World War, the influence of Virginia Woolf, Maynard Keynes, Roger Fry and others lived on, but Bloomsbury as a collection of eccentric individuals was largely forgotten until the publication of Michael Holroyd's biography of Lytton Strachey in 1967. Partridge objected to the manner in which various authors and films subsequently reduced her husband to a caricature. Her principal contribution to the reputation of Bloomsbury was to demonstrate through her published diaries how the values of one age still had meaning for a later generation confronting such issues as unilateral nuclear disarmament and Vietnam—and still later for those who protested against Thatcherism and the Falklands War, for that matter the first Gulf War. Just as the original Bloomsbury group had rebelled against the artistic, social, and sexual restrictions of Victorian society, so their descendants re-embraced the cause of pacifism and the virtues of friendship. Partridge was not a creative or innovative writer. She recognized herself that she lacked imagination and that her talent lay in observation and descriptive writing. She was exact and unsentimental. Her writings helped to make clear the reasons that the values associated with Bloomsbury continued to have meaning in the latter part of the twentieth century.

The lecture by **Niall Ferguson** begins the historical sequence by reflecting on the origins of the First World War. A. J. P. Taylor used to remark that wars happen more by accident than by design. Yet Taylor himself in *The Struggle for Mastery in Europe*—and the distinguished editors of the *Documents of the Origins of the War*—traced the war's antecedents to the last decades of the nineteenth century and some historians have found underlying causes extending even further back. How did people at the time view the origins of the war? More specifically, how did those who stood to lose most from the war—the financiers—see it? This line of inquiry returns to the issue analyzed by J. A. Hobson and seized upon by personalities as different as Lenin and Wilson. In their various ways, these commentators suspected financial interests not only of benefiting from international conflict but perhaps even of fomenting it. Shorn of ideological assumption, this type of inquiry is useful because of its focus. Those who invested in financial markets would, it is often assumed, be most sensitive to the possibility of war. But what does this approach to the economic causes of war actually yield if examined against the historical sources? This is Niall Ferguson's point of departure. After tracing the evolution of comment in *The Economist*, then as now the principal news magazine in English concerned with financial issues, he concludes that the war came as a surprise to the bankers and shareholders as much as to the statesmen, soldiers, and general public. Yet such a conclusion must also take into account the contemporary view that war had long been regarded as inevitable. Answers are as difficult to find as ever, but one certainty is that it is best to be on guard against fixed ideological assumptions such as those about financiers and war. The theme of this lecture thus fits closely to that of the next.

Oh! What a Lovely War is the play by Joan Littlewood that successfully ran in Britain and America in the 1960s and later continued, through the film with the same title, to have an immense influence on the popular understanding of the First World War. But though the subject of the play is war in the early twentieth century, its passion is that of the anti-Vietnam movement. The aim of **Brian Bond**'s lecture is to rescue the interpretation of the First World War from the ideological commitment of a later age. A year or so before the play's first performance the world had been on the brink of catastrophe because of the Cuban missile crisis. The Vietnam war increasingly fuelled anti-American, anti-empire, and anti-authority protest. The anti-war movement held passionately that all wars were futile and unjust. *Oh! What a Lovely War* is a dramatic statement against the war's pointlessness, unspeakable suffering, unacceptable casualty figures, and incompetent generalship. It is a savage satire. But there is a sentimental dimension to it, too. The poignant songs of the 1914–18 era and the nostalgia they aroused took the edge off the ferocious and angry political drive of the play. Many people who saw it, or the film, probably concluded that the war had no cause other than the irrational pride of those controlling Europe's destinies at the time, and that the leadership of the war was not only incompetent but criminal in its disregard for human life and the sacrifice of a generation of young and brave soldiers. The radical argument presented in the play may be regarded as a general reflection on the 1960s, with the circumstances of one era being seen through the ideological prism of another. This lecture has a direct connection with the one by Gertrude Himmelfarb on the Whig interpretation of history.

Sir Alan Brooke (Lord Alanbrooke) was the Chief of the Imperial General Staff during most of the Second World War. **Alex Danchev** traces the evolution of his historical reputation against the background of Churchill's memoirs, in effect Churchill's own history of the war, and the publication of Sir Arthur Bryant's two-volume work which draws extensively from Alanbrooke's diaries. Neither did Brooke justice. Churchill slighted him while Bryant portrayed him as an omniscient Elizabethan-Wellingtonian swashbuckler. In fact Brooke was one of the great military figures of the war, certainly one of the few who could stand up to Churchill. Churchill himself wrote: "When I thump the table and push my face towards him what does he do? Thumps the table harder and glares back at me." Brooke's diaries, even in the grotesque form published by Bryant, provided a counter-Churchill perspective, never denying that Churchill was the savior of his country but suggesting that there were different ways of looking at British wartime operations and especially Churchill's interfering ways. The rounded portrait of Brooke had to await access to the manuscript diaries, which reveal a soldier remarkably close to the powerful, decisive, honest, brilliant general of Anthony Powell's miniature mentioned in Ferdinand Mount's lecture. Brooke gave the impression of being imperturbable, but in fact he was lonely and vulnerable, a profoundly human figure. He used his diary much in the same way as his contemporary in the Foreign Office, Sir Alexander Cadogan—to record but also to vent his pent-up emotions and frustrations, not least about Churchill. At one point Brooke wrote that he was "chained to the chariot of a lunatic." He had words no less scathing for Eisenhower and de Gaulle. To his diary he was fiercely honest about his own sentiments. At the same time he was deeply religious in a way that few contemporaries suspected. He once wrote in his diary: "I pray God that the decisions we arrived at may be correct, and that they may bear fruit." Historical reputations have a way of settling after five decades or so. Alanbrooke emerges from the historical record as an altogether admirable figure.

As the title suggests, the "The Strange Death of Puritan England" by **Simon Green** bears a resemblance to G. N. Dangerfield's *Strange Death of Liberal England*. Just as Dangerfield demonstrated the unexpected consequences for British politics that followed the outbreak of war in 1914, so Green deals with the change in moral tone during the Second World War as a transformation that few would have predicted as late as 1939. To many in the inter-war period, puritanism continued to represent the best of English civilization. In this positive sense it meant upholding the ethical ideals of the nation and the rejection of the Bloomsbury code of behavior, especially its emphasis on sexual freedom. As a study in ideas and of the relationship between church and state from the Victorian era to the 1950s, the lecture focuses on certain key issues such as drink, sexual habits, women's rights, and the frequency of church-going. Contemporary attitudes were complex and by no means as sharply divided as in the caricature of villagers torn between chapel and public house. (As caricatures go, there is at least a comic value to the contemporary Italian view of British men as tea-drinking snobs and apathetic towards women.) What can be said with certainty is that in the inter-war years most Britons were puritans and some were more puritan than others. A substantial part of the population, especially in Scotland and Wales, still believed in lifelong marital fidelity, temperance, and the duty to go to church on Sundays. These traditional values sometimes came into conflict with emergent political trends. Christabel Pankhurst perhaps best caught the convergence of politics and morality in her slogan, "Votes for women and chastity for men." As Simon Green says, we should beware of ridiculing contemporary views that served a purpose at the time but in retrospect seem confused, naïve, comical, and embarrassing. Historical analysis can itself be a source of confusion. Historians usually deal with the 1960s as the century's critical period of social and cultural change whereas the seminal decades were the 1940s and 1950s.

Katharine Whitehorn takes the reader on a romp through the 1950s. She reinforces the point made by Simon Green: during the Second World War sexual restraint often went by the board, setting the stage for the late 1940s and 1950s. Even though the contraceptive pill was not available until ten or so years later, the 1950s was a decade of much greater sexual openness than is usually believed. In a certain sense it was a time of paradox, reflecting both gaiety and anger, both the exquisite politeness of Sir Anthony Eden and the exhibitionism and violence of the Teddy Boys. With the coronation of the young Queen in 1953 there was a general sense of the country entering a new Elizabethan age. Although the period is often remembered as one of stultifying conformity, John Osborne's *Look Back in Anger* and John Braine's *Room at the Top* created a new literary genre and led to the cult of the "Angry Young Men"—perhaps the cultural symbol of the decade—as well as the iconoclastic demand for changes in a still stratified society. For the public at large it was a time when much of the drudgery of everyday life was reduced because of the washing machine and the refrigerator—and the general mood changed because of the advent of television. Britain seemed to stand on the threshold of mass abundance. The public moved away from austerity and puritanism into an era of rising expectations. Yet the cold war and troubles abroad were never far from mind. In 1956 the British faced one of the great political crises of the century when Eden led the nation into the bitter clash at Suez. The *Observer*—the newspaper for which Katharine Whitehorn wrote for many years—took the lead in protesting British aggression. In the 1960s, writing against a background of cultural explosion—the flower children, the campaigners for nuclear disarmament, and those who condemned the war in Vietnam—she penned a column for women that was personal, irreverent, and serious. She assumed that women had higher concerns and aspirations than domesticity and children. Her column came to symbolize the human warmth of the *Observer* in its golden age.

Gertrude Himmelfarb reappraises the career of Herbert Butterfield and his reputation as a "public intellectual" many decades before that phrase acquired currency. Butterfield was Regius Professor at Cambridge and Master of Peterhouse. She is concerned with his attitude of pro-appeasement before, during, and after the

Second World War. In the latter part of his career Butterfield became preoccupied with the relationship between Christianity and history. He came to take the view that Providence rather than the intentions and ideas of men provided the best explanation for the meaning of human history. To Butterfield, in Himmelfarb's view, Providence also took the place of moral responsibility. In any event Butterfield confounded his admirers, who believed that he stood for a firm commitment to the independence of academic history from religion and ideology. Paradox was a theme that ran through his career, which many believed to be characterized by great and perhaps singular originality. Himmelfarb, on the contrary, judges that his historical work was neither great nor original. Butterfield was in fact more of an essayist or lecturer than a writer of historical works of substance. Much of his writing was repetitive, loosely structured, and superficial. The spontaneity of his ideas may have had its attraction to an earlier generation of readers but the lack of focus now distracts rather than commends. Nevertheless he did write one work for which he will be forever remembered. It is not a book but an essay of 134 pages written when he was thirty years old. *The Whig Interpretation of History* declares that history must be understood in its own terms and not viewed through the lens of the present. Butterfield had in mind historians who assumed that history had a purpose, who believed that it demonstrated a movement towards progress and liberty, and who used it for the purpose of moral judgment. The very name "Butterfield" came to represent the view that ideological commitment should play no part in the historian's job of trying, as impartially as one might be able, to assess the past: "The true historical fervour is love of the past for the sake of the past." Two cheers for Butterfield's *Whig Interpretation*! May it long be read by graduate students!

John Darwin does for Jack Gallagher what Himmelfarb does for Butterfield. This lecture is a study in the history of ideas and of the writing of history, but it also traces Gallagher's life. He was the son of an Irish railway worker living in Liverpool. From the humblest of backgrounds he won a scholarship to Trinity College, Cambridge, and remained loyal to Trinity throughout the rest of his life. Even though in the 1960s he become the Beit Professor at Oxford and lived in Balliol, his heart remained in Cambridge. Regarding Oxford as a sort of Siberia, he successfully conspired to return to Cambridge in 1971. During the war he had fought as a tank soldier in the North African campaign. After the war he proposed marriage to Katharine Whitehorn (the future Agony Aunt declined, but they maintained a close friendship). He remained a bachelor. In the post-war years he met the historian who became his comrade-in-arms, Ronald Robinson. Together they plotted a revolution in the interpretation of the history of the British Empire. They brought it off in two stages, first with a famous article published in 1953 entitled "The Imperialism of Free Trade" and then eight years later with their book, *Africa and the Victorians*. Their achievement can be summed up by stating that they explained how the empire functioned—sometimes indirectly but effectively through informal control—as a coherent economic and military system throughout the world. Robinson's contribution to the partnership was that of a powerful mind seeking a single, driving argument while Gallagher's was that of a subtle, imaginative intellect that was literary as well as historical. The pen portraits in *Africa and the Victorians* are Gallagher's, rich in color and wit and depicting life as a comic spectacle of ambition and vanity. Gallagher was a lovable, inspiring human being. "Sweet Jack, kind Jack, true Jack, valiant Jack," wrote one of his former students in a Falstaffian dedication to a book. Very few scholars can claim such affection from their former students and colleagues. Part of the reason for this was his breadth of reading and intellectual curiosity combined with an unexpected humility, but Gallagher together with Robinson also attracted disciples because of what they represented in the intellectual and moral culture of post-war Britain: both were working class, and both were as suspicious of the red claw of American capitalism as of the sickle of Russian communism.

John Darwin's lecture begins a sequence on British imperialism. **Avi Shlaim**, who describes himself as an expatriate Iraqi Jew, examines the origins and consequences of the Balfour Declaration. It should be said at the outset that not all readers are going to agree with its conclusion, but it follows logically from his premise and from an examination of sources in both Arabic and Hebrew as well as archival material in the Middle East Centre at St. Antony's College, Oxford. His argument is that the British from the outset favored the Jews and that the creation of the Jewish state in 1948 was the direct consequence of the promise in 1917 to support the establishment of a national home. On the other hand, many scholars hold that the British at least tried to be even-handed and some believe the administration in Palestine itself to have been biased in favor of the Arabs. Shlaim thus plunges into controversy. He bases his case in part on a rereading of the literature, notably the landmarks in the history of the subject by Leonard Stein and Mayir Vereté, but he also follows the lead of Tom Segev, the author of a popular revisionist account written in 2000. Shlaim likes revisionist history in the positive sense of seeking to test new evidence and arriving at fresh conclusions. He agrees with Segev that Lloyd George, the Prime Minister in 1917, lies at the heart of the story. Lloyd George has often been accused of pandering to the Jews in order to win the war. Shlaim concurs that this is certainly true but that Lloyd George did so out of ignorance, prejudice, and a considerable amount of arrogance. The Prime Minister and others within the British government went forward with the Balfour Declaration on the basis "of an absurdly inflated notion of the power and influence of the Zionists." Lloyd George actually thought that the Jews could turn the wheels of history to Britain's advantage. The preconceptions of A. J. Balfour, the Foreign Secretary under whose name the Declaration was issued, were, Shlaim argues, just as crude. Balfour believed that the Arabs of Palestine hardly deserved a second thought. And so the dice were loaded: those responsible for the Balfour Declaration foresaw a Jewish state from the outset. By favoring the Zionists they helped to ensure the actual creation of Israel in 1948. What of the decision itself to issue the Declaration in 1917? Shlaim goes beyond Elizabeth Monroe in her celebrated judgment that, calculated in terms of the interests of the British alone, the Balfour Declaration was the worst mistake in their imperial history. Shlaim believes that it was a catastrophe for all parties concerned, not least the Jews.

The lecture by **Erez Manela** delineates another great declaration of the First World War era, President Wilson's proclamation of the principle of self-determination. Manela represents a new breed of historian. He is fluent in Chinese and Arabic as well as Hebrew and European languages, and he has worked in Indian and other Asian archives and at the Public Record Office (in these changing times now called The National Archives). Self-determination is one of the great guidelines in modern history: from its acceptance as an implicit principle in the Covenant of the League of Nations to the present, one can see the evolution towards today's 191 sovereign states of the United Nations. This was not the vision of the future that had been seen at the close of the First World War by the British, and certainly not by Wilson himself. Until as late as the 1950s the British worked towards larger configurations of territories that would be economically as well as politically viable as independent states. Wilson had not disagreed with this view. When he said that countries should have the right to determine their own future, he meant primarily the nations of Europe. He belonged to the tradition of colonial reform, not liberation. But as Manela demonstrates in his case study of Indian nationalism, nationalists throughout the world seized on Wilson's principle to advance their own aims. They were bitterly disappointed that Wilson not only ignored them but even seemed to be oblivious to the implications of his own statements. The "wild delirium of joy" expressing the hope that he might assist the nationalists to throw off the yoke of European imperialism proved to be short-lived. The young Nehru wrote that "President Wilson's brave words have remained but words," just as he would later lament that President Roosevelt's promises were as empty as those of his predecessor. But self-determination proved to be the wave of the future. We live today in its wake. The year 1919 was its defining moment, in Manela's phrase, the "Wilsonian moment."

One of Avi Shlaim's quotations reveals some of the underlying connections between the lectures dealing with the aftermath of the First World War: "The problem of Palestine is exactly the same as the problem of Ireland, namely, two peoples living in a small country hating each other like hell." In Ireland no less than in Palestine and India, the question ultimately became one of whether partition might be averted. The answer, when it came—at about the same time in both cases, in the late 1940s—was that there could be no other solution. Here was self-determination with a resounding vengeance. **Deirdre McMahon** pursues a similar theme as she sketches British views of how the American Irish had joined the "Indians, Egyptians, Bolshies" to bring about Irish independence "by murder and outrage." The American-born de Valera, the nationalist leader who became prime minister and later President of the Irish Republic, believed that Ireland possessed the inalienable right to determine her own destiny. In 1948 Ireland seceded from the Commonwealth while Northern Ireland remained a part of the United Kingdom. Could there have been a different outcome? McMahon argues that "Dominion Status," which set the constitutional relations between Ireland and the United Kingdom, would have offered the Irish the same sovereign independence possessed by other Dominions such as Canada but to the Irish it contained an insurmountable difficulty: the oath of allegiance to the British Crown. Had the Irish been offered unequivocal membership in the Commonwealth as a Republic, as India was in 1949, the fate of the Irish people, at least within the Commonwealth, might have been different. The problem lingered on. A decade later de Valera broached the issue of rejoining the Commonwealth if the question of partition could be resolved. Harold Macmillan commented that a united Ireland with de Valera as "a sort of Irish Nehru" would do no one any good. The times were out of sync, the 1940s were not the 1920s: the British offered too little, too late—though one might ask in retrospect what difference did the Commonwealth make after all? Deirdre McMahon's answer is that it could have meant a lot to Ireland.

Antony Best deals with similar retrospective questions in his lecture on British intellectuals and the Far East by focusing his inquiry on western knowledge of China and Japan and how the British might have preserved their economic and military power in that part of the world. In the fine arts, literature, and history, British writers certainly held their own in comparison with those from other western countries. For example, Harold Acton lived in Peking in the 1930s and wrote on Chinese theater and poetry. George Samson of the British Embassy in Tokyo, the author of *Japan: A Short Cultural History*, was the foremost western authority on Japan. Because of the treaty ports, above all the great industrial port city of Shanghai with its 9,300 British subjects, Britain remained the dominant western trading power in China despite the civil war. With Japan however relations had deteriorated. Churchill's attitude may be taken as a weather-vane. In the late 1920s he viewed Japan's expansion into China as a stabilizing force on the side of civilization, but when Japan began to drift towards Germany his assessment changed. In 1936 he wrote on the need to contain Japanese aggression. The theme of appeasement and anti-appeasement played itself out in Asia no less than in Europe. Here, too, there was a parallel to the proposition that Britain's true enemy was not Germany but the Soviet Union. In Asia, Japan had been Britain's valiant ally until 1922 and — so believed those on the right of the political spectrum — the termination of the Anglo-Japanese alliance had been a grievous miscalculation. The champion of the idea of reviving the alliance, or at least Anglo-Japanese friendship, was the Prime Minister, Neville Chamberlain. It seemed obvious to him that the British informal empire of trade and commerce in China, not to mention the colonies of Hong Kong and Malaya, would be vulnerable to Japanese attack in the event of war. Moreover, Chamberlain mistrusted the United States. The logic was the same for Asia as for Europe. Friendship with Japan, as with Germany, would preserve the British Empire. Why should Japan's move into Manchuria be of concern to Britain? Was it not comparable to the British occupation of Egypt in 1882? Would Manchuria not deflect Japan's attention away from South East Asia? There were powerful reasons for Britain to appease Japan and they might have prevailed if it had not been for the slightly more powerful calculation that, come what may, the British had to remain on as good terms as possible with the United States. It is easy to forget how finely drawn were the lines of fate before the Second World War.

Where in the world could there be two competing whorehouses called the Oxford and the Cambridge? **Richard Drayton**, a

Guyanese, does not pursue which of the two was preferred by the CIA, but he does make it clear that Georgetown, the capital of British Guiana and the location of the whorehouses, was also the location of a combined operation by the intelligence agencies of Britain and the United States to overthrow the democratically elected Cheddi Jagan. So far as the British Empire was concerned, this was a rare event. One thing that that was "special" about Anglo-American relations was that the CIA usually did not run operations in British territories nor did the American government usually interfere in British colonial administration. The exception was the Caribbean and Latin America, which were to the State Department as Africa was to the Colonial Office. In the early 1960s Jagan was the Premier of British Guiana (the title given to a colonial prime minister before independence). He had made the unforgivable mistake of visiting Cuba. Jagan in American eyes would become the instrument of Castro and Khrushchev, and British Guiana the beachhead of Communism in Latin America. The CIA began a campaign of destabilization, which included acts of sabotage and the detention of key political leaders. Though the extent to which the British themselves were aware of the full sweep of CIA subversion is still uncertain, in 1964 they were able to replace Jagan with the anti-Communist Forbes Burnham. The irony is that within a decade Burnham began to court the Soviet Union. His corrupt, despotic regime lasted until 1985. There were however short-term gains. In return for allowing the CIA to take the initiative, the British received American support in the Honduras boundary dispute and a more tolerant American attitude towards the problems facing the British with the emergence of a white settler regime in Rhodesia. Such were the secret politics of the cold war, which itself has a relevance to the post-September 11 world. One lesson, Drayton concludes, is that the word "terrorist" is used today in the same way as the word "Communist" was used against Cheddi Jagan.

There is a connection between the novelists and poets of the Caribbean of the Second World War era and the African writers whose work began to appear in the late 1950s and early 1960s. The intellectual vitality and exuberance of the Caribbean was infectious. The lecture by **James Currey** is an account of publishing in Africa in the first quarter century after independence. It deals with such writers as Ngugi wa Thiong'o, the Kenyan novelist who found inspiration in Caribbean authors, and Chinua Achebe, the Nigerian writer who perhaps more than any other single person helped to launch the African Writers Series and build it into an unlikely success. Achebe's *Things Fall Apart* sold over nine million copies. Yet no one at the time would have placed much of a bet on Achebe and certainly not on a commercial list of African writers. Creating an African series was an inspired risk on the part of Heinemann, the London publishing house. It had one unexpected thing going for it; the post-colonial education authorities, the new examination boards, and the schools and universities from Nigeria to Uganda eagerly adopted novels and other works by living African writers for the new curricula. Nevertheless it was expensive and exacting work. When James Currey flew to Africa in 1959 his air ticket cost the equivalent of his annual salary. He had to be sure that the series made a profit, and he went to ingenious lengths to ensure reviews. Despite a patronizing attitude in London and elsewhere, African writers found an audience as far away as Canada, India, Australia, and not least the Caribbean. The writers themselves benefited further because Currey encouraged them and conscientiously sent them copies of readers' reports. "Writing is a lonely business," in Currey's view, "and some advice is better than a cold rejection slip." In the post-colonial period, some of the authors were censored by their governments. In 1977 Ngugi was taken in chains to a maximum-security jail and held without trial. While in prison he wrote *Devil on the Cross* (1982) on sheets of toilet paper. This lecture in some respects records a triumph of the human spirit as well as a significant intellectual and cultural achievement.

The concluding lecture, by **Scott Lucas**, returns to the theme of the cold war and its present-day consequences. Lucas is an American from Birmingham, Alabama. Through a quirk of fate he teaches in Birmingham, England, where he directs the American Studies program. American Studies might seem an unlikely subject to be of interest to the CIA and its British counterpart, but as will be seen the influence of intelligence services in cultural affairs over the past fifty years has been pervasive. The story begins with Ernest Bevin, the post-war Foreign Secretary with an all-encompassing mind and a determination to reassert Britain's place in the world as a "Third Force" balancing the United States and the Soviet Union. In 1948 the Foreign Office created a new section called the Information Research Department, a bland title concealing its purpose of waging cultural warfare against the Soviet Union and promoting the idea of British social democracy as preferable to either Russian communism or American capitalism. George Orwell was a willing recruit. Though his motives remain controversial, he revealed the names kept in his notebook of 135 "crypto-Communists" including Cecil Day Lewis, Stephen Spender, and A. J. P. Taylor. Spender, along with Irving Kristol (incidentally the husband of Gertrude Himmelfarb), became an editor of *Encounter*, the intellectual journal secretly subsidized by the CIA and MI6. Spender, then and forever after, disclaimed all knowledge of CIA sponsorship when the cover was blown in 1967. The facts of the *Encounter* case have long been known. The new dimension of the story is the extent of MI6 involvement and the way in which the British tried to follow their own line, until they were forced to bow out. They forfeited their plans to be a "Third Force" championing "Social Democracy" and the true values of western civilization not because of a failure of will but because they lacked the necessary resources. By contrast, the US government, if not the CIA, continued to sponsor cultural activities including the creation of American Studies programs in Britain. Biting the hand that fed it, American Studies proved to be recalcitrant and ungrateful, as the US Ambassador William Crowe discovered in 1995. Lucas's point is that, despite overt and covert subsidy, British writers and academics cling ferociously to their independence. British culture could not and cannot be reduced to the role of cheering on the Americans. The Iraq war is a case in point. In spite of the British government's support of the United States, protest in Britain is bitter. To many in Britain the "Special Relationship" now simply means "Most Favoured Client State."

New York skyscraper under fictional attack in 1910

An imaginary anarchist attack on Big Ben in 1920

1

'Oo Let 'Em In?
Asylum Seekers and Terrorists
In Britain, 1850–1914

BERNARD PORTER

The picture reproduced on page 21 shows an aircraft hi-jacked by anarchists and loaded with dynamite attacking the tallest New York skyscraper of its day. "Ground zero" is in the foreground. The year is 1910. The peculiar shape of the aircraft is because they have hardly been invented yet. This is taken from one of a number of sensational novels based on this kind of theme that came out around the turn of the twentieth century. The second illustration on page 22 is from another, set in 1920 but published in 1893. Other novels of this genre feature a Fenian "super-gun" that can bombard Britain from the eastern seaboard of America; bombs exploding on the London underground; anthrax bacilli put into the water systems of Britain's great cities; and a "dirty bomb" that kills everyone in London without destroying buildings. Almost all the terrors that afflict us at the beginning of the twenty-first century, in fact, were anticipated in the cheap fiction of a century ago.

Some of them were anticipated in reality, too. Not the "9/11" scenario, of course—that was too much over the top to be credible; though the "conquest of the air" more generally had worrying implications for a country like Britain whose whole defense strategy was based on the understanding that enemies could only shoot from ground level. Submarines were feared for the same reason. Alarmists pictured the entire Royal Navy becoming sitting ducks to attacks from above and below. The other dangers, however, were real and immediate. Science had a lot to do with this. It shifted the odds on

what today would be called "terrorism." (Then the term was more often applied to governments.) Developments in science meant that a
small group of people could now wreak damage enormously disproportionate to their numbers or physical strength. The big break-
through here was the invention of dynamite—so much more stable
than the old gunpowder—that was the favorite weapon of the new
generation of "anarchists by the deed," as they called themselves,
who came on the scene from the 1880s. The other frightening thing
about the anarchists was that they did not mind killing innocent
civilians. Some of them held that there was actually no such thing as
an innocent civilian; if you lived in a capitalist society, you were com-
plicit in it. In any case the whole idea was to create "terror" in order
to force either the breakdown of all formal government (the extreme anarchist position), or its replacement by something that ac-
corded more with your own will. Here we have the two essential components of the terrorist "threat" at all times: great destructive power,
and indiscriminate targeting. These too, of course, can and should
apply to governments.

Europe and America suffered grievously from anarchist attacks,
especially in the 1890s. Some were directed at specific political enemies: a secret police chief in Moscow in 1890; a French president in
Lyons in 1894; the Austrian Empress in Geneva in 1898; the King of
Italy in Monza in 1900; a US president in Buffalo in 1901, all killed—
and there are others. Among the more indiscriminate ones were the
Haymarket affray in Chicago in 1886; the bomb that was detonated
in the Café Véry in Paris in 1892; a bomb thrown into the front stalls
of the Liceo Theatre in Barcelona in 1893; and an explosion that
killed twelve in a religious procession in the same city in 1896. Britain was less affected. In the 1880s she had experienced a brief burst
of Fenian bombings in London and elsewhere. Those bombers succeeded in killing only three, and luckily those were of their own
number. The Fenians incidentally also tried to build a submarine,
but, of the two prototypes they completed, the first would not float
and the second would not steer. In the 1890s Britain felt some ripples from the Continental and Russian anarchist campaigns. A bomb
was discovered being manufactured in Walsall in 1892, and a second
detonated accidentally in Greenwich Park in 1894, killing the anarchist who had been carrying it. Joseph Conrad's *The Secret Agent* is
based on this affair. In 1897 a third bomb exploded in an Inner
Circle line underground train near Aldersgate station, though that
was probably put there by an ex-employee with a grievance. In 1894
a London weekly paper claimed to have been tipped off by a Metropolitan Police Special Branch officer of a genuine plot to poison wa-

ter supplies with anthrax.[1] That may have been a false alarm. Others certainly were: "bombs" that turned out to be a packet of Mazawat-tee tea in one case, for example; a baby's feeding bottle left on a bus in another; and in a third, bomb shells stuffed with copies of a mag-azine and sent to government offices in 1894 in order to win a prize offered for the most original way of advertising the magazine. A few years later the "anarchist threat" revived when a group of Latvian revolutionaries went on the rampage in the course of a series of rob-beries (the revolutionary word for it was "expropriation") in the East End of London, shooting a small boy and several policemen dead, culminating in the famous "Siege of Sidney Street" of January 1911, where after a dramatic gun battle two of them were burned alive when the house went up in flames, but "Peter the Painter" escaped. Alfred Hitchcock based a film on this: *The Man who Knew Too Much.* "Peter" and the rest were members of a large community of recent eastern European immigrants living in the East End, whose alienness (most of them were Jewish, though not the Sidney Street gang) and supposedly extreme political opinions raised apprehensions among some native Britons. A comparison could be made with perceptions of the Muslim community in present-day Bradford, say, though one should not press the analogy too hard.

In the case of present-day Bradford such fears have led to significant anti-Islamism in Britain, and cries for tighter immigra-tion control. In the 1890s and 1900s this did not happen. There was a burst of anti-Semitism, but it was mainly confined to the East End. There were also calls for "asylum seekers" to be more rigidly vet-ted, especially during the Sidney Street affair—Winston Churchill, the Home Secretary at the time, was greeted with cries of "'Oo let'em in?" when he went down to see the excitement for himself—but they soon died down.[2] In fact the most notable thing about Brit-ain's response to these events in the late nineteenth and early twen-tieth centuries was how liberal it remained. There was no call to bomb countries which harbored terrorists. This would have meant bombing Boston: most of the Fenians came from the United States. Churchill did not tighten up the immigration laws. Britain's pol-icy of "asylum" for refugees remained as rock-solid as it had al-ways been.

It is worth spelling out the full extent of this. Britain's right of asy-lum was absolute. No one arriving in Britain and claiming to be the victim of political persecution could be denied entry. They did not even have to prove it; the mere assertion was enough. Before 1906 this was part of the general right that Britain offered to anyone to immigrate to Britain for any reason whatsoever; there were, quite simply, no laws on the statute book that would allow governments to deny entry to anyone. There were also no checks made on people coming in; they did not, for example, have to carry passports. This carries a disadvantage for the historian; we have no means of knowing for sure how many refugees lived in Britain. There is an 1853 figure for those in London of 4,380, which seems fairly precise, until it is learned how it was arrived at: by policemen going round pubs in likely areas and asking how many foreigners had been seen there.[3] In the 1890s Britain was far more open and liberal in this regard than the United States. In 1905 she caught up with the latter a little way, with a new Alien Act, operative from 1906, which allowed certain kinds of immigrants to be turned back, partly as a response to nativist agitation in the East End. That was implemented only very mildly by the new Liberal government of that year, however—hence the "'Oo let 'em in?" cries. In any case the Act specifically exempted anyone claiming—again, simply *claiming*—political asylum. Britain's extradition laws and treaties mirrored this. All of these, too, exempted political crimes. That included even crimes which were crimes by any definition, but committed for political motives; hence, a foreigner accused of murdering a politician abroad, or even a theater audience if it were out of political principle, could not be extradited in any circumstances. There is one minor exception. In 1894 an anarchist murderer called Meunier was extradited, on the ingenious grounds that because anarchism was against all politics, it could not be defined as a "political" creed. And "politicos" could be tried in Britain for their offences, theoretically at least. Even there, however, they had advantages. One was the right early on to be tried by a jury half made up of foreigners. They usually forewent this right, trusting "to the good sense of twelve honest Englishmen," as they typically put it, in order to ingratiate themselves with them (it often worked); another was a certain liberal prejudice in favor of foreign politicos, as we shall shortly see. Even if they were convicted, as some were, they probably ended up better off than in their own countries. British prisons were pretty barbaric at this period; but at least you were in no danger of having your fingernails torn out there, as had happened apparently to one of the Sidney Street gang in a Russian jail. So Britain was the safest possible haven for even the most violent of terrorists.

Britain as a country of asylum was under considerable foreign pressure to modify this line. Other countries suffered more from the terrorists' activities than Britain. Resentment at her for harboring these firebrands went back a long way. In the early 1850s it may have nearly sparked a war between Britain and those continental governments whose revolutionaries had fled to Britain after the suppression of the 1848 uprisings, and whom Britain declined to return. Continental governments could scarcely credit it. They believed Britain was as vulnerable to these men as themselves. Reports flooded in to the Foreign Office warning of specific refugee plots against her, especially during the Great Exhibition of 1851, when thousands of foreign malcontents would be there. (One had the refugees dressed as match-sellers, using their unsold matches to set fire to London at night. That was a joint plot by American Catholics and European socialists to make Bishop Hughes of New York the Pope. Another claimed that Karl Marx, no less, was plotting to assassinate the Queen. A third had the refugees cunningly disguised as trees—the Exhibition, of course, was held in Hyde Park.) But Britain refused to act. "Every civilised nation on the face of the earth," proclaimed *The Times,* "must be fully aware that this country is the asylum of nations, and that it will defend the asylum to the last ounce of its treasure, and the last drop of its blood. There is no point whatever on which we are prouder and more resolute."[4] One French writer smelled a plot here. Britain was using the refugees, he claimed; having only a pathetic army, she was hiring these foreigners to subvert her enemies from within. That explained why 1848 had largely passed her by: if everyone's house in a village is ablaze except one, he asked rhetorically, where do you look for the incendiary?[5]

In 1858 the row flared up again when one of the conspirators in the failed Orsini plot to kill Napoleon III, Simon Bernard, fled to England, and the British government refused to send him back. In this case the government buckled a little: it put Bernard on trial, and moved a bill in Parliament to make it easier to prosecute foreigners for crimes committed abroad. But the results were disastrous. Bernard was acquitted—though he was clearly guilty—by a jury that did not like being told what to do by the French, and the "Conspiracy to Murder" bill was defeated, bringing Palmerston's government down with it. Bernard's defense hinged entirely on the pressure that was supposed to have come from the French Emperor:

> Tell him [the emperor] that you will acquit the prisoner—and that though 600,000 French bayonets glitter in your sight; though the roar of French cannon thunder in your ears, your verdict will be firmly and courageously given—careless whether that verdict pleases or displeases a French despot. . . .[6]

And so on. It is rousing stuff. (Bernard's barrister had started off as an actor.) This is a description of the scene in the gallery when Bernard was finally acquitted:

> The moment these words [Not Guilty] were uttered the excited audience raised a loud and continued cheer, such as had seldom been heard in a court of justice, and this they repeated again and again, and in which even some members of the bar joined. Men, in their frantic joy, raised their hats, and ladies in their wild enthusiasm stood on their seats and waved their handkerchiefs, and cheered and cheered again.[7]

That showed what happened when you "truckled to foreigners," as it was usually put. Governments might not be averse to a bit of truckling. It would have made their lives easier diplomatically. But "the people" would not brook it.

All this was quite early on; but the memory of these events remained in the minds of ministers on every subsequent occasion when foreign governments put pressure on them to act against the refugees: after the Paris Commune, for example, and in the wake of all those assassinations in the 1890s. If they gave in to a recent Russian demand on Britain to keep a police watch merely on Russian exiles in Britain, wrote a Home Office Under-Secretary in 1878, citing the 1858 precedent directly, "no-one can say how the present feeling against Russia, & the long-established feeling on the subject of absolute government, right of asylum, & secret police would not carry the public, when inflamed by political and social agitators."[8] In 1898 an international "Anti-Anarchist Conference" was convened in Rome to discuss common measures that might be taken against terrorism: easier extradition, stricter immigration controls, tougher "homeland security" laws, closer police co-operation, and so on. Britain stood almost alone in refusing to go along with any of this. There was some closer police co-operation, but it was kept secret. Her continental neighbors huffed and puffed against this, but without any joy. Britain stood firm.

THE CONTRAST WITH THE PRESENT DAY IS GLARING. What were the reasons for it? A couple are obvious. First, Britain was strong enough to defy the other powers. It would be more difficult now, even if she wanted to. Second, the situation *vis-à-vis* terrorism was not the same around 1900 as it is today—it was not as threatening. A proto-9/11 never seemed really likely (any more, probably, than it seemed on 9/10). Science had not yet come up with most of the horrors that plague us now: nerve agents, computer viruses, and nuclear bombs.

Anarchists of all kinds, violent and peaceful, were far more of a minority in the 1890s than fundamentalist Muslims of all kinds are in the 2000s. Britain was only a peripheral target then, except for the Irish-American Fenians, who were too incompetent to do any real damage. All this goes a long way to explain how Britain could afford to stick to her tolerant and principled line over these questions in the earlier period. It does not altogether, however, tell us why she did.

The reasons lie in her liberal traditions. Most Britons were inordinately proud of their asylum policy, which went back—certainly in their national mythology—for centuries. The French Huguenots had been the first substantial group of refugees that had fled to Britain, in the sixteenth and seventeenth centuries. Most of them, incidentally, had initially settled in exactly the same area of London that the east European Jews were coming into in the late nineteenth century. Descriptions of them always emphasized the enormous contribution that they had made thereafter to British life. The same was true of many of the political refugees who came to Britain in the early nineteenth century, who included, for example, Gabrieli Rossetti, Professor of Italian at London University and the father of Dante Gabriel and Christina Rossetti; and Antonio (later Sir Anthony) Panizzi, the greatest ever Librarian of the British Museum. That was one reason for welcoming them. Obviously, though, it did not apply to all of them: the Marxes, Mazzinis, Bakunins, Kropotkins, and Lenins for example, as well as the Simon Bernards and Peter the Painters, who also took advantage of Britain's great generosity in the nineteenth and early twentieth centuries. No one believed that *they* would become Chief Librarians of the British Museum. They were, quite frankly, a pain. But this was the point. The fact that they were a pain made it so much more flattering to Britain that she could tolerate them. There is no particular virtue in giving a home to a house-trained kitten. A wild tiger, however, is something else. Britain could take in tigers. That showed how truly liberal, and also how resilient, she was.

More important than this, however, was that it showed how much *better* she was than her neighbors. This was the real attraction of her asylum tradition: it displayed her virtues in direct contrast to others' deficiencies. It was an instrument of popular chauvinism, even xenophobia, as well as of simple pride. The Bernard trial exemplifies this well. Bernard's jurors (and the MPs who voted down the Conspiracy Bill) were not going to give in to a lot of foreigners. This was also a reason why they objected to extradition: they simply did not trust foreign courts. In this case, unlike today, national chauvinism worked

in the asylum-seekers' favor. It operated at the time of the Sidney
Street business as well. However much people deplored the activities of "Peter the Painter" and the rest, they loathed the Tsar far
more. They also tended to explain and even excuse the former in
terms of the latter. Stories of the terrible tortures suffered by these
men and women in Russia were circulating widely in the 1900s.
That was what had turned them into such monsters. You could not
help but have some sympathy for them. Even in the sensational
fiction of the day they are not always portrayed unsympathetically.
A common convention was to have anarchist gangs "led" by beautiful and aristocratic-born women with noble souls, but twisted by
Tsarist atrocities. One of them, called Zalma, is portrayed with "puls-
ing busts, which hid behind the down of fur and lace, as though they
were moons about to appear from masses of feathery clouds."[9] It
must have been difficult to work up a proper rage against her. Similarly, and in real life, Peter the Painter's "Wanted" poster portrays a
very refined, handsome man. It would not do to send these poor
victims back.

More important was *why* Britain could tolerate them more. It was
because she was so liberal. That made her safer. Other countries
were less safe because they were more tyrannical. Furthermore, it
was their tyranny that gave rise to the "terrorism" (or whatever else
it might be called) in the first place. Terrorism was a response to
bad—that is, illiberal—government. That was why Russia was so
afflicted by it. Liberal countries did not spawn such monsters.
Everyone was born a kitten; whether he or she grew up into a cud-
dly cat or a tiger depended on how kindly and well he was ruled. By
the same token, tigers, wherever they came from, could do damage
only to tyrannies, not to liberal states like Britain. Palmerston in
1852 expressed this with another metaphor:

> A single spark will explode a powder magazine, and a blazing
> torch will burn out harmless on a turnpike road. If a country be in
> a state of suppressed internal discontent, a very slight indication
> may augment that discontent, and produce an explosion; but if
> the country be well governed, and the people be contented, then
> letters and proclamations from unhappy refugees will be as harm-
> less as the torch upon the turnpike road.[10]

He also noted how safe and happy the Queen had been when she
came to open the Great Exhibition in May 1851, despite all those
hairy revolutionaries and the lurid rumors that surrounded them.
Terrorists could do no harm to Britain. If they could harm other
countries, then it was those countries' own fault: almost—though

no one quite came out with this—what they deserved. It was the result of repression; ironically, and perhaps counter-intuitively, because it was the repression, of course, that was supposed to stamp it out. Hence Britain's response to Irish terrorism—her only home-grown variety (and we have seen that even that was not truly home-grown)—was to offer the Irish more freedom, or "home rule." One word for this is "appeasement," which ought to give those who always use that word derogatively pause for thought. That shows a certain consistency. The best prophylactic against revolution and terror was not less freedom—the Russian way—but more.

The British people were tolerant of the refugees, partly to feed their national *amour propre;* but they were not exactly welcoming. The refugees were cold-shouldered. There were some exceptions. The better class of early Italians—men like Rossetti and Panizzi—was lionized by the Whig establishment. The Poles had a number of high-class friends and sponsors in Britain, including most notably Lord Dudley Stuart, who organized a "society" dance annually to provide some charity for them. To mark this event *The Times,* which was not so fond of the refugees, used to come out with leading articles sneering at Stuart and "his Polish balls."[11] The 1848ers were befriended by the more "Fraternal"—that is, internationalist—of the Chartists, including James Julian Harney and Ernest Jones. Harney in fact serialized Karl Marx's *Communist Manifesto* in his *Red Republican* newspaper in 1850. But these were exceptions. Most of the refugees found themselves friendless. The French were probably the least popular, though in their case this was partly because they never showed the gratitude the British thought was owed to them for saving their lives. Almost the first thing Alexandre Ledru-Rollin did on stepping off the boat was to write a long book attacking Britain, *La Décadence d'Angleterre.* That was not polite. Many refugees struggled to survive, by begging or stealing, for example—they were always appearing in police courts—or by writing (like Marx) for American newspapers. A few resorted to murder. One, called Emmanuel Barthélemy, murdered twice: the first time he was let off because the judge thought that, being French, he probably did not understand that murder was illegal in Britain; the second time, however, he was hanged—and ended up in effigy in Madame Tussaud's. (He was an atheist, and his last words on the scaffold were "Now I shall learn whether I am right".)[12] For many of the refugees this neglect, or worse, must have been all the more painful, after the fame (or notoriety) they had bathed in at home. "The life here," wrote the Russian exile Alexander Herzen, "like the air here, is bad for the weak, for the frail, for one who seeks a prop outside himself, for one

who seeks welcome, sympathy, attention; the moral lungs here must
be as strong as the physical lungs, whose task it is to separate oxygen
from the smoky fog."[13] Elsewhere he called it "as dull as the life of a
worm in a cheese" (though who is to say how a cheese appears to a
worm?).[14] Most refugees huddled together with other refugees, often in little ghettoes—London's Seven Dials earlier, the East End
later—for the support they found lacking in their host community;
but even this was not as comforting as it should have been. The exile groups were riddled with (their own) police spies. "Peter the
Painter" was suspected of being one—otherwise how was he able to
escape so easily after Sidney Street? This unfriendliness was the reverse side of Britain's famed liberalism.

They were, however, faces of the same coin. Victorian British liberalism was never about friendliness. It was about the free market,
and individuals finding their places in that. Immigrants were let in
indiscriminately because that was what the law of the market dic-
tated: no restraints on the movement of anything, in order to mini-
mize cost and maximize value. Hence "free trade." Hence also the
absolutely free movement of men and women in the labor market,
which implied no restrictions on immigration from abroad, even if
the result was to undercut wages at home. That was just the God of
the market ruling. The argument is familiar. Refugees were inci-
dental beneficiaries of it—in one way. It meant that Britain had to
allow them in. It also meant, however, that she was not obliged to do
anything for them after that. The idea was that people were attracted
in for economic reasons: usually to work. Those who came for other
reasons were anomalous to that. No provision was made for them;
indeed, it hardly occurred to anyone that it should be. Earlier in the
nineteenth century, before free market ideology had caught on
fully, Parliament had voted "grants" to relieve certain groups of
exiles—Poles, Italians, Spaniards—presumably out of sympathy for
their political views and situations; but by the 1850s this had more or
less stopped. Private charity never filled the gap. The money raised
by Lord Dudley Stuart's balls, for instance, was never enough. An attempt by Harney to collect money from the working classes for the
relief of the '48ers had to be abandoned when only £69 11s—a de-
risory sum even in those days—was raised. For Harney this was bitter proof of "the absolute indifference of the great mass of the British people to the claims of the political exiles."[15] But then why
should the working classes subsidize these exiles, when they were
only subject to the same market disciplines as themselves? It is not as
though there was any discrimination. The British working classes
had to struggle to live as well. There seemed no logical reason why
foreign immigrants should be privileged over them.

This had a number of implications. The first, of course, was un-
happiness and real suffering among the refugees: some because
they could not find work (it was difficult for Polish speakers, for example); others because they were unwilling even to look for it. That
was something to set against the "toleration" they enjoyed. The German Joanna Kinkel, for example, was full of praise for the latter—
for Britain's remarkable political liberties; but, she wrote home in
1854, "one must work terribly hard here."[16] Second, this was undoubtedly a deterrent for many refugees against coming to Britain
in the first place, in preference to certain other western European
countries, which were usually more generous towards exiles of
whom they approved. That probably lessened the flow. (Those who
went to America were different; most of them had given up on their
political ambitions in their homelands. They mutated into "settlers,"
rather than strict "refugees.") On the other hand—third—it meant
that those who did come to Britain were often the fieriest ones:
those of whom France, Switzerland and the other "asylum" countries of Europe did not approve, and felt they could not contain.
Unfriendly Britain may have been a last resort, but she was the *only*
resort for these. Many of them—"Peter the Painter," for example—
had tried several of the other countries first. That made the refugee
community in Britain more potent and also more volatile than
those in other countries, which might have been expected to alienate the natives, but did not, as we have seen. One additional reason
for this may have been a fourth ramification of Britain's lack of
charity: that no one could object to them on the grounds that they
were "scrounging" off the British state. This is one of the arguments
that is often leveled against asylum seekers in Britain today—that
they are milking her welfare system, or even choosing Britain in the
first place in order to benefit from her generosity. It is called "welfare tourism." That argument could not be deployed in pre-1914
Britain. Refugees were not taking anything from the native Britons.
With so few being willing to work, they were not even undercutting
wages. If they could not make it on their own, or with help from
their own communities, they starved—like the rest of the British
working class population. No one could reasonably object to that.
And if they did manage to find work—this is the fifth and last
ramification—it probably meant they had less time for their more
dangerous activities. They were too tired at the end of the day. This
was one way in which capitalism was supposed to tame people and
neutralize radicalism. It was another reason for all those blazing
torches burning out harmlessly on Britain's turnpike road.

The uncanny contemporary resonance of that 1910 New York
picture might suggest that there are practical lessons to be drawn

from that period for today. But that is too much to expect. History does not repeat itself; or if it does, then it is, as Marx claimed, differently. He suggested first as tragedy, then as farce. (He was thinking of the two Napoleons; the second—Napoleon III—a refugee in Britain himself at one stage.) In the present case these appear to be reversed. Cheap sensation in 1910 became grim and horrifying reality in 2001. That changed perceptions of the "terrorist threat" everywhere. No country could any longer afford to be as liberal and tolerant of potential terrorists as Britain was before 1914. There are no safe turnpike roads any more. And the convenient theory, that only countries which deserve it are vulnerable to terrorism, may be less convincing now than it was in the nineteenth century. Even if not, it must be less of a comfort to anyone who lives in a less perfect polity than Britain prided herself on being in Victorian times.

As for our 1910 terrorists: here there was a happy ending—not for them, but for humankind generally. The anarchists overreached themselves. After subduing most of America and Europe, mainly with poison gas this time, they decide to go exploring, becoming the first to discover the North Pole, for example, where they discover the source of the aurora borealis—a great "radium lake"; and then are the first to scale Mount Everest. They prang their aircraft on the summit of that, however, and all die through lack of oxygen. It may be too much to hope that their present-day successors will do the same.[17]

Spring Semester 2004

Sources

The "9/11" picture is taken from George Glendon, *The Emperor of the Air* (London, 1910); the one of Big Ben falling down from E. Douglas Fawcett, *Hartmann the Anarchist, or the Doom of a Great City* (London, 1893). The Fenian "super-gun" features in Donald Mackay, *The Dynamite Ship* (London, 1888). Fergus Hume, *The Year of Miracle: A Tale of the Year One Thousand Nine Hundred* (London, 1891), has London destroyed by something very much like a "dirty bomb." The villain of W. L. Alden's "The Purple Death," originally published in *Cassell's Magazine,* February 1885, threatens to wipe out two-thirds of the world's population with a virus. The social justification for this is that it will treble wages. The same theme, of anarchists destroying or controlling the world through deadly science, is found in George Griffith, *The Angel of the Revolution: A Tale of the Coming Terror* (London, 1893); Hume Nisbet, *The Great Secret: A Tale of Tomorrow* (London, 1895); T. Mullett Ellis, *Zalma* (London, 1895); Robert Cromie, *A New Messiah* (London, 1902); and W. Holt White, *The Earthquake: A Romance of London in 1907* (London, 1906).

More "respectable" contemporary novelists who explored this theme less sensationally were Joseph Conrad, *The Secret Agent* (London, 1907), mentioned in the text; Henry James, *The Princess Casamassima* (London, 1886), its anarchist refugee villain also based on a real case; Robert Louis Stevenson, *The Dynamiter* (London, 1885); and G. K. Chesterton, *The Man who was Thursday: A Nightmare* (London, 1908).

The secondary sources for the historical part of this essay are Hermia Oliver, *The International Anarchist Movement in Late Victorian London* (London, 1983); Richard Bach Jensen, "The International Anti-Anarchist Conference of 1898 and the Origins of Interpol," in *Journal of Contemporary History,* 16 (1981); and Bernard Porter, *The Refugee Question in mid-Victorian Politics* (London, 1979), and *The Origins of the Vigilant State* (London, 1987).

1. *Tit-Bits*, Mar. 14, 1894, p. 404.

2. Donald Rumbelow, *The Houndsditch Murders and the Siege of Sidney Street* (London, 1973), p. 119.

3. Police report of Mar. 19, 1853, Public Record Office PRO HO 45/4816.

4. *The Times*, Feb. 28, 1853.

5. Charles de Bussy, *Les Conspirateurs en Angleterre 1848–1858* (Paris, 1858), p. 78.

6. State Trials, n.s., Vol. VIII, c. 1024.

7. *People's Paper*, Apr. 24, 1858, p. 3.

8. Henderson memorandum, Oct. 15, 1878, in PRO HO45/9473/A60556.

9. T. Mullett Ellis, *Zalma* (London, 1895), p. 38.

10. Palmerston in House of Commons, *Parliamentary Debates* (Lords), Apr. 1, 1852, cc. 511–12.

11. E.g. *The Times*, Dec. 11 and 19, 1848, Oct. 28, 1850, May 21, 1853.

12. Charles Hugo, *Les Hommes de l'Exil* (Paris, 1875), pp. 38–42.

13. Alexander Herzen, *My Past and Thoughts* (1968 ed.), Vol. III, p. 1025.

14. Quoted in Monica Partridge, "Alexander Herzen and the English Press," *Slavonic and East European Review*, 36 (1957–58), p. 470.

15. *Reynolds's Newspaper*, Aug. 8, 1852, p. 13.

16. Rosemary Ashton, *Little Germany: Exile and Asylum in Victorian England* (London, 1986), p. xii.

17. As this book was in press, the following report from Guantanamo Bay appeared in the Guardian newpaper (Jan. 22, 2005). "Mr. [Moazzem] Begg, who says he has been tortured by the US while in captivity, is reported to have confessed to a plot to bomb the Houses of Parliament with remote controlled planes full of anthrax. His supporters say that such a plan is technically impossible, and that he confessed to try to stop the ill treatment he was suffering." But it may also be thought to carry an uncanny resonance from the "Big Ben" picture on p. [?].

2

The Pax Britannica, American Hegemony, And the International Order, 1793–2003

PATRICK K. O'BRIEN

Τhis lecture will argue that since the Roman Empire no other state, especially not Britain, has deployed hegemonic power or anything comparable to the combination of domination by force and leadership by consent exercised by the United States between 1941 and 2001.[1] Indeed, before the entry of America into the Second World War, no emperor, monarch, ruling oligarchy, or sovereign assembly pretended to formulate and enforce rules designed to shape and stabilize an international order for the operation of competition and co-operation among states. Even when policies pursued by other leading powers of their day had some discernible but unintended consequences of curbing the violence and mitigating the inefficiencies associated with an otherwise anarchic system of geopolitical relations and international commerce, the scale, scope, intensity, and duration of their actions cannot be compared with those of the United States over the past seven decades.

Only the United States has ever created conditions, allocated resources, and displayed intentions to enforce rules for a stable and effective operation of political, economic, and cultural relations between states. Nevertheless, social scientists have supposedly perceived (and some purport to have measured) increases in security and prosperity that they have correlated with actions taken by a succession of "hegemonic" states going back as far as Sung China (960–1279).[2] In search of validation from history, they have associated demarcated periods or cycles of instability and insecurity in world history with the absence of a hegemonic power capable of restoring some semblance of order to an otherwise malfunctioning system of interstate relations.[3] Their best, indeed their only conceivable, example is the British Empire. Thus a paradigm has been constructed and widely accepted that, after an interregnum of interstate violence and neo-mercantilism, the United States succeeded to the benign hegemonic role that Britain had played in the geopolitical and economic order from the time of the French Revolution down to the Great War of 1914–18.[4] Analogies in the history of great power politics are not difficult to display. Nevertheless, this lecture will substantiate the case that contrasts between the roles played by Britain between 1793 and 1914, and the United States from 1941 to 2003, overwhelm superficial similarities. The argument is that the contexts and circumstances in which these two great powers emerged and operated are singular. The commonplace representation of the Pax Britannica is a self-serving myth, sustained by an Anglo-American political and intellectual elite who have gained most from propagating it since the Second World War.

Obvious contrasts are immediately apparent when the histories of the international relations preceding the assumption of "hegemony" by the United States and "primacy" by Britain are placed side by side.[5] Before 1917 (and perhaps as late as 1941) the geopolitical context in which governments in Washington operated was virtually confined to the Americas, north and south. In 1823, prompted by George Canning (Britain's Foreign Secretary), President Monroe explicitly reserved the entire Western hemisphere as a sphere of influence for the new Republic.[6] Tacitly protected by the Royal Navy from all further attempts at colonization by an Iberian, Dutch, French, or any other European power seeking territory and wealth in the Americas, confrontations thereafter between the United States and other powers were overwhelmingly with its wary and rejected mother country. Over Texas, Oregon, California, Venezuela, Panama, even Canada, as well as the far more serious issue of the Confederacy, governments in London invariably appeased Washington.[7] After the war of 1812–14, Britain complied with the Monroe Doctrine and the Royal Navy virtually enforced it because Britain's command of the seas meant that other European powers had no option but to allow federal governments in Washington to hold the Union together and to concentrate on the exploitation of a sparsely populated continent, rich in natural resources, with enormous potential for economic growth. Even after the closing of the internal frontier and when the American navy moved (as European navies had done for centuries past) to secure the new nation's "home waters" by establishing bases (Puerto Rico, Cuba, Guam, Hawaii, and the Philippines) in the blue waters of the Pacific and Atlantic oceans, only Mexico, Spain, and, in a farcical fashion, France under Napoleon III, challenged its manifest destiny and precocious ambitions to secure both continental and oceanic power.[8]

Meanwhile American business, operating within an evolving framework of law and institutions highly conducive to private enterprise, realized the inherent potential in the continent's massive and accessible endowments of fertile land and minerals. That potential was already obvious to European observers before the American Revolution, when labor productivity and per capita incomes were perhaps already close to British standards.[9] Thereafter, a constellation of highly favorable forces led to the almost inexorable growth of the economy. American success rested upon territorial expansion (sometimes at the expense of France, Mexico, and Russia); the exploitation of slave and black labor in the old south; rapid demographic growth complemented by a large influx of healthy skilled and semi-skilled adolescents from Europe; highly favorable and seemingly unlimited endowments of natural resources which attracted funds available for investment on London and other European capital markets; and finally the diffusion of homogeneous tastes and mass markets, reinforced after the Civil War by an intensified process of ideological, linguistic, legal, and cultural assimilation to the aims of American capitalism.[10] Relatively unencumbered by social distinctions, protected from external aggression, unhampered by problems of internal security, very lightly taxed and regulated, provided with ready access to European skills, capital, and technology, the integrated economy of the United States could hardly fail to grow more rapidly than the economies of its industrializing rivals in Western Europe.[11]

Shortly after the Civil War, the US national output exceeded the combined outputs of Britain, France, and Germany. By the 1870s there is little doubt that the United States offered the majority of its white citizens higher standards of living and prospects for upward mobility than anything available in Europe. By the 1890s the gap in real per capita incomes had become significant and it increased steadily until the middle of the twentieth century. Over the late twentieth century the average differential in real incomes between Europe and the United States has narrowed but in scale and scope the American economy still remains larger and technologically more sophisticated than the now integrating European Union.[12]

No doubt Europeans have only themselves to blame for their failures to keep up and then catch up with the economy of the United States. Their barbaric and highly destructive wars of 1914–18 and

1939–45 (separated by an interregnum of antagonism and neo-mercantilism 1919–39) surely account for more of Europe's relative retardation than any resort to crude binary comparisons which posit superior American technologies, scales of production, institutions, cultural values, and other non-quantifiable factors. There were obstacles but never barriers to the diffusion of American know-how.[13] Furthermore, it is not clear when and how far the techniques and scales of production, designed to exploit the North American continent's rich portfolio of natural resources and to produce goods and services for mass consumption, became optimally efficient for European industries to adopt.[14]

Class struggles within, together with internecine warfare and imperial rivalry among European states, certainly held back the development of their economies and created the economic conditions as well as the political instability, predation, and violence which encouraged and allowed for the emergence of a unique form of hegemony over a world in which European power had been on the rise since the Portuguese conquered Ceuta in North Africa in 1415. Indeed the economic strength and the naval and military capacity required to assume such a role had already become apparent during the war of 1914–18, when the United States intervened late, and profitably, to prevent Germany from becoming the dominant power on the mainland and leaving, as the Germans suggested, Britain to continue as the preponderant power at sea.[15] Thereafter, for roughly a quarter of a century, the American stance towards an international system of weaker, economically retarded, politically unstable, and mutually antagonistic powers vacillated between a retreat towards isolation (within its own already vast hemisphere of influence and oceanic expanse of home waters) and the actions of a global hegemon in waiting.[16]

For example, after the Great War, America funded relief operations that helped towards the recovery of Europe. Furthermore, its plans (Young and Dawes) represented laudable attempts to rebuild a stable monetary system. But on the negative side, Washington's insistence on the full repayment of the loans and credits extended to help its allies defeat the Central Powers complemented the uncertainties surrounding the whole system of international exchange rates and the servicing of foreign debts after the most serious global war since the Napoleonic era. American rhetoric in favor of open trading was hardly congruent with the imposition of controls on immigration and protective legislation against imports passed by Congress.[17] Finally, and most damaging of all, came the Wall Street crash, followed by the collapse of the American banking system which led to the Great Depression of 1929–32 and delivered a severe blow to a fragile international monetary system, to overseas trade, and to a world economy struggling with the aftermath of the disruptions and interruptions that flowed from Europe's first great civil war of 1914–18.

Although debate continues about the causes of the Great Depression, the view that it constituted a crucial political as well as economic conjuncture in world history, that it originated in the United States, and that the New Deal did little to assist recovery outside American borders remains tenable after more than fifty years of modeling and research in economics and economic history.[18] Yet in the realm of political economy one outcome of the Depression was to reorder the perspectives of American elites responsible for the formation of economic policies affecting the vitality of their continental economy. Under Franklin Roosevelt their vistas widened to include foreign trade, exchange rates, and international financial flows as integrated components of their thinking about the economic interests of the United States.[19]

Britain's rise to primacy in a world dominated by European power politics looks very different from America's. As rulers of a small and not particularly advanced economy, located on an offshore island, the Tudor and Stuart regimes (1485–1688) had always taken full cognizance of their realm's place in a wider, largely European and Atlantic, economy as well as its vulnerability to attacks and invasion from the sea. Before the Glorious Revolution of 1688 they lacked the fiscal resources to play anything but a peripheral role in geopolitics on the mainland and relied on the sea together with a modest allocation of national resources to a partially privatized Royal Navy to defend their kingdom against external aggression.[20] England's detached position in the hierarchy of contending European states and economies began to change after the Civil War in the 1640s when its rulers (Republican and Royal alike) reconstructed a fiscal system capable of providing the state with the taxes and loans required to invest in naval power, to hire mercenaries, subsidize military allies on the continent, and to play an altogether more active role in power politics.[21] Between 1651 and 1802 the British state fought ten wars against major European rivals (the Netherlands, Spain, and above all France) to maintain the security of the realm, to preserve its highly inegalitarian system of property rights, to shore up the nation's share of the gains from trade and profits from servicing an expanding global economy, and to safeguard the kingdom's growing portfolio of assets: concessions, territories, natural resources, and colonies in the Americas, Africa, and Asia.[22]

At the Congress of Vienna in 1815 (and after twenty-two years of warfare against Revolutionary and Napoleonic France) Britons emerged with a recently united kingdom; the largest navy in the world; the most extensive occidental empire since Rome; extraordinary shares of the profits derived from overseas commerce; and a domestic economy that was in the throes of the first industrial revolution. Even then, in global terms, the economy of the realm remained small, but its exceptional endowments of fertile land, cheap energy, and a skilled workforce (together with an extraordinary navy) had enabled the offshore island to reallocate more of its national resources to manufacturing industry and to convert inputs into outputs somewhat more efficiently than its European rivals.[23]

The rivals' problems in contending with the rise of Britain (1651–1815) emanated in part from inferior natural endowments (especially deposits of coal) and marginally weaker economies. Retardation persisted and widened because the fiscal and financial systems could not provide the mainland states of *ancien régime* Europe with the taxes and loans required to match British expenditures on naval and military power. Between 1688 and 1815, when real expenditures on the army and navy multiplied by a factor of 15 while domestic product increased just three times, the Hanoverian state appropriated and borrowed a rising share of national resources which it used overwhelmingly to secure strategic, political, and related economic gains. Neither France, Spain, the Netherlands, nor any of Britain's competitors or clients could match London's ever-expanding capacity to tax, borrow, and spend on ships, arms, and troops, basically because fiscal arrangements and inefficient organizations for the assessment and collection of taxes constrained the powers of central governments (monarchical and oligarchical alike) to raise revenues. Furthermore, after three centuries of active engagement in state formation, re-formation, wars of religion, and imperial ventures overseas, by 1648 the fiscal systems had become almost impossible to reform. Resistance to the rulers' ever-increasing demands for revenues became entrenched, and the capacities of most European states to tax and to borrow declined. Thus in geopolitical terms the Hanoverian regime and its domestic economy benefited as a latecomer to power politics and rivalry for colonies and trade overseas.[24]

Toward the end of the four centuries of mercantilism (1415–1815), the entire system of international relations was rent apart by nearly twenty-five years of disruptive warfare associated with the French Revolution and the attempt of France to dominate continental Europe. When Napoleon's ambition was finally thwarted the British state, its fiscal and financial system, the Royal Navy, and its domestic economy emerged from the most destructive of European conflicts in a much better condition than the devastated economies, dilapidated fiscal bases, and defeated armed forces of its rivals. Plenipotentiaries, gathered at the Congress of Vienna in 1815 to re-establish some kind of stable international order, recognized that the one clear outcome of the French Revolution had been to elevate British trade, commerce, finance, industry, and naval power to unmistakable positions of primacy in Europe, Asia, Africa, and the Americas. They looked to the recovery of their economies, the reconstruction of their financial systems, and the rebuilding of their armed forces. They even supported the reconstruction of monarchical government in France to bring back a balance of power that might preserve the status quo ante and check any latent British ambitions.[25]

Nevertheless—and despite the fact that Britain had cobbled together four coalitions, subsidized the armies of Austria, Prussia, Russia, and several minor powers, committed troops to campaigns in Iberia and Flanders, provided the bulk of the naval power to defeat France and its allies at sea—when Napoleon was finally defeated no European state looked to Britain to play the role of hegemon. Furthermore, Britain's rulers never contemplated or presumed to occupy the place assigned to them retrospectively by social scientists whose theories implicitly "predict" that the systemic properties of a "Hegelian system" of international relations would prompt them and their rivals to do just that at the Congress of Vienna.[26]

Nothing like a post-Vienna reversion to normal power politics followed the Second World War, when an alliance of states, dominated and heavily funded by America, had inflicted crushing defeats on Germany, Italy, and Japan. Years before the unprecedented unconditional surrender of its enemies, Washington had already taken the lead in drawing up plans for the post-war reconstruction of an international economic and political order that would avoid the division of the world economy into competitive and potentially antagonistic British, French, Dutch, Portuguese, and Soviet empires. At the end of a destructive war, when its mobilized economy had fully recovered from the long depression of the 1930s, the United States possessed fiscal capacity, financial strength, a benign history in power politics, and above all the political confidence acquired from managing an alliance of powers that had won so decisive a victory over European fascism and Japanese militarism. Washington was able and willing to take the lead in promoting economic recovery and maintaining political stability. With Britain, still burdened with imperial responsibilities, afflicted by delusions of grandeur, and with illusions of a "special relationship," among the leading supplicants for aid, only the Soviet Union, whose strategic frontiers had been extended by the Red Army into the heartlands of central Europe, resisted American aspirations for a new international order.[27]

Within a year the two opposing ideologies of communism and capitalism (latent in wartime) led to the beginnings of a "Cold War." For four decades international relations were dominated by the division of the world into antagonistic coalitions of armed powers led by the Soviet Union on the one side and the United States on the other. Most other states, explicitly or tacitly, and with varying degrees of solidarity, reluctance, and episodes of disloyalty, opted to accept protection from the latter. In the middle of a barbaric century, and with the collapse of all pretensions that Europeans could provide more benign and civilized forms of alien rule for Asia, Africa, and the Middle East, only the Americans were confident in their liberal ideology, historical record, and capability to manage the international economic and geopolitical order. An American (largely east coast) establishment offered governments and their citizens an alternative to fascism, communism, and re-incorporation into the Soviet or some other European empire. Resistance to the exercise of a well-funded hegemony by a power ostensibly untainted by prior histories of imperialism and aggression in great power politics matured, despite the rhetorical stance taken by some third world leaders against American dominance, into tacit compliance.[28]

Clearly the defeated axis powers, Germany, Italy, and Japan (as well as Fascist Iberia) had virtually no alternative to incorporation into a "Western" alliance. In addition, scores of ethnically diverse countries, recently emancipated from colonial rule and preoccupied with state formation, the forging of national identities, and economic development, also looked to Washington for all the loans and credits they could obtain, particularly for the training and funding of their armed forces. Naturally, conditions were attached to programs of aid funded and managed by Americans.[29]

Among European states only Britain and France maintained the pretence of possessing nuclear capability. Aligned but also other non-aligned "Bandung" powers such as India made the plausible assumption that they were explicitly or implicitly part of a nuclear protectorate and that Washington would in the last resort defend them from threats of takeover by the Soviet Union or by Communist China.[30]

Since 1941 the United States has signed an unparalleled range of agreements to defend the sovereignty and territorial integrity of an astonishing number of regimes of every conceivable political persuasion located on every continent. American taxpayers have now witnessed six decades of unprecedented levels of peacetime expenditures to maintain a military and naval presence around the world. The majority of the American electorate acquiesces and, with occasional lapses into skepticism, usually applauds patriotically the day-to-day involvement of their politicians, diplomats, armed forces, and security services in the formulation, funding, and execution of policies designed to protect far-away and otherwise sovereign governments against threats of external aggression, internal subversion, and more recently from terrorism. Presidential programs defending the allocation of resources to contain communism, to isolate potentially disruptive regimes such as North Korea, Cuba, Libya, and now Iraq usually attract an overwhelming national consensus.[31]

For a society with a long fiscal tradition of opposition to imperial and federal taxation, the proportion of US national income appropriated in peacetime by democratically elected governments for expenditures on strategic objectives has been extraordinarily high. Although Washington's fiscal base penetrates into a highly productive continental economy, America's hegemonic role could not and has not been sustained from tax revenues alone. Economists and political scientists can usually be mobilized by Presidents to assure the electorate that any reduction in America's expenditures on preserving stability for the international system as a whole would lead to further costs. Federal expenditures on strategic policy, however, have been covered only intermittently and partially by taxation. Budget deficits emerged during the Second World War and persisted into the last decade of the twentieth century. They have now reappeared during the war on terrorism.

If "British hegemony" can be located anywhere in the historical record from 1793 to 1914 it appeared briefly in the sphere of foreign trade (though largely in the guise of diplomacy and ideological persuasion), rather than in the form of power. The Kingdom's policy of free trade in an international economy prone to protectionism and degenerative bouts of mercantilism is famous. It first appeared as a geopolitical strategy after the American War of Independence under Pitt the Younger but went sharply into reverse during the last great European conflict of the mercantilist era (1793–1815) and was not even placed on the table at the Congress of Vienna in 1815. At that point Prime Minister Castlereagh concentrated on securing a political settlement and no European state attempted to address the problem of reconstructing an international economic order.[32]

Nearly three decades later tariff reform and free trade reappeared on Britain's own political agenda, but they did so almost entirely as an expedient designed to resolve a serious constitutional split between agrarian and other interests over the protection of grain farming. Britain's famous Corn Law controversy provided its aristocratic Tory and Whig elites with an opportunity to restrain demands for further constitutional reform, to tidy up the fiscal system by restoring an income tax, and (too late) to meet responsibilities to Ireland by alleviating what was the most serious famine to afflict any European population during the nineteenth century. Ministers at the time of the "Hungry 'Forties" saw the repeal of the Corn Laws and Navigation Acts, along with imperial preferences, as nothing more than a response to Britain's own social, constitutional, political, and administrative problems. Neither Robert Peel nor any other statesmen involved in the reformation of fiscal policy ever pretended to be offering "public goods" for the international economic order as a whole.[33]

Although the Royal Navy had not (as some powers had feared) been used to interfere with the trade of competitors, and Britain had even relinquished the right to interdict neutral shipping trading with its enemies in wartime, the subsequent formulation and implementation of a British diplomatic program for the extension of open trading among nations matured slowly. That project really came on stream during the third quarter of the nineteenth century as a sequence of bilateral treaties which invariably included "Most Favored Nation" clauses.[34]

Free trade then became part of Britain's enduring national ideology. Thereafter, and down to the Ottawa agreements of 1932, the success of the Victorian and Edwardian economy as well as the stability of Britain's parliamentary constitution and the nation's status as a great power all became linked to free trade policy. Once again, Britain's classical economists and their popularizers (such as Richard Cobden) could be mobilized to demonstrate rigorously that open trading was the only rational policy to pursue for their homeland and its vast empire, and the rest of the world as well. For roughly three decades that message gained sympathy not merely among European and American liberals but with the autocratic rulers of France, Spain, Prussia, and the Romanov and Habsburg Empires as well. Impressed with British economic success, anxious to avoid costly bouts of warfare, in search of cheaper food for their potentially disorderly urban working classes, and short of revenues, they lowered tariffs. Smaller trading powers (Holland, Portugal, and Switzerland) made moves in a British direction entirely congruent with their interests. "Clients" in South America found British pressures irresistible, while the weak Qing, Ottoman, Tokugawa, and Siamese empires could be intimidated by actual or threatened use of gunboat diplomacy.[35]

During a liberal interlude in world affairs, Britain took the lead and promoted open trade. Unfortunately, that limited program of persuasion, pressure, and occasional use of naval power collapsed with the 1870 unification of Germany and the Franco-Prussian War of 1870–71. Thereafter, in a more dangerous geopolitical climate marked by rearmament, the scramble for colonies in Africa and Asia, and intensified competition on world markets, British statesmen virtually withdrew from any active promotion of open trade on a global scale. Confronted with the revival of protectionism, they convened no international congresses to seek agreements on trade, tariffs, or commercial codes of conduct. Although the Foreign Office negotiated a few bilateral treaties to help British exports, the Cabinet adhered rigidly to a unilateralist version of free trade, declined to barter, and hoped that Britain's moral example and the transparent economic rationality of her policies would restrain the rising tide of nationalism and neo-mercantilism which had, to their annoyance, surfaced in the Dominions.[36]

The British government's persuasive defense of a popular tradition led the electorate to reject campaigns for fair trade and imperial preference which might have provided the state with the power of sanctions required to bargain with France, Germany, America, and other major powers for the preservation of an open trading regime.[37] Even in the sphere of international relations that the British elite and the electorate at large (for economic and ideological reasons) cared most about, the imperial state in London remained circumspect and even timorous in the use of power (or any strategic trade policy) to constrain the reversal to protectionism. Furthermore, those infamous episodes of gunboat diplomacy to prop up the Ottoman and open up the Qing Empires occurred largely for geopolitical reasons. The first was part of a strategy to contain the expansionist ambition of the Romanov Empire. As for the second, the British Navy fought two "opium wars" to preserve the substantial revenues that the Government of India derived from taxing the export of hard drugs to China.[38] In contrast, the policies of the United States of maintaining more open trade have relied less on diplomatic and ideological persuasion coupled with moral example and far more on sanctions mediated through the International Monetary Fund and the World Bank, but above all on clear threats of retaliation against foreign exports to the world's richest market.[39]

Circumspection and acts of appeasement marked Britain's foreign as well as commercial policies for most of the century after the Congress of Vienna. The Victorian state maintained a navy equal in scale and technical capability to the combined fleets of any two rival powers. It had committed troops to the mainland during the closing years of the war against Napoleon and refrained from continental commitments before the rise of Germany. Nevertheless the elite in charge of foreign relations remained acutely aware of serious constraints on their capacity for decisive action overseas.

Their preoccupation moved from geopolitical to imperial concerns. First and foremost (especially after Britain took over from the Mughal empire in India), the British found themselves responsible for the day-to-day governance and defense of an enormous empire which included territories, assets, and diverse populations on every continent. Year after year the frontiers of that Empire lengthened and bumped willy-nilly against the borders or zones of influence of rival European and Asian powers. What had been before 1815 a preoccupation with the security of the realm and the protection of overseas trade matured into responsibilities for a vulnerable and ever-expanding empire from which there could be no escape and for whose management and defense the fiscal base of the domestic economy remained woefully inadequate.[40]

Furthermore, the ever-increasing resources appropriated by the Hanoverian regime between 1688 and 1815 for the protection of trade and the achievement of a geopolitical primacy were no longer available to its Victorian and Edwardian successors. After the enormous sums borrowed as loans and expropriated as taxes to defeat the French between 1793 and 1815, it became extremely difficult for any nineteenth-century government to persuade Parliament to sanction further accumulation of debt. To restore trust in aristocratic rule, to achieve fiscal sobriety and treasury control became akin to articles of an unwritten constitution. Britain's *ancien régime* survived down to the Great War, but it was fiscally emasculated. It had no serious engagement in power politics except for policies that could be presented as entirely necessary. Cheap expedients were designed to preserve the security of the realm, defend an overseas empire, and protect trade.

These underlying structural constraints on the size and actions of the state can be represented as the reflexive reactions to 164 years of mercantilism going back to Cromwell's first Anglo-Dutch War of 1652, which came to an ostensibly triumphant end with Nelson's victory at Trafalgar and Wellington's close run thing at Waterloo. Britain's heritage of successful mercantilism and imperialism matured into a historical myth that sustained an ideology of distrust and antipathy towards the state among both an expanding electorate and parliaments bent on constitutional reform. Cabinets of aristocrats in control of foreign policy could only contain them by embracing prudence, parsimony, and *laissez faire*.[41]

Britain's unwritten fiscal constitution goes a long way to account for the anxious and circumscribed role played by an ostensibly powerful state in international relations from 1815–1914. Foreign Secretaries before Sir Edward Gray consistently avoided any entanglement in European power politics. They renounced all claims to territory (including Hanover) across the channel. British influence on the redrawing of frontiers, movements for national unification, democracy, and independence in mainland Europe can be represented as largely diplomatic and rhetorical. Continental commitments of troops to theaters of war in Europe, North America, and China were resolutely avoided, apart from that restricted conflict in the Crimea (1854–56), which could be regarded as a misallocation of troops and naval power to prop up the Ottoman Empire and to check Russian ambitions in the Balkans.[42]

Outside the Indian sub-continent and Africa, British troops were rarely deployed against other powers. When coercion was required to secure or defend a national objective, naval power was invariably the preferred option. Like air power today, navies operated at a distance (offshore) which constrained what could be achieved by bombarding coastal fortifications and ports hostile to British interests. Even sea power was used with circumspection in order to preclude the expensive naval arms races that had marked the long era of mercantilism 1415–1815.[43] Meanwhile, for the defense and expansion of empire the British state relied on an elite corps of officers recruited from the aristocracy and gentry and on unskilled, poorly paid, white soldiers from the urban underclass and the Celtic fringe. But the state depended overwhelmingly (in terms of numbers) on a large army of Indian mercenaries—paid for from taxes collected in India—drafted from time to time for imperial service in spheres of conflict beyond the sub-continent. Thus the "forces of the crown" were equipped up to, but not beyond, European standards of technical proficiency. They were managed by amateur or at best semi-professional officers, manned by an underclass of white troops, and dominated in numerical strength by Indians whose reliability after the Mutiny remained a matter of anxiety to Ministers in London as well as Viceroys in Delhi.[44]

Britain's military and naval primacy depended far more on the persistent weakness of defeated European rivals (France, the

Netherlands, and Iberia), the absorption of Prussia and Piedmont with the unification of Germany and Italy, and the compensations of overland expansion pursued by other rival territorial empires (run from St Petersburg, Vienna, and Washington) than any extraordinary economic, military, or cultural institutions. Britain's position in great power politics continued to depend on the Royal Navy, the decline of the Ottoman and Chinese Empires, and the geopolitical preoccupations that prevailed and evolved within Europe for roughly a century after the Congress of Vienna.[45]

Aristocratic and imperial rulers of the Victorian and Edwardian state seem, moreover, to have been aware that any attempts to move from primacy to hegemony would be risky, expensive, and (given the pressures for democracy) could lead to the demise of their adaptable, but essentially *ancien régime*. They appreciated that their privileged social and political position was vulnerable because of a declining tradition of deference to birth and status.[46]

The British ruling elite lacked the confidence displayed by the American East Coast and Texan establishments since 1941 in the economic mission of the United States for the exercise of global hegemony.[47] Although the far smaller British economy was progressive, the government's ability to appropriate revenues and raise loans suffered from sharply diminishing returns after the Napoleonic War. In their diplomatic efforts to maintain a balance of power and to attenuate envy of their country's stake in global commerce and colonies overseas, appeasement of major powers in Europe and North America seems to have been a constant in British foreign policy down to its apogee in the 1930s.[48]

The British elite represented their state as peaceful and tolerant and themselves as democratic, cultivated gentlemen. Liberals everywhere found them and their constitutional regime attractive. Nevertheless, French "style" retained its prestige and Albion was also widely regarded as "perfidious." The urban degradation, yob-like xenophobia, and imperialistic jingoism of the English populace did not convey images of a culture that other societies would want to emulate.[49]

This intangible contrast between British and American cultures cannot be underestimated as a novel component of twentieth-century power. For decades, images of American standards of living, individualistic behavior, as well as evidence of the republic's military might and technological capabilities have been seen across the globe thanks to modern communications: radio, television, films, and the internet. Such seductive images of the United States are disliked by intellectuals, mullahs, academics, and nationalists of all kinds, because they erode religious, as well as local and traditional identities that support rival states.⁵⁰ Nevertheless the appeal of America is clear and is conveyed to their leaders: any society that aspires to a higher standard of living and "modernization" must somehow adapt to (if not accept) American values.

The emergence of cultural power certainly has historical roots in British liberalism, tolerance, and science, which also possessed international appeal before 1914. Yet the significance of that kind of influence is distinctively modern and represents a discontinuity in international relations that is the product of mass consciousness, popular democracy, and advanced communication. Cultural power provides Washington with a real supplement to its already massive economic and coercive powers, not merely to compel others to do what the hegemon wants, but to embrace what it wants.⁵¹

The architecture of theories that represent the long-term history of geopolitical relations in terms of a succession of hegemons lacks the bricks and the buildings of history to provide it with plausibility. Attempts to apply the label of hegemon to the Genoese, Venetian, and Dutch States, let alone to China, carry almost no conviction. The perception of hegemonic succession from Great Britain to the United States can be degraded by a sequence of exercises in history: comparing the circumstances surrounding the emergence of each state to a position of leadership; contrasting the economic and cultural bases available to them to support the deployment of coercion and influence; treating seriously the proclaimed intentions of two very different political elites; and examining the ramifications of hegemonic power exercised by the United States since 1941 compared to Britain from 1793 to 1914. What seems to be left of hegemonic successions?

Anglo-American intellectuals continue to find the notion of a tradition of civilized leadership of the world exercised by two English-speaking states since 1815 entirely pleasing to contemplate and profitable to pursue.⁵² Yet whether they conceive of the geopolitical role played by their countries as benign or malign, the representation of the Pax Britannica as an antecedent or precedent for the hegemony of the United States is virtually a myth.⁵³

Spring Semester 2004

1. For a parallel argument in the context of decolonization, see Wm. Roger Louis and Ronald Robinson, "The Imperialism of Decolonization," *Journal of Imperial and Commonwealth History,* 22 (Sept. 1994), pp. 462–511.

2. William R. Thompson, *The Emergence of the Global Political Economy* (London, 2001).

3. Robert Gilpin, *The Political Economy of International Relations* (Princeton, N.J., 1987).

4. Joseph Nye, *Bound to Lead* (New York, 1990); Paul Kennedy, *The Rise and Fall of the Great Powers* (London, 1988).

5. Charles P. Kindleberger, *World Economic Primacy 1500–1990* (Oxford, 1996).

6. Howard Temperley, *Britain and America Since Independence* (Basingstoke, 2002).

7. H. C. Allen, *Great Britain and the United States: A History of Anglo-American Relations, 1783–1952* (London, 1952).

8. David Traxel, *The Birth of the American Century* (New York, 1998).

9. Richard K. Vedder, *The American Economy in Historical Perspective* (Belmont, 1976); Robert William Fogel and Stanley L. Engerman, eds., *The Reinterpretation of American Economic History* (New York, 1971).

10. Richard Nelson and Gavin Wright, "The Rise and Fall of American Technological Leadership: The Postwar Era in Historical Perspective," *Journal of Economic Literature,* 30 (1992), pp. 1931–64.

11. S. N. Broadberry, *The Productivity Race: British Manufacturing in International Perspectives 1850–1990* (Cambridge, 1997).

12. Angus Maddison, *The World Economy: A Millennium Perspective* (Paris, 2001).

13. Gavin Wright, "The Origins of American Industrial Success, 1879–1940," *American Economic Review,* 80 (1990), pp. 651–68.

14. Moses Abramovitz and Paul A. David, "Convergence and Deferred Catch-up," in Ralph Landau and others, eds., *The Mosaic of Economic Growth* (Stanford, 1996).

15. Kathleen Burk, *Britain, America and the Sinews of War 1914–18* (London, 1984).

16. Charles S. Maier, *In Search of Stability: Explanations in Historical Political Economy* (Cambridge, 1987).

17. Gilbert Ziebura, *World Economy and World Politics, 1924–31: From Reconstruction to Collapse* (Oxford, 1990).

18. Michael A. Bernstein, *The Great Depression, Delayed Recovery and Economic Change in America 1929–39* (Cambridge, 1987).

19. Frank Costigliola, *Awkward Dominion: American Political and Cultural Relations with Europe 1919–33* (Ithaca, N.Y., 1984).

20. David Bayne Horn, *Great Britain and Europe in the Eighteenth Century* (Oxford, 1967).

21. Richard Bonney, ed., *Economic Systems and State Finance* (Oxford, 1995).

22. Patrick K. O'Brien, "Political Preconditions for the Industrial Revolution," in Patrick K. O'Brien and Roland Quinault, eds., *The Industrial Revolution and British Society* (Cambridge, 1993).

23. Francois Crouzet, *A History of the European Economy 1000–2000* (Charlottesville, Virginia, 2001).

24. Patrick K. O'Brien, "Fiscal Exceptionalism: Great Britain and its European Rivals," in Donald Winch and Patrick K. O'Brien, eds., *The Political Economy of British Historical Experience, 1688–1914* (Oxford, 2002).

25. Kalevi J. Holsti, *Peace and War: Armed Conflicts and the International Order 1648–1989* (Cambridge, 1991).

26. C. K. Webster, *The Congress of Vienna 1814–15* (London, 1963).

27. Charles S. Maier, *Recasting Bourgeois Europe* (Princeton, N.J., 1975).

28. Thomas J. McCormick, *American Half Century: U.S. Foreign Policy in the Cold War and Beyond* (Baltimore, 1995).

29. Alan S. Milward, *The Reconstruction of Western Europe 1945–51* (London, 1984).

30. David Reynolds, *One World Divisible: A Global History Since 1945* (London, 2000).

31. Stanley Hoffman, *World Disorders* (New York, 1998).

32. Patrick K. O'Brien and G. A. Pigman, "Free Trade, British Hegemony and the International Economic Order in the Nineteenth Century," *Review of International Studies,* 18 (1992).

33. Anthony Howe, *Free Trade and Liberal England* (Oxford, 1997).

34. Bernard Semmel, *Liberalism and Naval Strategy* (Boston, 1986).

35. Bernard Semmel, *The Rise of Free Trade Imperialism* (Cambridge, 1970).

36. George L. Bernstein, *Liberalism and Liberal Politics in England* (London, 1986).

37. Aaron L. Friedberg, *The Weary Titan: Britain and the Experience of Relative Decline* (Princeton, N.J., 1988).

38. W. C. Costin, *Great Britain and China 1833–60* (Oxford, 1968).

39. Peter H. Lindert, "United States Foreign Trade and Trade Policy for the Twentieth Century," in Stanley L. Engerman and Robert E. Gallman, eds., *The Cambridge Economic History of the United States* (3 vols, Cambridge, 1996) Vol. 3.

40. Patrick K. O'Brien, "The Security of the Realm and the Growth of the Economy," in Peter Clarke and Clive Trebilcock, eds., *Understanding Decline, Perceptions and Realities of British Economic Performance* (Cambridge, 1997).

41. Winch and O'Brien, eds., *British Historical Experience.*

42. Kenneth Bourne, *The Foreign Policy of Victorian England* (Oxford, 1970).

43. Cited in Paul M. Kennedy, *The Rise and Fall of British Naval Mastery* (London, 1983).

44. Patrick K. O'Brien, "The Imperial Component in the Rise and Decline of the British Economy," in M. Mann and F. Halliday, eds., *The Rise and Decline of Nations* (Oxford, 1991).

45. Muriel Chamberlain, "Pax Britannica?" *British Foreign Policy, 1789–1914* (London, 1988).

46. Ronald Hyam, *Britain's Imperial Century 1815–1914* (Basingstoke, 1993).

47. D. Cameron Watt, *Personalities and Politics* (London, 1996).

48. Friedberg, *Weary Titan.*

49. P. J. Taylor, *The Way the Modern World Works: World Hegemony Impasse* (Chichester, 1996).

50. Donald W. White, *The American Century* (New Haven, Conn, 1996).

51. Olivier Zunz, *Why the American Century?* (Chicago, 1998).

52. D. Cameron Watt, *Succeeding John Bull: America in Britain's Place 1900–75* (Cambridge, 1984).

53. Corelli Barnett, *The Verdict of Peace* (Basingstoke, 2001). I am also grateful to Niall Ferguson for allowing me to read his unpublished paper, "British Imperialism Revisited: The Costs and Benefits of Anglo-globalization" (Stern School of Business, New York, 2003).

3

"In the Advance Guard": Evelyn Waugh's Reputation

GEOFFREY WHEATCROFT

However aloof he holds himself, Evelyn Waugh wrote in 1948, "the artist is always and specially the creature of the Zeitgeist; however formally antique his tastes, he is in spite of himself in the advance guard."[1] He was writing about Graham Greene, in a review of *The Heart of the Matter,* but those words—"formally antique . . . in spite of himself"—plainly intended the reviewer also. Waugh is not often thought of as a creature of his time, or an advanced writer. Far from it: even at his centenary in 2003, his name was invoked once again as a synonym for reaction, obscurantism, snobbery, and bigotry, and he still inspires a personal dislike which is almost impressive.

He would not entirely have minded. Waugh recognized—he almost insisted—that artists in contemporary society must expect to live "under a fusillade of detraction and derision; they accept it as a condition of their calling." This was by way of contrast with Hollywood, where all, as he dryly noted, "is a continuous psalm of self-praise."[2] To put it another way, maybe he asked for it. Throughout his life he enjoyed something of a *succès d'animosité,* a self-inflicted unpopularity that has pursued him beyond the grave. But even if he practiced a kind of deliberate bloody-mindedness, and relished the response, he might have been less pleased by the kind of detraction to which his work is still subjected, a blind determination to misunderstand and depreciate a great writer.

In that centennial year, William Boyd in the *Daily Telegraph* and Christopher Hitchens in the *Atlantic Monthly* derided him at length with a common theme. Waugh wrote some sparkling early farces, it is conceded, but he failed when he tried to write anything weightier. Hitchens is gravely disappointed by the war trilogy, *Sword of Honour,* and Boyd not only conventionally disdains *Brideshead Revisited,* but more unusually he disparages *A Handful of Dust* as well. He also quaintly asserts that *Scoop* is Waugh's "real masterwork,"[3] which can only be a conscious slight, rather like saying that *The Merry Wives of Windsor* is Shakespeare's greatest play or *Eine kleine Nachtmusik* the best thing Mozart ever composed. But the thrust of it all is clear enough: Waugh was a funny fellow, to be sure, but he was something less than a great writer, or even a serious one.

Personal hostility informs full-length biographies. Martin Stannard denigrates Waugh relentlessly over two volumes, and even Selina Hastings, much the best of his biographers to date, begins her book by addressing what she calls his twin reputations: that he was one of the great prose stylists of the twentieth century, and that "as a man he was a monster."[4] And no sooner had Stephen Fry filmed *Vile Bodies* as *Bright Young Things* than he chipped in to say that, although Waugh's prose was splendid, "he was a howling shit."

Was he? That he was a difficult and complicated man is impossible to deny, by turns offensive and self-hating, obsessed and depressed, with a core of madness that erupted on one occasion: the episode recorded in *The Ordeal of Gilbert Pinfold.* He could behave odiously to those too weak or too inarticulate to answer back, he was quarrelsome even with friends, and those who managed to like him often had to put up with a good deal. His eldest son, the late Auberon Waugh, fiercely defended his father at the time of his death in 1966, and for years after, but gradually changed his tune before his own death in 2001. His claim that his father's last ten years "were probably the most mellow and tranquil of his life" became impossible to sustain when the evidence of Waugh's diaries and letters showed a man consumed by gloom.[5] Auberon Waugh also pretended for years that his relationship with his father had been warm, until in his memoirs, published in 1991, he finally admitted that his childhood had been starved of affection and that, although he revered his father, he had only begun to like him a short time before he died. Despite all his conscious efforts to mend his ways, and all his remorse when he failed, Waugh can sometimes seem one of those men— one of those Englishmen?—in Philip Larkin's brutally honest lines, "too selfish, withdrawn / And easily bored to love."[6]

And yet he was in many ways a notably virtuous man. He was an affectionate and faithful husband and as doting a father as his temperament allowed. He devoted himself to raising a large family, and he was a loyal friend to a small group of men and women. In a spirited and touching defense written shortly after his death (by which time the denigration had already begun), Greene affirmed that Waugh was "the greatest novelist of my age" while emphasizing this "rare quality of criticising a friend harshly, wittily and openly to his face, and behind the friend's back of expressing only his kindness and charity . . . Evelyn Waugh had an unshakeable loyalty to his friends, even if he may have detested their opinions and sometimes their actions. One could never depend on him for easy approval or a warm weak complaisance, but when one felt the need of him he was always there."[7]

He was—and is—endlessly accused of snobbery and social ambition, and to deny this would be pointless. In a cleverly worded letter to the Dublin magazine *The Bell* in 1947, Waugh even admitted that "I think perhaps your reviewer is right in calling me a snob," before denying that this was "necessarily an offence against Charity, still less against Faith," or that it had had any influence on his becoming a Catholic. He had known none of the old Catholic aristocracy at the time of his conversion in 1930: "My friends were fashionable agnostics and the Faith I then accepted had none of the extraneous glamour your reviewer imputes to it."[8] (The reviewer in question was the sharp-witted and vehement young Irish writer "Donat O'Donnell," otherwise Conor Cruise O'Brien.)

That was certainly true about Waugh's religion, which was held with passionate sincerity, and was not at all the "ancestor-worship" of which critics had accused him. His social ascent before and during the Second World War was, all the same, brazen and unmistakable even to his friends: he married two aristocratic women; he enjoyed a *vie de château* around English and Irish country houses; and he became a slightly ambiguous member of the Society which he so penetratingly observed and chronicled. But although he acquired a set of highborn drinking cronies and a small group of close women friends—patrician but declassed, uneducated but clever, fond of him but capable of standing up to him, Nancy Mitford, Diana Cooper, Ann Fleming—his real friends were other writers. And as Noel Annan perceptively observed, he didn't really have an "upperclass" life to speak of in his last twenty years.

As a young man, he had found his family dowdy and unglamorous, something of which his father, the loveable but fusty and embarrassing publisher Arthur Waugh, was painfully aware. There are even confessional overtones in the writings of Waugh's later years, as when he admitted obliquely that he hadn't thought his own background quite good enough, and when he wrote with audible self-reproach that his father had shunned elegant society and had had "no wish to move among people richer than himself."[9] To be fair to Waugh, his love of the *beau monde* was not especially reprehensible in itself, and anyway it placed him in a familiar category. A certain kind of gifted and romantic young writer "could not but be dazzled by the aristocracy, as Balzac, or Wilde, or Proust were . . .," Isaiah Berlin once wrote, "when he came into contact with what seemed, and perhaps was, a freer, gayer, more confident world."[10] The high society in which Waugh delighted, at least some of the time, was not only more amusing than that which he had known as a boy, it gave him his subject: would he still be read if he had written novels about a publisher's family in Hampstead Garden Suburb?

Just as striking as all that, and far more attractive, is Waugh's sheer generosity, personal, financial and literary. A small example of his practical and very endearing charity is found in a 1951 letter to Catherine Walston, Graham Greene's mistress, who was worried that Waugh would disapprove if they stayed in his house as an illicit couple. He replied with great tenderness: "I met you first as a friend of Graham's but I hope I can now look on you as a friend in my own right. I should love you to come if you can bear the discomforts. . . . Please believe that I am far too depressed by my own odious, if unromantic, sins to have any concern for other people's. For me, it would be a delight to welcome you here."[11] A howling shit?

Such kindness cost nothing, but very few writers of the past century can have given away more money than Waugh did. This was partly a game, as indeed much of his life was. Before the war he was only moderately prosperous, and the huge success of *Brideshead Revisited* in 1945 coincided with ferocious rates of income tax. When Greene also hit the jackpot with *The Heart of the Matter,* Waugh told him that: "it is impossible now to be rich but it is possible to be idle, and this American coup relieves you of work for about fifteen years."[12] He viewed his own success somewhat sarcastically: "In a civilised age this unexpected moment of popularity would have endowed me with a competency for life. But perhaps in a civilised age I should not be so popular."[13]

More signs of vexation at his own success are found in his occasional writings from the period. Waugh was contemptuous of the Century of the Common Man and its prevailing belief that something was only of value if valued equally by all: "In the old days a play which ran a hundred nights was a success, a book which sold 5,000 copies might influence a generation. Even now a writer who sells more than 20,000 copies, instead of being elated, begins to wonder what has gone wrong with his work."[14] At any rate, having sold many copies and made a great deal of money, he was determined to out-wit the Inland Revenue. One way was to make over the royalties on foreign editions to Catholic charities whenever he could, or when-ever they were accepted—when the Archbishop of Utrecht was of-fered the Dutch royalties on *The Loved One,* he waited until he had read it, and then politely declined.

Almost more impressive than his financial largesse was Waugh's professional generosity to other writers. Sometimes this meant help-ing them by stealth and encouraging them to write (more than one writer was effectively rescued by him), sometimes it meant bestow-ing his own fame. When Eric Newby, who did not know him, told Waugh that an American publisher would only take his engaging book *A Short Walk in the Hindu Kush* if it had a preface by a notable writer, Waugh asked his agent to check that the appeal was genuine, added that "Terms don't matter. I should be doing it as a kindness," and then wrote the preface.[15] Anyone who has dallied in literary life will know that such kindness is not found on every side. Over and again, Waugh went out of his way to commend authors whom he ad-mired even when he had no personal affinity with them.

When Angus Wilson's masterpiece *The Old Men at the Zoo* was slightingly reviewed in the *Spectator* in 1961, Waugh wrote a com-pletely disinterested letter to the magazine by way of second opin-ion, which is both a good deed and a miniature jewel of literary crit-icism: "But writing is the expression of thought. There is no abstract writing. All literature implies moral standards and criticisms—the less explicit the better."[16] When Waugh regretted the way the crit-ics had only praised those parts of the book which were most like Wilson's previous work, and said that "reviewers should welcome variety and development in a writer," it was also a rebuke to his own detractors, then and now.[17] Critics are "lazy brutes and hate having to think," he said on another occasion. "They can't bear to see a writer grow up."[18]

Waugh's letters as well as his essays scintillate with warm and intel-ligent appreciation of other writers, as well as honestly acknowl-edged differences. His close, always warm, sometimes tense, rela-tionship with Greene apart, he had another fascinating literary friendship with George Orwell. They were not intimates, but they knew and greatly admired one another; in one review Waugh got Orwell just right when he praised his "unusually high moral sense and respect for justice and truth."[19] He wrote him a fan letter about *Animal Farm,* and another about *Nineteen Eighty-Four* which is a model of how one writer should address another, intelligently, ap-preciatively, but critically. He recognized the strengths of the novel, and was delighted by scenes like the "delicious conversation in the pub when Winston tries to pump the old man for memories of pre-revolutionary days." And yet "the book failed to make my flesh creep." Its metaphysics were wrong, Waugh thought, while "Winston's rebellion was false . . . And it was false, to me, that the form of his revolt should simply be fucking in the style of Lady Chatterley— finding reality through a sort of mystical union with the Proles in the sexual act."[20]

Quite as interesting as his literary discernment is his political insight, for which he is rarely given credit. Waugh may not have been politically correct, but he was politically acute. Much as he disliked the post-war "Attlee terror," he knew perfectly well that England was going to remain a plutocracy. After Sir Stafford Cripps's "austerity" budget in 1948, his beloved White's Club in St James's had become uninhabitable, he wrote. He found it full of men who in truth had no money screaming that they were ruined, but he also saw "the dozen or so really rich men smoking quietly in corners having made themselves registered companies in Costa Rica years ago."[21]

His analysis of the Suez adventure in 1956 reads with painful relevance after the Iraq adventure of 2003 (and they compare indeed more closely than Iraq does with Vietnam): "It cannot be justified on moral or legal grounds," although "practically no recent action of any British government can be justified morally." While "any troup of Boy Scouts can defeat the Egyptian army," the country was now awash with arms and zealots to use them, and would be ungovernable after military conquest; the populace could doubtless be subdued by starvation, but "a more humane solution is to stop motor traffic."[22] It might be a model left-wing environmentalist speaking.

Service in Yugoslavia towards the end of the war had imbued Waugh with a bitter enmity towards Tito; he was determined to think the worst of the Partisans and the best of the Croats. He even defended Archbishop Stepinac from what he called the "often refuted" accusations against him, about his complicity in Ustasha massacres of Serbs and Jews, accusations which were alas all too irrefutably true. And yet, for all his bias, Waugh's delineation of Yugoslavia past and present reads with more painful relevance now that we have seen the country tear itself apart.

In the first place, Yugoslavia was the aberrant creation of the peacemakers after 1918. "From the first years of the peace disruptive forces were apparent. Croats and Slovenes almost unanimously sought independence of the Serbs."[23] In 1941, the country did collapse, with the invader's brutal rule opposed by small bands of guerrillas. This happened in a way which made it easy for interested parties to represent Tito as the only determined resister, or even a national hero, although Waugh rubbed in Tito's total lack of chivalry and inability ever to say a good word of any opponent: "Even Stalin, no Bayard, was shocked by his grossness in this matter."[24] As a lighter side to his loathing, Waugh always insisted that Tito was a female transvestite, leading to the wondrous moment when they met, and Tito told his translator to "ask Captain Waugh why he thinks I am a woman."

Despite all this knockabout, Waugh grasped exactly what had happened in 1948, when "Stalin decided to destroy Tito and for a variety of reasons did not succeed." The Russians wanted to establish their secret-police rule in Yugoslavia as they already had in Bulgaria, and proposed a federation of the two. "But Tito had observed and assisted in too many 'purges' to be caught so easily," and he outwitted Stalin.[25] Five years later Waugh added a very telling footnote: "I am becoming a Russian imperialist, in reaction to the politicians." If the countries of Eastern Europe were going to be Communist, it was much better for Russia to rule them. The one sure way to start another world war would be "to establish half a dozen independent atheist police states, full of a fatuous nationalism and power hunger."[26] It could almost be E. J. Hobsbawm talking.

That time in Yugoslavia inspired *Unconditional Surrender*, the final volume of his war trilogy, which provides an ironic comment on his reputation as a blinkered know-nothing. When it appeared, reviewers on either side of the Atlantic quite missed its point. Philip Toynbee in the *Observer* was not only obtuse about Waugh's writing in general—to say that "*The Loved One* was the most perfect of Mr Waugh's books since *Decline and Fall*" is even sillier than to call *Scoop* his masterwork—but snorted at one particular detail.[27] There is a subplot in the book about Communists in high places within the British forces and the Foreign Office. One is the repellent army officer Gilpin, who gloats over the execution by Tito of the Jewish couple whom the hero Guy Crouchback has tried to rescue, and who ends up as a Labour MP in 1945. Another, in a smaller way is De Souza, Guy's young friend from their early days in the Halberdiers. Then there is Sir Ralph Brompton, a patrician diplomatist of homosexual tastes and fellow-traveling inclinations. He has been likened to Anthony Blunt, though Waugh said, maliciously if privately, that he was modeled on Sir Harold Nicolson.

"What are we to make of all the high officers and others who appear to be involved in a widespread Communist conspiracy?" Toynbee sarcastically wondered. "Satire, or some kind of lunatic McCarthyism?"[28] And Gore Vidal in the *New York Times* sneered

that: "Waugh's account of the British Communists' successful conspiracy to establish Tito is fascinating; admirers of Robert Welch's
[the leader of the John Birch Society] will be gratified that their
worst suspicions are confirmed."[29] But it is Waugh's own worst
suspicions—or novelist's intuitions—that have been confirmed: we
now know for an historical fact that there were numerous Communists, some of them Soviet agents, exactly where he depicted them,
not least in the sections of intelligence dealing with Yugoslavia; and
if Orwell is to be believed, there were also not a few covert Communists elected to Parliament under Labour colors. Today it is
Waugh who looks like the social realist.

Even his least good books contain profound passages. *Robbery under Law* was written after a visit to Mexico in 1938 which was clandes-
tinely, and not very creditably, sponsored by someone he referred to
as a very rich chap, in the form of Clive Pearson, whose family business was being expropriated by the leftist Cardenas regime. The best
thing in it is a "Conservative Manifesto" much more lucid than anything likely to come from any Tory or Republican today:

> I believe in government; that men cannot live together without
> rules but that these should be kept at the bare minimum of safety;
> that there is no form of government ordained by God as being
> better than any other; that the anarchic elements in society are so
> strong that it is a whole-time task to keep the peace. I believe that
> inequalities of wealth and position are inevitable and that it is
> therefore meaningless to discuss the advantages of their elimina-
> tion; that men naturally arrange themselves in a system of classes;
> that such a system is necessary for any form of co-operative work,
> more particularly the work of keeping a nation together.[30]

And those who regard Waugh as a mere *farceur* should read these
words: "Barbarism is never finally conquered; given propitious circumstances, men and women who seem quite orderly will commit
every conceivable atrocity."[31] They were written shortly before a war
in which every conceivable atrocity was witnessed from one end of
Europe to the other.

Anyone who wants to find evidence of casual bigotry will not
need to spend much time with Waugh's published letters. But then
the bigot-hounds, nowadays as zealous as the smut-hounds of old,
are philistines at heart. They want us to join them in clucking cen-
soriously over the nastier passages in Larkin's letters, rather than
reading "High Windows"; we could just as well cluck over *Das Ju-
dentum in der Musik,* rather than listen to *Tristan und Isolde.* Like
most of us, Waugh had a dark side as well as a better, and he de-

serves to be judged by the humanity that shines through many noble passages.

He disapproved of the cult of Simone Weil, not because she was "a
young, highly intelligent French Jewess" but because, although she
recognized the truths of Christianity, she refused to follow the logic
of this by becoming a Catholic, and he made a contrary cult of Edith
Stein, "a highly intelligent German Jewess" who not only became a
Catholic but a Carmelite nun. That did not save her under the New
Order. In the summer of 1942, "Edith was arrested and driven off
with the other victims of the Terror; somewhere, quite soon probably, she was killed in one of the extermination camps in the east. . . .
She disappeared bodily in the total, hellish darkness," a death which
touches us because it still lies "at the heart of contemporary disaster.
The aimless, impersonal wickedness which could drag a victim from
the holy silence of Carmel and drive her, stripped and crowded,
to the gas chamber and the furnace, still lurks in the darkness." It is
not necessary to share the sectarian sympathies that inform Waugh's
peroration—"She did not sit, waiting on God. She went out alone
and by the God-given light of her intelligence and strength of purpose, she found Him"—to be moved by them.[32]

In Maryland, while traveling to write about Catholicism in America, Waugh was deeply affected by "the heroic fidelity of the Negro
Catholics. The Church has not always been a kind mother to them.
Often they could only practice their religion at the cost of much humiliation . . . for here the persecutors were fellow-members in the
Household of Faith. But, supernaturally, they knew the character of
the Church better than the clergy. Today [in 1949] all this is fast
changing. Catholics are everywhere leading the movement to make
amends." But in the efforts to forget those scandals, "honour must
never be neglected to those thousands of coloured Catholics who
so accurately traced their Master's road amid insult and injury."[33]

There is an ethnic or national prejudice lurking here, but not the
one people generally complain about. That same essay contains a
bravura and brutal passage. Some descendants of Catholic immigrants to America, Latin or Slav, were ashamed of their origins and
even of their ancestral religion; but "the Irish, on the other hand,
present a precisely contrasting problem . . . the further they move in
time and place from their homeland the louder they shout about
it. . . . The problem with the Irish is to guard them from the huge presumption of treating the Universal Church as a friendly association
of their own." That problem had not been resolved, least of all in
Boston where "the stranger might well suppose that Catholicism was
a tribal cult."[34] (Waugh's original draft, now at the University of

Texas, had a nice alternative touch: ". . . suppose that England is behind the Iron Curtain.") Although the Irish had learned the superficial habits of "good citizenship" as they were turned into townsmen, "at heart they remain the same adroit and joyless race that broke the heart of all who ever tried to help them." Even more insulting words had to be toned down before publication: "It is one of the functions of an upper class to see that the clergy do not get above themselves," and anyone might understand "why there is often a distinct whiff of anticlericalism where Irish priests are in power. . . . [M]any live out their lives in a painful state of transition; they have lost their peasant simplicity without acquiring a modest carriage of their rather modest learning."[35] At one time Waugh thought of settling in Ireland; perhaps it was as well that he did not.

One of his last books, possibly the worst he ever published, and the one of which he was most openly ashamed, was *A Tourist in Africa,* written in return for a "freebie" trip. But even this contains pearls of wisdom, which once more belie the idea of its author as no more than a racist and imperialist. In Tanganyika he gives an admirably droll account of the groundnut scheme, that supreme folly under the Attlee Government of socialist planning, which wasted so many careers and so much taxpayers' money. He attributes the failure to pride, "the hubris which leads elected persons to believe that a majority at the polls endues them with inordinate abilities," but then adds delightfully that, if the scheme "had been conceived and executed by natives, everyone would point to it as incontrovertible evidence that they were unfit to manage their own affairs."[36]

In South Africa, he saw apartheid as the spirit of egalitarianism gone mad, replacing the infinitely subtle gradations of a healthy society with one crazy dividing line based on the irrelevance of skin color. In one aside, which Daniel Patrick Moynihan liked to quote, and which applies today with excruciating relevance from the Balkans to central Asia to central Africa, he said that, "The foundations of Empire are often occasions of woe; their dismemberment, always."[37] Then in Southern Rhodesia (to whose founder he did not warm) he remarked that slavery and tribal warfare had been endemic in Africa before whites arrived, and "no doubt they will break out there after they leave," a prediction which has since come true. Meantime, in the first half of the twentieth century, Europeans had already waged on African soil wars far more bloody and destructive than anything known to marauding spearmen, "and a generation which has seen the Nazi regime in the heart of Europe had best stand silent when civilised and uncivilised nations are contrasted."[38] But then it takes an intelligent conservative to see that.

In the end, Waugh's reputation must depend on his novels, and here the denigration is at its most wrong-headed. Boyd dismisses *A Handful of Dust* as an act of revenge on Waugh's faithless first wife (but shouldn't we stick to the text?). It is true that the book is not quite the faultless masterpiece others have claimed: the final section, with Tony Last trapped in the jungle, should have been a separate story, and it is preceded by a tedious travelogue. But up to that point it is surely one of the most perfect English novels written between the wars.

Many people affect to deplore *Brideshead Revisited,* the book that Waugh sardonically said had lost him such reputation as he possessed among his contemporaries. This was the first time he seriously attempted a grave theme, divine love working among fallen humanity or some such, and he may have failed in such an apologetic purpose. Does that matter? Great art transcends its immediate origins and works separately from its conscious intention, otherwise only medieval Tuscans could understand *The Divine Comedy* and only pious Lutherans could love the *Saint Matthew Passion.* As to the distress that the setting and characters of the book cause puritans, this is another form of philistinism. Proust could have written a long *roman-fleuve* about factory life in Boulogne-Billancourt, but he didn't, and he is not treated as a reprobate in consequence. It is a pity that those who find a book about a nobleman's house and family unbearably distasteful cannot at least admire it for technical reasons, as a masterly work of construction and compression.

What is true is that *Brideshead Revisited* illustrates Waugh's shortcomings as a novelist. One concerned half the human race. His loving and admiring friend Nancy Mitford said perceptively after reading *Men at Arms,* with its unaffectionate portrait of Virginia, "You see women through a glass darkly don't you?" and so he did.[39] His female characters are either bitches or witches, or just wraiths. As Orwell said of Thackeray, his good women are simply intolerable, and in *Brideshead Revisited,* even Julia, who is meant to be personally and sexually fascinating, is wishy-washy on the page compared with her emotionally destructive, completely convincing mother, or the ghastly Celia.

But then Waugh had a more general difficulty with creating large, virtuous characters. This seems almost to be a tradition among English novelists. Thackeray apart, Waugh shared Dickens's inability to make good people attractive; and his heroes and narrators are usually his least interesting creations. Tony Last and Guy Crouchback are such drips that you can almost forgive the women who betray them, and Charles Ryder manages to be both dislikable and unmemorable; his cousin Jasper, who appears for two short, dazzling scenes, is unforgettable by comparison. Then again, Waugh belonged to that great tradition of English fiction in another way: his best creations are his secondary and often monstrous characters. It is hard to think of any other writer of his age who has left behind so many we recognize as part of our mental furniture: Captain Grimes, Lord Copper (and "Up to a point"), Basil Seal, Anthony Blanche, Rex Mottram, Ritchie-Hook (and "biffing"), Apthorpe, and Trimmer.

To list those last three names might seem to suggest that the *Sword of Honour* trilogy is another piece of Waugh-like farce, rather than the finest English fiction to come out of the war; its only serious rival is the wartime trio within Anthony Powell's *A Dance to the Music of Time*. This is truly Waugh's masterwork, as more appreciative readers have seen. A. J. P. Taylor wrote that "if future generations want to know what the Second World War was like for English people, they can safely turn to *Sword of Honour* by Evelyn Waugh, the greatest work of art by a great English novelist."[40] It may be that being an historian helps: Hobsbawm also transcends political prejudice to call Waugh "the greatest British novelist of the period."[41]

Not only a magnificent work of imagination, the trilogy is a brilliant record of an immensely important historical moment. The account of military life is (according to those who should know) faultless in its often surreal detail, and the description of the rout in Crete is perhaps the best battle scene in any novel from any country set in that war. But this is not just a chronicle. Although Waugh was not writing a *roman à thèse,* the trilogy does have a theme; no literary masterpiece should be reduced to a trite "message," but *Sword of Honour* is, among other things, a great "anti-war" book, greater than *All Quiet on the Western Front* or *Catch-22.*

It begins in a mood of elation, or at least hope. Guy is exhilarated by the Nazi-Soviet Pact in August 1939: "The enemy at last was plain in view, huge and hateful, all disguise cast off. It was the Modern Age in arms. Whatever the outcome there was a place for him in that battle."[42] He sees the war as a way of repaying a debt of honor incurred by birth, of giving meaning to his empty life, of finding fulfillment at last. Over the next five years he discovers that war is morally empty or worse, "a Holy Land of Illusion in the old ambiguous world, where priests were spies and gallant friends proved traitors and his country was led blundering into dishonour."[43] He learns not so much Wilfred Owen's "pity of war" as the futility of war, and he realizes that his private mission was ignoble.

The crucial moment of the whole trilogy is towards the end, when Guy is in Croatia talking to the Jewish woman he has befriended. Too many people had hoped for war and thought that it would bring some public gain or personal redemption, she says:

> "Even good men thought their private honour would be satisfied by war. They could assert their manhood by killing and being killed. They would accept hardships in recompense for having been selfish and lazy. Danger justified privilege. I knew Italians— not very many perhaps—who felt this. Were there none in England?"
> "God forgive me," said Guy. "I was one of them."[44]

To the extent that Waugh deserves his reputation as a reactionary pessimist, he also justifies David Gilmour's astute words in his recent biography of Kipling: "Pessimists and reactionaries make the best prophets because . . . they can see behind as well as beyond contemporary viewpoints."[45] And yet Waugh was not only a pessimist, he was a great writer; he was not only an embattled conservative, he was—and could only have written his masterpieces if he had been— a "creature of the Zeitgeist"; he was not behind his time, but in many ways far ahead of it.

Spring Semester 2002

A version of this lecture appeared in the *Times Literary Supplement,* Oct. 24, 2003.

1. *Commonweal,* July 16, 1948, in Donat Gallagher, ed., *The Essays, Articles and Reviews of Evelyn Waugh* (London, 1983), p. 360.
2. "Why Hollywood is a Term of Disparagement," *Daily Telegraph,* Apr. 30 and May 1, 1947, in Gallagher, ed., *Essays,* p. 325.
3. *Daily Telegraph,* Oct. 4, 2003.
4. Selina Hastings, *Evelyn Waugh* (London, 1994), p. 1.
5. *Spectator,* May 6, 1966.
6. Philip Larkin, "Wild Oats," in *The Whitsun Weddings* (London, 1964), p. 41.
7. *The Times,* Apr. 15, 1966.
8. Mark Amory, ed., *The Letters of Evelyn Waugh* (London, 1980), July 1947, p. 255.
9. Evelyn Waugh, *A Little Learning* (London, 1964), pp. 64–65.
10. Isaiah Berlin, *Against the Current* (London, 1979), p. 265.
11. Amory, ed., *Letters,* Aug. 25, 1951, p. 355.
12. Ibid., May 3, 1948, p. 278.
13. "Fan-fare," *Life,* Apr. 8, 1946, in Gallagher, ed., *Essays,* p. 300.
14. "Why Hollywood . . . ," in Gallagher, ed., *Essays,* p. 329.
15. Amory, ed., *Letters,* Aug. 6, 1958, p. 511.
16. Ibid., p. 573, n. 7.
17. Ibid., Oct. 13, 1961, p. 574.
18. Ibid.
19. "A New Humanism," *Tablet,* Apr. 6, 1946, in Gallagher, ed., *Essays,* p. 306.
20. Amory, ed., *Letters,* July 17, 1949, p. 302.
21. Ibid., April 7, 1948, p. 276.
22. Ibid., Nov. 7, 1956, pp. 477–78.
23. Christie Lawrence, "Introduction" to *Irregular Adventure* (London, 1947), p. 12, in Gallagher, ed., *Essays,* p. 322.
24. "The Voice of Tito," *Commonweal,* May 8, 1953, in Gallagher, ed., *Essays,* p. 439.
25. Ibid., p. 438.
26. Amory, ed., *Letters,* Mar. 14, 1953, p. 395.
27. *Observer,* Oct. 29, 1961, in Martin Stannard, ed., *Evelyn Waugh: The Critical Heritage* (London, 1984), p. 435.
28. Ibid., p. 437.
29. *New York Times Book Review,* Jan. 7, 1962, in Stannard, *Critical Heritage,* p. 441.
30. Waugh, "Conservative Manifesto," in *Robbery Under Law* (London, 1939), pp. 16–17, in Gallagher, ed., *Essays,* p. 161.
31. Ibid., p. 162.
32. "Edith Stein," *Catholic Mother* (Christmas 1952), in Gallagher, ed., *Essays,* pp. 432–35.
33. "The American Epoch in the Catholic Church," *Life,* Sept. 19, 1949, in Gallagher, ed., *Essays,* p. 383.
34. Ibid., p. 384.
35. Ibid., 384–85 & n.
36. Evelyn Waugh, *A Tourist in Africa* (London, 1960), pp. 86 and 111–12.
37. Ibid., p. 164.
38. Ibid., p. 151.

    39. Nancy Mitford to Waugh, Sept. 27, 1952, quoted in Hastings, *Evelyn Waugh*, p. 550.
    40. A. J. P. Taylor, *English History 1914–1945* (Oxford, 1965), p. 467.
    41. E. J. Hobsbawm, *The Age of Extremes* (London, 1994), p. 190.
    42. Waugh, *Unconditional Surrender* (London, 1961), p. 1.
    43. Ibid., p. 4.
    44. Ibid., p. 300.
    45. David Gilmour, *The Long Recessional: The Imperial Life of Rudyard Kipling* (London, 2002), p. 310.

4

A Time to Dance:
Anthony Powell's *Dance to the Music of Time*
And the Twentieth Century in Britain

FERDINAND MOUNT

It must have been in the summer of 1950 that I first met Anthony Powell. He and his wife Violet, my mother's sister, were living in a painfully tall and narrow house at the entrance to Regent's Park, No. 1 Chester Gate. It stood more or less on its own then because one of Hitler's bombs had burnt its twin next door down to the ground floor. Everything about this house was novel to me. I had never seen a London town house before: the endless twisting stairs, the dumb waiter creaking up from the kitchen with the decanters, and at full length on the *chaise longue,* my uncle, a shortish, dapper figure wearing a bow tie and a jacket which, even if not actually made of velvet, gave the decided impression of being a smoking jacket, a garment I knew only from books. I always think of him reclining thus like Madame Récamier throughout the long conversations we were to hold for the next fifty years down at the house they soon moved to, the Chantry, a Regency villa in Somerset. This house was of the same style and date as the Nash terrace they had moved from, and since they had taken all their furniture with them, not least the *chaise longue,* it was as though my uncle had never moved an inch in all these years. Indeed, the only time I ever remember conversing with him when he was actually sitting upright was in his extreme old age when, frail in body and increasingly in mind, he used to be pushed about the house in a wheelchair—the reversal of the normal pattern of life in which we sit up for the best part of it and only lie down at the beginning and the end.

My mother had brought me up to see the Sherlock Holmes exhibition which was a few hundred yards round the corner at what purported to be 221B Baker Street, although in fact no such address ever existed. So in my mind Holmes's rooms became confused with No. 1 Chester Gate with its old portraits of Powell ancestors and the gilt sphinxes and eagles of its Empire furniture. Something too of the same curiosity, the interest in exact particulars, the emphasis on getting things right, seemed to link the fictional detective and the real-life novelist. Holmes, you will recall, not only notices details that most of us miss, he also notices people to whom we all too often don't give a second glance: the boy who delivers a message, the woman who serves you at the check-out. Powell had what I would call a miraculous evenness of curiosity. His writings epitomize Pascal's remark: "the more intelligent a man is the more originality he discovers in men. Ordinary people see no difference between men." The mysterious Mrs. Erdleigh says in Powell's novel, "no human life is uninteresting."[1] Or as the narrator Nicholas Jenkins muses in an earlier volume, "I reflected, not for the first time, how mistaken it is to suppose there exists some 'ordinary' world into which it is possible at will to wander. All human beings, driven as they are at different speeds by the same Furies, are at close range equally extraordinary."[2] Even as a little boy Powell obviously had that love of detail. In his great novel sequence—he was about to publish the first volume, *A Question of Upbringing,* when I came to stay—he records a conversation in which the ancient General Conyers comes to lunch and quizzes the narrator about army uniforms, cap badges, and regiments. The narrator, then aged eight, is flawless. The conversation sounds as if taken directly from life.

Not far from Chester Gate, the other side of Marylebone Road, lay the Wallace Collection and Poussin's picture, "A Dance to the Music of Time," which gave the title and set the theme for the twelve-volume sequence. *Dance,* as I shall call it from now on, covers a large expanse of time and experience in the history of Britain, not just England, for some of the most memorable passages cover Powell's wartime service in Wales and Northern Ireland. The first scene, in which General Conyers tests the narrator on army cap badges, takes place on the eve of the First World War. The narrator's unreliable Uncle Giles arrives unexpectedly after lunch and immediately pours scorn on the General's motor-car and indeed cars in general:

> "Never driven one in my life," said Uncle Giles. "Not too keen on 'em. Always in accidents. Some royalty in a motor-car have been involved in a nasty affair today. Heard the news in Aldershot. Fellow I went to see was told on the telephone. Amazing, isn't it, hearing

so soon. They've just assassinated an Austrian archduke down in Bosnia. Did it today. Only happened a few hours ago."

Uncle Giles muttered, almost whispered these facts, speaking as if he were talking to himself, not at all in the voice of a man announcing to the world in general the close of an epoch; the outbreak of Armageddon; the birth of a new, uneasy age. He did not look in the least like the harbinger of the Furies.[3]

Uncle Giles, a restless, unsuccessful, retired army officer, is one of my favorite Powell creations. Always popping up when least wanted, leading a strange, nomadic life in residential hotels, he embodies the dissatisfied spirit of the age. Shortly before he expires of a stroke in the Bellevue Private Hotel in 1939, he "continued to enjoy irritating his relations" by remarking quite casually, "I like the little man they've got in Germany now."[4] But the sequence goes on far beyond Uncle Giles's death to cover the post-war period, and the hippie era. We first glimpse the villain of the series, Kenneth Widmerpool, on a drizzly December afternoon in 1921 on an exercise run trotting across the plough back to school. We hear of him last expiring of a heart attack in the autumn of 1971, collapsing after a run led by the sinister cult leader Scorpio Murtlock—the modern version of Dr. Trelawney, the magician who used to lead his acolytes on jogs across Aldershot Heath in Jenkins's boyhood.

The sense of patterning is strong. "In the end most things in life—perhaps all things—turn out to be appropriate."[5] People have a way of repeatedly turning up in the narrator's life. He says of Widmerpool, "I should never have gone out of my way to seek him, knowing, as one does with certain people, that the rhythm of life would sooner or later be bound to bring us together again."[6] Some critics have objected to the way Powell's characters do constantly bump into each other, complaining that, if true at all, these repeated coincidences may be true only of the English upper classes and certainly would not be true in a vast country like the United States, where life is a procession of strangers. That is for the reader to judge, though I should have thought that in academic life, at least, there is quite a bit of eternal recurrence anywhere one goes.

At any rate, *Dance* is based on the principle that what goes around, comes around. In Poussin's scene:

> the Seasons, moving hand in hand in intricate measure: stepping slowly, methodically, sometimes a trifle awkwardly, in evolutions that take recognisable shape: or breaking into seemingly meaningless gyrations, while partners disappear only to reappear again, once more giving pattern to the spectacle: unable to control the melody, unable, perhaps, to control the steps of the dance.[7]

Powell tells us: "nothing in life is planned—or everything is—because in the dance every step is ultimately the corollary of the step before; the consequence of being the kind of person one chances to be."[8]

These patterns do not imply that things are foreordained. Indeed, they constantly recombine to produce dramatic surprises. What seemed built on the most solid foundations turns out to constitute only a temporary conjunction. In fact, this applies even to the image of the Four Seasons. To remind myself of the picture, I pulled down from the shelf the *magnum opus* on Poussin by Sir Anthony Blunt—referred to by my uncle as "the traitor Blunt." I found to my surprise that scholars now agree that the clumsy maidens dancing their measure are not the Four Seasons at all but rather the figures of Poverty, Industry, Wealth, and Luxury representing stages through which man passes in an eternal series of revolutions. It's a sort of wheel of fortune and one which would in fact serve just as well as an emblem for the gyrations in *Dance*. One should also not ignore the two putti, the one holding an hourglass to show that it's later than it seems and the other blowing a bubble to indicate that pretty things can exist and grow, but they cannot last. Eventually the bubble must burst—the dotcom episode has been a very good illustration of this point.

On looking at the picture again, I also detected a certain resemblance in the figure of Time to the author. If you subtract Time's whiskers and ignore his nakedness, there is something about the figure—his ironic smile, the way he watches the other figures with such amused detachment while plucking at his lyre—which recalls Powell's relationship to those around him. Perhaps all novelists are a bit like that.

My intention in this lecture is to concentrate not so much on the dancers as on the landscape they are dancing in, and the way its lights and shadows reflect back on the quartet treading their awkward measure. I do not intend simply to point out how the novel records in passing so many of the high and low points of British history in that half century—Sarajevo, the Slump, the Spanish Civil War, the Abdication, Munich, the Katyn Massacre, D-Day, VE Day, the Labour government of 1945—although as a matter of fact these events and many more are indeed set in the text, often as free-standing milestones, to remind us of where we have got to. My mission here is rather to try to draw attention to how what you might call the temporal atmospherics—the *Zeitgeist* or the vibes—are rendered in the book and what light they shed on that extraordinary period in our history.

Powell was a soldier's son. His father, Lieutenant Colonel Philip Powell, was engaged in the early open fighting of 1914 before the armies settled down to trench warfare, and narrowly missed commanding the Welch Regiment because ill-health prevented him taking an overseas posting. As a result, Powell and his parents (he was an only child) led the usual nomadic life of service families. His mother had to move house nine times during the first two years of their marriage. Powell did not get on well with his father, an increasingly short-tempered and disappointed figure. As the narrator remarks in *The Kindly Ones:* "my father . . . grew easily tired of hearing another man, even his own cook, too protractedly commended."[9] Yet Powell inherited an ineradicable military gene, an obsessive fascination with all the routines, shibboleths, and impedimenta of military life. Why did this regiment have Fishguard on their battle honors, the only British place name to be so signaled in the British army? What is the correct term for becoming a full colonel? Surely not "go red,"[10] as Widmerpool absurdly boasts, but "taking flannel" or putting on "a red hat."

This interest in military matters was not simply a playful thing. As a young man in the late 1920s, perhaps the least militarist period in British history, Powell was spending much of his time in brightest bohemia—night clubs like the Gargoyle and the pubs of Fitzrovia—but at the same time he joined the Territorial Army and would sneak off for exercises to the Royal Artillery's barracks down in South London to meet a very different crowd. And when war comes in 1939, he hastens to join his father's old regiment, the Welch, with a "c," of course, not an "s." And he serves throughout the Second World War, in rainswept barracks in Pembrokeshire and Belfast, in the bureaucratic warren of the Cabinet Office, then finally as Liaison Officer to the smaller Allied nations whom he leads on a mission to Montgomery's HQ in France.

There is an interesting comparison to be made here with his friend Evelyn Waugh's treatment of military life in the *Sword of Honour* trilogy. Waugh, too, joined up in a spirit of high idealism but was disillusioned by the shabby behavior of his superior officers on the evacuation of Crete. It is not the least of Waugh's savage ironies that he should have dedicated *Officers and Gentlemen* "to Major General Sir Robert Laycock that every man in arms should wish to be," when twenty years later he was still referring to "Laycock's and my ignominious flight" from Crete, leaving their men to face death or capture. The words of Madame Kanyi, one of the Jewish refugees under the care of Guy Crouchback in *Unconditional Surrender,* come to mind:

"There was a will to war, a death wish, everywhere. Even good men thought their private honour would be satisfied by war. They could assert their manhood by killing and being killed. They would accept hardships in recompense for having been selfish and lazy. Danger justified privilege. I knew Italians—not very many perhaps—who felt this. Were there none in England?"

And Crouchback's reply:

"God forgive me," said Guy, "I was one of them."[11]

That is the recantation of a crusader, an amateur soldier who goes to war for a cause. In total contrast, Powell remains steadily fascinated by the soldier's profession and the ups and downs that must be endured. The second two of the three books in the trilogy covering the war refer to this—*The Soldier's Art* and *The Military Philosophers*. Only the first, *The Valley of the Bones*, refers to the terrible punishment that the fates are preparing. Powell discovers Alfred de Vigny's *Servitude et grandeur militaires:* "the soldier is a dedicated person, a sort of monk of war."[12] He quotes, too, the maxim of General Lyautey, who pacified North Africa for the French, that "the first essential of an officer [is] gaiety."[13]

For Powell, it is this mixture of stoicism and romance that has always characterized the soldier's life, producing results that are at once touching and absurd. In cleaning up the effects of Uncle Giles after his death at the Bellevue Hotel, at the bottom of a Gladstone bag he comes upon a roll of parchment tied up with red tape:

"VICTORIA by the Grace of God, of the United Kingdom of Great Britain and Ireland, Queen, Defender of the Faith, Empress of India etc. To Our Trusty and well-beloved Giles Delahay Jenkins, Gentleman, Greeting. We, reposing especial Trust and Confidence in your Loyalty, Courage and good Conduct, do by these Presents Constitute and Appoint you to be an Officer in Our Land forces..."

Trusty and well beloved were not the terms in which his own kith and kin had thought of Uncle Giles for a long time now. Indeed, the Queen's good-heartedness in herself greeting him so warmly was as touching as her error of judgment was startling. There was something positively ingenuous in singling out Uncle Giles for the repose of confidence, accepting him so wholly at his own valuation. No doubt the Queen had been badly advised.[14]

While shaking his head over his uncle, the narrator is deeply moved by these great rolling phrases, so compelling in their beauty and simplicity and indeed their intimacy.

Or take Captain Rowland Gwatkin, the narrator's company commander in the Welch battalion posted to Northern Ireland. Like the rest of the battalion's officers, he is a bank manager in civilian life (the soldiers are all miners) and being impractical and liable to flap is not expected to go far. Yet he has unshakable dreams of military glory; "he aspires to be a military saint." In a novel by Evelyn Waugh he would be a purely comic character, like, say Apthorpe in *Men at Arms,* yet in *Dance* he is a sympathetic—even touching—figure:

> [Gwatkin] had draped a rubber groundsheet round him like a cloak, which, with his flattish-brimmed steel helmet, transformed him into a figure from the later Middle Ages, a captain-of-arms of the Hundred Years War, or the guerrilla campaigning of Owen Glendower. I suddenly saw that was where Gwatkin belonged, rather than to the soldiery of modern times, the period which captured his own fancy. Rain had wetted his moustache, causing it to droop over the corners of the mouth, like those belonging to effigies on tombs or church brasses. Persons at odds with their surroundings not infrequently suggest an earlier historical epoch. Gwatkin was not exactly at odds with the rest of the world. In many ways, he was the essence of conventional behaviour. At the same time, he never mixed with others on precisely their own terms. Perhaps people suspected—disapproved—his vaulting dreams.[15]

It is this understanding of the unchanging aspects of soldiering that throws into relief the sudden alarming arrival of mass warfare. General Conyers is a pivotal figure here. As a young subaltern on the North-West Frontier, according to Uncle Giles, he had armed the palace eunuchs with rook rifles, and in the Boer War he took part in Sir John French's charge across the Modder River. Now nearly eighty, he is prophesying war, but on an infinitely greater scale than any he has himself fought in: "One of these fine mornings the Germans will arrive over here. . . . And when the Germans come, it will be a big show—Clausewitz's Nation in Arms."[16]

It is a new and terrifying world, for which the British are hopelessly unprepared. The narrator remembers seeing as a child how:

> squads of recruits began to appear on the Common, their evolutions in the heather performed in scarlet or dark blue, for in those early days of the war there were not enough khaki uniforms to go round. Some wore their own cloth caps over full-dress tunics or marched along in column of fours dressed in subfusc civilian suits.[17]

The Army, too, is transformed by total war from a professional, secluded brotherhood fighting far-off colonial wars that, to the civilian population, have the character of sporting events. Nothing brings home to the narrator the imminence and certitude of the Second World War more than the appearance of Widmerpool in the midst of the revels at the country house of the tycoon Sir Magnus Donners:

> A man stood on the threshold. He was in uniform. He appeared to be standing at attention, a sinister, threatening figure, calling the world to arms. It was Widmerpool.
>
> By that date, when the country had lived for some time under the threat of war, the traditional, the almost complete professional anonymity of the army in England had been already abrogated. Orders enacting that officers were never to be seen in London wearing uniform—certainly on no social occasion, nor, as a rule, even when there on duty—being to some extent relaxed, it was now not unknown for a Territorial, for example, to appear in khaki in unmilitary surroundings because he was on his way to or from a brief period of training. Something of the sort must have caused Widmerpool's form of dress. His arrival at this hour was, in any case, surprising enough. The sight of him in uniform struck a chill through my bones.[18]

After war has passed, there is a grim toll to be counted. Not simply in terms of those who have been killed, although a remarkable number of characters are killed: among them the narrator's earliest friends, Stringham and Templer, two of his brothers-in-law, and one of his sisters-in-law who is killed by a bomb the same night as her estranged husband is among those slaughtered by the bomb that destroys the Café de Madrid—the fictional version of the bomb on the Café de Paris that put an end to so many gilded lives.

But many of those who survive are never quite the same— exhausted, restless, hollowed out:

> There was something else about Umfraville that struck me, a characteristic I had noticed in other people of his age. He seemed still young, a person like oneself; and yet at the same time his appearance and manner proclaimed that he had had time to live at least a few years of his grown-up life before the outbreak of war in 1914. Once I had thought of those who had known the epoch of my own childhood as "older people." Then I had found there existed people like Umfraville who seemed somehow to span the gap. They partook of both eras, specially forming the tone of the post-war years; much more so, indeed, than the younger people. Most of

them, like Umfraville, were melancholy; perhaps from the strain of living simultaneously in two different historical periods.[19]

Umfraville's old drinking partner, Ted Jeavons, who leads a strange dim existence shuffling around the edge of the ill-assorted parties given by his wife Lady Molly, confides to the narrator one night over the deafening din of a trio playing in the dismal club Umfraville has just opened:

> "People don't think the same way any longer," he bawled across the table. "The war blew the whole bloody thing up, like tossing a Mills bomb into a dug-out. Everything's changed about all that. Always feel rather sorry for your generation as a matter of fact, not but what we haven't all lost our—what do you call 'em—you know—. . ."
> "Illusions?"
> "Illusions! That's the one. We've lost all our bloody illusions."[20]

Nor does this post-war gloom lift as the 1920s give way to the 1930s. Here is Dicky Umfraville again. He has settled in Kenya with the other wealthy refugees of Happy Valley but we find him in the smoky surroundings of Foppa's club in Soho:

> "Got rather tired of [Kenya] lately. Isn't what it was in the early days. But, you know, something seems to have gone badly wrong with this country too. It's quite different from when I was over here two or three years ago. Then there was a party every night— two or three, as a matter of fact. Now all that is changed. No parties, no gaiety, everyone talking in a dreadfully serious manner about economics or world disarmament or something of the sort. That was why I was glad to come here and take a hand with Foppa. No nonsense about economics or world disarmament with him. All the people I know have become so damned serious, what? Don't you find that yourself?"
> "It's the slump."[21]

This sense of national exhaustion is recalled again at the end of the Second World War, when the narrator concludes that the Victory Service in St Paul's:

> had somehow failed to take adequate shape, to catch on the wing those inner perceptions of a more exalted sort, evasive by their very nature, at best transient enough, but not altogether un-known. . . . Perhaps that was because everyone was by now so tired. The country, there could be no doubt, was absolutely worn out.[22]

Rereading the whole sequence after a long time, perhaps twenty years, I was struck by the worn-out quality, the inescapable shabbiness of almost all the places in which the action is set between the wars as well as after 1945.

Think, for example, of the Ufford, the private hotel in a latent, almost impenetrable region of Bayswater where Uncle Giles lurks. The place has an:

> air of secret, melancholy guilt. The passages seemed catacombs of a hell assigned to the subdued regret of those who had lacked in life the income to which they felt themselves entitled; this suspicion that the two houses were an abode of the dead being increased by the fact that no one was ever to be seen about, even at the reception desk. The floors of the formerly separate buildings, constructed at different levels, were now joined by unexpected steps and narrow, steeply slanting passages. The hall was always wrapped in silence; letters in the green baize board criss-crossed with tape remained yellowing, forever unclaimed, unread, unchanged.[23]

Or take Foppa's Club, a single smoky billiard room over Foppa's restaurant, reached by a "narrow staircase, over which brooded a peculiarly Italian smell: minestrone: salad oil: stale tobacco: perhaps a faint reminder of the lotion Foppa used on his hair."[24] Or the mournful pubs of Soho and Fitzrovia, such as the Mortimer, later bombed in the war. Or the dismal surroundings of the Maida Vale canal where the writer X. Trapnel finds his manuscript dumped by his fiendish lover Pamela Flitton.

Nor is the English countryside in much better state. Thrubworth Park, the seat of the narrator's in-laws, the Tollands, is kept under dustsheets. The owner, Lord Erridge, the Left-wing peer, lives in a state bordering on squalor in the servants quarters. Financial insecurity racks most of the characters. Money comes and goes. Wealth, if anticipated at all, is expected to come from some deal in South America or the Middle East. There is little or no suggestion that Britain is capable of self-regeneration.

In the UK paperback edition, *Dance* is grouped into four volumes of three books each, named after the Seasons. I think this is unfortunate—and not just if Sir Anthony Blunt was right about the iconography—but because it promises a certain fresh, optimistic quality to the opening volume which we expect to be supplanted in turn by the riper glow of summer, the fading tints of autumn and the chilly pallor of winter.

In reality, the whole sequence is riddled from the start with restlessness, apprehension, and nostalgia. Describing the garden at Stonehurst, the bungalow rented by the narrator's parents when his father is stationed at Aldershot, the narrator has something in mind beyond the military aspect of the terrain:

Beyond the white-currant bushes, wild country began again, separated from Stonehurst civilisation by only a low embankment of
turf. This was the frontier of a region more than a little captivat-
ing—like the stables—on account of its promise of adventure.
Dark, brooding plantations of trees; steep, sandy slopes; soft, velvet expanses of green moss. . . . Here, among these woods and
clearings, sand and fern, silence and the smell of pine brought a
kind of release to the heart, together with a deep-down wish for
something, something more than battles, perhaps not battles at
all; something realised, even then, as nebulous, blissful, all but
unattainable: a feeling of uneasiness, profound and oppressive,
yet oddly pleasurable at times, at other times so painful as to be almost impossible to bear.[25]

These apprehensions in their most alarming form revive at the outset of Hitler's war when:

war towered by the bed when you awoke in the morning . . . its
tall form, so far from dissolving immediately, remained, on the
contrary, a looming, menacing shape of ever greater height, ever
thickening density. The grey, flickering sequences of the screen
showed with increased persistence close-ups of stocky dema-
gogues, fuming, gesticulating, stamping; oceans of raised fore-
arms; steel-helmeted men tramping in column; armoured vehicles
rumbling over the *pavé* of broad boulevards.[26]

Politics in the narrow sense plays little part in *Dance* and, we are led
to assume, has little to offer. A couple of MPs have walk-on parts,
for example the narrator's brother-in-law Roddy Cutts who retains
"the forceful manner, half hectoring, half subservient, common to
representatives of all political parties, together with the politician's
hallmark of getting hold of the wrong end of the stick."[27] Widmerpool is also briefly a Labour MP after the war. Having found much
to admire in Hitler in the 1930s, he has been steadily moving to the
Left and is greatly impressed by Stalin. When the massacre of Katyn
Forest is uncovered, he sees no point in jeopardizing the Soviet alliance in the interests of a few thousand Polish exiles. Gypsy Jones,
La Pasionaria of Hendon Central, who has a one-night stand with
the narrator, actually joins the Communist Party (unlike most of
the fellow travelers with whom the book teems) and is seen ha-
ranguing an anti-war meeting from a soapbox in 1939. The narrator himself has no illusions that the settlement reached at Munich
will stave off hostilities. When he hears the news that Germany has
invaded Russia, "an immediate, overpowering, almost mystic sense
of relief took shape within me. I felt suddenly sure everything was

going to be all right."[28] Of course the victory can come only at the
cost of millions more lives and destruction on a scale unprecedented in human history. Even at this moment of cataclysmic relief,
the implications of the narrator's perspective are bleak, to say the
least.

Yet the overall effect of *Dance* is far from one of unrelieved melancholy. On the contrary, it is the background of decay and exhaustion
that shows the human will at its most unstoppable and inspiriting.
Powell was a great admirer of Stendhal, and he has Stendhal's fascination with willpower and with those individuals who live by the
power of the will. These characters vary widely: the upwardly mobile
Marxist writer J. G. Quiggin, for example, or his landlord, the reclu-
sive and ascetic peer Erridge, who goes off to the Spanish Civil War.
Erridge is a marvelous character, to outward appearance seedy and
down-at-heel, yet inwardly iron-willed in his determination to get his
own way. "He belonged to the class of egoist who dislikes the taste of
food and drink."[29] On entering a room in his patched old tweed coat
and infinitely filthy corduroy trousers, he appears diffident: "I forgot
at the time that this inability to penetrate a room is a particular form
of hesitation to be associated with persons in whom an extreme egoism is dominant."[30]

But the most memorable egoist is Widmerpool, whose determination to live by the will alone propels him, despite an endless series
of comic humiliations, to success in business, the rank of colonel,
and a life peerage:

> There was something impressive in his total lack of interest in the
> fate of all persons except himself. Perhaps it was not the lack of in-
> terest in itself—common enough to many people—but the fact
> that he was at no pains to conceal this within some more or less
> hypocritical integument.[31]

He dispatches Stringham to the Far East and Templer on a dangerous mission to the Balkans and is unmoved when both are killed as
result. Widmerpool is an immortal, one whose name has more or
less entered the language as a synonym for a clumsy, ambitious, un-
scrupulous character. He has joined that fictional Valhalla inhab-
ited by Fagin, Sherlock Holmes, and Jeeves.

Yet we are not to regard Powell as simply hostile to the exercise of
willpower. He is an analyst not a preacher, and to show the application of the will to necessary ends I would like to quote two fine portraits of the military will in action. The first is of the CIGS, Sir Alan
Brooke, coming up the stairs of the Cabinet Office. My attention:

was at that moment unequivocally demanded by the hurricane-like imminence of a thickset general, obviously of high rank, wearing enormous horn-rimmed spectacles. He had just burst from a flagged staff-car almost before it had drawn up by the kerb. Now he tore up the steps of the building at the charge, exploding through the inner door into the hall. An extraordinary current of physical energy, almost of electricity, suddenly pervaded the place. I could feel it stabbing through me. This was the CIGS. . . . Vavassor [the hall porter], momentarily overawed—there could be no doubt of it—came to attention and saluted with much more empressement than usual. Having no cap, I merely came to attention. The CIGS glanced for a split second, as if summarizing all the facts of one's life.

"Good morning."

It was a terrific volume of sound, an absolute bellow, at the same time quite effortless.[32]

This, then, contrasted with the narrator's encounter a little later with Montgomery in Normandy:

I tried to reduce to viable terms impressions of this slight, very exterior contact. On the one hand, there had been hardly a trace of the almost overpowering physical impact of the CIGS, that curious electric awareness felt down to the tips of one's fingers of a given presence imparting a sense of stimulation, also the consoling thought that someone of the sort was at the top. On the other hand, the Field Marshal's outward personality offered what was perhaps even less usual, will-power, not so much natural, as developed to altogether exceptional lengths. No doubt there had been a generous basic endowment, but of not the essentially magnetic quality. In short, the will here might even be more effective from being less dramatic. It was an immense, wiry, calculated, insistent hardness, rather than a force like champagne bursting from the bottle. . . . One felt that a great deal of time and trouble, even intellectual effort of its own sort, had gone into producing this final result.[33]

If I had to pluck out a single phrase to characterize the philosophical tone of the whole book, it would, I suppose, be a classical Stoicism. There is no hint of Christian redemption in the book. Indeed, there is little about Christianity at all, even as a departing presence from the scene. I can remember only a couple of ordained priests in the entire cast of 350 characters, and very few of the characters seem much troubled by questions of faith. But endurance, pleasure, melancholy—all those elements of the Stoic worldview—haunt the pages of *Dance*. Above all, there is a clear-eyed, unsen-

timental rendering of things as they are and a celebration of the
ordinary as extraordinary. Thus the shabby, uncertain, apprehen-
sive character of British life throughout much of the period is not
blurred or minimized. At the same time, there is no quarter given to
despair. It is no accident that Powell was a firm admirer of Margaret
Thatcher and also found her remarkably physically attractive.

He was fond of saying that with every writer there is always
something you have to put up with. Some readers prefer Powell's
lighter novels of the 1930s and do not care for the denser texture of
Dance: the long sentences, the heavy adverbial structures, the adjec-
tival impasto and, most remarkable and then unfashionable, the substantial participial clauses moored alongside the main sentence. At
its most successful, the entire sentence manages to give the broadest
possible expression to a moment of experience, containing within it
the awkward contradictions, the blurrings, and slippery undermin-
ings which abound in real life. It is at the opposite end technically
from the pared-down style of, say, Ernest Hemingway (whom, I
should add, Powell admired). At its worst it is liable to topple over
into ponderousness and even pomposity. Yet in its sheer richness of
effect, it offers to me an unrivaled picture of British life as it was and
is lived. Those scenes which I happen to have experienced myself,
even though it is now thirty or forty years later, I remember exactly as
they are given in the novel: a winter's afternoon in an English public
school, an evening in a Soho pub, a debutante dance, the offices of
a literary magazine. While in no sense posing as a chronicle of the
twentieth century in Britain, I cannot think of any better fictional
guide to it.

How much of the book and its characters are based on the writer's
own experience? This is a subject on which Powell has something to
say in the first volume of his memoirs, *Infants of the Spring.*[34] Most
novelists, he agrees, draw their characters and scenes in some degree from "real life"—to use the characteristic Powell quotes. Characters who bear no resemblance to any human being one has ever
met are liable to have something wrong with them. But the real person who "sets going" the idea of a major character always requires
change, addition, development if he or she is to acquire substance,
not so much from the author's calculation as from the uncontrolled
subconscious instinct that gives life to a character. While Erridge
certainly bears some of the characteristics of Powell's brother-in-law
and my uncle, the late campaigning Labour peer Lord Longford—
the obsession with causes, the egoism, the indifference to material
pleasure or comfort—so too does Widmerpool. Indeed, my Uncle

Frank—being also obsessed with celebrity—proudly claimed that he *was* Widmerpool, since Widmerpool was easily the most famous character in the book. To which Powell used to say that: "if someone is good for being a character, he is probably good for many characters. You can form the basis of perhaps half a dozen people from one human model." Dickens certainly did with his father.

I am perhaps too close to my subject to form any reliable estimate of the enduring merits of Powell's works. I can only say for my own part what may sound like a backhanded compliment but is in reality a fervent tribute: of all novelists in English I have found his the most difficult influence to get away from, such is the cumulative power of his stylistic richness, his powers of observation and above all his humor. Powell is certainly not averse to the one-liner that tickles you in the ribs, but he specializes in the slowly building, comic crescendo, in which the absurdity of the action and its baroque elaboration on the page can leave you brimming with laughter.

When I begin a novel myself, I have always his shadow behind me, insisting on the importance of *dwelling*, of giving full value to a place, however superficially unmemorable, a moment, however seemingly inconsequential, a person, however dim or marginal they might be in the eyes of the world. The accusation of snobbery, made by several hasty critics, needs not so much rebutting as standing on its head.

His admirers were certainly not confined to dyed-in-the-wool conservatives. On the Left, his fans included the playwright Dennis Potter, the Marxist historian Perry Anderson, and the socialist firebrand Tariq Ali. Powell's fascination was not at all with the smug connections of a closed caste, but rather with the remarkable anarchic openness of English life, its quirks and eddies and, indeed, with the ups and downs of life generally—as conveyed in the torrential quotation from *Burton's Anatomy* with which he closes the twelfth and last volume of *Dance*. As a matter of fact, his fiction was extraordinarily democratic in a way few other writers of his time could claim. The light plays evenly on each personage—not merely on the beautiful, elusive Jean Duport, or the charming, doomed Stringham or even the monstrous Widmerpool, but on Alfred Tolland, the dim aphasic relation who only appears at family parties, on Le Bas, the awkward housemaster with a weakness for late Victorian poets, on Eleanor Walpole-Wilson, the dogbreeding dyke, on Uncle Giles.

Every dance comes to an end. The Wheel of Fortune must eventually spin to a halt. Well into his late eighties Powell was a remarkable advertisement for not taking exercise. But there succeeded a rather long, unhappy period of frailty. At three in the morning on

March 28, 2000 he took a turn for the worse, and the doctor was summoned. The doctor was new, youngish and turned out to be called Powell, too. While they were waiting, the novelist's elder son, the film director Tristram Powell, chatted to Dr. Powell about what part of Wales his ancestors came from. It was a typical Powellian moment: unexpected, genealogical, comical, melancholy. Anthony Powell died later that night. He had left instructions that his ashes should be scattered on the lake below the Chantry. While the rest of us gathered on the bank, his sons rowed the ashes out to the middle of the water. As he scattered them, Tristram read "Fear no more the heat o' the sun." The moment was, I think, less reminiscent of *Cymbeline* than of Tennyson's *Morte d'Arthur,* a favorite of Powell's. Snow was gently falling, as it does at the beginning and the end of *A Dance to the Music of Time.*

Fall Semester 2003

1. Anthony Powell, *The Military Philosophers* (London, 1968), p. 134.
2. Anthony Powell, *The Acceptance World* (London, 1955), p. 85.
3. Anthony Powell, *The Kindly Ones* (London, 1962), p. 69.
4. Ibid., p. 142.
5. Anthony Powell, *Casanova's Chinese Restaurant* (London, 1960), p. 2.
6. Ibid., p. 103.
7. Anthony Powell, *A Question of Upbringing* (London, 1951), p. 2.
8. Powell, *Acceptance World,* p. 63.
9. Powell, *Kindly Ones,* p. 56.
10. Powell, *Military Philosophers,* p. 110.
11. Evelyn Waugh, *Unconditional Surrender* (London, 1961), p. 300.
12. Anthony Powell, *The Valley of the Bones* (London, 1964), p. 107.
13. Ibid., p. 152.
14. Powell, *Kindly Ones,* p. 157.
15. Powell, *Bones,* p. 76.
16. Powell, *Kindly Ones,* p. 54.
17. Ibid., p. 73.
18. Ibid., pp. 133–34.
19. Powell, *Acceptance World,* p. 153.
20. Anthony Powell, *At Lady Molly's* (London, 1957), p. 178.
21. Powell, *Acceptance World,* p. 156.
22. Powell, *Military Philosophers,* p. 217.
23. Powell, *Acceptance World,* p. 1.
24. Ibid., p. 144.
25. Powell, *Kindly Ones,* p. 9.
26. Ibid., p. 87.
27. Anthony Powell, *Books do Furnish a Room* (London, 1971), p. 40.
28. Anthony Powell, *The Soldier's Art* (London, 1966), p. 227.
29. Powell, *Lady Molly's,* p. 116.
30. Ibid., pp. 12–13.
31. Powell, *Soldier's Art,* p. 192.
32. Powell, *Military Philosophers,* pp. 53–54.
33. Ibid., pp. 183–84.
34. Anthony Powell, *Infants of the Spring* (London, 1976), pp. 51–52.

5

Philip Larkin's "Elements"

DAN JACOBSON

Philip Larkin died in 1985, at the age of sixty-three. Even before his death he had come to be regarded in Britain as a kind of national institution rather than as just another distinguished writer. His poems were the most widely quoted and anthologized of any Englishman whose career fell within the second half of the twentieth century. He had (grumblingly) received innumerable awards, prizes, medals, and honorary doctorates; been made the subject of various television and radio programs and collections of laudatory essays; twice been decorated by the Queen; elected to a Visiting Fellowship of All Souls' College and an Honorary Fellowship of St John's College, both in Oxford; and, finally, offered the post of Poet Laureate by Margaret Thatcher during her period as Prime Minister. (He declined the offer on the grounds that he had by then already dried up as a poet.) Despite his well-advertised insularity of outlook and distaste for "abroad," he had also gone to Hamburg to receive that city's Shakespeare Prize for his contribution to English literature. (He once said that he wouldn't mind going to China provided he could come home the same day.) The memorial service held soon after his death took place in Westminster Abbey: an acknowledgement of services rendered that is granted only to the country's most prominent public figures.

Given all that, the early unveiling of a plaque to his memory in Poets' Corner, Westminster Abbey, might have been expected; or, conceivably, even a move to have him buried there, along with Dryden, Tennyson, Browning, among others. Not only was his work unusual in being so highly regarded by general readers and university critics alike; more remarkably still, in both his verse and critical prose he had taken to expressing quasi-"nationalistic" sentiments that his century's most important English poets had on the whole eschewed—or even despised. Having got over his adolescent infatuation with the poetry of W. B. Yeats and W. H. Auden, Larkin had programmatically opposed the international "Modernism" (manifest above all in the work of Eliot and Pound, "those culture-mongering American expatriates," as he described them) that had seemed to carry everything before it during the first half of the twentieth century. In contrast, he had asserted the moral and literary values of a specifically homegrown tradition of English verse-making which, he believed, was characterized by clarity, directness, modesty, accessibility, and truth to locality.

"Plain language, the absence of posturing, sense of proportion, humour, abandonment of the dithyrambic ideal"—that was one of Larkin's rapid sketches of the ideal he ostensibly set for himself and others. Naturally there were critics in England and elsewhere who for these very reasons dismissed his poems as "provincial," "timid," and "unadventurous"; but the suffrage of almost all dedicated readers of poetry in Britain went against them. Towards the end of his life the sense that English readers had of him as peculiarly and intimately "their" poet was reinforced by the elegiac tone of many of his later poems. In "Homage to a Government," "Going, Going," "Show Saturday," and others like them he spoke with sorrow of a country that appeared to have lost a living sense of its domestic and imperial past, and that was discarding its own ways and traditions—whether "folk" or "high" or both at the same time—without even knowing that it was doing so.

Yet it was precisely in this context, with its implicit and explicit view of what England was or had been, that his *Selected Letters,* edited by Anthony Thwaite (1992), and Andrew Motion's biography *Philip Larkin: A Writer's Life* (1993), produced an outcry against everything he had done and was believed to represent. How could anyone think of him as a poet and public figure worthy of a memorial in Poets' Corner when in letters and remarks to his friends he had repeatedly written and spoken in such vile terms of Britain's new, dark-skinned immigrants and of the countries they came from? His distaste for "niggers" and "coonland" was bad enough; no better, for many readers, was his longstanding addiction to pornography and to fantasies about underage girls—especially as these ran alongside litanies of complaint against the grown-up women in his life for being calculating and irrational, weak and strong, stupid and crafty, humiliatingly indispensable to someone like himself yet always taking up more time than they were worth. In the poetry his misogynistic murmurs—and more than murmurs—had usually been taken to express nothing worse than a half-humorous, half-serious bloody-mindedness, his version of that "harmless rebellion against virtue" which George Orwell (in writing about saucy seaside postcards) had affectionately described as "a permanent tendency in the human mind . . . which is always there and will always find its own outlet, like water."[1] But the letters and biography suggested that something darker was at work here, more obsessive, less assimilable to anyone's idea of knockabout fun.

Nor did such outbursts and nagging complaints exhaust all that readers found disconcerting in the two memorial volumes. There was his habitual use of foul language, particularly but not exclusively in earlier years, that comes across at times like a kind of scribal Tourette's Syndrome, afflicting not the victim's tongue but his writing hand. There was his inexhaustible, claustrophobic preoccupation with himself—his health, his work, his lodgings, his dislikes, his women (or their absence)—alternating with equally elaborate expressions of self-disgust and self-deprecation (those too being just another form of self-absorption.) There was his manifest jealousy of contemporary poets on his side of the Atlantic (Ted Hughes, Seamus Heaney) whose fame threatened to outstrip his own; and his tireless attempts—in reverse mode, so to speak—to foster the reputations of comfortably middlebrow writers of much less consequence than himself (John Betjeman the poet, Barbara Pym the novelist) who clearly presented no threat to him or to his own reputation.

THE RUMPUS THAT FOLLOWED THE PUBLICATION of the Thwaite and Motion volumes took a predictable form. On one side were readers who adopted a hearty, what's-all-the-fuss-about attitude towards the belated "revelations" which, they claimed, had revealed nothing of consequence. Nothing, anyway, that had a significant bearing on the merits of his poetry or even on his character as a man. The reactionary views, abusive remarks and scabrous bits of unpublished verse appearing in the letters showed Larkin putting on a performance, taking up attitudes which he knew would amuse right-wing friends like Kingsley Amis and Robert Conquest, and would scandalize all the solemn liberals and *bien-pensant* Lefties he despised—exactly the kind of people who were now doing their best to destroy his reputation. In critical debate and in his everyday dealings with others he had invariably been courteous and kindly. His poems about the women he cared for showed great delicacy and intensity of feeling, and so did his letters to them. Throughout his working life he had been a skilled and conscientious university librarian who had won the affection of the scores of men and women who worked under him—always a severe test of a person's character. Whatever he may have said about "niggers" privately, in public he had always made plain his sense of gratitude, even of reverence, towards the black jazz musicians (Armstrong, Bechet, Ellington, and others) about whom he produced a sustained body of critical writing; and in relation to whom he had argued that their great art-form of the blues did not reveal a "natural melancholy" on the part of African-Americans, as some (white) people liked to imagine, but was a consequence of their entire race having been "cheated and bullied and starved" over the centuries. Finally, his defenders pointed out, if we were all to be as uninhibited as Larkin in putting on paper our hidden selves, our private resentments and involuntary lusts, how many of us would emerge any more attractively from our posthumously published scribblings than he had? And how many of us would reveal in them anything like his wit and inventiveness?

So much for the defense. Ranged on the other side were those who claimed that the near-idolization of the man and his work by the British Establishment revealed the truth about its real attitudes towards foreigners, women, the working-class, and the country's newly arrived minorities. In effect, his detractors asserted, Larkin had devoted his life to flattering his white, middle-class readership and assuaging—while reinforcing, too—its anxieties about the revolutionary changes that had overtaken the country's social order and international standing. His nostalgia for the cozy domesticities and marauding imperial certainties of the past was mirrored perfectly in his programmatic detestation of Modernism and in the unreconstructed, old-fashioned prosody of his verse. Ultimately, perhaps, little more needed to be said about the man than that he was the favorite modern poet of the hated, reactionary, "warmongering" Mrs. Thatcher. In the excited words of Tom Paulin, himself a writer and a teacher of literature in Oxford and elsewhere, the publication of Larkin's *Letters* and *Life* had starkly revealed "the sewer under the national monument [that] Larkin became."

And there the matter rests; or rather, slumbers uneasily. The website of his fan-club, the Philip Larkin Society, with its headquarters in Hull, the city in which he had made his home, continues to offers to members and visitors a variety of "study days," "Philip Larkin walks," evenings of "readings, anecdote and reminiscence (glass of wine included)," conferences and the like. All of which, I am sure, would have pleased Larkin greatly and provoked him to volleys of scathing adjectives, obscene and otherwise. But canonization? No. Elevation to the status of a great and blessedly comprehensible English poet? Doubtful. The launching of a campaign to have a plaque bearing his name put up in Poets' Corner? I suspect not. Not for a long time, anyway.

W. B. YEATS ONCE WROTE THAT OUT OF A POET'S QUARREL with others he produces rhetoric; out of his quarrel with himself, poetry. It is an often-quoted remark, but like others of its kind it doesn't stand up to inspection. "Poetry" and "rhetoric" are not antithetical terms. The better a poem is the less distinguishable from each other will be its "poetic" and "rhetorical" elements. For all the conversational intimacy of tone that marks so many of Larkin's poems, they are again and again given to making what the late Ian Hamilton, one of Larkin's most astute critics, described as "great, haunting statements about love and death."[2] Such statements often come at the end of a poem, as in "An Arundel Tomb" (". . . to prove / Our almost instinct almost true: / What will survive of us is love"), or the title-poem of his last collection, "High Windows," where what can be seen beyond the eponymous windows is only "deep blue air, that shows / Nothing, and is nowhere, and is endless"). Yet as often as not statements of this kind will be undercut in the poem itself by a dismissive shrug, or a lewd phrase, or a bleak gesture of acceptance, each of these being, in context, both rhetorical and poetic, the record of one more episode in the author's never-ceasing arguments with both himself and others. In the phrases quoted above from "An Arundel Tomb," for example, we hear the undermining going on within the sonority of the poem's conclusion—which speaks with unflinching precision of an *almost* instinct that is *almost* true. Nothing more.

Larkin's mature poetry is seldom obscure, but it is always more complicated than either his admirers or detractors generally wish to believe. Even the most simple-seeming of his poems emerge from positively Nietzschean depths of self-contradiction; they are born out of thoughts, impulses and emotions in a state of internecine conflict with one another. From his letters it is clear that nothing mattered more to him than his writing: it was his refuge from his unsatisfactory relations with friends, lovers, and members of his family; and (as he was ready to admit from time to time) the reason why such relationships were bound to remain unsatisfactory. Or, to put it more strongly still, why he felt compelled to keep them in that state. Morally and psychologically it seems to have been impossible for him to reach forward—for a woman, for a mood, for self-transcendence in any form—without retracting; and he could not retract without sorrowing for whatever he had just felt himself compelled to renounce.

For all their translucence, the poems by Larkin most worth going back to—and there are a large number of them, relative to his overall output—do not merely arise from self-division but are explicitly *about* self-division. Each recreates an irresolvable, tripartite argument between the poet's delight in the shapes and satisfactions of this world ("reaching forward"); his pre-emptive withdrawal ("retraction") from them in the face of the certainty of death, which takes everything from everyone, himself included; and his hunger for a realm (by definition unattainable) where this three-way tug-of-war is replaced by a consciousness of "infinity and absence, the beauty of somewhere you're not . . . where there's neither oppressed nor oppressor, just freedom."[3] For him, this imaginary realm can be approached only through the creation and enjoyment of art—through poetry, fiction, and music. (Though a poem like "The Card-Players" and various scattered references in his letters suggest that he spent a great deal of time, in his youth especially, looking at pictures.)

Denial as a form of affirmation (and vice versa); disappointment as the condition of creativity (and vice-versa) . . . Couplings and transformations of this kind can be found at every level of Larkin's work. Take, for example, the apparently "abstract" issue of his espousal of an anti-Modernist poetic ideology. Yes, he prided himself on being typically, old-fashionedly "English" in his insularity, his aversion to going abroad, his indifference to what foreigners got up to in the unfortunate parts the world they were condemned to live in. Yes, he spoke disdainfully of the Modernist revolution in poetry and chose in his own verse to cling to traditional English rhyme and stanza forms. Yet the debts he owed to his Modernist predecessors reveal themselves again and again in the subjects, syntax, and patterns of imagery in his verse. (Not to speak of the four-letter words he used in the poems whenever he needed them: a freedom which Modernists like Joyce, Lawrence, Henry Miller and others had made it possible for him to employ—and enjoy.) It is wholly typical of him that he should say about the last line of one of his own poems, "Absences," that "it sounds like a slightly unconvincing translation from a French symbolist"—and then add wistfully, "I wish I could write like that more often." (The line in question, consisting of just seven words and two exclamation points, refers to the sea and sky as "Such attics cleared of me! Such absences!"[4]) Parallel passages and poems abound in the three major volumes of verse he left behind. "Sad Steps," for instance, opens unpromisingly with the speaker of the poem "Groping back to bed after a piss" and then, after parting the curtains, finding himself staring in astonishment at the full moon—"High and preposterous and separate – / Lozenge of love! Medallion of art!" In a companion poem, "Solar," the sun makes its appearance in the first line simply as "Suspended lion face," with no explanatory gloss or preceding article; and the poem ends with this supposedly most cautious and fretful of poets finding an unexpected, ungrudging, and wholly human term of praise for the inhuman power he has been apostrophizing throughout: "Unclosing like a hand, / You give forever."

LARKIN IS TODAY ALMOST AS FAMOUS AS Thomas Hardy (his chief poetical mentor) was for his "pessimism." It is true that Larkin himself once remarked ironically that "desolation" was to him what "daffodils were to Wordsworth." Yet how characteristic it is of him, too, that he should write with more passion than any other poet known to me of the unstable splendors of the English summer: its heat, its fullness, heaviness, leafiness, the sultriness of its airs and the ever-changing density of its light. Look at such poems as "Cut Grass," "Here," "The Whitsun Weddings," "Solar," even the visionary "The Explosion." In a poem written early in his career and left unpublished until the appearance of his posthumous *Collected Poems,* he described himself as "summer-born / And summer-loving"—and so he was, though in that same poem he confesses how inadequate he feels himself to be to "the emblems of perfect happiness" that summer days should represent.

In an essay on Hardy's poetry Larkin wrote that:

> it cannot be denied that the dominant emotion in Hardy is sadness. Hardy was peculiarly well equipped to perceive the melancholy, the misfortunate, the frustrating, the failing elements of life. . . . Any approach to his work, as to any writer's work, must seek to determine what element is peculiarly his, which imaginative note he strikes most plangently; and to deny that in his case it is the sometimes gentle, sometimes bitter, but always passive apprehension of suffering is, I think, wrong-headed.[5]

Is this just a thinly disguised portrait of Larkin himself? Only up to a point. One notices the self-revealing suggestion that readers would normally search in the first instance for the most "plangent" note struck by the author. Certainly that was Hardy's "peculiar . . . element." But why shouldn't readers look also for the notes which "a writer" strikes most strongly, most cheerfully. There are some writers—Byron, for example—whose plangent note is the one they might least wish to listen to. And as for the "passive apprehension of suffering"—no, for all the regret which pervades so much of Larkin's work, that is not really its most characteristic element. Its "apprehensions" are pervaded by regret, certainly, but they are qualified also by rebelliousness and angry humor; his verse is attentive not so much to suffering—not as we ordinarily think of it, anyway—but to the pains of change and impermanence, the pathos of our fleeting experience of the world.

As a young man Larkin aspired to follow Hardy in becoming both a novelist and a poet, and in his early twenties he published two colorless, spiritless novels, *Jill* and *A Girl in Winter*. In a conversation I had with him almost three decades after the appearance of the second of those books, he confessed that his failure to complete a third novel, which he had been intermittently working on for several years, led to what he described as "the unhappiest part of my life, creatively." (He did not know then that the last dozen years of his life were to be almost as unhappy, creatively speaking, and that he would produce in them no more than a tiny handful of poems worth collecting—though one of them, "Aubade," is among the finest he wrote.) One result of his abandonment of his ambition to write novels was a conscious decision to bring into his verse the interests and range of emotions that he had previously believed could be expressed only in novels (including the right to be "colloquial . . . funny or flippant if I felt like it," as he said on the same occasion.) Some of his funny or flippant poems are brilliantly successful—both in themselves, as it were, and for reaching a public that would generally swerve away from poetry of any kind.[6] Others appear too easily content with putting the boot into life in general, or, with even greater zeal, putting the same boot into the "indigestible sterility" of the "I" who speaks in the poems. (Who of course both is and is not the person *writing* them.)

Anyway, once he had made up his mind that he had no choice but to draw into his poems a wider range of experience than he had previously thought they could contain, Larkin set about developing a diction that could move easily from the quotidian to the elevated and back again—and could do it in a multitude of tones and contexts. With hindsight one can see that this ambition became indistinguishable in his work from the ability to sustain grammatically elaborate sentences over lengthy, formal stanzas of various kinds, without the "voice" of the poem losing either its intimacy or power. Not all his poems fulfill these demands, of course, but a high proportion do. Again and again the reader becomes aware that the voice he is listening to has changed in key without any apparent change of emphasis, and that what might have sounded casual a moment before has become passionate, melodic, unforgiving. The improbable musical parallel I am most insistently reminded of in reading many of Larkin's poems is not his beloved jazz, but opera, with its busy, continuing life and its unpredictable swellings and lapses of emotion.

Shifts of this kind can probably best be illustrated by focusing on a single poetic "device" which Larkin uses repeatedly in both longer and shorter poems. "The Building," for example, is a long poem of nine stanzas, each consisting of seven lines—aside from a final, detached line standing on its own—that rhyme irregularly not only with lines in the same stanza but also with others that come much earlier or later in the poem. Of the nine stanzas in "The Building" only the first ends with a punctuation point; all the others "cross over," with no break in grammar or meaning, from the last line of one stanza to the first line of the next. The effect of these enjambments is to slow the pace of the entire poem while simultaneously giving it a sense of irresistible momentum. The "building" of the poem's title turns out to be a huge hospital, which is seen at first from a distance ("Higher than the handsomest hotel . . ."), and moments later viewed from within one of its waiting rooms. The room is described in terms that could hardly be more quotidian in detail and neutral in tone ("There are paperbacks and tea at so much a cup . . ."); and the same matter-of-fact language is used about the random selection of people gathered there. Yet from one neutral-sounding line to the next a significant shift in tone takes place; something grimmer and more foreboding enters the poem ("outdoor clothes and half-filled shopping bags / And faces restless and resigned . . ."). Then, at the end of the third stanza and the beginning of the fourth, comes this—

> some are young,
> Some old, but most at that vague age that claims
> The end of choice, the last of hope; and all
>
> Here to confess that something has gone wrong.

It is extraordinary that such grave music can be wrung from a sequence of simple monosyllables (twenty-nine in total, with just two bisyllables among them), following without incongruity on the dropped gloves and shopping bags mentioned just a moment before. Remarkable too is the deftness with which the solemn assonances ("that vague age that claims / The end of choice, the last of hope . . .") are combined with the crucial verb "confess" to put into the reader's mind the notion of a judgment, perhaps a last judgment, fateful for the person involved. These elements would have much less effect than they do, however, if it were not for the white, hanging, unpunctuated space between the two stanzas that makes for a sudden suspension and resumption of the narrative, and thus gives a wholly unpredictable weight to the sundered yet inseparable little words "all" and "Here."

There are eight such "crossings-over" between stanzas in this poem, each of them both faltering and resolute in the same manner; each rather like a bird choosing a particular branch to settle on— only for it to change direction at the last moment and take off again unexpectedly. Here is another example from the same poem, in this case marking the crossover between the sixth and seventh stanza of the poem—

> Look down into the yard. Outside seems old enough:
> Red brick, lagged pipes, and someone walking by it
> Out to the car park, free. Then, past the gate,
> Traffic; a locked church; short terraced streets
> Where kids chalk games, and girls with hair-dos fetch
>
> Their separates from the cleaners— O world,
> Your loves, your chances, are beyond the stretch
> Of any hand from here!

From Chaucer onwards poets have run stanzas without a grammatical break from one to the next, either because they found themselves with no choice in the matter or "on purpose," as it were. (Technically they go by the name of "interstrophal enjambments"— a mouthful in itself.) But I know of no one who uses the technique as frequently and boldly as Larkin. The transition can strike one like a sudden catch of breath under the stress of emotion; or, as in "Sunny Prestatyn," a poem about a girl on an advertising poster for a seaside resort, it can be used for comic effect. (Yet—need it be said?—not for comic purposes only.)

> She was slapped up one day in March.
> A couple of weeks, and her face
> Was snaggle-toothed and boss-eyed;
> Huge tits and a fissured crotch
> Were scored well in, and the space
> Between her legs held scrawls
> That set her fairly astride
> A tuberous cock and balls
>
> Autographed *Tich Thomas,* while
> Someone had used a knife
> Or something to stab right through

The moustached lips of her smile.
She was too good for this life.
Very soon, a great transverse tear
Left only a hand and some blue.
Now *Fight Cancer* is there.

SOCIALLY — AS I REMEMBER FROM THE THREE or four times I met him
(only once *tête-à-tête*) — Larkin was reserved, courteous, witty, ironically unassuming both about his poems and his librarianship. As an
artist, however, he was ravenously ambitious from the start. At the
age of sixteen or seventeen, he told me, he suddenly began to write
"furiously" (with Virginia Woolf, of all people, as a "remote model"),
though previously he had shown no particular literary inclinations.
From then on, it would seem, he was done for: "arrogant eternity"
had taken him under its eye, and he would never escape its scrutiny.
The phrase I have just quoted is taken from a late, desperate poem,
"Love Again," which was found among his papers after his death. In
it he blames the intensity of his artistic ambitions for what he knew
to be his manifold failures as a human being. Those ambitions were
to bring him a degree of recognition that must have exceeded most
if not all the extravagant dreams of his youth; but no one knew more
bitterly than the poet himself that they had not made him a better
or a more complete man. On the contrary.

> Isolate, rather, this element
>
> That spreads through other lives like a tree
> And sways them in a sort of sense
> And say why it never worked for me.
>
> Something to do with violence
> A long way back, and wrong rewards,
> And arrogant eternity.

We will never know what exactly Larkin had in mind in speaking of
the "violence" and "wrong rewards" that had maimed his youth. But
the demands that "arrogant eternity" made of him are another matter. Of them we remain the beneficiaries.

Summer Semester 2004

1. George Orwell, "The Art of Donald McGill," in *The Collected Essays, Journalism and Letters* (London, 1968), Vol. 2, p. 165.

2. Ian Hamilton, "Philip Larkin: The Biography," in *Walking Possession* (London, 1994), p. 140.

3. Philip Larkin, "An Interview with John Haffenden," in Anthony Thwaite, ed., *Further Requirements* (London, 2001), p. 59.

4. Philip Larkin, "Absences."

5. Philip Larkin, "Wanted: Good Hardy Critic" in *Required Writing* (London, 1983), p. 172.

6. Think of "This Be the Verse," which Larkin once said was going to be his equivalent of Yeats's "The Lake Isle of Innisfree"—the one poem by him which everyone would recognize. He expected, he said, that he would one day hear it recited by a chorus of a thousand Girl Guides. Its first verse reads:

> They fuck you up, your mum and dad.
>   They may not mean to but they do.
> They fill you with the faults they had
>   And add some extra just for you.

and its last verse:

> Man hands on misery to man.
>   It deepens like a coastal shelf.
> Get out as early as you can,
>   And don't have any kids yourself.

6

C. P. Snow:
"The Two Cultures" and the "Corridors of Power" Revisited

DAVID CANNADINE

The growth of a reputation, C. P. Snow once opined to his life-long friend and near-contemporary J. H. Plumb, "is oddly mysterious." This was a quintessentially Snovian remark: ostensibly knowing, mildly portentous and undeniably well-meaning, but on closer examination neither particularly profound nor especially significant. For in his own case at least, there was no mystery at all about the rise—or the later fall—of his reputation. By 1956, when he penned these words, Snow's position in British life seemed set on an irreversibly upward trajectory, and it peaked during the next ten years, when he was widely regarded as the Arnold Bennett or H. G. Wells of his day, when he coined such famous phrases as "the two cultures" and "corridors of power," when he was made a peer of the realm as Lord Snow of Leicester, and when he was briefly a minister in Harold Wilson's Labour Government.[1] Thereafter, his stock declined rapidly and inexorably, so that by 1985, scarcely half a decade after his demise, Plumb could lament "the great drop in Snow's reputation since his death." Nor has it recovered in the years since then. Today, his novels go largely unread, and his once-influential public utterances are derided and scorned—most recently by W. G. Runciman who, when addressing the British Academy at its centenary dinner in 2002, dismissed the very idea of there being "two cultures" as "intellectually crass, politically naïve, historically short-sighted, and rhetorically inept."[2]

Accordingly, and in modified extension of Snow's original comment, it might be better (but no more profound) to observe that, like the stock market, reputations can go up, and reputations can go down. They can also, as Shakespeare put it more felicitously, be "got without merit, and lost without deserving," and this may also be said of Snow, who was over-praised at some stages of his career, and under-appreciated at others. The purpose of this lecture is to explore in greater detail the (far from "oddly mysterious") means by which he propelled himself from provincial obscurity to national renown and international fame; to explain how his writings and pontifications made him so quintessentially 1960s a figure during the early years of that decade; and to show how his youthful hopes and middle-aged triumphs disintegrated in the disillusions of the 1970s and the disappointments of old age. As such, it views Snow in a more searching light than was usually directed on him in his glory days, but also with more sympathy than he has generally received since then. Nearly a quarter of a century after his death, it is time his life was seriously evaluated and set in a broader historical perspective, and not just at the length offered here, but also in full-dress biographical form.

Charles Percy Snow was born in 1905, and thus belonged to what Noel Annan, following Maurice Bowra, called "our age," by which he meant that generation of clever, well-educated Britons who grew up between the end of the First World War and the late 1940s, who thereafter joined what became known as "the Establishment," and who wielded power and influence until the advent of Margaret Thatcher in 1979.[3] But in one significant way, this characterization is inappropriate. Most of the men about whom Annan wrote (and they were nearly all *men*) boasted metropolitan connections, came from upper-middle-class backgrounds, were educated at public schools, and went on to Oxford, Cambridge, or the London School of Economics as undergraduates. By contrast, Snow was very much an outsider—geographically (he was provincial), sociologically (his family background was modest), and educationally (he was a grammar school boy who stayed at home for his first degree)—circumstances he would later evoke, both movingly and leadenly, in his novel *Time of Hope*. He was born in Leicester, his father was a clerk in a shoe factory, and he attended the local grammar school, Alderman Newton's, where he was taught by an inspirational mentor, H. E. Howard, whom he later immortalized as George Passant in his "Strangers and Brothers" novels. Snow enrolled at his local university college to study physics and chemistry, and having obtained a First Class degree there, he won a scholarship to Cambridge as a research student at Christ's College in 1928.

This account of Snow's early career might suggest that inter-war Britain was a more mobile society than it is sometimes fashionable to think. As a young man of ambition, spirit, and ability Snow made his way on his merits and little else, but compared to most members of "our age," Snow's was scarcely a gilded path. Although "a brilliant boy from the Midlands," he came up the hard way, and all his life he was appropriately hungry for fame, recognition, and success (though not, significantly, for the real substance of power). Indeed, when he became a peer, he took as his motto *Aut Inveniam Viam Aut Faciam*— "I will either find a way out or make one"—words he had chosen in adolescence for this very purpose and cherished ever after.[4] Not surprisingly, the themes of class and social mobility loom large in Snow's novels, especially in the case of Lewis Eliot, the central character in the "Strangers and Brothers" books, who is a thinly disguised version of himself. He is born in similarly humble circumstances, he is eager to make his way in the world, he is determined not to die unknown, and he encounters many gradations of English society along the way, from the provincial petty bourgeoisie to the traditional landed aristocracy, via the professional middle classes. All his life, Snow was fascinated by the many nuances of class in England. At the same time he was ensnared by them. He was sensitive to what he regarded as metropolitan condescension, and he always saw himself as championing the robust tradition of the English provincial novel against what he regarded as the self-indulgent pretentiousness of Bloomsbury.

Having got himself to Cambridge, Snow began research in infrared spectroscopy, he was awarded the Ph.D. in 1930, and he was immediately elected a Fellow of Christ's College, the place that would provide both the background and inspiration for three of his later novels, *The Light and the Dark*, *The Masters*, and *The Affair*. But the three figures who most influenced him at the time came from elsewhere in the university and beyond Cambridge. The first was Ernest Rutherford, the Cavendish Professor of Physics and a Nobel Prizewinner, who presided over what Snow regarded (and increasingly romanticized) as the heroic days of "big science" as embodied in experimental physics. The second was his close friend and near contemporary, J. D. Bernal, a brilliant, progressive, left-wing scholar, who embodied Snow's democratic, meritocratic, optimistic, internationalist ideal of the scientist, and who believed that science was not just an academic activity, but must also contribute to the general public good.[5] The third was H. G. Wells, whom Snow also befriended at this time, a radical novelist who was passionate about science, and who used his fiction to champion and advance its cause.

Thus inspired, and in addition to his time-consuming laboratory experiments, Snow began to write novels: *Death Under Sail*, a conventional whodunit; *New Lives for Old,* a Wellsian work of science fiction; and *The Search,* a more experimental work about the joys and frustrations of scientific discovery, with a central character, Constantine, who was modeled on Bernal.[6] "By twenty," J. H. Plumb once wrote, "Snow wanted to be a great man; by thirty he was fairly confident that he was going to be one." Yet despite his early hopes and promise, he did not realize his ambition to be a scientist of outstanding distinction. At its best, his work was good, but it was not in the same league as that of his friend, Bernal, or of such other dazzling contemporaries as Patrick Blackett, John Chadwick, Alan Hodgkin, and John Cockroft. Even worse, in 1932 Snow suffered a major setback when his much-trumpeted claims (initially reported in *Nature,* and subsequently made at a meeting of the Royal Society) to have synthesized Vitamin A turned out to have been based on faulty calculations and misleading results.[7] From this reverse he never recovered professionally. His academic career stalled for the rest of the decade, and he soon abandoned laboratory research altogether. Some scientists never took Snow seriously thereafter, and while his sense of being an outsider was naturally intensified, so, too, was his desire to succeed, even though it must be by different routes. Accordingly, he became editor of *Discovery,* a middle-brow magazine devoted to the appropriately Wellsian enterprise of popularizing science; and he conceived the ambition of writing a great novel cycle, as it were by Trollope out of Proust, which would be about his own life and times and experiences. The first installment of this cycle, bearing the series title "Strangers and Brothers," appeared in 1940.

By then, Snow's ailing academic career had been brought to a merciful quietus with the advent of the Second World War, and his professional life acquired a wholly new impetus in an unexpected direction. Like many clever young men from Oxford and Cambridge, he was summoned to Whitehall, although he was also allowed to keep his College Fellowship for the duration of the war. There he found an ideal and unusual niche, not (like most of his colleagues) as a code breaker, or as a bureaucrat, or as a boffin, but as the recruiter of scientific personnel for secret work at the highest level, initially on radar and subsequently on the atomic bomb. To this end, Snow went round the country interviewing and befriending many young scientists, and for this work he was awarded the CBE in 1943, at the unusually early age of thirty-eight. He later drew on these experiences for two of his novels, *The New Men,* and *Homecomings,* and these wartime activities also influenced him in other ways. They encouraged his tendency to see himself as someone unusually knowing and worldly wise, at ease with scientists while writing novels in his spare time. They also brought him into contact with what he later called the "corridors of power," though in a less influential or engaged or comprehending way than he himself would subsequently think.

By the end of the war, Snow had shaped and settled his life to his own satisfaction, taking on two part-time jobs which gave him an adequate income and left him with ample time to write. He was appointed a Civil Service Commissioner (with responsibility for recruiting scientists), and became a Director of the English Electric Company (with essentially the same remit), and he duly resigned his College Fellowship in 1950. In the same year, he married the novelist Pamela Hansford Johnson. The reception was held at Christ's, J. H. Plumb made all the arrangements, and H. E. Howard was best man. With his wife's encouragement, Snow continued work on his "Strangers and Brothers" novels, publishing seven of them between 1945 and 1960, and they established his reputation as one of the most important and influential writers of contemporary fiction. In their form and structure, they harked back to nineteenth-century realist novels, especially Trollope's, and like his work, they often evoked "privileged and secretive social groups unknown to outsiders." In their content, though, they were entirely up-to-date, dealing with science, education, and government, with the "closed politics" of committees and personality clashes, and with the manipulation of power by men drawn from a wide variety of social backgrounds, who were outwardly successful but whose inner lives were often troubled and unhappy.[8] To his admirers, these were serious and significant works of creative literature, engaging with some of the most important issues of the time in a way that most writers lacked the courage or imagination to do. At the same time they were criticized, especially by the metropolitan intelligentsia, for being excessively knowing, for their ponderous and pedestrian prose, for their excruciating dialogue, and for their two-dimensional characters.

Nevertheless, this sequence of novels established Snow as a major voice with new things to say, and this in turn helped buttress his parallel and developing careers as both politician and pundit. In the early 1950s, he changed publishers, migrating from Faber to Macmillan, at the behest of Harold Macmillan, who thereafter became a staunch friend and admirer, who probably helped obtain Snow a knighthood in 1957, and who would be Conservative Prime Minister from that year to 1963. Ever since the 1930s, most of Snow's political friendships had been on the left, and they were now extended and reinforced by his membership of the Labour Party's Science Advisory Group, which put forward the radical agenda that science and technology provided the key to social progress and economic regeneration—the agenda originally formulated by Blackett and Bernal back in the 1930s, and now thoroughly approved of by Harold Wilson.[9] By this time Snow was also writing in newspapers and journals on both sides of the Atlantic on education, science, and government in Britain, and on the problems and prospects of the United States, the USSR, and the Third World, and it was in the late 1950s that he coined the two phrases that he would soon propel more vigorously around the world. Sensing that his hour was coming, he resigned his two jobs to devote himself exclusively to his fiction, his politics, and his punditry. His timing was perfect: the 1960s were nigh, and in this new and brief time of hope he established himself as an early prophet and influential voice.

The decade of the 1960s has never been an easy one to define or describe: indeed, according to Arthur Marwick, the 1960s probably lasted from 1958 to 1974.[10] Their most significant characteristics may be easily summarized, however. In Britain, thirteen years of Conservative rule ended in 1964, to be followed by six years of Labour, after which the Tories returned to power again. Under Macmillan (1957–63) and Douglas-Home (1963–64) the Conservatives had increasingly seemed an effete and fading establishment incapable of dealing with the many challenges facing Britain, both at home and overseas. Harold Wilson, by contrast, claimed he would get the country moving again, by wresting control from the public-school amateurs and by putting power in the hands of managers, scientists, and technologists who would be produced in the new universities and technical colleges recommended by the Robbins report in 1964. By modernizing Britain's outdated educational system, social structure, and business attitudes, he hoped to increase productivity and revive the nation's faltering economic performance; and in the post-Suez era of decolonization and imperial retreat, he also sought to create a new, more forward-looking role for Britain on the world stage. Meanwhile the recently emancipated colonies needed all the help the West could provide. Massive injections of capital were necessary: to jump-start fledgling industrial economies, to finance irrigation schemes, nuclear power stations, hospitals, and universities, and to provide the manpower—scientists, planners, economists, and doctors—to run the countries. This was partly to bring to them the benefits of modern, developed civilization, but it was also to ensure that they allied with the West, rather than the Communist bloc.[11]

The state of education, the state of the nation, the state of the Third World: these were some of the issues that were bubbling up in the early Macmillan years, and which Snow sought to define and address in his Rede Lecture on "The Two Cultures," delivered in Cambridge in May 1959. As he saw it, the British education system was deeply flawed because of the entrenched divisions between the arts and the sciences—two "polar groups" living in a state of mutual ignorance and misunderstanding. And it was clear where the blame principally lay. The arts had signally failed to appreciate the significance or momentum of science. Indeed, most humanists were reactionary, elitist, and irresponsible—natural Luddites opposed to the very idea of material self-betterment—whereas the scientists tended to be progressive, meritocratic, and internationalist: the men "with the future in their bones."[12] If Britain was to move forward, Snow insisted, then the scientists and technologists must have more resources and more influence: jam today and jam tomorrow. Yet there was also a global dimension. In many parts of the non-Western world, Snow observed, there were too many people with not enough to eat. Their best hope lay in an industrial and a technological revolution for, as the British experience had shown, this was the one means whereby the mass of the population might improve their standard of living. And the only professionals who could bring about such a narrowing of the gap between the rich and the poor were the trained experts—the scientists and the technologists. At home and overseas, they were both the new men and the necessary men—the only people who could bring what he termed "social hope" to the majority of mankind.[13]

In drawing attention to the great divide between the arts and the sciences in contemporary Britain, Snow was endowing a debate which dated back to T. H. Huxley and Matthew Arnold with a contemporary significance that was both national and international. He emphasized the deficiencies of the British education system compared to that of the United States and the USSR, he urged the need for the nation to modernize if it were to avoid relegation to the margins of global affairs, and he insisted that the West must confront and help solve the pressing problems of the Third World. As a piece of panoramic punditry it was a *tour de force* of synthesis, simplification, and speculation, and it consolidated Snow's reputation as a public commentator with important things to say. Thus encouraged and emboldened, and freed from the constraints of his two jobs, he took to the international lecture circuit to expound and expand his views. As Lord Rector of Aberdeen University he told the undergraduates that the proper application of science and technology meant that global poverty could be eradicated in two generations. As Godkin Lecturer at Harvard he argued that governments needed responsible scientific advisers with a sense of future directions: men such as

Sir Henry Tizard rather than Lord Cherwell. And in a speech to the American Association for the Advancement of Science he insisted that scientists were "the most important occupational group in the world today" who, and notwithstanding their creation of the atomic bomb, still held out the best hopes for improving and transforming the future of mankind.[14]

Snow did not have things all his own way, however, for not everyone was in thrall to what soon became derided in some quarters as "1960s fashionableness," and of no critic was this more true that of F. R. Leavis, who denounced the "Two Cultures" lecture, three years after it had been delivered, in one of the most celebrated and vitriolic attacks ever mounted by one Cambridge figure on another. Far from Snow's being a master mind or a great sage, wisely and compassionately pronouncing on the pressing problems of contemporary civilization, Leavis insisted that he was "portentously ignorant" of history and literature, and was intellectually as undistinguished as it was possible for any man to be. What claims did he have to be so knowing, so all-seeing, so worldly-wise? Who was *he,* a failed scientist and a mediocre novelist, to presume to act as a bridge between the sciences and the humanities? What did Snow know of high culture or creative thought or civilization? On what grounds could he possibly claim that scientists had "the future in their bones"? Instead of offering profound insights into the human condition, Snow rode on "an advancing swell of clichés" of which the notion of "social hope" was the most absurd. The prospect that Britain's tomorrow might resemble America's today filled Leavis with gloom and alarm, and he had no time for the view that industrialization and material improvement should be humanity's ultimate goal. "Who will assert," Leavis concluded, "that the average member of modern society is more fully human, or more alive, than a Bushman [or] an Indian peasant?"[15]

Snow was personally wounded by this savage and splenetic diatribe, but in the short run, it did his public reputation little damage. He did not reply directly to Leavis, but instead he refined, modified, and embellished his original views on "the two cultures," though in its essentials, his argument remained unaltered.[16] As higher education expanded, he came to believe that a third culture was developing, situated mid-way between the traditional arts and the hard sciences, which combined the insights of a revived humanism with a more rigorously scientific methodology. As Snow came to appreciate them, these fledgling social sciences—demography, sociology, economics, political science, psychology, and social history—offered a new, exciting, and relevant way of understanding the present. Of all these subjects, it was social history that most interested him, especially the debate on the standard of living in the English industrial revolution where, urged on and advised by J. H. Plumb, he sided with the optimists.[17] It seemed to Snow that they were approaching the past in a more imaginative and wide-ranging way than high-political obsessives such as Lewis Namier or Marxist-romantics such as E. P. Thompson; and their work also reinforced Snow's conviction that "traditional" life was miserable, that "no one in his senses would choose to have been born in a previous age unless he could be certain that he would have been born into a prosperous family," and that the only escape from such primitive deprivation was by going through an industrial revolution. In a world increasingly polarized between "the rich and the poor" (the alternative title, he now revealed, for the original lecture), only industry, technology, and science might bridge the gap.[18]

Here, in the 1960s, was Snow in full blizzard as a public man, drawing on his own varied experiences, interpreting the arts and the sciences to each other, offering sage advice to young and old alike, and setting Britain's domestic problems in a broader global context. His words were invoked in support of many progressive 1960s causes: the inauguration of A-level courses in General Studies, the reform of the Oxford and Cambridge undergraduate curriculum, and the creation of a Ministry of Technology and a Ministry of Overseas Development.[19] And the publication of his latest novel, *Corridors of Power*, at almost the same time, further reinforced his reputation as a public commentator and national sage, as he produced what seemed to be a wholly plausible picture of Westminster politics and Whitehall infighting. "You have really broken through at the world level," Plumb told him, insisting that Snow had become "a voice of authority . . . in tune with all that is restless, intellectual, creative." This was not just a matter of public fame. He seemed to have real political influence, too, with the Labour opposition. "Through Blackett," Snow explained to Plumb, "I am closely in touch with Wilson and Co. I have the distinction of being a grey eminence behind a grey eminence." Indeed, it was widely thought that if Labour won the general election that must take place no later than 1964, Snow's chances of government office would be high.[20]

So, indeed, it proved. Harold Wilson won in October that year, and one of his first actions was to establish a Ministry of Technology which, it was hoped, would give effect to the progressive Bernal-Blackett agenda. Snow was duly appointed Parliamentary Secretary, given a peerage, and was thus responsible for representing the Ministry in the Lords—inhabiting the corridors of power in fact just as he had recently evoked them in fiction. There had been nothing like it since John Buchan, another self-made novelist with political ambitions, had been ennobled in 1935 to become the Governor-General of Canada. "I'm delighted you've got power," Plumb wrote exultantly. "There are few men I would rather see wield it." "This job," Snow replied, "may be mildly useful, and certainly will have its points of interest."[21] In his well-received maiden speech in the Lords, he urged the need for industry and academe and government to work together, and he insisted that it was only by the application of science and technology that national decline could be halted. He returned to these subjects on many subsequent occasions, especially when welcoming the Robbins Report, which recommended a massive expansion in higher education, so as to produce more qualified scientists and technologists, and which he acclaimed as "one of the great state documents of our time."[22]

Here was Snow at his mid-1960s zenith, the lower-middle-class boy from Leicester who had indeed found his own way out—and up—to what seemed the very heart of a radical government that was determined to transform a flagging nation by the sustained application of "the white heat of technology." Yet despite these high hopes and great expectations, the triumph was short-lived. This was partly because the Ministry of Technology was fundamentally misconceived. As some critics had warned, it made no sense to separate science and technology in this way, with the result that Snow's department never had much clout in Whitehall, but it was also because Snow (like the Minister himself, Frank Cousins) was unhappy and unsuccessful in the corridors of power. Yet despite his reputation as a knowledgeable insider, he had no first hand experience of running a large department or organization, his executive abilities and administrative talents turned out to be minimal, and he was far too deferential to his civil servants. Nor was he taken seriously by senior Labour figures. Richard Crossman regarded him as a lightweight, and even Harold Wilson unkindly admitted that the appointment had been largely "public relations."[23] And while Snow had made a good start in the Lords, speaking cogently and convincingly, with neither text nor notes, he was fatally tripped up by Viscount Eccles, who wanted to know why a minister in a government that championed comprehensive schools had decided to send his own son to Eton. Snow was visibly discomfited by this attack, and his parliamentary reputation never recovered.[24]

After scarcely a year in office, he decided to resign, and he did so in April 1966, returning with much relief and no regrets to his novels, his writing, and his punditry, though with his reputation somewhat diminished by his failure in Whitehall and by the lingering and increasingly damaging impact of Leavis's attack.[25] As befitted the self-appointed bridge between the "two cultures," who had also been a government minister, Snow's next book, *Variety of Men*, provided warm and vivid pen portraits of writers (Frost, Wells), scientists (Rutherford, Einstein, Hardy), and statesmen (Lloyd George, Churchill, Stalin, and Hammarskjöld). However his main preoccupation for the rest of the decade was the completion of the "Strangers and Brothers" sequence. *The Sleep of Reason* appeared in 1968, and the aptly (though uninspiringly) named *Last Things* followed two years later. Their reception was "out of proportion" better than Snow had expected, and the completion of eleven novels across thirty years was a triumph of sustained stamina and indefatigable effort. Snow, however, felt little elation. "It's been a rough ride . . .," he wrote to Plumb. "I shouldn't like to start it again."[26] As the titles suggested, these two last books were among the bleakest in the series, and they were preoccupied with student rebellion among the young, and with infirmity and death among the old. Only in one revealing way did Snow lighten this darkening scene: when Lewis Eliot is offered a government job in *Last Things,* he, unlike his creator, wisely turns it down on the grounds that nothing he could do in the post would make any real impact.

It was not only Snow's later novels that were more pessimistic: so was his punditry. By the time he was freed from ministerial responsibility, the early hopes and mid-decade euphoria of the 1960s had largely collapsed, as the Johnson administration in America and the Wilson government in Britain both ran into unprecedented difficulties: Vietnam in the one case, and devaluation in the other. There were riots and protests on both sides of the Atlantic, while the "permissive society" of drugs and sex and violence seemed to be spinning out of control. This was not how Snow had hoped the decade would end. "The external world," he lamented to Plumb in 1967, "is remarkably bleak. . . . I can't remember a time when sensible and robust people were feeling so helpless."[27] Once again, he tried to catch and crystallize the very different public mood. In a lecture he delivered at Fulton, Missouri, entitled, somewhat apocalyptically, "The State of Siege," he had, he declared, "been nearer to despair in this year, 1968, than ever in my life." The West was in turmoil; the global problems of poverty and population had not been solved; and by 2000 there would be either a nuclear war or a catastrophic famine. But while "The Two Cultures" had resonated with the hopes of the early 1960s, "The State of Siege" made much less impact on the end-of-decade pessimism. Indeed, Snow grudgingly admitted that his later efforts to alert the world to what he regarded as its impending doom had been a "total failure," and with the publication of his collected pronouncements in 1971, he effectively retired as a public sage.[28]

The 1970s were very different from the 1960s, and Snow was not comfortable in this dismal decade, when the Heath, Wilson, and Callaghan administrations came and went, amidst mounting inflation, economic crisis, and trade union militancy. He no longer felt at ease in "intolerably parochial" Britain, and he did not "like the look of the world," but he continued to write, and also to demonstrate his unrivalled capacity to bridge the arts and the sciences.[29] There were three more novels, which were respectfully received, but made little impact. *The Malcontents* again dealt with student unrest, but unsuccessfully, since Snow could not catch the cadences of a younger generation. *In Their Wisdom* brooded on the infirmities and indignities of old age, and on Britain's decline as a great power, and concluded by observing that no one needed "humbling" who had lived in "our time." *A Coat of Varnish,* his last novel, explored the thin veneer separating civilization from barbarism, and was, like his first fiction, a whodunit. There were studies of other writers: a biography of his hero, Trollope, which made plain how closely Snow identified with him, and how much he owed to him; and a book of essays on six great realist novelists, which he concluded by lamenting that his own time was too pessimistic for the production and appreciation of such confident and creative fiction. Before his death he completed a book *The Physicists,* in which he once again harked back to the halcyon days of "big" Cambridge science in the 1920s and 1930s, when clever young men like himself—left-wing, meritocratic, internationalist—had been full of hope.[30]

By the late 1970s, this had long ceased to be his sense of things, or of himself. "I have," he told Plumb, "got used, or perhaps addicted, to being saddened." He still craved fame, recognition, and success in the great world where he had sought to make his way and striven to make his name. Although he had lived his life with the grain of events from 1946 to 1966, this was no longer true thereafter. On the completion of his "Strangers and Brothers" series, Snow had hoped that a grateful world might do him honor and pay him homage: perhaps with the Order of Merit, or maybe the Nobel Prize for Literature, or possibly the Chancellorship of a "new" university, or (at least) election to a Fellowship of the Royal Society—something which had been denied his hero H. G. Wells, but which he craved no less ardently for himself. No such recognition came his way, and he was obliged to console himself with a lecture established in his name at Christ's, and the Visitorship (effectively Chancellorship) of Hatfield Polytechnic.[31] In the era of Thatcher, which began in 1979, he increasingly seemed a figure from another age, and as he himself wrote of Trollope, there was "a strong impression that his reputation was slipping precipitately" in his last years. He died in 1980, a few months before what would have been the fiftieth anniversary of his election to the fellowship of Christ's College, which had launched him on his way. "He possessed," Plumb wrote in his obituary notice, "a largeness of heart and a capacity of mind beyond the common run of men."[32]

What in the end did it all add up to? Was it merely, as one critic alleged, "careerism" and little else?[33] Given his humble origins, Snow had achieved much, but given his great ambitions, he had not achieved enough. To be sure, he was an exceptionally gifted and versatile man, by turns a scientist and an academic, a company director and a civil servant, a pundit and a government minister, a novelist and a critic, a journalist and a biographer. Still, even in his great days during the late 1950s and early 1960s, he was never taken seriously in the corridors of power, and by the end of his life, it was clear, to borrow another of his own phrases, that his career had not quite "come off." Yet judged by less exacting standards, he was a man who mattered in his day. His novels no longer command a broad or appreciative audience, but for anyone interested in certain aspects of British life between the 1920s and the 1960s, they will always remain essential reading. "I have," he wrote to a friend in 1960, "a modest hope that a few people in the twenty-first century may perhaps read these books."[34] It seems likely that they will. And while his notion of "the two cultures" is still derided in some quarters with almost Leavis-like ferocity, it also remains an essential point of reference for those interested in our day in the issues that Snow raised and addressed: the arts and (or versus?) the sciences; the condition of higher education; the gap between the rich and the poor.[35]

In any case, Snow needs to be set in a broader context than that which is afforded by merely compiling a balance sheet of his failures and successes. For although he came from Leicester, he did not appear out of nowhere. Like Samuel Johnson and Sir Edward Elgar, he was a boy from the provinces whose talent, energy, and ambition carried him to fame and fortune and to the heart of the national establishment. Like John Buchan before him, and like Jeffrey Archer after him, he was a self-made novelist, who wanted to be accepted and respected in political circles, but who, despite his peerage, never carried the requisite weight.[36] Like George Eliot, Anthony

Trollope, George Gissing, and Arnold Bennett, he upheld the great tradition of the English provincial novel, and sought to revive it in his own time. Like Jules Verne and H. G. Wells, he possessed an almost childlike delight in scientific experiment and discovery, and saw fiction as the best way to evoke and promote them. Thus regarded, Snow may be seen as a more resonant and representative phenomenon in British cultural life than he is generally thought to have been. There are paradoxes and contradictions as well as precedents and parallels. In the early 1960s, Snow was deeply committed to the cause of national modernization, to moving Britain forward after thirteen "wasted" years of Tory torpor. Yet in many ways he was a time-bound product of the great industrial cities of Victorian England. He wrote novels that were nineteenth-century in their form and construction, and his notion of science never advanced beyond the 1930s. From this perspective, Snow was not so much a new man as an old man. Perhaps, in this regard, he was more a stranger in our midst than the brother he aspired to be?

Fall Semester 2002

Note on Sources

The two archival collections on which this study is based are the Snow MSS (Harry Ransom Humanities Research Center, University of Texas at Austin), and the Plumb MSS (Cambridge University Library). Obituaries of Snow appeared in the *Guardian,* July 2, 1980, *The Times,* July 2, 1980, *Daily Telegraph,* July 2, 1980, and *Christ's College Magazine* (1981) pp. 26–28 (written by Plumb). See also Lord Vaizey, "Charles Percy, Baron Snow (1905–1980)," in *Dictionary of National Biography, 1971–1980* (Oxford, 1986), pp. 788–89. J. Halperin, *C. P. Snow: An Oral Biography* (Brighton, 1983), printed much valuable information and reminiscence, though not always accurately or consistently; and Philip Snow recalled his brother affectionately in *Stranger and Brother: Portrait of C. P. Snow* (London, 1982) (reviewed by Plumb in *Cambridge Review,* Nov. 19, 1982, pp. 352–53), and more revealingly in *Time of Renewal: Clusters of Characters, C. P. Snow and Coups* (London, 1988).

The complete sequence of Snow's "Strangers and Brothers" novel cycle is as follows: *Strangers and Brothers* (London, 1940, later renamed *George Passant*)*; The Light and the Dark* (London, 1947); *Time of Hope* (London, 1949); *The Masters* (London, 1951); *The New Men* (London, 1954); *Homecomings* (London, 1956); *The Conscience of the Rich* (London, 1958); *The Affair* (London, 1960); *Corridors of Power* (London, 1964); *The Sleep of Reason* (London, 1968); *Last Things* (London, 1970). His other fiction was: *Death Under Sail* (London, 1932); *New Lives for Old* (published anonymously, London, 1933); *The Search* (London, 1934); *The Malcontents* (London, 1972); *In Their Wisdom* (London, 1974); *A Coat of Varnish* (London, 1979). His main non-fiction was: *The Two Cultures and the Scientific Revolution* (Cambridge, 1959) and *The Two Cultures: A Second Look* (Cambridge, 1964), republished together as *The Two Cultures,* with an introduction by Stefan Collini (Cambridge, 1988), which I have used here; *Variety of Men* (London, 1967); *Public Affairs* (London, 1971); *Trollope* (London, 1975); *The Realists* (London, 1978); *The Physicists* (London, 1981). See also P. Boytinck, *C. P. Snow: A Bibliography* (Norwood, 1977). Snow was a regular speaker in the House of Lords, and I have had frequent recourse to *Parliamentary Debates* (Lords).

1. Snow to Plumb, Apr. 2, 1956, Plumb MSS; Snow, "The Two Cultures," *New Statesman*, Oct. 6, 1956, pp. 413–14; Snow, "The Corridors of Power," *Listener*, Apr. 18, 1957, pp. 619–20.

2. Plumb to Donald Dickson, June 18, 1965, Plumb MSS; W. G. Runciman and R. M. May, *"Two Bodies, One Culture": Speeches Given at the Centenary Dinner of the British Academy, 4 July 2002* (London, 2002), pp. 2–3.

3. Hugh Thomas, ed., *The Establishment* (London, 1959); Peter Hennessy, *Whitehall* (London, 1990), pp. 540–46; Noel Annan, *Our Age: English Intellectuals Between the Wars: A Group Portrait* (New York, 1990), pp. 3–18; David Cannadine, *History in Our Time* (London, 1998), pp. 165–73.

4. J. Halperin, *C. P. Snow: An Oral Biography* (Brighton, 1983), pp. 15–16 and 24; A. Kazin, *Contemporaries* (London, 1963), pp. 171–77; Snow, *Strangers and Brothers*, pp. 161–62; Snow, *Time of Hope*, pp. 87–88; S. Gorley Putt, "Techniques and Culture: Three Cambridge Portraits," *Essays and Studies*, XIV (1961), p. 19.

5. C. N. L. Brooke, *A History of the University of Cambridge: 1870–1990* (Cambridge, 1993), Vol. IV, pp. 185–91; Snow, "The Age of Rutherford," *Atlantic Monthly*, 102, pp. 65–80; Snow, *Variety of Men*, pp. 1–2 and 9–11; Snow, *Parliamentary Debates* (Lords), Feb. 28, 1969, col. 858; Snow, "J. D. Bernal: A Personal Portrait," in M. Goldsmith and A. Mackay, eds., *The Science of Science: Society in the Technological Age* (London, 1964), pp. 19–29; Snow, *Parliamentary Debates* (Lords), Mar. 4, 1970, col. 405; Snow to P. M. S. Blackett, May 22, 1968, Snow MSS 58.18, recalling "the increase of social commitment among scientists in England during the 'twenties and 'thirties."

6. Snow, "H. G. Wells and Ourselves," *Cambridge Review*, Oct. 19, 1934, pp. 27–28; Snow, *Variety of Men*, pp. 49–64.

7. J. H. Plumb, *Cambridge Review*, Nov. 19, 1982, p. 352; J. C. D. Brand, "The Scientific Papers of C. P. Snow," *History of Science*, XXVI (1988), pp. 111–27; cf. N. Bezel, "Autobiography and the 'Two Cultures' in the Novels of C. P. Snow," *Annals of Science*, XXXII (1975), pp. 555–71.

8. Snow, "Science, Politics and the Novelist," *Kenyon Review*, XXIII (1961), pp. 1–17; Snow, *Trollope*, pp. 109–10; G. Watson, "The Future in Your Bones: C. P. Snow (1905–1980)," *Hudson Review*, LIV (2000), pp. 595–602; for early discussions of Snow's writings, see W. Cooper, *C. P. Snow* (London, 1959); M. Milgate, "Structure and Style in the Novels of C. P. Snow," *Review of English Literature*, I (1960), pp. 34–41; B. Bergonzi, "The World of Lewis Eliot," *Twentieth Century*, CLXVII (1960), pp. 214–25.

9. Alistair Horne, *Macmillan: 1894–1956* (London, 1988), Vol. I, pp. 63, 81, 295, 402; Ben Pimlott, *Harold Wilson* (London, 1992), p. 274; Philip Ziegler, *Wilson: The Authorised Life of Lord Wilson of Riveaulx* (London, 1993), p. 112.

10. Arthur Marwick, *The Sixties: Cultural Revolution in Britain, France, Italy and the United States, c. 1958– c. 1974* (Oxford, 1998), pp. 3–22.

11. Pimlott, *Wilson*, pp. 300–01; J. Tomlinson, "The British 'Productivity Problem' in the 1960s," *Past & Present*, 175 (2002), pp. 188–210; David Cannadine, "The Present and the Past in the English Industrial Revolution, 1880–1980," *Past & Present*, 103 (1984), pp. 149–58; Albert O. Hirschman, "The Rise and Fall of Development Economics," in his *Essays in Trespassing: Economics to Politics and Beyond* (Cambridge, 1981), pp. 7–13.

12. Notwithstanding these stereotypes, it should be mentioned that in *The Masters*, Snow's *alter ego*, Lewis Eliot, votes for the reactionary humanist (Jago) rather than the radical scientist (Crawford).

13. Stefan Collini, "Introduction" in Snow, *The Two Cultures* (Cambridge, 1988), esp. pp. 3–11, 44, 48.

14. Snow, "On Magnanimity," *Harper's Magazine* (July 1962), pp. 37–41; Snow, *Public Affairs*, pp. 99–150 and 187–98.

15. F. R. Leavis, "The Significance of C. P. Snow," *Spectator*, Mar. 9, 1962, pp. 297–303, reprinted in Leavis, *Nor Shall My Sword: Discourses on Pluralism, Compassion and Social Hope* (London, 1972), pp. 41–64.

16. Snow, "The 'Two-Cultures' Controversy: Afterthoughts," *Encounter* (February 1960), pp. 64–68; Snow, "The Two Cultures: A Second Look," *Times Literary Supplement*, July 9, 1970, pp. 737–40 [subsequently reprinted in Snow, *Public Affairs*, pp. 81–98].

17. Collini, in *Two Cultures*, pp. 70, 79, 82–84; Peter Laslett, *The World We Have Lost* (London, 1965); Harold Perkin, *The Origins of Modern English Society, 1780–1880* (London, 1969).

18. For Plumb's help to Snow on the standard of living and the industrial revolution, see: Snow to Plumb, May 24, 1962; Plumb to Snow, July 1, 1962, Dec. 7, 1962, 166.10; Snow to Plumb, Sep. 3, 1963, Snow MSS, 166.9. Plumb wrote the quotation "no one in his senses would choose to have been born in a previous age, unless he could be certain that he would have been born into a prosperous family, that he would have enjoyed extremely good health, and that he could have accepted stoically the death of the majority of his children," explicitly for Snow, and he used it: see Collini, in *Two Cultures*, p. 82.

19. Blackett to Snow, Feb. 11, 1965, enclosing "The Case for a Ministry of Technology," Sept. 1964, sent to Harold Wilson, Snow MSS, 56.16; José Harris, "The Arts and Social Sciences, 1939–1970," in Barbara Harrison, ed., *The History of the University of Oxford* (Oxford, 1994), Vol. VII, pp. 219 and 224; J. Roche, "The Non-Medical Sciences, 1939–1970," in *History of the University of Oxford*, Vol. VII, p. 287.

20. Plumb to Snow, Dec. 29, 1959; 166.10, Snow to Plumb, May 22, 1963, Snow MSS: 166.7; typescript article on Snow, undated [c. 1962], Plumb MSS.

21. Plumb to Snow, Oct. 19, 1964, Nov. 11, 1964; Snow to Plumb, Nov. 2, 1964, Snow MSS: 166.11; Janet Adam Smith, *John Buchan: A Biography* (Oxford, 1985), pp. 371–74.

22. Snow, *Strangers and Brothers*, p. 127; Snow in *Parliamentary Debates (Lords)*, Nov. 18, 1964, cols. 590–98; Dec 2, 1964, cols. 1117–25; Dec. 1, 1965, cols. 1293–1305.

23. Snow to Plumb, Jan. 26, 1955: "we've never been able to collect men of spirit together to run an institution, even for a short time," Plumb MSS. See also: Ziegler, *Wilson*, p. 176; Pimlott, *Wilson*, p. 328; R. Jenkins, *A Life at the Centre* (London, 1991), p. 178; R. H. S. Crossman, *The Diaries of a Cabinet Minister: Minister of Housing, 1964–66* (London, 1975), Vol. I, pp. 36, 42, 117.

24. *Parliamentary Debates* (Lords), Feb. 10, 1965, col. 161.

25. S. Gorley Putt, "The Snow-Leavis Rumpus," *Antioch Review*, XXIII (1963), pp. 299–312; Lionel Trilling, "The Snow-Leavis Controversy," in Trilling, *Beyond Culture: Essays in Literature and Learning* (London, 1966), pp. 145–78; Collini, in *Two Cultures*, pp. xxix–xxliii.

26. Snow to Plumb, Nov. 30, 1970, Plumb MSS.

27. Snow to Plumb, Feb. 15, 1967, Nov. 29, 1967, Plumb MSS; Snow to Plumb, Feb. 9, 1968, Snow MSS 166.13.

28. Snow to Plumb, Nov. 29, 1967, Plumb MSS; Snow to Plumb, Feb. 9, 1968, Snow MSS, 166.13; Snow, *Public Affairs*, pp. 8, 199–221, 223; Snow, *Parliamentary Debates* (Lords), July 6, 1966, cols. 1133–1140; Feb. 28, 1968, col. 862; June 18, 1968, col. 545; Mar. 4, 1970, cols. 406–08; Feb. 10, 1971, cols. 145–54, 222–24; Mar. 27, 1974, cols. 668–72. Snow was too pessimistic. By 2000 the global catastrophes he

had predicted had not (yet?) happened: David Reynolds, *One World Divisible: A Global History Since 1945* (New York, 2000), p. 536.

29. Snow to Plumb, Nov. 1, 1979, Jan. 9, 1980, Plumb MSS.

30. Snow, *Realists*, p. 254; Snow, *Physicists*, pp. 17, 35–39, 68, 138, 166.

31. Snow to Plumb, Aug. 24, 1970, Oct. 30, 1970, Plumb MSS; Lord Todd to Snow, Mar. 5, 1975, Snow MSS 197.4; Plumb to Snow, Oct. 31, 1979, Snow MSS 166.17; Philip Snow, *Stranger and Brother*, p. 173; Snow, *Time of Hope*, p. 171.

32. Snow, *Trollope*, p. 107; Plumb, *Guardian*, July 2, 1980.

33. Canon Charles Raven, *Spectator*, Apr. 19, 1960.

34. Snow to S. W. Grose, Apr. 19, 1960, Plumb MSS.

35. Snow, Noel Annan, M. Black, S. Rose, G. Steiner, "Symposium: The Two Cultures Revisited," *Cambridge Review* (March 1987), pp. 3–14; M. Kettle, "Two Cultures at Forty," *Prospect* (May 2002), pp. 62–64; Runciman and May, "*Two Bodies, One Culture*"; Collini, in *Two Cultures*, pp. xliii–lxxi.

36. Cannadine, *History in Our Time*, pp. 233–42.

7

Frances Partridge:
Last of the Bloomsberries

ANNE CHISHOLM

In the Introduction to the third volume in the *Adventures with Britannia* series, the editor commented that Bloomsbury, "for better or worse," is one of the standing interests of the British Studies Seminar. Bloomsbury is the theme of this lecture and Frances Partridge, the last of the Bloomsberries, is my topic. She died in February 2004 aged 103. What drew me to Frances Partridge was reading and reviewing, for the *Times Literary Supplement*, her diaries of the 1960s and 1970s, as they were successively published in the 1980s and 1990s. By the time I started to work on her biography, her sight and her energies were beginning to dwindle, which made her feel that perhaps the time was right. She had no intention of stopping work, but she sensed that the moment might have arrived when she needed to work with and through someone else. She was also positively pleased that someone with no particular Bloomsbury expertise or axe to grind was to write her life. After all, although her formative years, her youth and even her early middle age were certainly spent in the aura of Bloomsbury, she had lived for a very long time afterthat and had earned the right to hope that her biographer would not see her life and her achievements as entirely Bloomsbury-derived.

If Frances Partridge really was the last Bloomsberry, the only remaining survivor of the famous Group, then it must be of interest to ask whether she did, throughout her life, represent the qualities and achievements associated with Bloomsbury. Among the key values or precepts of the Bloomsbury Group were:

A belief in personal and sexual liberty;
A preference for the ties of love and friendship over the ties of family;
Freedom of speech and openness of expression;
Support for innovation and experiment in the arts and intellectual life;
A commitment to the truth in social and personal relationships;
A commitment to penal reform and to pacifism;
A distaste for all forms of jingoism and imperialism.

For its admirers, that list by and large represents the case for Bloomsbury. But there is also the case against, and it is important to remember that for many people, possibly indeed the majority, Bloomsbury at the time and ever since has stood for:

Promiscuous and casual sexual misbehavior;
Selfish neglect of the interests of parents, wives, and children;
Second-rate and derivative art;
Malicious and destructive gossip;
Wilful undermining of church and state;
Moral and physical cowardice.

It all began, of course, in Cambridge, with a group of clever young men under the influence of the philosopher G. E. Moore, around 1900. One of the clever young men, Thoby Stephen, had two beautiful and clever sisters, Vanessa and Virginia, who lived in Kensington with their eminent father, the quintessential man of letters, Leslie Stephen. Through Thoby, Vanessa and Virginia came to know those clever young men of Cambridge and their friends, who included John Maynard Keynes, E. M. Forster and Lytton Strachey. In 1904, after the death of their father, the Stephen sisters made a deliberate break with their solidly respectable Kensington past and moved to Bloomsbury, where they set up the first of a series of flexible, semi-communal households in the handsome Georgian squares near the British Museum north of Oxford Street and east of the Tottenham Court Road. Before the First World War changed everything, and brought an end to the first phase of Bloomsbury's artistic endeavors, Molly MacCarthy, wife of the critic Desmond MacCarthy, both of them insiders, coined the nickname the Bloomsberries, but it was not until the 1920s that the label gained a wider circulation and began to surface in the press, usually as a term of affectionate mockery. During the 1930s, it was more usually a term of abuse, suggesting, as Regina Marler, the editor of Vanessa Bell's letters and author of

Bloomsbury Pie, a study of the Bloomsbury phenomenon, has written, "everything from giggling effeminacy to political indifference."[1] During and after the Second World War, the Bloomsbury Group faded into a dim obscurity. This is not to say that Virginia Woolf's and E. M. Forster's novels were not admired, that Leonard Woolf's and Maynard Keynes' writings on economics and politics were not taken seriously, or that Duncan Grant and Vanessa Bell's paintings were not exhibited and sold; but it was not until after Michael Holroyd's biography of Lytton Strachey came out in 1967 that Bloomsbury as a movement and a set of relationships became of wide general interest.[2] Since then, there have been quiet patches, but on the whole that interest has been sustained.

As my subject, Frances Partridge, was not born until 1900, it is obvious that she could not have been part of the core of original Bloomsbury, who were adult and active before the First World War. On the other hand, she was, unlike many of them, born in the heart of Bloomsbury itself, physically and to some extent socially as well. Her father was William Marshall, a sought-after and successful— though now forgotten—architect, and the family lived in one of the tall, imposing grey and white Georgian houses on the east side of Bedford Square. William Marshall, whose antecedents were among prosperous linen merchants in the north of England, had as clients and friends some of the most eminent and celebrated Victorians such as Tennyson, Conan Doyle and even, at the end of the great man's life, Charles Darwin. Frances was the youngest child and fourth daughter of the six Marshall children. Her mother, Margaret Anne Marshall, always known to her children, partly because of her initials, as Mam, came from a well-connected Irish family, had been orphaned young in New Zealand and thereafter grew up with her uncle, the provost of Trinity College, Dublin.

Frances had an unusually serene and stable childhood. According to an unpublished memoir left by her mother, it had been hoped that she would be a boy, to balance the family; but the fact that she was a girl did not prevent her, as the youngest, from being the focus of a great deal of love and attention. Until 1908, when the Marshall family moved to the country, the large, and by today's standards quite grand, London house in Bedford Square, with its fine interconnecting first floor reception rooms with their molded plaster ceilings, and wide staircase leading past the main bedrooms to the children's and servants' quarters on the top and attic floors, was her home and Nan, the family Nanny, her constant and devoted companion. Her father was already sixty when she was born, and always seemed to her a little remote, but he was genial and kind, and encouraged her from a young age to read widely and to write. He once predicted that she would be the writer of the family. She loved her mother dearly, and Mam, although much occupied with the half dozen or so servants required to look after the house and the family, as well as the substantial social life of a successful upper-middle-class professional couple, never seemed too busy for her children. She was highly musical, and made sure all the children learned to sing well and play an instrument. When any of them were ill, as they frequently were, with the usual childhood diseases which in those days could be serious, even fatal, Mam liked to nurse them herself.

Frances Partridge observed that her mother was more liberal-minded and politically aware than her father, and she added: "It was because my mother was a keen Suffragist that an important stage of my education was reached—I got my first sight of Stracheys."[3] Three of Lytton Strachey's sisters were also in favor of votes for women, and made friends with Margaret Marshall. As it happens, William Marshall used to go walking with Leslie Stephen; thus Frances herself was not only born part of Bloomsbury in a geographical sense but grew up within easy reach of its two leading families.

Although she liked Bedford Square well enough, especially when the children were sent to play under the enormous plane trees in the central gardens, Frances's childhood paradise was the family's week-end and holiday retreat near Hindhead, on the borders of Surrey and Hampshire about fifty miles south west of London. Today, Hindhead has become a rather unattractive suburbanized bottleneck on the main road to Portsmouth, but in the last decade of the nineteenth century, when William Marshall designed his dream house at the junction of three roads on a wooded hilltop between Hindhead and Haslemere, and gave it the slightly unfortunate name of Tweenways (later a source of some embarrassment to Frances), it was situated in one of the most desirable stretches of unspoiled countryside near London. The sandy, gorse-covered hills with their pine trees, bracken, and fine views were sometimes referred to as the English Alps, and many of London's writers, artists, and intellectuals chose to spend holidays or settle there, enjoying long walks in the fresh air, golf, riding, tennis, and boisterous evenings of music and charades. Gradually, as his family grew and grew up, William Marshall added extra rooms until the original gabled, tiled cottage became a quite substantial country house. It is still standing, not much changed, and has become a residential music school. For Frances, who lived there from the age of eight to eighteen, it was near perfection, although she also had a passion for the much wilder hills and streams of the Lake District, where the Marshalls went regularly for summer holidays.

It was at her day school near Hindhead that she made her own first and lifelong, despite occasional ups and downs, Strachey friend. This was Julia, the daughter of Lytton's brother Oliver, and it was because Julia went on to Bedales, the already famous and distinctly progressive coeducational boarding school nearby, that Frances persuaded her parents when she was fifteen to send her there as well. She never much cared, at the time or in retrospect, for the wholesome food, communal lavatories or naked bathing favored by the school, but she made several more good friends and learned enough to follow her sister Eleanor to Newnham College, Cambridge, where she arrived to read English in 1918, just before the end of the First World War. It is thus clear that although Frances's background and childhood were far from bohemian, indeed were in all material ways quite conventional, she was lucky enough to be born into a family interested in intellectual and artistic pursuits, well off, and open-minded enough to send its daughters as well as its sons to good schools and to university—by no means the norm at the time.

At Cambridge, where although women were allowed to follow the same course of study and take the same examinations as the men they were not able to take a degree, Frances discovered two crucial facts about herself: she was genuinely interested in ideas, and she was attractive to the opposite sex. She changed from English to Moral Sciences half way through her studies, and found she particularly enjoyed logic and ethics; she always counted Bertrand Russell's *Problems in Philosophy* as one of her favorite books. She met Russell, of course, but she knew the young Wittgenstein better; he was a friend of another brilliant young philosopher called Frank Ramsay, who fell in love with and later married one of her Bedales friends, but tragically died soon after. Although the war had helped to loosen some of the conventions that governed relations between male and female students, Frances found it convenient to invent a chaperone when asking her principal for permission to meet a man. Still, she loved dancing, and collected a string of partners and admirers. Photographs show her to have been strikingly pretty, small and slender, with large dark eyes, a wide forehead, and a gleaming smile; she was also athletic, and loved long walks, swimming, and energetic games of tennis. She had several flirtations, but no real love affairs.

Her father died during her time at Cambridge and her mother sold the Hindhead house and moved back to London, to a house in Bloomsbury in Brunswick Square. By the time Frances finished

her studies at Cambridge in 1921, her favorite sister, Rachel, always
known as Ray, who had been to art school and was a published illus-
trator, had married David Garnett, who was always known as Bunny.
He was a young man from a scholarly and bookish family—his father
was a force in publishing and his mother, Constance, the renowned
translator of Russian classics. Bunny had already become involved
with Bloomsbury through his literary aspirations, his pacifism, and
his brief youthful love affair with Duncan Grant. It was thus through
her sister that Frances took the first step which was to lead her, almost
literally, into the heart of Bloomsbury. She was offered, and accepted, a job in the bookshop known as Birrell and Garnett, set up by
her brother-in-law and his friend Francis Birrell, in Taviton Street.

It was in the bookshop, in 1923, that Frances met Ralph Partridge, the handsome, extroverted young man who was working at
the time for Leonard and Virginia Woolf at the Hogarth Press and
so was a regular visitor to Birrell and Garnett to take and deliver
orders. Ralph also happened to be married to Dora Carrington, a
fair-haired, blue-eyed, pigeon-toed painter trained at the Slade,
and they shared a house, Tidmarsh Mill, near Pangbourne on the
Thames in Berkshire, with Lytton Strachey himself. Strachey was
at the height of his fame as an essayist and biographer—*Eminent Victorians* (1918), his iconoclastic look at, among others, Florence
Nightingale and General Gordon had not long been published—
and he was at work on his study of Queen Victoria. One of the two
characteristic and perennially fascinating triangular relationships
of Bloomsbury operated between Strachey, Partridge, and Carrington. (The other operated at Charleston in Sussex and involved
Vanessa and Clive Bell and Duncan Grant). Carrington, as she always called herself, was deeply in love with Lytton Strachey, despite
the fact that he was much older than she was and an active homosexual. Ralph had fallen in love with Carrington in 1918, and met
Lytton through her. Lytton was truly fond of Carrington, but not
prepared to share her life or set up house with her without the permanent presence of a congenial man; he was, for a while, greatly attracted to Ralph, but knew that Ralph was, as Frances was to put
it, hopelessly heterosexual. Nevertheless, Ralph was devoted to and
greatly influenced by Lytton Strachey and happy to share Carrington's love with him. For all the familiarity of this story, it is not easy
to summarize, or to understand—which partly explains why it continues to intrigue.

By the time Frances Marshall met Ralph Partridge and began to
be drawn into this complex tangle of emotions, the triangle had begun to show signs of strain. They all still loved each other as friends,

but sex, as it is wont to do, regularly led to complications. None of the three had been faithful to any sexual partner for very long. Carrington had nearly broken Ralph Partridge's heart by becoming involved with his great friend Gerald Brenan not long after their marriage. Ralph had retaliated with several affairs. Carrington did not really care for sex anyway, but enjoyed intense flirtations with women as well as men. Love affairs with a succession of young men were vital, it seems, to Lytton just as sex was very important, by all accounts, to Ralph. The arrangement at Tidmarsh, and then at Ham Spray, the house near Hungerford in Wiltshire to which the trio moved in the summer of 1924, just about worked as long as none of them fell so seriously in love with a fourth party that the precarious balance was put at risk. However, by the time of the move to Ham Spray just that had happened: Ralph had fallen in love with the dark-haired girl described by Carrington as "the beautiful princess who works in Birrell and Garnett's bookshop," and she was beginning to return his love.

But who and what, exactly, was Ralph Partridge? It is worth, I think, taking a new look at him. When I embarked on her biography, I asked Frances what she thought needed to be added to the Bloomsbury story, and what she thought a biography of herself should include that had not already been explained ad infinitum. "No one has got Ralph right," she said at once. "He was not at all like the picture that has been given of him, by Michael Holroyd or anyone else."[4]

In 1923, Ralph Partridge was twenty-nine. His name was really Rex, and he came from a completely un-Bloomsbury background. Both his father and his grandfather had joined the Indian Civil Service, the elite body of imperial administrators who governed India; Ralph was born and spent his early childhood in India. According to his family, Lytton Strachey made him change his name to Ralph because he disliked the name Rex and thought it had imperialist and monarchist connotations. Ralph's family's reaction to his relationship with Strachey's circle revealed the great gulf that existed then, and can still be found today, between Bloomsbury values and conventional English middle-class society. His parents and two older sisters, as I learned from one of his surviving nieces, were profoundly and permanently shocked and distressed when their son, hitherto a model clean young Englishman, a large, strapping, fair-haired public schoolboy who had won a scholarship to Oxford to read law, rowed for his college and been a potential rowing blue when the First World War sent him to the trenches in France, suddenly fell into the clutches of the subversive, suspiciously effeminate Lytton Strachey. They were horrified when he married the very peculiar, arty, bohemian Carrington. They felt their hitherto entirely satisfactory son, their gallant, straightforward, promising Rex, had become "depraved."

Ralph Partridge, unlike so many of his contemporaries and friends, was lucky; he came back from the war, in which he served with conspicuous gallantry and courage. He was wounded twice, buried alive once and only rescued by his batman, awarded the Military Cross and Bar, and was reputed to have been the youngest major in the British Army at the time. Frances believed that the war changed him forever in two vital ways: it removed from him all conventional ambitions, and it made him into a pacifist. One can argue, as Michael Holroyd does, that in fact it was not until Ralph met Lytton and Carrington and fell for them both that he really became a pacifist; there is some evidence in letters and diaries that he was far from being one at the outset of their acquaintance.[5] He was certainly, however, a firm pacifist by the time he met Frances.

It was probably Ralph's aura of classic English masculinity, his broad shoulders, keen blue eyes, forthright manner, and air of command learned in war that made him so attractive to both Lytton and Carrington. No doubt it also amused them to help transform his opinions; he was intelligent and well read, but Lytton, a brilliant thinker and teacher who loved to instruct, was able to broaden his intellectual and emotional horizons a great deal. And something in Ralph must have been longing to be transformed, or it would not have happened so fast and so permanently. Nevertheless, something of "The Major," as he was teasingly nicknamed at first by his new friends, always hung around Ralph, and this whiff of heartiness and conventionality was instantly observed and sharply disapproved of by the preternaturally perceptive and waspish Virginia Woolf. Ralph worked for the Woolfs at the Hogarth Press for about two years, and it is clear in her diaries that although she was for a time quite fond of him she soon became exasperated and uneasy in his company. He was altogether too solid, too forthright, too masculine, and too large for her. All her diary references to him, especially during the several emotional crises surrounding his courtship of Carrington, make her distaste for his strong emotions and sexuality very plain. This image of Ralph as a bully and a bit of an oaf, later reinforced by the writings of his rival for Carrington's love, Gerald Brenan, was unfair, but it was tenacious, and explains why Frances has always disliked the way he has been portrayed in successive biographies and films.

There is no doubt at all that Frances fell almost at once deeply in love with Ralph, although he was, technically, a married man and she was being seriously pursued by several suitable young men at the time. She also found herself from the first at home in the Bloomsbury world she entered via the bookshop; something in her nature responded with delight to them all, and she soon made strong and lasting friendships with Bunny Garnett, Raymond Mortimer, Clive Bell, and James and Alix Strachey in particular. Unlike Ralph, she had not had a particularly conventional or repressive background, but nevertheless, as she later put it, when she met them: "it was as if a lot of doors had suddenly opened out of a stuffy room which I had been sitting in for far too long."[6] She particularly loved their passion for talking about ideas and saying what they meant. "In my home circle," she wrote, "even the more civilized had shied away from words like 'good,' and 'beautiful,' and would veil their appreciation of works of art in phrases such as 'That's rather a jolly bit,' or 'Isn't this amusing?' But the Bloomsburies called spades spades and said what they thought; they didn't keep afloat in a social atmosphere by the wingflapping of small talk—if they were bored by the conversation they showed it."[7] Frances loved this atmosphere; more naturally than Ralph, she was in her element.

I propose only to summarize the saga of how, eventually, Ralph and Frances became lovers, and how, not without considerable tension and some pain, she was accepted as part of their lives and their household by Lytton and Carrington so that from late 1925 onwards Ralph and Ham Spray became the center of her life. It mattered to her very little, if at all, that she could not marry Ralph; she was, however, amazed and impressed that her mother was able to accept the situation, although she did have to pretend to Nan, her former nanny, that a secret marriage had taken place. She did want a child, though, and knew that this would present difficulties; but before the matter became really pressing, fate took a hand. Lytton Strachey died of undiagnosed stomach cancer early in 1932, and Carrington, unwilling to live on without him, shot herself a few weeks later.

This double tragedy left Ralph emotionally shattered, but his love for Frances and hers for him endured; in 1933 they married, and in 1935 their only son Burgo was born. They continued to live at Ham Spray, where Carrington's studio became Burgo's nursery. Their Bloomsbury friends continued to visit; Lytton's library and Carrington's decorations remained unchanged, and Ham Spray became, after Charleston, the main focus for the circle for the next twenty-five years. Ralph and Frances, after working together for ten years on editing and indexing the Greville Diaries, a project initiated by Lytton, both occupied themselves with literary tasks.[8] Ralph reviewed

regularly for the *New Statesman,* specializing in history, detective stories, and criminology and wrote a book about Broadmoor, the hospital for the criminally insane. Frances took on the daunting task of
indexing, for the Hogarth Press, successive volumes of the writings
of Sigmund Freud, as they were translated and presented by Lytton's
psychologist brother, James Strachey. They traveled frequently to
Europe, especially to Spain, where their friend Gerald Brenan lived
for most of his life. They were both open pacifists for the whole of
the Second World War, not a popular or easy position to take in that
of all wars. They built an unusually stable and happy marriage, although their son Burgo, as he grew up, became moody and difficult
and caused them considerable anxiety.

During the 1950s, Ralph's health began to fail. He developed
heart problems, and died at Ham Spray in November 1960. Anyone
who has read her diaries for that time will know how much Frances
suffered, but also how composed, realistic, and positive she managed to remain. By the summer of 1961 she had dismantled and sold
the house and moved to a smallish flat near Belgrave Square in central London; she moved twice to similar flats in the same street and
lived there to the end of her days, surrounded by Bloomsbury treasures—Lytton's furniture and his portrait by Carrington, Spanish
plates, paintings by Duncan Grant, drawings by Augustus John and
Henry Lamb, and a great many marvelous books. She took up her
violin again, joined an orchestra, started looking for translation
work and, at sixty, began a new stage of her life with exemplary fortitude and determination.

In 1962, another Bloomsbury alliance took place. Her son Burgo
married Henrietta Garnett, whose mother Angelica, Vanessa Bell's
daughter, had married Bunny Garnett after Ray's death. The Ham
Spray and Charleston branches of Bloomsbury were thus united by
a younger generation, and Frances began to feel her new life had
found a focus again when Burgo and Henrietta's daughter Sophie
was born in the summer of 1963. A few weeks later, Burgo was talking to a friend on the telephone when he was struck by a catastrophic
and completely unexpected heart problem. Frances arrived to find
her son dead on the floor and her infant granddaughter asleep on
the bed.

How she managed to survive even that appalling blow is best told
in her own words in her later diaries. She not only survived, but
found the energy and strength to make three new careers for herself as she grew older: as a well-regarded translator from French and
Spanish; a memoirist and diarist of outstanding quality; and as the
prime source and adviser for a succession of biographers and social

historians. She lived long enough to see her life and times become the stuff of literary history, not always an easy or comfortable process but one in which she shared to the best of her very considerable abilities.

How do Frances Partridge's life and attributes appear in relation to the values held by the Bloomsbury Group? On the matter of personal and sexual liberty, there can be no doubt that she always strongly believed in it. As far as her friends were concerned, she never cared in the least whether they were heterosexual, homosexual, or bisexual, believing, she once told me, that most people are a bit of everything. She had a great many homosexual friends, and supported the legalization of homosexuality in Britain. She disliked dishonesty much more than infidelity. She was, I believe, entirely faithful to Ralph; he had a few flings over the years, which she knew about, and was able to tolerate. Unlike Bloomsbury, however, she believed strongly in marriage, not in the legal sense but as the lifelong union of kindred spirits.

Friendship was one of the most important elements in her life, at every stage. There is no doubt that Bloomsbury, reacting against Victorian and Edwardian rules and conventions, did not admire or emulate traditional family loyalties. For example, Frances told me that Ralph really did not like his mother. Soon after she had died, he was at a party: when someone remarked that he looked very cheerful, he replied "Yes, I am, my mother has just died." Was that some kind of a joke, I asked nervously? "Oh no," said Frances. "He really meant it."[9] As for her own family, Frances only kept up, after she met Ralph, with her brother Tom, who became a Cambridge academic, and her sister Ray. Bunny Garnett had taken up with the much younger Angelica Bell before Ray died, indeed during her prolonged and painful death from cancer. I asked Frances whether this behavior had angered or upset her, or altered her feelings for Bunny. She looked at me in genuine surprise; no, it had not, that was just what Bunny was like. She added that perhaps because she and Ralph had been for some time an illicit couple, they always thereafter supported lovers in awkward positions.

It has to be said that many of the children and grandchildren of Bloomsbury had a difficult time, and even Frances and Ralph, whose marriage was so solid, were not particularly successful as parents. Bloomsbury made few allowances for the needs of what Lytton would refer to with distaste as "*le petit people.*" His contemporaries remember Burgo as a troubled and confused boy, who went through periods of dramatic and open hostility to his parents, especially to his father. But Frances helped to look after her mother in her old age, and remained close to her daughter-in-law, granddaughter, and two great-granddaughters. She did indeed build her later life largely around her friends, and relied on them as they did on her, but she never ignored or neglected her own close family.

As far as the artistic and intellectual achievements of Bloomsbury are concerned, it is obvious that Frances was not a creator or an innovator. She said of herself that she lacked imagination, that her talents lay in observing, organizing, and classifying, not in original creation, but her sharp eye for natural beauty and human behavior and the excellence of her uncluttered prose are remarkable enough. Her diaries have won her a following among readers who know little and care less about Bloomsbury; nevertheless, the truthful, unsentimental, precise and humorous way Frances wrote about herself and her circle owes much to a certain Bloomsbury tone.

Although Frances never played a part in public life, she observed it and thought about it for some eighty years. The social and political attitudes she had absorbed as a young woman remained remarkably constant, even though she regarded herself as non-political, as was Bloomsbury in general, with the two great exceptions of Maynard Keynes and Leonard Woolf. Even so, in her old age she joined the Labour Party and rejoiced when Labour came to power in 1997. She never wavered in her support for the libertarian causes dear to the heart of the liberal left. Specifically, she was against censorship, in favor of nuclear disarmament, and opposed to capital punishment. She grew to dislike ostentation and snobbery more and more and could be outspokenly critical of the spoiled ways and exploitative behavior of the rich, while somehow remaining, as even her admirers could not resist pointing out, happy to accept their hospitality.

As her renown grew in the last two decades of her life, Frances Partridge was much interviewed. She would take every opportunity to turn questions away from her personal life and towards discussion of her beliefs, especially her enduring belief in pacifism. She continued to explain her conviction that war breeds, rather than cures, violence and hatred. She was much disturbed by the Falklands War of 1982; her diaries record her profound antipathy to Margaret Thatcher's martial rhetoric. The first Gulf War filled her with horror and alarm. Above all, in her writings and among her circle of younger friends—who included senior diplomats and influential journalists—she never ceased to stand up for the opinions and values she had learned through her association with Bloomsbury.

1. Regina Marler, *Bloomsbury Pie* (London, 1997), p. 11.

2. Michael Holroyd's biography of Lytton Strachey was originally published in two volumes: *The Unknown Years, 1880–1910* (London, 1967), and *The Years of Achievement, 1910–1932* (London, 1968).

3. Frances Partridge, *Memories* (London, 1996), p. 32.

4. Conversation with the author, April 1999.

5. In 1994 Michael Holroyd published a new, one-volume edition of his biography of Strachey, containing much new material. He discusses the young Ralph Partridge in *Lytton Strachey: The New Biography* (London, 1994), pp. 445–47.

6. Partridge, *Memories,* p. 75.

7. Ibid., p. 76.

8. After Lytton Strachey's death in 1932 Roger Fulford took over as editor of the Greville diaries, which were eventually published in eight volumes by Macmillan in 1938. Although as he later confirmed much of their work appeared under his name, and they were entirely responsible for the index, Frances and Ralph Partridge received no acknowledgment in the text. (Conversation between Frances Partridge and the author, Sept. 2000.)

9. Conversation with the author, June 2000.

8

A Bolt from the Blue?
The City of London and the
Outbreak of the First World War

NIALL FERGUSON

Historians have tended to portray the two decades before the outbreak of the First World War as a time of "mounting tension" and "escalating crises." War, we are assured, did not burst onto the scene in the summer of 1914; rather, it "approached" over a period of years, even decades. A not untypical example of the way historians have ordered events more or less teleologically is the structure of the eleven-volume official series, *The British Documents on the Origins of the War, 1898–1914,* published between 1926 and 1938. The titles of the individual volumes offer a clear narrative framework of the war's origins, extending over seventeen years:

This elegant structure can be compared with the more compact but not dissimilar way in which A. J. P. Taylor organized the concluding chapters of his *Struggle for Mastery in Europe:*

XVIII. The Last Years of British Isolation: The Making of the Anglo-French Entente, 1902–05
  XIX. The Formation of the Triple Entente, 1905–09
   XX. The Years of Anglo-German Hostility, 1909–12
  XXI. The Balkan Wars and After, 1912–14
 XXII. The Outbreak of War in Europe, 1914

Nearly all books about the origins of the War are variations on these themes. Some authors go back further. For example, Immanuel Geiss has portrayed the outbreak of war as the last of a succession of nine diplomatic crises directly or indirectly involving Germany: the 1875 Franco-German "War in Sight" crisis, the 1875–78 Eastern crisis, the 1885–88 Bulgarian crisis, the 1886–89 Boulanger crisis, the 1905–06 Moroccan Crisis, the 1908 Bosnian crisis, the 1911 Agadir crisis and the 1912–13 Balkan crisis.[1] Hew Strachan also traces the origins of the war back to the foundation of the German Reich in 1871, emphasizing in particular the Anglo-German naval competition after 1897.[2] Others (notably those interested in the pre-war arms race on land) have tended to concentrate rather more on the immediate pre-war decade. Thus, David Herrmann begins his account of the "making of the First World War" at the time of the 1905–06 Moroccan Crisis,[3] while David Stevenson identifies the period after 1907 as having witnessed the "breakdown of equilibrium" in the European military balance.[4] Those historians who center their accounts on the policy of Austria-Hungary tend to start the "countdown" to war even later, with the annexation of Bosnia-Herzegovina in 1908.[5] But no one today seriously claims that the war was a "bolt from the blue" in the summer of 1914. Though it begins by evoking an idyllic summer abruptly shattered by an unexpected war, David Fromkin's *Europe's Last Summer* quickly retraces its steps to restate the now familiar case that the war was the culmination of a calculated German policy dating back to the 1890s.[6]

The idea of a gradually approaching war accords well with the idea, propagated by numerous cultural historians, that European "voices" had been "prophesying war" for so long before the summer of 1914 that its actual outbreak was more of a relief than a surprise. The Left had predicted for decades that militarism and imperialism would eventually produce an almighty crisis; the Right had been almost as consistent in portraying war as a salutary consequence of Darwinian struggle. European societies, it is widely agreed, were "ready for war" long before war came.[7] The question, however, is how far narratives of escalating crisis have been retrospectively devised by historians in order to create an explanation of the war's origins commensurate with the vast dimensions of the event itself. One way of addressing this question is to look more closely at contemporary attitudes to the diplomatic crises so familiar to historians.

If any social group had a strong interest in detecting the approach of a world war, it was international investors and the financial institutions that served their needs in the City of London. The reason is obvious. They had a great deal to lose in the event of such a war. In 1899 the Warsaw financier Ivan Bloch estimated that "the immediate consequence of war would be to send [the price of] securities all round down from 25 to 50 per cent."[8] The journalist Norman Angell made similar points about the negative financial consequences of great-power conflict in his best-selling tract, *The Great Illusion.*[9] Both authors expressed the hope that this consideration might make a major war less likely, if not impossible. But investors—and especially investors with holdings of bonds issued by the great powers—could scarcely afford to take this for granted. We would therefore expect any event that made such a war seem more likely to have had a detectable effect on investor sentiment. To be precise, if the Moroccan, Balkan, and other crises truly were harbingers of an approaching world war, investors should have reacted to them by marking down the prices of the bonds issued by the expected combatants. Fortunately, because bond prices were so regularly published after the middle of the nineteenth century, it is not difficult to find out whether or not this actually happened. This lecture uses quantitative and qualitative data, drawn principally from *The Economist* weekly magazine, to show that it did not.

THE FIVE GENERALLY ACKNOWLEDGED "GREAT POWERS"—Britain, France, Germany, Russia and Austria-Hungary—were by no means financially alike. Russia and possibly Austria might be regarded as "emerging markets" in this period, since both still had large and backward agricultural sectors and the former in particular relied heavily on foreign capital. Britain and France, by contrast, were plainly mature economies with surplus savings available for investment abroad. Constitutionally, too, the five great powers were quite different, ranging from republican France to absolutist Russia. However, as the world's most powerful empires, the five were not only territorially but also militarily in a league of their own—a league which Turkey had long since left and which Italy (to say nothing of the United States and Japan) had not yet joined. It was this "pentarchy" that determined whether or not Europe and much of the rest of the world were at peace or at war. Precisely because of their histories of warfare and their large military and naval establishments, the five empires had another thing in common: each had accumulated a large public debt in the course of the nineteenth century. More than half of sovereign fixed-income securities quoted in London were bonds issued by the five great powers. By 1905, bonds issued by the other great powers (France, Russia, Germany, and Austria) accounted for nearly two-fifths (39 per cent) of the total, or half (49 per cent) of all foreign sovereign debt. It is the regularly quoted market interest rates—the yields—on these bonds that allow us to infer changes in investors' expectations of war in the years up to and including 1914.[10]

What exactly do bond yields capture? In economic theory, the yield on a bond is the real, underlying rate of interest plus a premium for uncertainty that takes into account, first, the risk of default by the borrower and, secondly, the lender's expectations of inflation and currency depreciation. In addition, yields tend to be influenced by the liquidity of markets and the availability and relative attractiveness of alternative assets, as well as by legal rules and restrictions (such as those obliging pension funds and life assurance companies to hold government bonds) and by any taxation levied on investment income. Thus bond price fluctuations will reflect changes in investors' expectations not only of growth and inflation, but also of default and currency depreciation, as well as rates of return in other asset markets and changes in legislation and taxation. The significance of wars is that they generally increase the likelihood of defaults or currency depreciations on the part of the affected countries. That is because wars almost always lead to large government deficits, which can be financed either by selling new bonds to the public (which will tend to depress the price of the existing stock of bonds and hence to raise bond yields) or by discounting short-term bills at the central bank (which will increase the volume of currency in circulation, which in turn will raise both inflationary expectations and bond yields). As government debt rises, so generally does the probability of default. As banknote circulation rises, so does the probability of inflation. These increased risks are priced into bonds, pushing up yields. The same also applies to the *possibility* of wars, since investors will seek to anticipate the actual outbreak of hostilities. It is therefore expectations of events as much as the events themselves that drive financial markets.

Political events were especially important to investors before 1914 because news about them was more readily and regularly available than were detailed economic data. Modern investors tend to look at a wide variety of economic indicators such as budget deficits, short-term interest rates, actual and forecast inflation rates, and growth rates of gross domestic product. They are inundated on a daily basis with information about these and a host of other measures of fiscal, monetary and macroeconomic performance. In the past, however, there were far fewer economic data on which to base judgments about default-risk, future inflation and growth. Prior to the First World War, investors in the major European economies had fairly good and regular information about certain commodity prices, gold reserves, interest rates, and exchange rates, but fiscal data apart from annual budgets were scanty, and there were no regular or reliable figures for national output or income. In non-parliamentary monarchies even annual budgets were not always available or, if they were published, could not be trusted. Instead, investors tended to infer future changes in fiscal and monetary policy from political events, which were regularly reported in private correspondence, newspapers and telegraph agencies. Among the most influential bases for their inferences were three assumptions:

1. that any war would disrupt trade and hence lower tax revenues for all governments;
2. that direct involvement in war would increase a state's expenditure as well as reducing its tax revenues, leading to substantial new borrowings; and
3. that the impact of war on the private sector would make it hard for monetary authorities in combatant countries to maintain the convertibility of paper banknotes into gold, thereby increasing the risk of inflation.

Bond yield data and financial commentary for the period 1850–1880 illustrate these points clearly. The outbreak of the Crimean War had a significant effect on the bonds of all the great powers. Between June 1853 (when the British and French fleets were sent to the Dardanelles) and March 1854 (when the two powers declared war on Russia), the yield on British consols[11] rose by 52 basis points.[12] The yield on French rentes rose by 106 basis points; and the yield on Russian bonds by 175 basis points. When British yields rose again in November 1854, *The Economist* attributed the movement to "the impression that there was a great deal more work for the English troops to do in Crimea than had previously been expected."[13] Interestingly, however, it was Austrian bonds that were worst affected by the outbreak of war. By March 1854 Austrian yields had risen by 243 basis points because investors discerned the greater financial vulnerability of the Habsburg Empire in the event of war. This differential between a manifestly over-stretched Habsburg regime and its rivals widened disastrously in the wars of 1859 and 1866. Austria's defeat by France and Italy pushed yields up by more than 400 basis points, and her defeat at the hands of Prussia by just under 300.

In 1870, however, it was the turn of France to succumb to Prussian arms. The speed and completeness of the French defeat was evidently not anticipated by investors. To be sure, *The Economist* noted nervousness of the Paris market as early as July 8, 1870: "Securities on the Paris Bourse fell on the news that a Prince of Hohenzollern had been offered and had accepted the Spanish Crown, and by the solemn declaration of the French Government that it would go to war to prevent him from taking it."[14] But this did no more than push the yield on French rentes to around twelve basis points above their level prior to the announcement of the Hohenzollern candidacy (which had been 4.09 per cent). The actual declaration of war on July 19 drove yields up to 4.62 per cent, but they then fell back in anticipation of French military successes. As late as August 13, *The Economist*'s Paris correspondent could still report a market rally based on a (bogus) rumor of a French victory.[15] It was not until the news of the French defeat at Sedan that yields soared to 5.68 per cent, more than 150 basis points above their pre-crisis level; they remained above 5.60 per cent until July the following year.

By contrast, the bond market reacted with extreme nervousness to the possibility of a war between Russia and Britain arising from the Eastern crisis of 1876–1878. On the eve of the crisis, in May 1876, Russian yields stood at 5.10 per cent. When the Russians formally declared war on Turkey (on April 24, 1877), they rose to 7.35 per cent, an increase of 225 basis points. Russian yields did not fall back below 6.00 per cent until after the Congress of Berlin, which began in June 1878. So nervous was the market about an Anglo-Russian war that even Russian military successes caused yields to rise if they were thought to increase the likelihood of British intervention. As *The Economist* noted on February 15, 1878, shortly before the Russians imposed the Peace of San Stefano on Turkey:

> The decline in Russian stocks [i.e. bonds], with an army in possession of the Turkish capital, is remarkable. Peace might enable Russia to acquire a large war indemnity, to disband its troops, and to cease extra expenditure. On the other hand, war with Austria or England would increase and prolong those extra expenses, would probably interfere with the chance of an indemnity, and would tend further to exhaust the tax-paying capacity of the population—a new campaign would lead to a financial disaster. Although

the risk of this is very small, this has, nevertheless, depressed Russian stocks.[16]

Not only war, then, but even the mere *possibility* of war could significantly affect the yields on great power bonds.

By the mid-1880s, therefore, it had become "obvious" to financial experts that a great power war spelt trouble for financial markets, and especially for the international bond market centered on the City of London. As the editors of *The Economist* carefully explained:

> To begin with, [war] must necessitate Government borrowings on a large scale, and these heavy demands upon the supplies of floating capital must tend to raise the rate of discount. Nor is it only our own requirements that will have to be provided for. . . . From other quarters demands are likely to be pressed upon us. There is a very general conviction that if war is entered upon . . . other Powers . . . will almost inevitably be, in some way or other, drawn into the contest. The desire, therefore, in all European financial centres, will be to gather strength, so as to be prepared for contingencies. Thus the continental national banks will all be anxious to fortify their position, and as they can always draw gold from hence by unloading here the English bills they habitually hold, the probability is that gold will be taken. And the desire on the part of the continental banks to be strong will, of course, be greatly intensified by the precarious condition of the Berlin and Paris bourses. At both of these centres it would take little to produce a stock exchange crisis of the severest type; and . . . it is to the Bank of England, as the one place whence gold can promptly be drawn, that recourse must be had. The outbreak of war, therefore, would in all probability send a sharp spasm of stringency through our money market . . . [that] would pretty certainly leave rates at a higher level than that at which it found them.
>
> . . . There is, of course, one [other] way, apart from the depressing influence of dearer money in which war, should it break out will prejudicially affect all classes of securities. It will . . . necessitate Government borrowing on a great scale, and the issue of masses of new stock will lessen the pressure of money upon existing channels of investment. . . . And as it is to the volume of British . . . securities that the additions would be made, these would naturally be specially affected.
>
> . . . With European Government stocks . . . a more or less heavy depreciation, according as war circumscribed or extended its sphere, would have to be looked for. . . . For Russia . . . war can mean little else than bankruptcy, possibly accompanied by revolution, and those who . . . have become her creditors, have a sufficiently black outlook.[17]

Events nearly thirty years later would bear out the accuracy of this analysis.

THE PUZZLE IS THAT BETWEEN AROUND 1880 and 1914 the magnitude of financial responses to political crises steadily *declined*—the reverse of what conventional historical accounts would lead us to expect. The diplomatic crisis caused by the British occupation of Egypt in 1882 had no effect at all on consols and only a trivial effect on French rentes (a rise of just 9 basis points). The Afghan (Penjdeh) crisis of 1885 was more significant; it pushed up Russian yields by 61 basis points, though consols rose only 5 points. But the Bulgarian crisis of 1886 was responsible for at most an increase of 20 basis points on Russian bonds; the effect on consols was nil. The Boulanger crisis is often associated with Bismarckian "sabre-rattling" and press speculation that war was "in sight," but the effect on French yields was to increase them by just 20 basis points, and the effect on German bonds was even less. The breakdown of relations between Russia and Germany between 1888 and 1891 in fact coincided with a substantial decline in Russian yields, while the rise in German yields was little more than 17 basis points. The celebrated Fashoda incident of 1898, which supposedly brought Britain and France to the brink of war, had almost no effect on the London and Paris bond markets. The Boer War pushed up consol yields, but had no significant implications for any other power, Germany included. Even if one tries to portray the whole period from the beginning of the German naval construction program until the end of 1901 as a time of growing Anglo-German friction, the effects on the bond market were negligible (and impossible to distinguish from other non-political factors at work in the same period). The same goes for the second bout of naval rivalry between 1906 and 1908. Remarkably, neither the two Moroccan crises nor the successive Balkan crises had significant bond market repercussions. Indeed, until the assassination of the Archduke Francis Ferdinand on June 28, 1914, events in the Balkans coincided with *falls* in both Russian and Austrian bond yields. These events may have been important to diplomats. They have certainly been important to historians. They do not seem to have been very important to investors.

Bond prices *did* fall sharply once investors realized that a great power war was a real possibility. But the striking thing is that this did not happen until the last week of July 1914—to be precise, in the week after the publication of the Austrian ultimatum to Serbia, which demanded co-operation with an Austrian inquiry into the Sarajevo assassinations. That ultimatum was delivered on July 23.

Between July 22 and July 30 (the last day when quotations were published), yields on consols rose by 26 basis points; yields on French rentes by 22 basis points; and yields on German bonds by 17 basis points. The increases were twice as large for Austrian and Russian bonds, yields on which rose by nearly half a percentage point. Even so, these were not by any means unprecedented market movements. The explanation is simple: when the London market closed on July 31 the magnitude of the crisis had still not become fully apparent. Had the market remained open that day, prices of all securities would have fallen much further.

Evidence that the City was slow to appreciate the seriousness of the crisis is plentiful. On July 22, 1914, Lord Rothschild told his relatives in Paris that he "rather fanc[ied] the well founded belief in influential quarters that unless Russia backed up Serbia the latter will eat humble pie and that the inclination in Russia is to remain quiet, circumstances there not favouring a forward movement."[18] The following day he wrote that he expected "that the various matters in dispute will be arranged without appeal to arms."[19] Before the details of the Austrian ultimatum to Serbia were known, he anticipated that the Serbs would "give every satisfaction."[20] On July 27 he expressed "the universal opinion that Austria was quite justified in the demands she made on Serbia and it would ill-become the great Powers if by a hasty and ill-conceived action they did anything which might be viewed as condoning a brutal murder." He was confident that the British government would leave "no stone . . . unturned in the attempts which will be made to preserve the peace of Europe."[21] "It is very difficult to express any very positive opinion," he told his French relatives on July 29, "but I think I may say we believe [French opinion] . . . to be wrong . . . in attributing sinister motives and underhand dealings to the German Emperor[;] he is bound by certain treaties and engagements to come to the assistance of Austria if she is attacked by Russia but that is the last thing he wishes to do." He and the Tsar were "corresponding directly over the wires in the interests of peace"; the German government sincerely wished any war to be "localised."[22] As late as July 31, Rothschild continued to give credence to "rumours in the City that the German Emperor [was] using all of his influence at both St. Petersburg & Vienna to find a solution which would not be distasteful either to Austria or to Russia." Only at this late stage did he show signs of grasping the scale of what was happening. "The result of a war . . . is doubtful," he noted, "but whatever the result may be, the sacrifices and misery attendant upon it are stupendous & untold. In this case the calamity would be greater than anything ever seen or known before."[23]

Rothschild was by no means exceptionally slow on the uptake. *The Economist*—which had been more concerned about "the continual suspense over Ulster" a week previously—echoed his sentiments in its issue dated August 1:

> The financial world has been staggering under a series of blows such as the delicate system of international credit has never before witnessed, or even imagined. . . . Nothing so widespread and so world-wide has ever been known before. Nothing . . . could have testified more clearly to the impossibility of running modern civilisation and war together than this . . . collapse of prices, produced not by the actual outbreak of a small war, but by fear of a war between some of the Great Powers of Europe.[24]

The key phrase here is "fear of a war." Although Austria had declared war on Serbia on July 28, even at this stage it was still far from certain that the other great powers would join in. It was not until July 31 that Russia, after three days of indecision, began general mobilization and the German government issued its ultimata to St Petersburg and Paris. The Germans declared war on Russia only on August 1; the declaration of war on France came two days later. Britain did not enter the fray until August 4—a decision strongly opposed by both the Rothschilds and the editors of *The Economist*.[25] In the eyes of these strongly interested parties, then, what happened between July 22 and July 30 was essentially a sharp rise in the perceived probability of a great power war on the continent; "Armageddon" was still not seen as a certainty.

As the probability of war suddenly rose, the financial crisis long ago foreseen by *The Economist*—to say nothing of Boch and Angell—unfolded with terrible swiftness. What happened was a classic case of international contagion. The Vienna and Budapest markets, which had been sliding for more than a week, were closed on Monday, July 27, St. Petersburg followed two days later, and by Thursday *The Economist* regarded the Berlin and Paris bourses as closed in all but name. The closure of the continental stock markets caused a twofold crisis in London. First, foreigners who had drawn bills on London found it much harder to make remittances; those British banks that had accepted foreign bills suddenly faced a general default as bills fell due. At the same time, there were large withdrawals of continental funds on deposit with London banks and sales of foreign-held securities. As Lord Rothschild nervously reported to his French cousins on July 27, "All the foreign Banks and particularly the German ones took a very large amount of money out of the Stock Exchange to-day and . . . the markets were at one time quite demoralized, a good many weak speculators selling *à nil prix* . . ."[26] London became, as *The Economist* put it, "a dumping ground for liquidation for the whole Continent of Europe."[27] On July 29, with the clearing banks declining to accommodate their hard-pressed Stock Exchange clients, trading effectively ceased—"jobbers in every part of the Stock Exchange declined to deal, declined even to quote nominal prices"—and the first firms began to fail. The next day the news broke that the well-known house of Derenburg & Co. had been "hammered" (i.e., declared bankrupt); this, coupled with the Bank of England's decision to raise its discount rate from 3 to 5 per cent, deepened the gloom. On the morning of the July 31 came what *The Economist* called the "final thunderclap"—the closure of the Stock Exchange, followed by the Bank of England's decision to raise the discount rate to 8 per cent.[28] There is no need here to detail the subsequent steps taken by the authorities to avert a complete financial collapse: the extension of the scheduled bank holiday until August 6; the one-month (later three-month) moratorium on commercial bills proclaimed on August 2; the decision to issue emergency £1 and 10 shilling notes, as well as to discount pre-moratorium bills.[29] The crucial point is that by July 31 the crisis had closed down the London bond market, and it stayed closed until January 4, 1915.

The closure of the Stock Exchange could only disguise the crisis that had been unleashed; it could not prevent it. In the course of the war, large new issues of bonds as well as money creation through the discounting of treasury bills led to sustained rises in the yields of all the combatants' bonds.[30] These rises would have been significantly higher had it not been for a variety of controls imposed on the capital markets of the combatant countries, which made it difficult for investors to reduce their exposure to pre-war great power bonds, as well as by systematic central bank interventions to maintain bond prices.[31] Even so, they were substantial. The average yield on consols in the first half of 1914 had been 3.34 per cent. According to Morgan's figures, the peak of consol yields during the war was 4.92 in November 1917; the average for the period January 1915 to November 1918 was 4.29.[32] From peak to trough, consol prices declined 44 per cent between 1914 and 1920, an increase in yields of 251 per cent. The figures for French rentes were similar (a 40 per cent price drop and a 222 basis point hike). Moreover, Britain and France were the two great powers that emerged on the winning side of the war. The other three all suffered defeat and revolution.

The Bolshevik government defaulted outright on the Russian debt, while the post-revolutionary governments in Germany and Austria reduced their real debt burdens drastically through hyperinflation. For all save the holders of British consols, who could justifiably hope that their government would restore the value of their investments when the war was over, these outcomes were even worse than the most pessimistic pre-war commentators had foreseen. The fact that the financial markets do not seem to have considered such a scenario until the last week of July 1914 surely tells us something important about the origins of the First World War. It seems as if, in the words of *The Economist,* the City only saw "the meaning of war" on July 31—"in a flash."[33]

DID INVESTORS SIMPLY UNDERESTIMATE the potential impact of a war on their bond portfolios in the pre-war period, as the memory of the last great power war faded? One possibility is, of course, that the City was a victim of what has come to be known as "short-war illusion." No less an economic eminence than John Maynard Keynes evidently suffered from that condition. As he excitedly explained to Beatrice Webb on August 10, 1914,

> he was quite certain that the war could not last more than a year. . . . The world, he explained, was enormously rich, but its wealth was, fortunately, of a kind which could not be rapidly realized for war purposes: it was in the form of capital equipment for making things which were useless for making war. When all the available wealth was used up—which he thought would take about a year—the Powers would have to make peace.[34]

Yet the young don's jejune optimism was not widely shared in the City—which perhaps helps to explain why he clashed so violently with the bankers when he swept down to London from Cambridge to offer the Treasury his wartime services. As we have seen, the Rothschilds understood full well that the "calamity would be greater than anything ever seen or known before." On August 1, *The Economist*'s editors foresaw with trepidation "a great war on a scale of unprecedented magnitude, involving loss of life and a destruction of all that we associate with modern civilisation too vast to be counted or calculated, and portending horrors so appalling that the imagination shrinks from the task."[35]

A more plausible interpretation is that investors genuinely regarded the outbreak of a major European war as a highly unlikely occurrence for most of the period after 1880—indeed, until the very last week of July 1914. They correctly evaluated the various international crises before 1914 as local difficulties, rather than as milestones on the road to Armageddon. This is certainly one inference that can be drawn from sources such as the Rothschilds' correspondence and *The Economist*'s weekly editorials. Even to the financially sophisticated, the First World War came as a real surprise. Like an earthquake on a densely populated fault line, its victims had long known that it was a possibility, and how dire its consequences would be; but its timing remained impossible to predict and therefore beyond the realm of normal risk assessment.

If this view is correct, then much of the traditional historiography on the origins of the war has, quite simply, over-determined the event. Far from there having been a "long road to catastrophe," there was but a short slip. Such a conclusion does not tend to support those historians who still think of the war as an inevitable consequence of deep-seated great power rivalries—a predestined cataclysm.[36] But it certainly accords with this author's earlier argument that the outbreak of war was an avoidable political error.[37]

Fall Semester 2004

1. Immanuel Geiss, *Der Lange Weg in die Katastrophe: Die Vorgeschichte des Ersten Weltkrieges, 1815–1914* (Munich, 1990).

2. Hew Strachan, *The First World War: To Arms* (Oxford, 2001), Vol. I, pp. 4–35. The same author shifts his focus to the Balkans after 1908 in *The First World War: A New Illustrated History* (London, 2003), pp. 4–8. For another recent account that emphasizes the alleged blunders of German policy, see Gary Sheffield, *Forgotten Victory: The First World War, Myths and Realities* (London, 2001), pp. 22–40.

3. David G. Herrmann, *The Arming of Europe and the Making of the First World War* (Princeton, N.J., 1996).

4. David Stevenson, *Armaments and the Coming of War: Europe 1904–1914* (Oxford, 1996). In his most recent book, however, *Cataclysm: The First World War as Political Tragedy* (New York, 2004), p. 8, he dates the "crumbling" of the "bases of deterrence" from 1905.

5. See for a recent example, Samuel R. Williamson, Jr., "The Origins of the War," in Hew Strachan, ed., *The Oxford Illustrated History of the First World War* (Oxford, 1998), p. 14.

6. David Fromkin, *Europe's Last Summer: Why the World Went to War in 1914* (London, 2004).

7. See Niall Ferguson, "Introduction," in *The Pity of War: Explaining World War One* (London, 1998), for a full discussion.

8. Ivan S. Bloch, *Is War Now Impossible? Being an Abridgment of "The War of the Future in its Technical, Economic and Political Relations"* (London, 1899), p. xlv.

9. Norman Angell, *The Great Illusion: A Study of the Relation of Military Power to National Advantage* (London, 1913 edn.), p. 209.

10. Four technical points need to be borne in mind. First, when yields are cited below, they are based on London prices with the exception of the yields on French rentes. These are based on Paris prices, which was what *The Economist* usually published. Secondly, for the sake of simplicity, all the yields used here are calculated in an unadjusted form (the coupon rate as a percentage of quoted price), without taking into account either maturity or the regular fluctuations caused by the timing of dividend payments. The difference between these unadjusted yields and yields to maturity is not wholly insignificant, since British consols, French rentes and most Austrian bonds were virtually perpetual, whereas German and Russian bonds were not. Thirdly, an important distinction needs to be noted with respect to the currencies in which bonds were denominated. Britain, France and Germany were members of that exclusive "club" of countries which, for historical reasons, were able to issue bonds on international markets denominated in their own currencies. Austria and Russia were not, in the sense that their bonds issued abroad stipulated payment of interest and principal in silver or gold crowns or rubles. Fourthly and finally, it is important to remember that, in moments of acute crisis, trading in some bonds simply ceased so that no prices were available to be published or the prices published were purely notional quotations that did not reflect actual transactions.

11. The 3 per cent "consol" had been created by the Consolidating Act of 1751 and remained the benchmark British bond until the First World War. It was effectively a perpetual bond, with the proviso that the government had the option to redeem consols if they reached par (i.e. if their market price coincided with their face value).

12. 100 "basis points" are equivalent to one percentage point.

13. *The Economist*, November 17, 1854.

14. Ibid., July 8, 1870.

15. Ibid., Aug. 13, 1870.

16. Ibid., Feb. 15, 1878.

17. Ibid., Apr. 11, 1885.

18. Lord Rothschild, London, to his cousins, Paris, July 22, 1914, Rothschild Archive, London [RAL], XI/130A/8.

19. Ibid., July 23, 1914.

20. Ibid., July 24, 1914.

21. Ibid., July 27, 1914.

22. Ibid., July 28 and 29, 1914.

23. Ibid., July 31, 1914.

24. *The Economist*, Aug. 1, 1914. Cf. ibid., July 25, 1914.

25. The magazine made it clear that it had considerable sympathy with the terms of the Austrian ultimatum to Serbia: "It is fair . . . to ask . . . what Great Britain would have done in a like case—if, for example, the Afghan Government had plotted to raise a rebellion in North-West India, and if, finally, Afghan assassins had murdered a Prince and Princess of Wales? Certainly the cry of vengeance would have been raised, and can we be sure that any measure milder than the Note sent from Vienna to Belgrade would have been dispatched from London or Calcutta to Kandahar?" The editors saw the "quarrel" in the Balkans as "no more of our making and no more our concern than would be a quarrel between Argentina and Brazil or between China and Japan." They strongly urged the government to adopt a policy of neutrality: *The Economist*, Aug. 1, 1914.

26. Lord Rothschild, London, to his cousins, Paris, July 27, 1914, RAL, XI/130A/8.

27. *The Economist*, Aug. 1, 1914.

28. Ibid.

29. John Maynard Keynes, "War and the Financial System, August 1914," *Economic Journal*, 24 (September 1914), pp. 460–86. Cf. D. E. Moggridge, *Keynes: An Economist's Biography* (London, 1992), pp. 236–241.

30. Theo Balderston, "War Finance and Inflation in Britain and Germany, 1914–1918," *Economic History Review* (1989), pp. 222–44.

31. Clemens Kooi, "War Finance and Interest Rate Targeting: Regime Changes in 1914–1918," *Explorations in Economic History*, 32 (July 1995), pp. 365–82.

32. E. V. Morgan, *Studies in British Financial Policy, 1914–1925* (London, 1952), p. 152.

33. *The Economist*, Aug. 1, 1914.

34. Quoted in A. D. Harvey, *Collision of Empires: Britain in Three World Wars, 1792–1945* (London, 1992), p. 279.

35. *The Economist*, Aug. 1, 1914.

36. See most recently Paul W. Schroeder, "Embedded Counterfactuals and World War I as an Unavoidable War," in Philip Tetlock, Richard Ned Lebow, and Geoffrey Parker, eds., *Unmaking the West: Counterfactual Thought Experiments in History* (forthcoming).

37. Ferguson, *Pity of War*, chapters 1 to 5.

9

Oh! What a Lovely War:
History and Popular Myths
In Late Twentieth-Century Britain

BRIAN BOND

In my book *The Unquiet Western Front: Britain's Role in Literature and History* (2002) I argued that the First World War had been redis-covered in the 1960s and presented to a new generation which had a very different cultural and political perspective from that of the 1930s. Furthermore I suggested that later twentieth century notions of Britain's role in the First World War had been decisively influenced by the books, plays, and films of the 1960s. I devoted only a few pages to discussion of the play and film *Oh! What a Lovely War* and the pur-pose of this lecture is to expand on that brief discussion.

Let me first provide the context in which a new generation was in-troduced to the history of the First World War. There was a perva-sive fear of nuclear war which provided a grim undertone to the play under discussion. Only a year before the play's first showing in 1963 the Cuban missile crisis suggested that the world had teetered on the brink of annihilation. Far less dramatic, but of long-term social significance, National Service was ended in 1960, so the last con-scripts left the armed services in 1963. Thus ended a tradition by which the majority of the male population had some familiarity with the realities of army life, and many conscripts actually experienced war itself.

The decade was also notable for the emergence of an indepen-dent youth culture and of much greater freedom in sexual matters. Homosexual relations between consenting adults in private ceased to be a crime; while the outcome of the "Lady Chatterley" trial her-alded a more liberal era for the publication and open discussion of

formerly taboo topics. As Philip Larkin wistfully recalled in his poem
Annus Mirabilis:

> Sexual intercourse began
> In nineteen sixty three
> (Which was rather late for me)—
> Between the end of the *Chatterley* ban
> And the Beatles' first L.P.[1]

The same year, 1963, was also that of the John Profumo scandal,
in which the Secretary of State for War was disgraced for consorting
with expensive call girls whose clientele included Stephen Ward, a
society osteopath, and Captain Ivanov, a naval attaché at the Soviet
embassy. This affair had all the ingredients to titillate the popular
press: sleaze and hypocrisy in the Tory Party and high society with
the possibility of espionage. Profumo's political career was ruined,
Ward committed suicide, and the call girls became celebrities.

The increasingly dire plight of the American forces in Vietnam provided a focus for anti-American, anti-imperial, and anti-
authority protest, especially in British universities. Only experts (at
least in Britain) will now remember the rapid surge of the American
military commitment in Vietnam and its even speedier contraction.
In 1961 there were only some 3,000 American personnel in Vietnam
but by 1966 there were 385,000. In 1968 the "Tet" offensive against
southern cities was defeated, but so unpopular was the war that President Johnson decided not to seek re-election and to begin peace
negotiations. American forces in Vietnam reached a peak of 541,500
early in 1969 but the ebb tide was so rapid that the last personnel left
in March 1973.[2]

Radical student protest and rebellion culminated in violent
demonstrations and clashes with police in Paris and other European cities. In Britain, university lectures and administration were
widely disrupted. Even at the conservative and largely apolitical
King's College London, where I was then a young lecturer, we were
worried (needlessly as it turned out) that departmental signs indi-
cating "War Studies" would provoke hostile demonstrations. At
Field Marshal Earl Haig's former Oxford College his portrait in the
hall was given a new caption "Murderer of One Million Men," while
the College War Memorial was temporarily removed.

All this may seem beside the point since Britain was not involved
in Vietnam, but as a teacher of military history I can assure you that
the fallout was profound and enduring. For students who could not
remember the Second World War, Britain's humiliation over the
Suez crisis in 1956 and America's own involvement and eventual

failure in Vietnam created a strong impression that even wars fought by democracies were unjust and futile.

It was in this generally anti-war setting that the entertainment *Oh! What a Lovely War* was put together and first performed in March 1963. Initially inspired by the soldiers' songs of the First World War, the play also drew heavily on anti-war historical writings of the inter-war decades, either directly or via their reappearance in derivative popular works of the early 1960s such as Alan Clark's *The Donkeys* (1961). I believe that the play (often revived) [3] and the film of *Oh! What a Lovely War* (1969) have had a significant role in shaping British beliefs and myths about the First World War from the 1960s to the present.

In my book I attributed the remarkable revival of interest in the First World War that occurred in the 1960s partly to the sense among publishers and television producers that the reading and viewing public needed a break from saturation coverage of the Second World War, followed by a sharp commercial perception that the imminent fiftieth anniversaries (1964–1968) would provide a splendid opportunity for re-visiting the First World War. But we need to explore further if we are to account for a new, more radical and even savage de-bunking approach to the First World War in the 1960s. Daniel Todman (who has generously allowed me to read part of his unpublished doctoral thesis), makes an interesting case for a demographic shift; his argument being that until the 1960s the generation of bereaved parents of soldiers killed in the First World War "set boundaries on what was acceptable public discourse about the war"; i.e., criticism in books, plays, or films would be tacitly restrained by fear of causing further distress to this vulnerable group. This is a plausible argument but, as Dr. Todman admits, it is difficult to document. [4]

I should like to offer a different kind of explanation based on the British public's perception of the nation's role in the two world wars. Paradoxically, Britain's role in the Second World War made it harder to understand, and appreciate, her role in the earlier conflict. The Kaiser's regime, though militaristic, was patently not such an evil force as Hitler's, and German atrocities in the First World War, seen after 1918 to have been exaggerated for propaganda purposes, were dwarfed by Nazi barbarism in the Second. Moreover, Nazi Germany had posed a more direct threat to Britain's survival with intensive aerial bombing and rocket attacks following the failure of the projected invasion in 1940. Thus, by the 1960s, Churchill's heroic leadership and the nation's "finest hour" had acquired the status of myth, accompanied by the retrospective justification of a crusade to end the

Holocaust. The radical historian A. J. P. Taylor concluded a popular history with the surprising verdict that, for all its suffering and destruction, the Second World War had been a "good war." By contrast, the First World War now seemed to many Britons to have been a very "bad war"—in its origins, its conduct and its consequences.

The original program of the play *Oh! What a Lovely War* describes it as "a musical entertainment based on an idea of Charles Chilton." In 1958 Chilton had visited Arras military cemetery to take a photograph of his father's grave but was confronted with the bitter truth that his father had no grave: his name was included in the collective memorial to 35,942 officers and men with no known grave who had died in that area alone—and there were nearly twice as many names on the memorial at Thiepval for the Somme campaigns.[5] Reflection on this horrific statistic led to Chilton's celebrated 1961 radio program *The Long, Long Trail,* based on soldiers' songs of the period, and his passionate determination to portray the fate of the rank and file on the Western Front. Hence his collaboration with Joan Littlewood, a radical founder of Theatre Workshop, whose aim was to present politicized drama to working class audiences. It was her idea to stage the show in a music hall setting and performed by a troupe of pierrots. She insisted on a didactic, extreme left-wing perspective. For this reason, in Dr. Todman's words, "[s]he rejected scripts which offered a realistic depiction of life in the trenches. The result is a black and white picture in which officers at all levels are stupid, callous cowards while their men are sardonic heroes."[6]

The third, vital contributor to the stage production was Raymond Fletcher, military history buff and devotee of Liddell Hart, military commentator for the socialist journal *Tribune,* sometime Labour MP, and more recently revealed as a Soviet agent. Fletcher had no time for the generals or "brass hats"; his sympathies were entirely with the ordinary soldiers. More ideologically committed than Charles Chilton, he fervently believed that the play should also convey a warning about the dangers of war in the nuclear age. Thus he described his three-hour harangue to the Theatre Workshop Group on the play's purpose as "one part me, one part Liddell Hart, the rest Lenin!"[7]

The play was first performed at Stratford, in the East End of London, on March 19, 1963 and later transferred to the West End. As someone who saw an early performance, I can testify that the experience was not only highly entertaining, but also deeply moving. The puerile sneering at the generals and staff officers (mostly cribbed from Alan Clark) was partly offset by marvelous one-liners. For example:

> *The Master of Ceremonies (re the slide into war in August 1914):*
> "Whenever there's a crisis, shoot some grouse, that's what I always say."
> *Briton:* "I understand President Wilson is a very sick man?"
> *American:* "Yes, he's an idealist!"
> *Haig reads a letter:* "Better conditions needed for officers. The other ranks don't seem to mind so much."
> *Haig (at prayer):* "I ask thee for victory, Lord, before the Americans arrive."[8]

But the overwhelming sense of sadness and nostalgia was mostly conveyed by the songs, thirty-one of which were listed in the program. These ranged from the music hall knockabout comedy of "Belgium put the Kibosh on the Kaiser" and the bawdy "I'll make a man of any one of you," to the solemn "Heilige Nacht," the poignant "Chanson de Craonne," and "They'll never believe us." The majority, however, were irreverent and bitter tirades against the soldiers' predicament in the trenches including "If you want the old battalion," "I don't want to be a soldier," "When this lousy war is over," "I want to go home," and "Forward Joe Soap's Army" sung to the hymn tune of "Onward, Christian Soldiers." The play's serious propaganda message was hinted at in various places in the text—such as the accidental nature of the war's outbreak, its unexpected duration and enormous casualty list—but it was spelt out in the author's notes, which read more like a political tract than the usual theater program.

Raymond Fletcher, like Joan Littlewood, was deeply concerned that the errors and miscalculations of 1914–1918 should not be repeated in the nuclear age. He was impressed by Herman Kahn's massive study *On Thermonuclear War* (1960), which was one of the many bizarre sources pressed on the Theatre Workshop players who were encouraged to contribute.[9] Before 1914, according to Fletcher, people had believed that the Balance of Power could preserve peace; today they believe in the Balance of Terror: "But accident and miscalculations are still possible—and a third, nuclear world war could kill as many in four hours as were killed in the whole of World War One." A series of notes drove home the lesson, the final one stating that "[o]ne atom bomb in 1945 caused as many casualties as the entire Battle of Arras. One Polaris missile is twenty-five times as destructive as the bomb that destroyed Hiroshima."

General Douglas MacArthur was quoted as saying in 1961: "Global war has become a Frankenstein to destroy both sides. . . . It [war] contains now only the germs of double suicide." According to another note, "[i]n 1960 an American Research Team fed all the facts of World War I into the computers they use to plan World War III (sic). They reached the conclusion that the 1914–1918 war was impossible and couldn't have happened. There could not have been so many blunders nor so many casualties." Regarding the play's text it was stated (in italics): *Everything presented as fact is true.* This preposterous claim will be challenged later in this lecture, but for the moment we need only note Derek Paget's assertion that, from a Marxist viewpoint, Joan Littlewood's mode of representing war "became dominant in historiography as well as in drama." The play's historical sources provide a view "now recuperated into the dominant cultural understanding of the great war."[10]

The play's most original feature was its presentation of the war from what was assumed to be the common soldier's viewpoint: a revolutionary inversion of class authority in the 1960s though since then a much more common approach. A new generation in the 1960s was provided with the disturbing argument—later to be comically trivialized in the 1989 BBC television series *Blackadder Goes Forth*—that the Great War represented a betrayal of the ordinary people by the ruling class.[11] As will be suggested later, in discussion of the film version, these strident denunciations of the military leaders' incompetence have gradually achieved the status of popular myth, so much so that to many people it now seems perverse to contend that the majority of soldiers did not see themselves as hapless victims in a pointless war; that there were numerous brave and popular subalterns; and that most of the senior officers were neither callous nor incompetent.[12]

The anti-historical nature of the play is evident in its structure. There are only two Acts. The first dramatizes an innocent hope of victory in a spirit of optimism; the second presents recognition of defeat in a mood of despair and pessimism. The play draws heavily upon three popular texts: Barbara Tuchman's *August 1914* (for the accidental outbreak of war in that year), Alan Clark's *The Donkeys* for 1915 (and the battle of Loos), and Leon Wolff's *In Flanders Fields* for 1917 (and especially Passchendaele). Significantly, from a historian's viewpoint, it has almost nothing to say about 1918, thus avoiding having to explain how "the donkeys" had secured victory. Indeed it was a crucial part of the play's message that there had been no winners. As early as page 61 of the text (cleverly transferred to the final scene in the film) a slide depicts a vast field with white wooden crosses stretching as far as the eye can see. This is what the war was "about" and how it has ended—in desolation and mass slaughter.

The play, moreover, deliberately subverted traditional accounts of the war as related from the officers' standpoint, such as the hugely popular drama *Journey's End,* by giving a voice to a lower class (the rankers) who were supposed only to be able to express themselves through irony and humor. Irony is indeed the prevailing mode throughout, above all in the songs. The line taken was that the war as a whole was inflicted upon a compliant lower class by an upper class which assumed a superiority it had failed to justify. This is to take a breathtaking liberty with historical truth in the light of the disproportionate number of officer casualties, which included the Prime Minister's son, Raymond Asquith, killed on the Somme. These obtrusive political concerns, as Derek Paget damningly concludes, "make the play a poorish source of knowledge about the Great War, (yet) such an excellent source of knowledge about the early 1960s."[13]

The play was a considerable box-office success, both in Stratford East and later in the West End, followed by several international tours and frequent productions by repertory theatres. But did the play realize the political expectations of its progenitors? In the short term, say over the next decade, probably not. As Daniel Todman has rightly pointed out, the majority of the audience, even at the Theatre Royal, Stratford, were almost certainly middle class regular playgoers and not members of the working class which Joan Littlewood had hoped to attract. This was even more the case when the play moved to Wyndham's Theatre on the Aldwych. One of Joan Littlewood's colleagues even complained that the critics' enthusiasm had attracted the wrong kind of audience which was tantamount to a betrayal of the Theatre Workshop's socialist aspirations. The play ran for a year in the West End but closed after only fifteen weeks on Broadway with a loss of about £30,000 to the Theatre Workshop. Presumably many of the characters and references were lost on an American audience.[14] British theatergoers would be well aware that the Theatre Workshop's productions were experimental and left-wing and would therefore be prepared for a swingeing attack on the First World War generals, provided they were also entertained. Reviewers' reactions showed that the gap between Chilton's aim of paying tribute to the humor, stoicism, and comradeship of the ordinary soldier and the more radical intentions of Littlewood and Fletcher had not been entirely bridged. In other words, the most enjoyable and memorable aspect of the entertainment was the wonderful songs which evoked emotions of pathos, nostalgia, and even sentimentality. The songs received even more emphasis in the West End version when a cynical ending was replaced by a jolly reprise.[15] These are my own recollections of that memorable evening, and most contemporary critics concurred that sentimentality had taken the edge off the savage satire. Thus the *Sunday Times* reviewer, J. W. Lambert, commented that "this immensely brisk charade gives nostalgia a top-dressing of belated anti-establishment respectability." David Pryce-Jones remarked of the Aldwych version that "showbiz has crept in to bespangle the poor relation from Stratford East" to the extent that audiences "could imagine themselves back in the days of good old musical shows."[16]

Few reviewers seem to have been worried by the play's blatant anti-military bias or its historical distortions, partly perhaps, as suggested earlier, because they gave priority to its entertainment value but also, I would argue, because the fundamental assumptions regarding the war's pointlessness, unspeakable conditions, unacceptable casualty figures, and incompetent generalship were already widely accepted. Liddell Hart, whose books were included in the source material, and who acted as a historical consultant, wrote to the *Observer* that there was "more of the real war in the play than in recent 'white-wash' history; it *did* faithfully reflect what his generation thought of the war." Correlli Barnett, however, struck a dissenting note in savaging the production in a BBC Third Programme radio talk. He stressed the gulf between entertainment and history. As entertainment it succeeded brilliantly, but in terms of history "[i]t is a highly partisan, and often grossly unfair, presentation of the war from an extreme anti-Brass-hat point of view. Its intent is serious—it wants to make propaganda."[17] Barnett made another telling criticism which applied to both the stage and film versions: while politicians were shown as responsible for the outbreak of war they were conspicuously absent during its conduct. There were "butchers" aplenty (i.e., the Generals) but where was "the Cur" (Lloyd George) asked Barnett rhetorically? If only officers were depicted, only officers could be charged—and their guilt was proven by the casualty figures.[18]

Richard Attenborough's film adaptation has largely eclipsed the original play in the public memory. It caused an immediate sensation when first shown in London in 1969, and on general release was acclaimed at international film festivals in the United States, Spain, and Japan. The film was one of the highest earners in Britain in 1969 but, interestingly, was outshone financially by *The Battle of Britain*.[19] Part of the appeal for regular cinema goers surely lay in the all-star cast. To mention just a few of the best-known actors: Jack Hawkins was a senile Emperor Franz Joseph; John Gielgud a cynical Count Berchtold; Michael Redgrave played Sir Henry Wilson; Laurence

Olivier an outrageously blimpish Sir John French; Ralph Richardson an aloof Sir Edward Grey; Maggie Smith the seductive recruiting siren and—starring throughout—John Mills was a cold and inflexible Sir Douglas Haig. Most of the play's songs and the dialogue were retained, but the setting was changed to Brighton Pier with the atmosphere and trappings of the 1914-era fairground and music hall. Attenborough also retained much of the stylized nature of the stage version, especially for Haig and his colleagues who remained on the pier, safely distant from the killing fields. The film made a strong impression by the frequent switches between the jolly scenes on the pier and the grim vignettes of front-line fighting, though from a critical historical standpoint the latter too were very unrealistic. A very successful innovation in the film was the introduction of a representative family, the Smiths, who provide continuity throughout from the five brothers' recruitment by the Maggie Smith character, through their experiences of battle, to their deaths in the trenches.

Attenborough's adaptation, though retaining the relentless critique of the officers and the upper classes in general (an elderly boss in his carriage cannot remember the name of his wounded employee, and wounded men on Waterloo Station are made to wait while wounded officers are at once whisked away), lacks Joan Littlewood's angry political drive. Feelings of nostalgia and sadness are evoked even more powerfully than on the stage. In a brilliant piece of symbolism, which can easily be missed, poppies—normally the emblems of remembrance—are here handed to those about to die.[20] Also, as Todman notes perceptively, the audience's perspective has been changed. In contrast to the play, where the theater audience is made to feel involved in a tragedy without end, in the film the viewers are detached spectators of a "war game" which ends with mass funerals and the same old statesmen (also located on the pier) re-drawing the map of Europe.

No one who has seen the film will forget the audacious final sequence. As hostilities draw to an end the remaining soldier of the Smith family (a ghost), is escorted from the battlefield and follows a tape which takes him back to England, past the peace-makers in session with the maps, and off the pier to emerge on the Sussex Downs. There he joins the reclining ghosts of his dead relatives and the female survivors who are enjoying a picnic on the hillside. When his small daughter asks the stock question "granny, what did daddy do in the war?" the scene is transformed. As Jerome Kern's nostalgic melody "They Wouldn't Believe Me" rises on the sound track, the dead soldiers dissolve into white crosses which are seen to stretch away into infinity, filling the whole screen. The effect is still powerful when viewed in solitude: in crowded cinemas the impression of sadness at the useless sacrifice of so many young men was reportedly overwhelming. Nevertheless it needs to be pointed out that this astonishing conclusion was not only deceitful as history but did a disservice to the memory of these young "lions" who were made to seem to have thrown away their lives for nothing. This was the meaning Richard Attenborough intended to convey. He remarked recently that watching the closing scene always brings tears to his eyes.[21]

In its supplement pre-viewing the film the *Observer* had displayed Field Marshal Haig (John Mills) on the cover amid this sea of white crosses with the comment: "the hated objects in this film turn out to be a parcel of imbecile aristocrats and politicians, and the British High Command—French and Haig especially." Its review noted that the film is on the side of the workers who do all the dirty jobs. Ironies are to be found everywhere. For example, the superficially glamorous lady who recruits Harry Smith and his pals with a broad hint of sexual favors to follow ("I'll make a man of every one of you"), is glimpsed off stage as "a raddled bag as hard as nails," suggesting that from the very outset the innocent recruits have been deceived by their social superiors. The *Sunday Telegraph*'s review described the film as "the most pacifist statement since *All Quiet on the Western Front.*" Derek Malcolm in the *Guardian* and Kenneth Allsop in the *Observer* both felt that the film was inferior to the play because its glossy production tended to elicit comfortable feelings of nostalgia. Malcolm also felt that the film-makers had been enamored as well as repelled by the terrible images of trench warfare. "In a way difficult to explain, it unwittingly indulges itself. . . . Its basic nostalgia is too comfortingly fond. . . . It seems almost ridiculous to admire it so much, but to be moved by it so little." Allsop admitted that: "The raw, caustic savagery which burned through the Theatre Workshop evening still haunts me. I esteem what Mr. Attenborough has done, but he hasn't disturbed my nights."[22] Between them the film and the play had managed to transform a terrible and devastating European tragedy into an entertaining "War Game."

Dr. Todman has thoughtfully analyzed the dilemma between the requirements for commercial success and the risks of brutal realism in comparing the film versions of *Oh! What a Lovely War* and *King and Country,* directed by Joseph Losey in 1964. The latter tells the story of the execution of a shell-shocked young British soldier called Hamp, and is "unremitting in its depiction of the horror of the Western front," culminating in the (improbable) scene of the defending officer, Captain Hargreaves, having to blow Hamp's head off with his revolver after the firing squad had botched its task. That film was a disaster at the box office whereas the phrase "Oh! What a Lovely War" has passed into popular language and both the play's and the film's contents and message are widely remembered. As Todman sums up: "For all that they might talk about the mud, blood and official stupidity, audiences would not accept such a bitter interpretation of the war (as Losey's) without a sugaring of sentimentality."[23]

In view of what was said earlier about the polemical intent and political bias of both the play and the film of *Oh! What a Lovely War*, it may seem otiose to make some detailed criticisms. I do so here because I believe that the media has had an insidious influence in shaping public opinion towards a view of the war that is largely false. I will concentrate on the film, partly because it has reached a wider audience, but also because I have been able to study it more carefully on video cassette.

The First World War can easily be portrayed as pointless if the Great Power rivalries before 1914 are completely ignored or the outbreak of war attributed to the mishandling of a petty incident at Sarajevo. Richard Attenborough has recently confirmed that he does indeed believe the war had no cause, that it resulted only from the pride of statesmen and diplomatic maneuvering.[24] While it would be unrealistic to expect a faithful adherence to chronology and an accurate depiction of the main events, the film's structure (following the play) creates enormous distortions. For example, so much time is devoted to scene setting and recruiting (on Brighton Pier) that nearly half the total time (one hour) is taken up with events in 1914, culminating in the Christmas Truce. This episode is given prominence to show that the ordinary soldiers on either side are reluctant to fight each other: the German spokesman, Fritz, actually says so. Indeed the Scots soldiers' real hostility is directed more towards "the bastard English" who end the truce with gunfire! After 1914 the rest of the war is drastically condensed. There is only brief coverage of Loos (September 1915), the first day of the Somme offensive (July 1, 1916) and the Third Ypres campaign in 1917.

Again, while it would be ridiculous to expect a fair and balanced portrayal of Sir Douglas Haig, still a controversial figure among historians, here he is crudely caricatured as completely unimaginative, stubborn, and inhuman in his calm acceptance of huge losses—a War Office official notice records, "British casualties on the Somme 600,000: ground gained nil." On a specific point, Haig is shown as complacent and overly optimistic about his troops' readiness before the Somme offensive, whereas we know that in fact he was very anxious about the inexperienced Kitchener divisions' inadequate training and tried in vain to persuade the French commander Joffre to postpone the start of the offensive.

The irony and pathos implicit in most of the soldiers' songs is fully exploited to engage the sympathy of the viewers, but the impression is created that pessimistic and anti-war lyrics should be taken literally, thus ignoring the traditional humor, grumbling, and stoicism of Tommy Atkins. It is ridiculous, for example, to place a disenchanted song as early as the battle of Mons in August 1914 where all the soldiers were regulars or pre-war reservists.

Although Richard Attenborough apparently felt that the stage production had been too harsh on the officers, his own depiction of officer-men relations was nevertheless an unhistorical caricature. No officers were shown leading their men in the trenches or in the attack; look for example at the officer-less group of Ulstermen stranded in an advanced position near Thiepval on July 1, 1916. The staff officer shown in the trenches at Loos is a pompous ass, ending his embarrassing harangue with the comforting words, "You're white men all," which indeed they were.

The British front-line soldiers are shown as passive, impotent cannon fodder who mostly die impersonally from shell fire and machine gun bullets. Their own role as attackers and killers is overlooked. Above all, they are portrayed as victims of their own incompetent staff officers and callous commanders, epitomized by the wooden characterization of Haig who believes that he is carrying out God's will.

The final criticism concerns the outcome of the war, on which both the play and the film were evasive. To be sure, the Allied victory was bought at a terrible price in lives, destruction, and the disruption of European society, and its political benefits soon came to seem disappointing. There was still a large gulf between victory and defeat, however, and this was generally appreciated by the generation that had fought, or endured, the war. In the film the only clue that the war on the Western Front has ended in an allied victory is a Tommy's remark that they are back at Mons where he and his brother fought in August 1914. There is an inference that the Americans' arrival in 1917 will lead to victory, hence of course Haig's prayer that God will allow *him* to win the war before the Americans become the dominant partner. The brief glimpse of the elderly statesmen redrawing the map of Europe after the Armistice suggests that they are again trying to establish a balance of power, having learned nothing since their failure in 1914. Finally the surreal closing scene on the Sussex Downs creates the impression that all the soldiers have been killed and have died in vain—an utterly negative conclusion which Attenborough still believes to be true.

In my book, *The Unquiet Western Front,* I may have exaggerated the extent to which the unsubtle polemical views of the play and film of *Oh! What a Lovely War* gained public acceptance in Britain in the 1960s and early 1970s. But the new, more insistent emphasis on the futility of the war and the vain sacrifice of a generation of brave ordinary young men by uncaring and incompetent upper-class officers put down deep roots which have since been continuously nourished in books, journals and, above all, television, until by the 1990s the farcical but enormously popular series *Blackadder Goes Forth* could be widely accepted as purveying the essential truths about the most unlovely war. In Derek Paget's perceptive analysis, "The myth of the Great Men of Empire with their tales of derring-do dissolved first into the Lions led by Donkeys, then into General Melchett and Captain Darling (the epitome of the incompetent commander and staff officer in *Blackadder*). . . . Crucial changes have taken place not only in representation, but also in national self-perception since 1963."[25] Furthermore, as Daniel Todman neatly puts it, "By the 1990s, the texts which had first arrived in the 1960s were themselves the subject of myths."[26] In August 2003 a reviewer could write, before addressing a book which robustly challenges these myths: "For many people, perhaps most people, 'futility' seems to be the word that best sums up Britain's martial endeavors on the Western Front. Few believe throwing away the flower of the nation's manhood for the gain of a few square miles of Flanders mud was worth it. . . . New Age pacifists, hip satirists and reactionary Edwardian summer sentimentalists all agree: the Great War came at too high a price."[27]

How is the military historian to react to what the majority of his professional colleagues regard as pernicious myths, misunderstandings, and misrepresentations which are blatantly out of touch with modern scholarship? He can shrug his shoulders and take the line that most people are not deeply interested in history and can be left to embrace any old myths that suit them. He can counterattack with righteous indignation as the likes of John Terraine and Correlli Barnett did in the late twentieth century and Gordon Corrigan is doing now. Or, as I tried to do in my recent book, and as Daniel Todman has explored in his doctoral thesis from a slightly different angle, they can trace the origin and development of myths as historical phenomena which acquire a life of their own. However in the case of such a huge and controversial subject as the First World War most military historians will feel that they have a professional duty to present "the truth" as they see it, based on the best documentary evidence and with as much objectivity as they can muster. As regards *Oh! What a Lovely War* and its pervasive influence, their task may be comparable to that of Sisyphus, forever fated to push an enormous boulder uphill. But, unlike him, they may eventually succeed when the First World War takes its place as just another great conflict in history and one in which Britain's very impressive contribution will be recognized.

Fall Semester 2003

I am indebted to Stephen Badsey, John Lee, and Daniel Todman for their help in preparing this lecture.

1. Philip Larkin, *High Windows* (London, 1979 pbk edn), p. 34.

2. Arthur Marwick, *The Sixties: Cultural Revolution in Britain, France, Italy and the United States 1958–1974* (New York, 1998), pp. 533–63 and 632–42. Some early American viewers of the film of *Oh! What a Lovely War* thought it "speaks as much for the young protesting generation of today as for their grandparents who survived the Great War." *Sunday Telegraph*, Apr. 6, 1969, Liddell Hart Papers, Liddell Hart Centre for Military Archives, King's College, London: hereafter LH. LH 13/61.

3. The play was performed in London's Regent's Park Open Air Theatre as recently as July 2002.

4. Daniel Todman, "Representations of the First World War in British Popular Culture, 1918–1998" (Ph.D. Thesis, University of Cambridge, 2003), Ch. 2, "Drama and the First World War, 1960–1998," pp. 41–45 and 80–84. A revised version of the thesis entitled *The Great War: Myth and Memory* will be published by Hambledon and London in 2005.

5. I have retained a copy of the original program. See also Alex Danchev's essay in Brian Bond, ed., *The First World War and British Military History* (Oxford, 1991), p. 281.

6. Todman, "Representations," p. 91.

7. Bond, *First World War*, p. 282. I owe the point about Fletcher's links with the Soviet Union to Dr. Gary Sheffield.

8. *Oh! What a Lovely War* (1965) pp. 46, 48, 49, 80, and 83. More than the film, the play stresses the evil influence of arms manufacturers and war profiteers. In the play, for example, an American profiteer remarks "Do you realise that there have been two peace scares in the past year? Our shares dropped 40 percent."

9. Derek Paget, "Remembrance Play: *Oh! What a Lovely War* and History," in Tony Howard and John Stokes, eds., *Acts of War* (1996), p. 83. For an example of the current interest in the "myths" rather than the "history" of the First World War, see Graham S. Galer, "Myths of the Western Front" (Ph.D. Thesis, University of Kent, 2002); Bond, *First World War*, p. 283. For a list of the historical sources consulted see Paget, "Remembrance Play," p. 91

10. Paget, "Remembrance Play," p. 83.

11. Ibid., p. 89.

12. John Bourne, "British Generals in the First World War" in Gary Sheffield, ed., *Leadership and Command* (London, 1997).

13. Paget, "Remembrance Play," p. 89.

14. *Sunday Telegraph*, Jan. 31, 1965, in LH 13/61.

15. Ibid.

16. I quoted some of these reviews from the Liddell Hart Papers (file LH 13/61) in my book, but I am grateful to Dr. Todman for his references to additional material in this file which I have subsequently checked.

17. Liddell Hart letter to the *Observer*, June 20, 1963 and typescript of Correlli Barnett's talk on July 10, 1963, both in LH 13/61.

18. Bond, *First World War*, p. 285.

19. Ibid., p. 283.

20. I owe this important insight to Dr. Todman. Richard Attenborough also mentioned this deliberate use of symbolism in a BBC 2 *Arena* program celebrating his career on Aug. 24, 2003.

21. Attenborough, *Arena* program.

22. Kenneth Allsop, "War Game Comparisons," *Observer,* Apr. 13, 1969; Derek Malcolm "Fun and Games," *Guardian,* Apr. 9, 1969. Copies of all the reviews mentioned are to be found in the Liddell Hart Papers LH 13/61. In re-reading this bulky file of press cuttings I was deeply depressed by the abysmal lack of historical understanding of the First World War, with the late John Terraine and Correlli Barnett honorable exceptions.

23. Todman, "Representations," p. 108.

24. Attenborough, *Arena* program.

25. Paget, "Remembrance Play," p. 86.

26. Todman, "Representations," p. 86.

27. Graham Stewart reviewing Gordon Corrigan's *Mud, Blood and Poppycock, Spectator,* Aug. 9, 2003.

10

Alanbrooke:
The Birdwatcher Who Saved Britain

ALEX DANCHEV

At the end of a long and difficult day at the War Office in London in 1943, the Director of Military Operations (DMO) was bidden to remain behind after a meeting with his master, the Chief of the Imperial General Staff (CIGS). When everyone else had filed out the CIGS, General Sir Alan Brooke, later Field Marshal Lord Alanbrooke, shut the door, opened a drawer in his desk, and took out a book. He handed it to the DMO and asked, in his characteristic clipped speech, "Have you read this? It is most remarkable." The DMO looked at it with disbelief. The title of the book was *The Truth About The Cuckoo*.[1] There was more to Alanbrooke, grand strategist, demon ornithologist, and closet diarist, than met the eye. Sixty years after their solitary composition, forty years after their sensational emasculation, the publication of his unexpurgated war diaries has brought into focus as if for the first time this profoundly human figure—resolutely formidable yet desperately vulnerable—author of the most important military document in modern British history.

Much commentary on the Alanbrooke diaries has fixed on the Tolstoyan relationship between the CIGS and the Prime Minister, Winston Churchill, a relationship as momentous as it was ambiguous. In keeping with a certain strain in the original source—"chained to the chariot of a lunatic" wrote the diarist of his own predicament—some of the commentary may be overcooked, but its radical potential may yet be underappreciated. The diaries are an intimate window on the Winston world: the cocooned world of the spoiled child running amok in the nursery. More than this, they represent an unsparing counter-Churchillian perspective on the war and by extension the nation and the bulldog who embodied it: a significant undermining of the founding myths of the British national past. Alanbrooke himself seems fated never to find a place in the popular pantheon (a brilliant miniature in Anthony Powell's novel *The Military Philosophers* is typically anonymous) but the gimlet eye of his diaries will mark the ones who do.[2] In the words of the columnist Simon Jenkins, "the unexpurgated Alanbrooke diaries have been trailed as the last unfinished business of the Second World War. They are said to be indiscreet, malicious and true, debunking Churchill, Eisenhower, Mountbatten, Marshall and de Gaulle. They are and they do. They offer an extraordinary insight into the conduct of a nation's leadership in war." Beyond the nation, they provide an eye-witness account of how the Grand Alliance learned to wage and eventually win the war, an account of lacerating authenticity, now indispensable to any serious study of that epic struggle. "At last," wrote Michael Howard with relief after surveying the textual terrain, "the Alanbrooke diaries, like those of his contemporary at the Foreign Office, Alexander Cadogan, are available as a reliable source for all historians of the Second World War."[3]

The diaries have a history of their own. They exist in several variations, accretions, or selections, and have been subject to dubious editorial practices. There were in effect four earlier versions. First, the handwritten original, written in little lockable books bought for the purpose in a cut-price job lot from W. H. Smith at the outbreak of hostilities, lodged periodically with his wife, and preserved in his papers. He wrote almost every night, at work, at home, in transit, and even in retreat. He kept the diary as he rose from Commander II Corps in France (1939–40), through his rescue of the rump of the British Expeditionary Force at Dunkirk, via Southern Command during the blitz and Home Forces at the height of anxiety about invasion (1940–41), to the lonely pinnacle: Chief of the Imperial General Staff (1941–46). The second version was a kind of transcript with added commentary, "Notes for my memoirs," written out again, in full, in his own execrable hand, as a source first for his eventual biographer and then for an interim edition of the diaries; this version, and the process of its creation, may also have acted as an *aide-memoire* for Alanbrooke himself. Some of the "Notes for my memoirs" have not survived, including those on 1944–45. The third version was a typescript copy of the foregoing, confusingly known as "Notes on my life," made by Marian C. Long, research assistant to the Royal Regiment of Artillery (Alanbrooke's Alma Mater) which was commissioning the biography, in 1954–56. This version is complete, but an unholy mix of guileless titivation and guiltless mistranscription means that it differs in detail from the "Notes for my memoirs." The last version is the most famous or notorious: an artful confection of the diaries and the notes, prepared by Sir Arthur Bryant, "the Tacitus of our time," and published as *The Turn of the Tide* (1957) and *Triumph in the West* (1959).[4] Bryant made much of the fact that these books were "based" on the material furnished by Alanbrooke: the jewel, as he said, cut and set in the paste of his own prose. Exposed now to the bright light of the unexpurgated edition, it is painfully obvious that they were a travesty of the original. All of this material, Alanbrooke's and Bryant's, is now secure and available to researchers in the Liddell Hart Centre for Military Archives at King's College, London.[5] Contemplating the plethora of documentation, it sometimes seems as if each successive version tried to improve upon its predecessor, artlessly and insignificantly in Alanbrooke's case, knowingly and egregiously in Bryant's.

Alanbrooke's improvements ran to a confetti of additional punctuation (more commas especially), not always helpful; a certain modulation of the telegraphese of the original (more definite and indefinite articles); some variations in usage; and brief insertions of a contextual character (titles, appointments, physical or geographical detail). Strikingly, and honestly, he was almost never tempted to modify the tone or retouch the painting of his diary, at the time or in retrospect: that is the internal evidence of the texts. He had occasional qualms the morning after about his immoderate expression of the night before—his vituperation of the somnolent First Sea Lord in 1942, his depression after the Quebec Conference in 1943—but these were very much the exceptions that proved the rule, and no more immoderate than many other nights that troubled him not at all. Considering his provenance and profession, in fact, Alanbrooke was astonishingly uninhibited in his diaries and notes. This was true of the notorious invective, so liberally applied and so rarely retracted, sparing neither colleagues ("seldom has a Supreme Commander been more deficient in the main attributes of a Supreme Commander than Dickie Mountbatten") nor allies:

> At the end of this morning's COS [Chief of Staff] meeting I cleared the secretaries out and retained only Pug [Ismay]. I then put before the meeting my views on the very unsatisfactory state of affairs in France, with no one running the land battle. Eisenhower, though supposed to be doing so, is detached and by himself with his lady chauffeur on the golf links at Rheims — entirely detached from the war and taking practically no part in the running of the war! Matters got so bad lately that a deputation of Whiteley, Bedell Smith

and a few others [from his Headquarters] went up to tell him that
he must get down to it and RUN the war, which he said he would.
Personally I think he is incapable of running the war even if he
tries.[6]

But it was true also in ways that seem to cut closer to his irreproach-
able persona. In the most secret matter of signals intelligence, for
example, Alanbrooke was a good deal bolder than Bryant. Thirty
years before the secret was out, the diaries make repeated and explicit reference to "intercepts," not to mention "the organization for
breaking down ciphers" (Bletchley Park), and the notes call attention to the remarkably detailed intelligence being provided. None of
this survived Bryant's blue pencil.[7] In his correspondence, too, Alanbrooke consistently broke the taboos of the time, to the evident disapproval of his straitlaced official biographer, General Sir David
Fraser. "Somehow the work has not decreased much," the CIGS
wrote to a friend shortly after the war was won, "but the responsibility is far less. I had some nasty moments wondering whether the
Boche would forestall us with the Atomic Bomb and snatch victory
from under our noses."[8]

Bryant's improvements are another matter altogether. Arthur
Bryant was a professional, as he did not shrink from reminding his
public. "In this volume even more than in its predecessor," he announced in *Triumph in the West:*

> I have based my book on the diary, quoting from it, wherever pos-
> sible, in preference to Alanbrooke's post-war commentary or my
> own narrative. The latter has been used only to set his daily jot-
> tings into the general framework of a global war, many of whose
> events he took for granted and whose details the ordinary reader
> has probably forgotten. Apart from providing this framework I
> have let the diary speak for itself. It has not been possible, of
> course, to print it in its entirety. Like all diaries it contains much
> that is repetitive or day-to-day routine of little general interest. It
> contains, too, as any diary must, material that might hurt personal
> feelings without adding anything essential to the record. Such
> passages, however, are less frequent than some reviewers of *The
> Turn of the Tide* assumed from the omission marks with which, out
> of a historian's habit, I indicated every omitted passage. I have
> therefore been less pedantic and have only used omission marks
> where substantial or important passages are missing.[9]

From this farrago two points only need detain us. In the first place,
any author who claims to let his subject "speak for himself" is claiming either too little or too much, usually for a purpose; and the usual
purpose is the not-so-subtle aggrandizement of the subject.[10] In this

instance there can be little doubt about Bryant's overall conception, which was of Alanbrooke as Happy Warrior in a sort of sea-faring Elizabethan-Wellingtonian tradition. "In one of my chapters in *The Age of Elegance,* I called Wellington 'Neptune's General,'" he wrote with typical address to his subject, "and the title might apply as aptly to you."[11] In the second place, Bryant's habits most definitely did not include pedantry—or, to give it another name, scrupulosity—as to omissions, excisions, or alterations in Alanbrooke's text, which are legion, and silent, throughout both volumes.

There is one complaint against Bryant, however, that can be dropped as misleading, at least in part. He is traditionally held responsible for over-egging the pudding, as the Chief of the Air Staff put it privately; that is to say for presenting Alanbrooke as the unerring master strategist, uncannily following his star, with a blue-water blueprint for winning the war in the West: the so-called Mediterranean strategy—in reality less a strategy than a straw man; or a stick used to beat Perfidious Albion, as amply represented by Pugnacious Winston. Much petted by the great and the good—one of the ironies of their association is that he was in many ways more favored than Alanbrooke—Bryant was nothing if not a shameless butterer and flatterer. On this argument he did the Happy Warrior a disservice by making him appear almost omniscient, especially by pointed comparison with his American opposite number, General George C. Marshall, and the clueless claque that surrounded him. "His plan does not go beyond just landing on the far coast!! Whether we are to play baccarat or *chemin der fer* at Le Touquet, or possibly bathe at Paris Plage is not stipulated!"[12]

Certainly Bryant presented Alanbrooke thus, but it was not his own idea. It was Alanbrooke's, as the unmediated diaries and notes serve to confirm. The vexatious presentation was in fact Alanbrooke's self-presentation, soused in Bryant's pickling panegyric. Bryant did prettify the record, as Gerhard Weinberg and other scholars have charged. Curiously enough, he had a certain authority from his subject so to do.

In documentary terms, Bryant's familiarity with the record was regrettably circumscribed. There is no evidence that he ever consulted the diaries themselves, or the handwritten "Notes for my memoirs." He appears to have worked solely from a typescript of "Notes on my life"—at two removes from the original—unwittingly incorporating the corruptions of that version straight into his own, where they happily multiplied. As the British historian Andrew Roberts has pointed out, the awful truth about Arthur Bryant is not only that he was obsequious, tendentious, and mendacious, but also remiss.[13]

The resulting volumes made a mint, nevertheless. On February 3, 1957 the *Sunday Times* began a lurid serialization of *The Turn of the Tide*. Two days later there was a star-studded book launch at the Dorchester. A first impression of 75,000 copies sold out within the month, a prelude to further vast sales in Britain and in the United States. For Alanbrooke, a man of few means, this was gravy. Reviewers, however, were not kind. The tone set by the British intellectual heavyweights was dismissive. The *Times Literary Supplement* called *The Turn of Tide* "a scrapbook"; *The Economist* thought *Triumph in the West* "neither fish nor fowl":

> The diaries, no doubt for perfectly sound reasons, are emasculated, and they have not been replaced by a mellow, reasoned autobiographical commentary. The reader can never quite catch the full tones of Lord Alanbrooke speaking. To his annoyance he finds he has to rely for many of the facts and not a few of the comments on Sir Arthur [Bryant]. Inevitably, he feels disappointed, far more so than if Lord Alanbrooke, using the diaries as his materials, had written his own account and even more so than if an editor more dispassionate and less partisan than Sir Arthur had stitched the pages of the diary together. Until the diaries can be published in full and until the confidential documents are made available, history will have to put up with this unsatisfactory compromise. . . .[14]

The almost personal sense of frustration running through these reviews was pithily expressed by the distinguished commentator Alastair Buchan in dispatching *Triumph in the West:*

> What one can legitimately complain of is that Alanbrooke himself . . . should not have addressed himself to personally reducing the wilderness of diaries and notes, which he handed over to Bryant, to a coherent set of judgements. . . . Part of his strength as CIGS clearly resided in his deep attachment to the ordinary things of life, but if he had devoted the last decade and a half to more important pursuits than becoming the definitive authority on the nesting habits of tomtits, he could have done much to enhance our own comprehension of one of the most difficult periods in our history, in a way that this book does not.[15]

Alanbrooke's priorities were not necessarily those of his reviewers. His collaboration with Bryant testifies to his essential simplicity, a quality manifest in surprising ways. For better or worse, he had placed himself in Arthur Bryant's hands. They were Bryant's books: that was the fiction or rationalization, and the professional soldier, at once proud and infirm, ceded precedence to the professional author. How this came about, why Alanbrooke, the pillar of propriety, elected to publish and be damned, what the illicit diary-keeping meant to this military diarist ("a whole little secret life over and above the other," as Sartre said of his own war diaries): these questions take us back to the very beginning of the story in September 1939.[16]

Alanbrooke wrote initially out of love and loneliness. Characteristically, he had made provision for both—hence the job lot of diaries. What he wrote was destined for his second wife, Benita Blanche Brooke, née Pelly, widow of Sir Thomas Lees. They were married in 1929, when he was forty-six, four years after his first wife had died, tragically, from an automobile accident with Alanbrooke at the wheel—a period shrouded in grief. Benita brought life. They had two small children, Kathleen and Victor (Pooks and Ti in the diary), who joined two older ones, Tom and Rosemary, from his first marriage. He loved Benita with a passion: a Gascon-Edwardian passion, a compound of his upbringing and education in Pau in the French Pyrenees, and his training and formation at "The Shop" (the Royal Military Academy Woolwich) and in the Royal Regiment of Artillery. Came September 1939, he wrote to his inamorata as he went to war. Construed as a perpetual love letter in the guise of a journal, delivered personally but sporadically at Hitler's pleasure, the diary was a form of communion, an exigent outpouring, a beacon to Benita.

The communion was at once remote and intense. In the early years it is that combination which feeds the more sustained passages of the work, exciting it, and giving it a distinctive character: part entreaty, part release. Alanbrooke's unimpeachable reputation was founded on "two qualities not readily interfusable," as Melville has it, "prudence and rigour."[17] As CIGS he could be prudent and rigorous all the long day—and it might seem, waltzing with Winston, all the long night—but not forever. In the still, small hour of duty to his diary, strong emotions welled up and spilled improvidently across the page: frustration, depression, betrayal, doubt. Keeping the diary may have begun as "just a little daily intimate talk" with his truly beloved, a function of enforced separation, but it evolved, as diaries do, into something more instinctual. It became a necessary therapy, even an offertory, for the diarist (no church-goer) was prone to thanksgiving, and, *in extremis,* prayer.

> I pray God that the decisions we arrived at may be correct,
> and that they may bear fruit.

Reflecting on this entry after the war, on the conclusion to a journey to the Western Desert to remake the command in August 1942, he wrote:

> One may be apt to overlook those ghastly moments of doubt which at times crowded in on me. Moments when one wondered whether one had weighed up situations correctly, arrived at the

right conclusion, and taken suitable action. This little short prayer of 2 lines was not just a figure of speech, it was a very real, deep felt and agonized prayer written at a moment of considerable mental and physical exhaustion at the end of 3 most memorable weeks!"[18]

Keeping the diary afforded some consolation, possibly, a measure of protection against "the melancholies, the morosities and the sadnesses of war."[19] When Alanbrooke inherited the mantle of CIGS from his friend and confessor Field Marshal Sir John Dill, as 1941 drew to its ignominious end, he was "temporarily staggered," not to say daunted, as his diary and notes movingly disclose. Except perhaps for Dill himself, no one would have known. By then the carapace was full-grown. For all his self-doubt, it protected a man who was temperamentally suited to the task he was called upon to fulfill. In a celebrated series of lectures delivered at Cambridge University just before the war began, that cerebral soldier Wavell defined the principal characteristic of "the Good General" as robustness. "Delicate mechanism is of little use in war; and this applies to the mind of the commander as well as to his body; to the spirit of an army as well as to the weapons and instruments with which it is equipped. All material of war, including the general, must have a certain solidity, a high margin over the breaking strain."[20]

"In his demanding and abrupt efficiency," offered *The Economist* appreciatively, "he knew when to scold, when to encourage, when to protect. Men admired, feared, and liked him: in that order, perhaps. He became, in peculiar, the conscience of the Army: a dark, incisive, round-shouldered, Irish eagle, the reluctant chairman of a council of war, frustrating, in selfless but far from patient service, those talents that could not otherwise but have forced him into the company of the great captains."[21] Existentially reassuring—Anthony Powell brilliantly caught "that curious electric awareness felt down to the tips of one's fingers of a given presence imparting a sense of stimulation, also the consoling thought that someone of the sort was at the top"—he presented a forbidding face to the world. His nickname in the War Cabinet Offices was an appropriate one: Colonel Shrapnel.[22] In debate his characteristic rejoinder was a bleak negative—"I flatly disagree"—accompanied by the snapping of a pencil. Alanbrooke had mettle. It was for this very quality that he was selected by Winston Churchill, who invited him to Chequers, dined him royally, interrogated him pitilessly, passed him the chalice, and tenderly wished him luck—a *modus operandi* with which he was to become excessively familiar over the next few years.

The Prime Minister's selection was not unpremeditated. Congenitally ardent, Churchill was tired of reverses and deadlocks, and tired too of the CIGS who had the misfortune to accompany them: Dilly-Dally, "the dead hand of inanition." Churchill had scrambled into supremacy in May 1940. His ambit was Elizabethan. "I myself will be your General, Judge and Rewarder of every one of your virtues in the field."[23] For some eighteen months he had been on short commons, unable to satisfy his craving. Finally, after wide inspection, he thought he had found his man. "When I thump the table and push my face towards him what does he do? Thumps the table harder and glares back at me. I know these Brookes—stiff-necked Ulstermen and there's no one worse to deal with than that!"[24] What Churchill craved was disputation. Disputation is what he got: more, much more, than he bargained for. That is the tale told by the Alanbrooke diaries—one might almost say enacted in the Alanbrooke diaries—a tale of schism and self-control in the secret heart of the machine. Churchill knew the Brookes of yesteryear: "the friends of my early military life."[25] How well he ever knew the one with whom he was yoked in harness for the greater part of the Second World War is a matter for speculation and skepticism.

High rank, Alanbrooke believed, carried a heavy obligation. The lacerations must not show. His performance of public impregnability was precisely that: a performance for others, just as Churchill performed the indomitable chauvinist-in-chief, complete with gesture and growl, and more props. Apart from Dill (excommunicated to Washington), who knew at first hand the purgatory of a Chief of Staff, Alanbrooke's only outlet was his diary, as he was at pains to convey. Ever since the appearance of *The Turn of the Tide* in 1957 this is the accepted answer to the question of motivation: a kind of psychological safety valve—the diaries as diatribe.[26] It is also the plea entered in mitigation, by Alanbrooke and his apologists, for their worst excesses: that is to say, for their shocking candor about Winston, the greatest Englishman, deep in his black dog dotage; about Ike, the chateau general, and then, lo and behold, the chateau President; and, not least, about Colonel Shrapnel himself, the charnel house of his criticism, and his mental state.

DOUBTLESS THE DIARIES ARE AN INVITING TARGET for such an explanation. The entry for July 6, 1944, for example, an entry heavily (and silently) censored by Bryant, records one late-night, late-war passage of arms:

> At 10 pm we had a frightful meeting with Winston which lasted till 2 am!! It was quite the worst we have had with him. He was very tired as a result of his speech in the House concerning the flying bombs, he had tried to recuperate with drink. As a result he was in

a maudlin, bad tempered, drunken mood, ready to take offence at anything, suspicious of everybody, and in a highly vindictive mood against the Americans. In fact so vindictive that his whole outlook on strategy was warped. I began by having a bad row with him. He began to abuse Monty because operations were not going faster, and apparently Eisenhower had said he was over cautious. I flared up and asked him if he could not trust his generals for 5 minutes instead of continuously abusing them and belittling them. He said he never did such a thing. I then reminded him that during two whole Monday Cabinets in front of a large gathering of Ministers, he had torn Alexander to shreds for his lack of imagination and leadership in continually attacking at Cassino. He was furious with me, but I hope it may do some good in the future.[27]

Despite its absolutist phraseology, the flavor of this entry is not untypical of the diary of that period, excepting only that it omits Alanbrooke's intermittent speculation that the Prime Minister, surely, could not go on like this—that Winston might not make it after all. The unspeakable corollary of the unspoken thought was that a swift death would be a several blessing, to his memory, to his coadjutants, and to the conduct of the war. Happily or otherwise, Churchill recovered, or was repaired, for a while, and so too was the professional relationship. Alanbrooke ruefully recanted. The old man of war was mightier than he thought. But the diarist had wished him dead, and something had dissolved in the process.

Alanbrooke was brought to such a pitch of aggravation by the cumulation of the war. After the alarums and excursions of 1942 and 1943 he was exhausted, as he frequently remarked. His diary fairly palpitates with exasperation at obtuse politicians, obstructive Americans, obstreperous Russians, obmutescent Chinese—to say nothing of the enemy—and, in a class of his own, Winston. The relationship between those two intimate adversaries changed over time. Churchill appointed Alanbrooke, in effect, as his minister-counselor. Taking the measure of his situation, Alanbrooke appointed himself Churchill's nanny, just as he appointed himself Montgomery's guardian. Uniquely, in each case, he was accepted in that role by both of these infantile tyrants, for his acumen, but above all for his rectitude. After two tempestuous years of it, however, Alanbrooke was sick of nannying. What sickened him was not so much that the spoiled child never learned grand strategy—Churchill's visionary vagabondage remained forever a mystery to the earthbound Alanbrooke—rather that, far from growing up, as nanny naively hoped, he appeared to regress, temperamentally, the longer the war went on. For Alanbrooke, this was at bottom a moral issue. By the winter of 1943–44, fuelled by a cocktail of medicine and alcohol, Churchill's moral degradation was such that he seemed no longer master of himself. Here the two men parted company. Self-mastery was Alanbrooke's cardinal precept. It is no coincidence that the strongest language in his diaries (invariably censored by Bryant) relates to Churchill's laxity.

To read the diary as a diatribe, a rage against the puerile and the pot-valiant, is very natural. But it is reductive. Alanbrooke's diary served a larger purpose. It was not simply an instrument of aggravation. Like André Gide's journal, to which it bears a passing resemblance, it was essentially a tool for recovering possession of himself—a means of self-mastery and survival, a mode of moral life.[28] Like Gide, too, Alanbrooke furnishes only a "mutilated me," a diary of telegrams and anger, the war of the outer world.[29] His children, especially the children of his first marriage, are mostly absent; even his wife, the ritual you, the witness of that life, becomes almost unmentionable, to be invoked only in the hushed tones of holy worship. In the everyday drama of the war diary their place is usurped by mewling ministers, the palimpsest of plans, and the high wire act of Churchill's traveling circus.

In the final analysis both Churchill and Alanbrooke were disposed to underrate each other, Moran thought, on account of their own limitations. In council they were an indispensable complement and foil; but it was a carefully bounded cohabitation, a marriage of convenience for the duration of the war. The doctor once asked Churchill, "'Don't you think Brooke is pretty good at his job?' There was rather a long pause. 'He has a flair for the business,' he grunted. That was all he would concede."[30] In his own notebooks Elias Canetti points a distinction between *illuminating* and *ordering* minds.[31] That was the PM and the CIGS. Intellectually and affectively, they were out of phase. Churchill's war memoirs, that enigmatic touchstone of his feelings, are eloquently silent on the subject of his relationship with the Brooke who really counted, who appears, if at all, as a stock character in a melodrama with one name above the title, bearing disappointments "with soldierly dignity" and rendering services "of the highest order." Alanbrooke's unexampled achievement is reduced to long service and good conduct, and dispatched in a paragraph. Unlike Churchill's "true comrade," Admiral Pound, he is not favored with oratory or eulogy. He is merely part of the retinue. It is evident that the pious motto of the work—"in victory magnanimity"—did not extend to Churchill's most intimate adversary, the CIGS and chairman of the Chiefs of Staff committee.[32]

Churchill's memoirs appeared, seriatim, over the years between 1948 and 1954. Alanbrooke read them carefully, and marked them well. He noted that Churchill put too much emphasis on the failure of the 1st Armoured Division in the Western Desert in 1941–42, rather than on the failure of the Commander-in-Chief, Auchinleck, to select appropriately for his senior staff officers. He corrected the account of their inaugural altercation, on the telephone, adrift in France, in June 1940. He revisited his own crushing disappointment when, in August 1943, the Prime Minister summarily withdrew the proposal he had made and repeated several times before, that Alanbrooke himself should have Supreme Command of Operation Overlord, and offered it instead to the Americans, for their gratification, and in cool anticipation of their preponderance. Churchill's exculpatory account of that inglorious episode was indeed as summary as the action itself, and it is clear that Alanbrooke was deeply wounded by it.

> "Not for one moment did he realize what this meant to me. He offered no sympathy, no regrets at having to change his mind, and dealt with the matter as if it were of minor importance! The only reference to my feelings in his official history . . . is that I "bore the great disappointment with soldierly dignity."

The involuntary deprivation hurt all the more, as Churchill well knew, because the CIGS had nobly foregone the offer of the Middle East Command a year earlier, feeling (rightly) that a substitute nanny would be hard to find. In the interim the bells had tolled a famous victory. Did he ever practice signing Alanbrooke of Alamein on his blotter, as did Montgomery of that ilk? It would have made a pretty handle. Self-possession was sorely tried.

Keen as it was—keener than we think—disappointment was not the vital spark. Alanbrooke's basic objection to Winston and his works centered on deprivation of a different sort. This was the highly combustible matter of recognition. It had been smoldering for some time. A diary entry in September 1944 contained one outburst:

> We had another meeting with Winston at 12 noon. He was again in a most unpleasant mood. Produced the most ridiculous arguments to prove that operations could be speeded up so as to leave us an option till December before having to withdraw any forces from Europe! He knows no details, has only got half the picture in his mind, talks absurdities and makes my blood boil to listen to his nonsense. I find it hard to remain civil. . . .
>
> And with it all no recognition hardly at all for those who help him except the occasional crumb intended to prevent the dog from straying too far from the table. Never have I admired and de-

spised a man simultaneously to the same extent. Never have such opposite extremes been combined in the same human being.[33]

An entry in January 1945 was less agitated and more specific:

> We had a fairly full COS which completed our record week for the maximum number of items handled in one week since war started!!! It is a strange thing what a vast part the COS takes in the running of the war and how little it is known or its functions appreciated. The average man in the street has never heard of it. Any limelight for it could not fail to slightly diminish the PM's halo! This may perhaps account for the fact that he has never yet given it the slightest word of credit in public![34]

How different it might have been if Churchill had delivered a more generous testament. As it was, to paraphrase Balfour's celebrated remark about his earlier memoirs, Winston wrote an enormous book about himself and called it *The Second World War*. The impact of that unscrupulously egocentric enterprise on his former CIGS was profound. "Winston's books hardened Alan's heart considerably," reflected Cynthia Brookeborough (wife of his cousin Basil), a shrewd and sympathetic witness, after asking Alanbrooke about it.

With appropriately tragedic irony for one whose whole life was triumph and tragedy, Churchill was the agent of his own nemesis. The weight of post-war commentary, much of it instinctively Churchillian, is that Winston was shocked and distressed by the publication of Alanbrooke's diaries, even as emasculated by Bryant. He may well have been.[35] Winston was wronged, the Churchillians impute, and his turncoat table-thumper was the culprit.[36] It is less often remarked that Alanbrooke was baffled and pained by the publication of Churchill's memoirs. In fact, his feelings mirrored his reaction to their face-to-face encounters, writ large in the midnight hours. His response was the same. He glared back. Publication of the diaries was a continuation of disputation by other means. It was a courageous step, though the courage was only half-conscious. It added new meaning to the recovery of self-possession: it was in effect a recovery of history—his story—the diaries as deposition. Churchill might have known what was coming, and perhaps he did. Moran was with him when he heard for the first time that Alanbrooke was going into print. "Winston looked up quickly. 'Is it a violent attack on me?'"[37]

As has been noted, a more subtle, not to say insidious, variant on the wronged Churchill was the injured Alanbrooke. "The more I read *The Turn of the Tide*," Lord Ismay wrote to his master a month after the book's publication, "the more certain I am that Bryant has done Brookie an injury almost as grievous as Henry Wilson's widow did to her husband."[38] The reference was to a predecessor CIGS (assassinated by the IRA), whose posthumously published diaries, edited and mediated in two reminiscent volumes, exposed the diarist as foolishly misguided and, worse still, actively disloyal.[39] Ismay himself peddled this line of self-injury assiduously, and there is a perceptible strain of it in contemporary reviews. In the overheated atmosphere of the time, both variants were damaging. When the book came out Alanbrooke sought to mollify by sending Churchill a copy personally inscribed, "To Winston from Brookie":

> With unbounded admiration, profound respect, and deep affection built up in our 5 years close association during the war. Some of the extracts from my diaries in this book may contain criticisms, and references to differences between us. I hope you will remember that these were written at the end of long and exhausting days, often in the small hours of the morning, and refer to momentary daily impressions. These casual day to day impressions bear no relation to the true feelings of deep-rooted friendship and admiration which bound me so closely to you throughout the war. I look upon the privilege of having served you in war as the greatest honour destiny has bestowed on me.

Churchill's reply was muted but unmistakable. "Thank you for sending me a copy of your book. On the whole I think I am against publishing day-to-day diaries written under the stress of events so soon afterwards. However, I read it with great interest, and I am very much obliged to you for what you say in your inscription." His darling Clementine was less restrained. "Alanbrooke," she exclaimed, "wants to have it both ways."[40]

Two years later Bryant returned to the fray with the effusive apologetics prefacing *Triumph in the West:*

> Some have questioned whether a diary so frank and revealing as Lord Alanbrooke's should have been published in the lifetime of its author. It was certainly not intended to be, for after his retirement he persistently refused to write his war memoirs or to allow any book to be written about him until after his death. Had others preserved the same silence the public would have had to wait many more years before his diaries saw the light of day or his part in the war became known. But during the first post-war decade a succession of widely read memoirs by American war leaders and Service chiefs appeared, presenting a very different view to Brooke's of the events which had brought about victory and reflecting on the judgement and competence both of himself and of the British commanders who served under him.

During this period the six volumes of Sir Winston Churchill's *Second World War* also appeared, giving in great, though not always complete, detail Sir Winston's version of the events in which he and Alanbrooke were so intimately and, after 1941, inseparably associated. The latter's viewpoint and the extremely important story of what he sought to achieve, and how, were thus in danger of being obscured or forgotten.[41]

This was a rearguard action, plainly enough, and not entirely successful. Bryant had been warned. P. J. Grigg, the downright former Secretary of State for War, read *The Turn of the Tide* in manuscript. "I don't suppose Winston or his toadies will like it very much but I hope that you will not make any major excisions or allow Norman Brook [the Cabinet Secretary] to frighten you with the Official Secrets Act, official etiquette and so forth." Grigg was wise in the ways of the velvet throttle. The Cabinet Secretary's considered response was an admonition exquisite in sentience and syntax alike. "I could have wished that the book was not to be published in Sir Winston Churchill's lifetime. And I cannot refrain from asking what steps are to be taken to prepare him for the kind of publicity which (if I am not mistaken) it will receive."[42] The question was left hanging in the air. But not for long. Innocent or overconfident, neither Alanbrooke nor Bryant was prepared for the furore of serialization or the odium of publication. In hindsight Alanbrooke was too passive for too long; no doubt Bryant should have known better. Despite an undercurrent of nervy anticipation both men failed to comprehend what they had done. By defacing a legend they had transgressed a norm. The legend, moreover, was still warm. His people were perplexed, and his friends were unforgiving. Alanbrooke may always have been beyond the Prime Ministerial pale. Now there was no way back.

Recognition did not evade Alanbrooke altogether, however. After the war, in time-honored fashion, he was created first a Baron (under Churchill's dispensation) and then, in tacit acknowledgement of a certain parsimony, a Viscount (under Attlee's); and in the Birthday Honours List for 1946, His Majesty was pleased to confer upon him the Order of Merit. This last, royal and select, was especially gratifying. Elevation to the peerage, on the other hand, was not an unalloyed pleasure. "We finished our COS with a private meeting discussing future of COS, our own successors and probable dates of our departures. . . . We then discussed the cost of becoming a Baron. Apparently I can't get out of it under £200 which appalls me."[43] The first Lord Alanbrooke was a noble pauper. His gratuity was a miserly £311 (Haig's was £100,000); his half-pay—a Field Marshal never retires—"inconsiderable." In the privacy of his diary he coveted the

Governor-Generalship of Canada, a position not merely dignified but remunerated, and was bitterly disappointed (once again) when it went instead to the effortless Alexander, at the behest of the King—so Churchill said. Correct to the end, Alanbrooke sported his stiff upper lip. "Alexander came to lunch and I had a chance to ask him afterwards how he liked the idea of the Canadian Governorship. He was delighted with the thought of it, and well he might be."[44] After a brief struggle he sold his house and moved into the converted gardener's cottage. "[I] am looking for some means of making money as I am broke (and forced to sell off bird books)," he wrote piteously to his confidante Cynthia Brookeborough in January 1946. "I hope to find something in the line of a directorship which will help me along."[45]

Apart from the precious bird books—a 45-volume set that realized around £3,000—he did have one undercapitalized asset: the Alanbrooke diaries.[46] How far he was aware of this, and how soon, it is difficult to be sure. Bryant spelt it out for him towards the beginning of their association, in 1954, when they were discussing the division of the spoils. "One thing to bear in mind is that if the book [*The Turn of the Tide*] should prove a success on this major scale [some £60,000, a colossal sum]—and Billy Collins [the publisher] feels that it well might—it would create a tremendous interest in the rest of your Diary and Notes and so increase their potential capital value, for in this volume we should only be using a very small proportion of the whole."[47] There were cues to be picked up well before that, however, not only from the cold war of memoirs which broke out almost immediately open hostilities were concluded, but even as the hot war was being waged. As early as April 1944, for example, Alanbrooke's incorrigible charge Montgomery mentioned the existence of his own secret diary in an interview with the American journalist John Gunther. When Gunther remarked that it would surely be an essential source for historians, Montgomery asked whether it would therefore be worth money one day. Gunther suggested a figure of at least $100,000. Once this had been converted into pounds sterling for him, Montgomery is supposed to have grinned and said, "Well, I guess I won't die in the poor house after all."[48] The pecuniary answer to the question of motivation is perhaps too easily overlooked, even among the monks of war.

Brother Brooke for his part, monkish in many ways, not least in his extreme self-containment, was happy to quit the monastery as often as he decently could. "Throughout my life," he wrote in 1953, "I have always held it as essential to cultivate some engrossing interest besides one's profession, to which one could turn for refreshment and rest whenever the exigencies of one's work admitted. In war the value of such a habit becomes more evident than ever. I sometimes doubt whether I should have retained my sanity through those long years of the last world war had I not had an interest capable of temporarily absorbing my thoughts, and of obliterating the war, even if only for short spells when circumstances permitted."[49] In other words, unlike the monomaniac Montgomery, Alanbrooke had a hinterland. His hinterland was populated with birds. Alanbrooke was one of the pioneers of wild life photography, whose fine appreciation and sheer determination made admiring experts gape. Throughout the war his search for bird books was unremitting—he seems to have been foiled on V.E. Day itself.

"Viscount Alanbrooke, I am quite sure, would prefer to be remembered as an ornithologist than as a soldier." Raymond Fletcher's verdict may have been a mischievous one, yet he may not have been far wrong. At sixty-eight, Alanbrooke stood for many hours knee-deep in water in the Camargue to film flamingoes. At seventy-four, he climbed a tall pylon hide on an expedition to the Coto Donana to glimpse the Spanish Imperial Eagle. For all the pleasure he may have taken in his professional mastery, his only real fulfillment was his recreation—his re-creation, as he said.

In truth, he was an unhappy warrior. That was his merit. It is what separated him from Churchill, ultimately, and from so many of his peers. Alanbrooke was always a little foreign to his fellows in arms. Unlike Vigny, he did not suffer from the disease of military ardor. Nor do his diaries. That is their rarity, and their fascination. "Let victory belong to those who made war without liking it."[50]

Fall Semester 2001

1. Major-General Sir John Kennedy, *The Business of War* (London, 1957), pp. 290–91.

2. Anthony Powell, *The Military Philosophers* (London, 1971), pp. 57–58.

3. Simon Jenkins, "Wartime Heroes Who Make Pygmies of Us All," *The Times,* May 18, 2001; Michael Howard, "Chained to the Chariot of a Gifted Lunatic," *Spectator,* June 2, 2001; see also Michael Carver, "Biting the Bulldog," *Literary Review* (July 2001); cf. David Dilks, ed., *The Diaries of Sir Alexander Cadogan* (London, 1971).

4. Arthur Bryant, *The Turn of the Tide* (London, 1957) and *Triumph in the West* (London, 1959); "The Tacitus of our Time," *Tatler,* Feb. 20, 1957.

5. The original handwritten diaries and the post-war typescript "Notes on my life" are in the Alanbrooke Papers, 5/1/1–12 and 5/2/13–31 respectively, housed at the Liddell Hart Centre for Military Archives, King's College, London. All subsequent citations from these papers unless indicated.

6. Diary, Nov. 24, 1944, p. 628, a passage that caused widespread offense in the United States when first published, even shorn of the last sentence (suppressed by Bryant).

7. Diary, for example Oct. 16, 17, and 24, 1940; notes to Aug. 18, 1942, in Alex Danchev and Daniel Todman, eds., *War Diaries 1939–1945* (Berkeley, 2001), pp. 116, 119, 309. Bryant coyly substituted "reports" for "intercepts," or excised the passage altogether.

8. Alanbrooke to Major Nigel Aitken, Aug. 26, 1945 (11/7); David Fraser, *Alanbrooke* (London, 1982), p. 280.

9. Bryant, *Triumph,* pp. 15–16.

10. As for example in the parallel case of the official biography of Winston Churchill, where a similar claim lies at the very foundation of the work. See Alex Danchev, "Dilly-Dally, Or Having the Last Word," *Journal of Contemporary History,* 22 (1987), pp. 21–44.

11. Bryant to Alanbrooke, Nov. 30, 1954, quoted in Bryant's "Epilogue" to Fraser, *Alanbrooke,* p. 544.

12. Diary, Apr. 15, 1942, *War Diaries,* p. 249.

13. Andrew Roberts, "Patriotism: The Last Refuge of Sir Arthur Bryant," in his *Eminent Churchillians* (London, 1994), pp. 287–322.

14. "At Churchill's Right Hand," *Times Literary Supplement,* Mar. 8, 1957; "The Other End of the Phone," *The Economist,* Nov. 7, 1959.

15. Alastair Buchan, "The Over-Sell," *Encounter,* 78 (1960), p. 88.

16. Cf. Jean-Paul Sartre, *War Diaries: Notebooks from a Phoney War,* Quintin Hoare, trans. (London, 1984).

17. Herman Melville, *Billy Budd: Sailor* (Oxford, 1997 edn.), p. 335.

18. Dedication in second diary, begun Apr. 12, 1940; diary and notes, Aug. 24, 1942, *War Diaries,* p. 314.

19. Jean-Paul Sartre, *Modern Times: Selected Non-Fiction,* Robin Buss, trans. (Penguin, 2000), p. xxv.

20. Lord Wavell, *The Good Soldier* (Penguin, 1948), p. 5. "It is sometimes said that British war material is unnecessarily solid," he adds, "and the same possibly is apt to be true of their generals. But we are certainly right to leave a good margin."

21. "Statesman and Soldier," *The Economist,* Feb. 23, 1957.

22. Powell, *Military Philosophers,* pp. 188–89; Alex Danchev, ed., *Establishing the Anglo-American Alliance: The Diaries of Brigadier Vivian Dykes* (London, 1990), p. 13.

23. Elizabeth I, speech to the troops at Tilbury on the approach of the Spanish Armada, Aug. 9, 1588, in Simon Schama, *A History of Britain* (London, 2000), p. 388.

24. Nye note, n.d., in Anthony Harrison, *Archie Nye* (privately published, London, 1980), p. 12.

25. Winston S. Churchill, *Second World War* (5 Vols, London, 1948–1953), Vol. II, p. 233.

26. Cf. Bryant, *Triumph,* pp. 36–42.

27. Diary, July 6, 1944, *War Diaries,* pp. 566–67; cf. Bryant, *Triumph,* pp. 229–30.

28. Cf. André Gide, *Journals 1889–1949,* Justin O'Brien, trans. (Penguin, 1967).

29. Gide, *Journals,* Jan. 26, 1939.

30. Lord Moran, *Winston Churchill: The Struggle for Survival, 1940–1965* (London, 1966), pp. 712 ff.

31. Elias Canetti, *The Human Province,* Joachim Neugroschel, trans. (New York, 1978), p. 200.

32. Churchill, *Second World War,* Vol. I, p. 321; Vol. II, p. 234; Vol. V, pp. 76, 145–46.

33. Diary, Jan. 10, 1945, *War Diaries,* p. 590; censored in Bryant, *Triumph,* pp. 270–71.

34. Diary, Jan. 20, 1945, *War Diaries,* pp. 647–48; excised by Bryant.

35. The fullest first-hand account is in Moran, *Winston Churchill,* pp. 716–17; echoed, among others, in John Colville, *Footprints in Time* (Salisbury, 1984), p. 188. "Triumph and Tragedy" is the sub-title of the sixth and last volume of Churchill's memoirs.

36. Churchill's official biography contributes to this vein of commentary a notably partisan attack on the diaries and a grace-note on the wronged Winston, "generous as usual." Martin Gilbert, *Never Despair: Winston S. Churchill 1945–65* (London, 1988), pp. 1232–33.

37. Moran, *Winston Churchill,* p. 716.

38. Ismay to Churchill, Mar. 5, 1957, in Gilbert, *Never Despair,* p. 1232.

39. Major-General Sir C. E. Callwell, *Field Marshal Sir Henry Wilson* (London, 1927).

40. Inscription and reply in Gilbert, *Never Despair,* pp. 1232–33; Clementine in Moran, *Winston Churchill,* p. 717.

41. Bryant, *Triumph,* pp. 25–26. Alanbrooke died in 1963.

42. Grigg and Brooke to Bryant, Sept. 16 and 18, 1956 (12/3); Bryant, "Epilogue" to Fraser, *Alanbrooke,* p. 558.

43. Diary, Aug. 23, 1945, *War Diaries,* p. 720.

44. Diary, July 4, 16 and 17, 1945, *War Diaries,* pp. 702 and 705–06; Bryant, *Triumph,* pp. 536–37; Fraser, *Alanbrooke,* p. 514.

45. Alanbrooke to Lady Brookeborough, Jan. 16, 1946 (11/9).

46. On the purchase and sale of the bird books (a matter of no small consequence for Alanbrooke) see diary and notes, June 22, 1943 and Apr. 11, 1946.

47. Bryant to Alanbrooke, Dec. 24, 1954 (12/1).

48. *Sunday Chronicle,* Apr. 16, 1944; Introductory Note to Montgomery Papers, Imperial War Museum, London.

49. Foreword to David Armitage Bannerman, *The Birds of the British Isles* (Edinburgh, 1953), p. xiii.

50. André Malraux, quoted in Sartre, *Modern Times,* p. 293.

11

The Strange Death of Puritan England, 1914–1945

S. J. D. GREEN

In 1935, at the very height of the Abyssinian crisis, as diplomatic relations between His Majesty's government and Mussolini's dictatorship soured and talk of League sanctions against Il Duce's regime charged the international atmosphere, an imaginative Italian journalist called upon his fellow countrymen to defend their new Roman Empire—simultaneously to take a principled stand against "perfidious Albion"—by collectively desisting forthwith from all such "pernicious British habits as tea-drinking, snobbery, golf-playing, Puritanism, clean-shaving, pipe-smoking, bridge-playing and that inexplicable apathy towards women" which so characterized the Anglo-Saxon male.[1] Whether his exhortation would ever have proved a sufficient basis for an effective modern imperial strategy may be doubted. But that it described widespread foreign views of the general character of Italy's newly intransigent enemy need not be questioned. Indeed, many in Britain itself would probably have acknowledged its positive description, even if they would have repudiated the normative judgement on their collective public persona. Yet just eight years later, with the allies on the verge of victory over what unexpectedly proved to be the weakest of the axis powers, Archbishop William Temple, Primate of All England, essayed a very different, if no less flattering, portrait of his compatriots. These were no celibate killjoys. On the contrary, they were a people increasingly characterized by a distressing capacity for sexual "self-indulgence." Nor did they maintain appropriate ethical standards in other aspects of life. Instead, they displayed an ever "easier common . . . morality."

In fact, through their perverse toleration of what had by then become a "positively rampant culture . . . of dishonesty," they had
degenerated to a point where domestic behaviour threatened to
"injure . . . the broader . . . war-effort itself."[2]

Could so much have changed so quickly? Amongst the English?
Probably not. After all, progressive prelate as he might have been,
Temple was still a Churchman. And this at a time when Anglican dignitaries still displayed a powerful inclination towards ethical nostalgia. Yet the censorious cleric was scarcely alone in observing a profound alteration in the moral tone of English life during the years of
total war. Indeed, by contemporary standards his was an unusually
subtle analysis, balancing criticism with praise, actually extolling the
"magnificent" spirit which the country had so recently displayed "at
least in some respects," whilst nevertheless insisting upon the necessity for wholesale "religious recovery" in others.[3] In a different way,
Fascism's ludicrous apologist at least succeeded in directing his An-
glophobic rage in the approximate direction of an altogether more
serious dimension of early twentieth-century European social criticism. This was the science of Anglo-Saxon studies; more specifically,
the tradition of scholarly enquiry into the English character: causes
and consequences.[4]

In an early essay on "political psychology," the distinguished
French social scientist, Emile Boutmy defined that genus in what
he took to be a unique, that is a nationally peculiar, capacity for
efficient—disciplined and galvanizing but also imaginatively constricting—self-control. He traced this quality to a peculiar form of
Christianity that informed the "national will." This he identified as "a
Protestantism of the most pronounced type."[5] Tapping into much
the same interpretative vein, Wilhelm Dibelius, Professor of English
at the University of Berlin, isolated a "religious force of incompara-
ble intensity" that, he believed, "dominated the English soul." He
called it "Puritanism." And he insisted that: "its life forms affect . . .
the entire nation from top to bottom . . . through aristocracy [to]
bourgeoisie and even proletariat . . . excepting [in fact] only those
of . . . the very lowest social grade.[6]

Influential Englishmen concurred. In 1923, J. C. C. Davidson,
then Chairman of the Conservative Party, wrote to a junior colleague, F. S. Jackson, assuring his doubting subordinate that "Puritanism" was something which "flowed" through an "English[man's]
blood."[7] Moreover, through every Englishman's blood; if Boutmy
had noted that its effects were "the monopoly neither of dissenters
. . . nor . . . protestants," Davidson went further still, suggesting that
its blessings were not even confined "to church or chapel-goers."[8]

That may have been true. Young Frank Leavis—no natural admirer of High Tories—proudly recalled that a "fierce protestant conscience . . . burned" through his father Harry. It struck him as in no way remarkable that this life-giving flame should have been entirely "divorced from any orthodox religious outlet."[9] And Harry, pianomaker and radical, was at least respectable. Yet the spell of Puritanism extended to the Edwardian libertines. Nothing else can quite explain Maynard Keynes's depiction of Bloomsbury as a "group of idealists . . . in the English puritan tradition," that is, men and women above all concerned "with the salvation of their souls."[10]

Perhaps the very elasticity of native understandings encouraged foreigners to believe in the apparent indestructibility of the phenomenon. Certainly, few outside observers noticed much change in characteristic English attitudes up to 1945. True, such survey material as then existed suggested that the natives had become even less of a church-going people during the intervening decades, but as French journalist, Pierre Maillaud, argued, that counted for little. For him, Attlee's England remained not merely a "Christian country," but a Protestant land. "Puritanism," he insisted, still "ran right through [it]."[11]

However, many locals now begged to differ. By the end of the Second World War, they had begun to notice something fundamentally different—indeed, recently altered—in collective moral life. To be sure, the England they observed still remained a Christian culture in some vague "ethical sense."[12] But it was no longer a puritan society. About this change, some were not merely sure but actually glad. Decrying the "prudish ascetic[ism]" that he took to be both characteristic of the type and alien to "the English people proper," George Orwell rejoiced that by 1947 "Puritanism" was in terminal decline amongst them, effectively reduced to the despised ranks of "small traders and manufacturers."[13] Would that his mind's eye had transported him to Councillor Roberts's grocer's shop in Grantham.[14] Others were content to describe their own liberation. Bitterly recounting "that denial of life" proclaimed in the "deplorable . . . Puritanism" of his Cornish Sunday School, A. L. Rowse ruefully remarked upon the "years which it had taken him to recover" from the insistent "effort to be good" that the teaching there had instilled.[15] We can rejoice in the knowledge that he succeeded.[16]

More subtle critics neither declaimed over the corpse nor gloated by the graveside. They did not, however, doubt the significance of what had happened. Attempting "a contemporary . . . perspective" on the "character of England," Ernest Barker noted the continuing presence of "the puritan within us." He even hazarded a guess that it would, in all probability, never "entirely leave us." But he contended still more forcefully that this stern taskmaster no longer represented "the only thing within us." More: it was no longer even the most important aspect of English ethical existence.[17] That view found widespread corroboration amongst subsequent commentators. So much so that by the time John Marlowe attempted perhaps the first self-conscious history of *The Puritan Tradition in English Life* less than a decade later, it had become axiomatic among the thinking classes that English Puritanism was a thing of the past.[18]

That view may have contained an element of wishful thinking, but it was grounded in many of the most basic realities of post-1945 life. For all the material austerity that necessity had forced upon them, the British, but most especially the English, were by then becoming a *culturally* permissive people.[19] This was true of their sexual habits. Naturally, these were not yet especially adventurous. An outbreak of bigamy failed to survive the years of hostilities.[20] Still, they were increasingly forgiving, at least about serial monogamy. A fundamental change in prevailing attitudes to the sanctity of marriage unmistakably outlived the re-establishment of peace. In 1913, there were just 577 divorces in England and Wales. In 1947, there were 60,000.[21] Injudicious wartime romance accounted for only a small part of that increase. In fact, the figure had begun to rise as early as 1920. It more than doubled during the years to 1940.[22] It has never really stopped rising since.[23] With such numbers came a certain moral leeway. The sure road to public ruin up to 1914, divorce was divested of much of its social stigma over the following thirty years. A "guilty party," George Riddell, was raised to the peerage in 1921, albeit in the teeth of opposition from George VI.[24] An innocent one, Josiah Wedgwood, was appointed to Cabinet in 1924; both were firsts.[25] Of course, there were limits to inter-war liberalism in this respect. Edward VIII all too obviously discovered them. Harold Macmillan preferred not to test their bounds.[26] But when Antony Eden dissolved his marriage in 1947, he did so in the reasonable hope that this would not prevent his eventual assumption of the premiership. And about that anyway, he was eventually proved correct.[27]

Then there was the question of drink. The Victorians had continually baulked at the possibility of their own "noble experiment."[28] But the idea of a "dry England" survived amongst the wilder passions of Edwardian liberalism.[29] And with the outbreak of the First World War, it entered into what one contemporary political commentator, David Willoughby, called the "borderlands of the practical."[30] Strict licensing laws, first introduced ostensibly to prevent interruptions of production, remained a long-term legacy of the conflict.[31] The nationalization—public houses and all—of the whole "brewing interest" was seriously discussed in cabinet throughout the spring of 1915.[32] Eventually thwarted in that plan, Lloyd George still persuaded the King to pledge himself not "to touch another drop of alcohol until the end of the war."[33] Denied her daily drop of Moselle, Queen Mary lamented, "we have been carted." All the same, their reluctant example proved mightily influential. It was quickly followed by Kitchener, then in short order by Haldane, and Runciman.[34] Bonar Law was a lifelong abstainer anyway.[35] With the removal of Asquith in 1916, the coalition cabinet became a more self-consciously abstemious administration than any to preside over this nation before or since. But that proved to be the sum of it. There were no more attempts at regulation, still less schemes for public ownership, and Britain fought the Second World War thoroughly well-oiled. Not only did a prodigious imbiber preside over national fortunes from 1940, he inspired a people by then officially guaranteed its favorite tipple.[36] The announcement of rationing on November 30, 1939 specifically excluded beer. National morale was further uplifted by a "helpful intervention from the brewing industry," just two weeks later, assuring armed forces and civilians alike that barley stocks were "ample" for the foreseeable future.[37] So they proved, right up to the bacchanalian revelries of May 1945.

Above all loomed the matter of the Lord's Day. Or rather, it once had. Certainly, nothing so defined Victorian Puritanism as its commitment to the Sabbath. This was because that commitment was so wide-ranging. Sunday was conceived not only as a day of worship, but also as a moment for domestic fulfillment, even as a simple opportunity for rest. As such, its spiritual promise precluded not only paid labor, but also private amusement.[38] Otherwise perfectly rational people took such obligations to extraordinary lengths. Some for specifically religious reasons: Viscount Simon remembered how his father had been brought up "to shave . . . last thing on Saturday night," thereby avoiding such labor as might despoil "the sanctity" of the following morning.[39] Others, on account of mere social convention: young Robert Byron's generally liberal-minded parents commonly refrained from the corrupting influence of card games.[40] Respectable children everywhere endured what one of them recalled as a strict injunction against "any play . . . anywhere, at any time."[41] These were never merely trivial restrictions. J. H. Thomas recalled how political activity ceased that day even amongst radicals. Military exercises were similarly frowned upon; amongst nonconformists, even after 1914.[42] Yet so-called "continental" habits crept up on the English during the inter-war years. Otherwise decent people not only skipped Church, but took part in organized sports, too. Roughs more obviously indulged their pleasures unmolested and increasingly unchastised.[43] So much so that by 1950, Parliament felt free to authorize that the "amusement parks" of the Festival of Britain remain "open to the public . . . on Sunday afternoon."[44]

All of these changes were obvious enough. What was more difficult was to explain them. Many contemporaries invoked the decline of denominational nonconformity in England after 1914. At least one contemporary historian—Denis Brogan—insisted upon its primary significance in the emerging "social landscape of the 1940s."[45] Others observed the still earlier and altogether more dramatic demise of the Liberal Party: seemingly triumphant as recently as 1906, effectively moribund by 1924.[46] Conventional wisdom suggested—and still suggests—that these organizational transfigurations must have played some part in the fate of Puritan England. Yet they neither were nor are in themselves sufficient to account for the passing of what had once been a national sensibility. That represented the eclipse of a form of common feeling whose particular strength had been rooted in what Davidson had himself called its essentially "private [even] latent quality."[47] It is not explained by the death of nonconformist liberalism. True, the loudest voice of Victorian Puritanism may well have bellowed out of the dissenting sects, but Arnold's depiction of a puritan ideal interchangeable with chapel nonconformity merely represented an error, not an insight.[48] By the same token, Puritanism's preferred political vehicle might indeed have been Gladstonian Liberalism after 1867. But any suggestion that the two were synonymous constituted no more than propaganda, whether for or against.[49]

In short, Victorian Puritanism was more institutionally flexible— and for that matter, more open to "sweetness and light"—than its critics ever acknowledged. And it only became more so during the twentieth century.[50] Its most eloquent champion in the inter-war years was Stanley Baldwin, himself a lifelong Anglican and Tory.[51] Yet its political possibilities also commanded the attention of his long-time socialist rival, Ramsay Macdonald.[52] Thus, Baldwin's famous essay on "Religion and National Life" presumed the compatibility of a universal Puritan sympathy with the one-nation conservative cause. Many accepted the logic of this argument. Think of the Chamberlain family.[53] But Macdonald's earlier "Plea for Puritanism" was conceived in the hope that others amongst the elect might be persuaded to turn their "admirable . . . private . . . characters" to still more deserving "social causes." Many were. Recall Arthur Henderson.[54]

Perhaps that was why a truly comprehensive contemporary understanding—both of the phenomenon and its passing—proved so elusive. That some kind of religious catastrophe had occurred, few doubted. Indeed, the crisis of 1940—that is, the eruption of a seemingly unstoppable because combined pagan assault from Germany and the Soviet Union—produced not only much sententious commitment to the defense of Christian civilization in England, but also many righteous denunciations of its failed witness there during the immediate past.[55] That alone can account for the extraordinary peroration—less against the Nazi threat and more about his country's "endangered . . . soul"—in Arthur Bryant's popular and influential *English Saga, 1840–1940,* published on the eve of the Battle of Britain.[56] Otherwise more restrained analyses still characteristically pointed to a vague but scarcely less malevolent moral degeneration in modern culture, all somehow embodied in what W. J. Blyton identified as "the mechanical conformation of society and the [attendant] rise of an easy-going average . . . which [together] . . . have dissolved the grand ideal of low living and high thinking." In that vein, the same writer went on specifically to blame "the inspector, big business; the job at a distance from home; slumps; inventions and new processes and [finally]—the replacement of men by machines."[57] Even Temple was reduced to grand generalizations. He traced the "loss . . . of old conventions" alternatively to the unfortunate results of "taking people away from their families" and then, still worse, to the mistake of bringing "men and women together in temporary artificial aggregations."[58]

Hindsight should beware of ridiculing contemporary confusion. It is not as if hindsight has done much better. Indeed, in many ways it has fared altogether worse. For it has all but forgotten the transformative crisis of the 1940s.[59] More: in its characteristically uncritical celebration of the presumed liberation wrought by the "Beatles Generation," it has bequeathed to its successors a caricatured understanding of Britain in the 1950s, still widely derided as a period of complacent—even reactionary—conservatism, rather than acknowledged for the era of rapid social change it truly was.[60] This has had a curious consequence. To consult the historiography of interwar Britain forged since the 1960s is, for the most part, to enter a world in which Sabbatarianism and the drink question, even marriage and divorce, seem barely to have aroused the appropriate passions, let alone defined the most important social and political questions of the day.[61] To recognize that they did, and that because, in Barker's words, "religion [then] remained . . . the key that

unlock[ed] most doors in English life," is to begin to appreciate
both the full extent and the real impact of the corrosion of Puritan
England in the years immediately up to 1945.[62] But fully to comprehend its final agony, it is important also to savor its salad days. And
in this respect, contemporaries retained a distinct advantage over
those who blithely followed them into the permissive paradise of
late years. They remembered them both.

Whatever their other shortcomings, the early elegists of Puritan
England knew one thing well. This was that they were themselves
living proof that a "pronounced Protestantism" was not constitutive
of the race—not even, as Boutmy had slyly insinuated, the necessary
religious palliative for its "natural . . . violence and brutality."[63]
Rather, English Puritanism was a historical phenomenon, one
whose had time both come and gone.[64] That said, most commentators during the pivotal years of the 1940s traced its origins a very long
way back into national history. Indeed, the Rev. A. T. P. Williams,
charged with the crucial chapter on "Religion" in Barker's famous
survey, actually identified a "strong . . . puritan . . . strain" within medieval English Catholicism.[65] Others, more conventionally, began
with the Elizabethan reformation.[66] But the "hot Protestantism" that
sixteenth-century ecclesiastical politics inspired barely survived the
1650s.[67] This was why the very notion of "Puritanism" was almost
completely absent from eighteenth-century English literature; similarly, from foreign accounts of domestic sensibility.[68] It had to be
rescued from virtual oblivion in the nineteenth century. Hence it
was a self-consciously revived and transformed ideal that became
the principal moral educator of the Victorians—the critical basis of
Sunday School teaching, self-help manuals, and *avant garde* social
and political criticism.[69]

This last observation is vital. It also needs to be fleshed out. Post-
war historiography located the modern efflorescence of Puritanism
first to the evangelical movement within the Church of England,
then to the uncontrolled force of new dissent beyond it.[70] This was
not so much incorrect as incomplete. To scarcely less an extent, Victorian Puritanism was the product of a literary as well as a religious
revival. Thus Bunyan was first restored by Southey, then championed by Macaulay, whence to become his countrymen's universal
teacher in the century up to 1918.[71] A similar story could be told
for Milton.[72] As a result, Puritanism re-emerged, indeed came to
prominence, in Victorian England almost as much beyond as within
the confines of conventional religious institutions. In the same way,
it grew out of, and achieved real social significance within, a recognizable dialogue between educated and popular contemporary

British culture. This, in turn, subjected what had once been little more than a sectarian creed to what Raphael Samuel has called a "vast metaphorical inflation." Removed from the traditional field of doctrine (given up to latitudinarianism), then abstracted from ancient quarrels about Church government (themselves diminished by the dissolution of confessional state), Puritanism became a kind of moral dogma increasingly made over to the regulation of "personal conduct."[73] This, at least in part, was what persuaded first John Caird, the Scottish cleric and then his most famous disciple, Stanley Baldwin, the English statesmen, to define religion itself as "consisting, not so much of doing sacred acts as doing secular acts from a spiritual motive."[74]

That made it universal. It also made it strikingly modern in outlook. This meant the rejection of the eighteenth century: not merely for its lax religious life, but also for its narrowly patrician notions of rank and fashion, polish and politeness, even of masculinity and femininity.[75] In their place, modern English Puritanism substituted not simply austere conceptions of piety (though it certainly did that) but also revolutionary notions of the soul (the repository of conscience), of character (the engine of improvement), and finally of mind, more particularly of high-mindedness (the rational basis of public duty and self-sacrifice). That intellectual revolution found perhaps its first—and certainly its highest—form in Carlyle's masterly *Letters and Speeches of Oliver Cromwell*. But it was also faithfully reflected in multitudinous examples of the new genre of working-class autobiography. It made a national hero of the Lord Protector. But it also opened the possibility of heroism to Everyman—at least to every Protestant Englishman.[76]

As such, the social sentiments that it expressed were as much democratic as bourgeois.[77] Yet in their alternate emphasis on duty and merit they could still pass muster among the more earnest sections of the nineteenth-century aristocracy. Put another way, it was what linked Samuel Smiles to Richard Cobden, and each, albeit tentatively, to Lord John Russell.[78] Thus Victorian Puritanism suggested something altogether more than a world made safe for manufacturers. It promised an unprecedented moralization of life; that is, of the whole of every life. This view may now seem rather constricting. Contemporaries found it, on the contrary, liberating. That was because it rejected both moral nostalgia and ethical elitism. Indeed, this understanding made the otherwise utopian end of a progressive purification of ordinary existence seem both necessary and possible. It was necessary because the sanctification of the commonplace also highlighted the latent devilry in normal things. It was possible because, for all the ubiquity of evil, Puritanism's egalitarian promise assured believers that God had endowed each man through his conscience with a capacity for what Carlyle called "soul-effort," or an ability for righteous striving. Not only extraordinary but also simple men, so armed, could confront the evil of the world and—to a degree anyway—replace it with good.[79]

That haughty goal informed the whole of Mr. Gladstone's "severe life."[80] But it also furnished lesser mortals with what Boutmy described as a "peculiar . . . fund of strength." This curious allocation granted each a divine measure of righteous resourcefulness, ready to be deployed in "practical life" for the regeneration of society as well as the salvation of each soul. Hence the unquenchable sense of optimism that accompanied this mindset and the ingenuous passion that it implied. To be sure, Victorian Puritanism tended to express itself through a certain kind of "personal austerity." As such, it "disdained . . . mere . . . forms." But it did so precisely because of its belief that frivolity represented missed opportunity, whilst superficial appearances concealed vital truths.[81] To reject them both was thus not merely to see things as they really were; it was to understand that "moral progress" was actually possible. By extension, it was to understand how moral pressure, righteously applied, could actually *increase* individual freedom. This was the English paradox; what Maillaud later described as "that peculiar acceptance of Church and chapel interference in their ways of living grounded in the conviction that in England anyway . . . the protestant religion is a powerful instrument of personal liberation."[82]

Not everyone agreed. John Stuart Mill wrote *On Liberty* specifically to warn his fellow countrymen about its potentially pernicious effects.[83] But to appreciate why so many did agree, it is important not to confine historical attention to those goals that have subsequently come to seem ethically quaint: lifelong marital fidelity, temperance, and sabbatarianism. They were scarcely more significant in their time than many that now appear eminently rational, such as women's rights, public health, and animal welfare. Recent research has highlighted the very close links between the suffrage movement of Edwardian England and the purity campaigns—for water, food, and fresh air—of the 1880s and 1890s. In the same way, the connection between political equality and sexual continence represented little more than a natural growth. As Christabel Pankhurst famously put it: "Votes for women and chastity for men."

To be sure, the regulation of individual existence through moral exhortation forged a world of severe ethical standards and strict cultural frontiers. This was grounded in an almost overwhelming preoccupation with work and by an indefatigable belief in the possibility of good money; one which explicitly rejected the inter-related evils of unearned inheritance, dishonest acquisition and, above all, gambling. It is unforgettably described in Arnold Bennett's Staffordshire sagas.[84] Even at its best, it necessitated a certain sancti-moniousness of manner. At its most repellent, it entailed simple hy-pocrisy. About that, foreign observers were insistent. As Dibelius put it: "Puritanism [may] have enriched the [English] people with lofty conception[s] of uprightness and decency [but] it is also the parent of English cant."[85] Still worse, the tight society of chapel, school, and lecture-hall often sustained not merely a moralistic but a morose existence. Dibelius again: "By insisting on looking at every issue, no matter how remote, from some religious or ethical angle, [Puri-tanism] has clothed English life in a universal matter-of-factness or joylessness.[86]

Hence, English philistinism: for in no respect did Puritanism ap-parently deny the broader possibilities of life more than in its repu-diation of art for art's sake. To be sure, this may have been a doctrine once nurtured in a profound iconoclasm, but it was often expressed in the language of common stupidity. Thus the legendary mayor of a Lancashire cotton town, on being presented two nude statues for civic display: "Art is art and nothing can be done to prevent it, but there is the lady mayoress's decency to be considered."[87] Yet even in this respect, puritan attitudes were altogether more complex than either contemporary or subsequent caricature allowed. A distaste for aestheticism did not preclude an appreciation of culture. In-deed, a certain distrust of the visual actually placed a premium on the literal. The early career of H. H. Asquith bore eloquent witness to that fact.[88] Considered even at its most extreme, the repudiation of licentious imagery never denied all the pleasures of the eye, cer-tainly none of those joys traceable largely to nature. Remember how "the Calvinist discipline" of John Buchan's home never dimmed his "sense of beauty and interest [in] the earth."[89]

Precisely because it comprehended the classes at a time of other-wise profound social division, more still, because it transcended de-nominational disputes in the first great age of religious pluralism, but, above all, because it consisted of the raw material of national self-definition and moral self-confidence, the puritan revival exerted an almost talismanic influence over early twentieth-century Britain, right up to the outbreak of the First World War. Moreover, to the 1920s and beyond its sway was not merely pervasive, it was also self-consciously progressive. Puritanism stood in the vanguard of change within a rapidly transforming society. At least in its own terms, it represented nothing less than the ethical dimensions of progress. In the same way, it symbolized the best—and the future—of British civilization. Yet at the same time, Victorian Puritanism char-acteristically assumed a paradoxically dichotomous *persona*. Its vital spirit pronounced a confident confrontation with the world. But its practical activities described a more subtle capacity for compromise with the complexity of things. It prevailed, but by negotiation.

This was especially so in the wider British context. Thus all true Britons were Puritans, but some were more puritan than others. And the most wholly uncorrupted were unusually found on the Celtic peripheries of United Kingdom. Writing to his friend H. T. Baker from north of the border in April 1898, Raymond Asquith remarked upon his recent subjection to "the rude assault of a Scottish sabbath." There was no need to explain any further. Every Englishman of the time would have instinctively known what he meant.[90] Those who ventured into contemporary Wales—and some did—found similar rigor by no means confined to the Lord's Day. Goronwy Rees recounted how Monday evenings in pre-war Aberystwyth were exclusively dedicated to the doings of the Band of Hope: "a temperance organisation designed to strengthen [us] against all kinds of temptation . . . in the form of solemn oath to abjure all forms of swearing and alcoholic liquor."[91] Then there were Wednesday evening prayer meetings, Thursdays *seints,* and so on.[92]

Such austere regimes were rarer in England. In part, this was because the peculiarly English form of Victorian Puritanism represented something of a social and political compromise in itself. It commanded the allegiance of the aristocracy more by public example than through private conviction. This was certainly true of the sophisticated within their ranks. For instance, "The Souls" avoided divorce. They scarcely abjured adultery.[93] In a slightly different way, it conquered only part of the educated English soul, which tempered its obvious Puritanism with an underlying Hellenism.[94] Finally, as everyone knew, many of the poor, especially the urban poor, had scarcely ever been exposed to its light. That, after all, was why the Salvation Army first came into existence.[95] Yet such compromises were as much a source of strength as of weakness to English Puritanism before 1914. To be sure, the more fervent among the Scots and Welsh periodically lamented the moral laxity of their English cousins, but the failings of the center more normally proved to the periphery only that they were more faithfully British—because more chaste, more teetotal, Sabbatarian—than their Anglo-Saxon counterparts. That invariably sustained their moral vanity. It rarely fed any underling sense of alienation.[96]

In other words, such relatively minor disparities in common British culture actually assured all three nations more about what they maintained in common. They also reminded still sterner Ulstermen of what bound them to the mainland. As such, they convinced all four nations of their opposition to Roman Catholic, Irish, nationalism.[97] In a different way, the limited tribute that English Puritanism paid to peculiar Anglo-Saxon realities also ensured its tight hold over domestic public opinion, more broadly conceived. This kept not merely atheists but also aesthetes and libertines firmly at the margins of national life, even at the fringes of intellectual life. Many amongst the self-consciously thoughtful were influenced by T. H. Green—new liberal, educational reformer, and temperance activist—up to 1914, few by Walter Pater—platonist, humanist, and Uranian.[98]

The balance of such advantage shifted subtly after 1918. This process was first traceable to a fundamental transfiguration within the geo-politics of the Union itself. Thus, the creation of the Irish Free State in 1922 initially assuaged Britain's Roman Catholic problem. Yet it also brought home to the remaining, British, peoples just how much their truer faith varied from one part of the kingdom to another. Certainly, it furnished an altogether broader significance for Welsh disestablishment after 1920.[99] These developments were only enhanced by more general movements of population, wealth, and even social caché to the south and east of Great Britain. To a previously unprecedented degree, England evolved differently, that is, more speedily and more prosperously, than the rest of the British Isles.[100] By the end of the Second World War, those differences had also come to describe a difference of outlook, especially of moral outlook. And that now amounted to more than an occasionally disagreeable Sunday.

In part, that transformation reflected the peculiarities of religious change in the south and east of Great Britain. Yet these were highly complex and far from clear-cut. Even according to the most unforgiving of statistical calculations, institutional Christianity as a whole held up pretty well in inter-war England.[101] However, both the superficial tone and at least some of the more important underlying realities of English faithfulness altered, to the permanent disadvantage of a kingdom-wide, puritan, consensus. Among the intellectually sophisticated, strident irreligion gathered renewed pace during these years. For a few, that permitted Hellenism with a vengeance, a celebration of Greek morality entirely removed from all Roman notions of duty.[102] For most, it entailed the more rigorous secularization of erstwhile righteous ends. In that way, many old puritan causes now found new atheistic promoters—notably in local government reform and the development of Britain's welfare state. Consider, for example, the ethical inspiration of William Beveridge.[103] Even among the religiously committed, a previously unbending Protestantism lost substantial ground to an increasingly emollient ecumenicalism. As organized nonconformity moved towards the center of national life—it was part of the official victory celebrations in 1945 as it had not been in 1919—many recognized this as an unambiguously good thing. They perhaps neglected to notice that the same process persuaded some of the more able and ambitious within denominational dissent back into the Anglican fold. Archbishop Joost de Blank was only the most candid in describing the process as a moment of "personal liberation . . . from an unreasonable and unreasoning Puritanism."[104]

More generally significant was the decline of the Sunday Schools. This proceeded precipitously after 1914. Enrollment figures peaked at around six million, or 16 per cent of the total British population, in 1906. They halved during the next thirty-five years, falling to just over three million, or around 8 per cent of the population, in 1941.[105] Naturally, this represented not just a collapse of collective conscience but also the growth of recreational choice. Mid-Victorian Sunday Schools were popular—accounting for up to 80 per cent of the relevant juvenile population—partly because of the lack of available alternatives.[106] Twentieth-century cities increasingly furnished the secular amusements capable of competing: parks, bands, and even organized games.[107] Technology contributed too—above all, the bicycle. Chapel sports could scarcely match the attractions of the emerging professional varieties.[108] These losses especially affected the nonconformist churches. They had invested more in the potential returns of Sunday School.[109] They lost more in their eclipse.[110]

It was Puritan England, however, that lost most of all, for the secularization of the Sabbath expressed in the decline of the Sunday Schools had broader social implications. Sunday School was the place, above all others, where ordinary people had learned the basic tenets of Protestant doctrine.[111] Fewer and fewer people now imbibed them. The lamentable results of that neglect were all too visibly highlighted in the infamous *Bishop's Report* of 1941. Huge swathes of urban youth no longer knew the faith, let alone practiced it. Sunday School had also been the place that had inculcated the idea of the purity of the upright, benevolent, and righteous life into Victorian and Edwardian children. That its success in so doing was not particularly great was altogether less remarkable than the fact that such an effort was ever made. The very attempt now appeared to have been abandoned. That sense of impending doom colored much contemporary denunciation of Sabbath-breaking and pleasure-seeking.[112]

Yet by now, every gloom merchant was matched by a contemporary celebrant. Indeed, Puritanism's newly emboldened opponents first began to make fun of their foe during the 1930s. The journalist Gerald Barry collected an anthology of not merely sanctimonious but actually ludicrous objections to increasingly permissive public habits.[113] For instance, in 1932, he recorded how Dr. J. A. Sharp, immediate past-president of the national Free Church Council, had argued in all seriousness that a Christian Sunday must be preserved "if necessary [by] some form of coercion." As an absolute minimum, Pastor Sharp had insisted that "cinemas should be met with stern repression."[114] Others found Satan lurking in still more innocent Sabbath amusements. One Councillor Jones of Rhyl opposed a suggestion arising that same year from his own Entertainment Committee that "diving experts . . . including one described as a Dare-Devil . . . be permitted to [provide] public displays in the [municipal] swimming pool . . . on Sunday." As he put it: "I knew that the devil was coming fast to Rhyl, but I did not think he would come in name."[115]

Underlying this apparent hysteria lay a more serious concern. It may be called a fear of the normalization of vice. It was rooted in the realization that Puritan England's road to ruin lay less in excess than through moderation, that is, in a superficially sensible accommodation with the powers of evil. This insidious process threatened not only the obviously indulgent but also the more righteous and restrained: potentially the whole community. That became a clear and present danger in pre-war Britain. Social science—righteous social science no less—proved as much.[116] In *An Autobiography,* published in 1934, Philip Snowdon recalled the West Riding village of his youth as a place strictly divided between "the chapel and . . . the public house."[117] The almost Manichean social analysis that such memories implied was grounded in something other than nostalgia. Indeed, it was largely corroborated in Seebohm Rowntree's rigorous study, *Poverty,* in late Victorian York. But Rowntree's later study, *Poverty and Progress,* undertaken in 1935, portrayed an altogether more complex place. The line between the righteous and the reprobate had become blurred.[118]

About no issue was this unfortunate departure more noticeable than concerning the question of drink.[119] Paradoxically, the news seemed good. The working classes of York spent a considerably smaller proportion of their income on alcohol than before—about one-tenth, rather than one-sixth.[120] Given that drink was more expensive, this meant that they were actually drinking less; moreover, less of what had become a progressively weaker brew.[121] Partly as a result of this, convictions for drunkenness fell far below the Edwardian average both in York and nationally.[122] But the old teetotaler was far from pleased with these developments. For the social scientist in him had discovered that this behavior was less the product of "self-restraint" than of financial discipline; still worse, of financial discipline tempered by the lure of sensual counter-attractions. True, publicans blamed falling trade primarily on the higher price of liquor, coupled with reduced licensing hours.[123] But the police pointed to alternative amusements such as cinemas, wireless sets, even gardens.[124] That explained for Rowntree how a decrease in the average quantity of alcohol consumed per head had been accompanied by an increase in the number of people actual drinking. To be sure, the young, that is, those born after 1901, had added little to the "class of drunkards" whom he so deplored. But, in so doing, they had effectively created a new class, that of the moderate drinker. This dismayed him scarcely less.[125]

There was something else. The nation of temperate imbibers had also become a race of occasional gamblers. Not that no one had ever had a flutter before 1914. But the institution of gambling had since assumed popular and permanent forms. The "modern craze" of football pools accounted for most of that development, but greyhound racing, introduced into Britain from the United States in 1926, became a regular part of life in many working-class communities. The result was that by 1935 the average family spent around 2s 6d per week on various forms of gambling.[126] That figure went on rising during the war. Indeed, G. M. Trevelyan argued that "[g]ambling now perhaps does more harm than drink" in his influential *English Social History*, published in 1944.[127] Just four years later, a Resolution of the 1948 Lambeth Conference drew particular attention to "the grave moral and social evil that [had] arisen through the [increased] prevalence of gambling."[128] Rowntree himself devoted an entire chapter to this "new . . . organised and . . . pernicious . . . rejection of reason [and] faith," in a further study, entitled *English Life and Leisure*, published in 1951. His conclusions were not optimistic.[129]

These were the people—less bridge-players than dog-fanciers, still perhaps tea-drinkers but unquestionably beer-swillers, too— who went to war against Italy and the Axis in 1939.[130] Their collective capacity for dignified endurance is not doubted here. After all, Temple never doubted it then.[131] Their Puritanism reasonably might be. That was what Temple feared for. Moreover, by 1943 it had been undermined still further by a new, unforeseen temptation. This was the "black market." The child of wartime rationing, it gave birth to a very different kind of moral order. Rationing, as the disgruntled Chairman of Mile End Conservative Association put it in May 1945, made "criminals . . . out of thousands of decent men and women . . . in all walks of life."[132] Of course, rationing had its proper function. For a few years it even won plenty of admirers. In the short-term at least, it fed an entire population, many better than they had ever been fed before. It also conserved precious resources for pressing purposes.[133] But it was continued, seemingly without an end, in a nation unthreatened by occupation after American intervention.[134] More importantly, it was maintained among a people by then enjoying a continuous rise in wages.[135] Officially, they had nothing to spend their money on, save National Savings Certificates.[136] Unofficially, they turned to the "spiv" and his products.[137]

More than anything else, this was what dismayed Temple in 1943. That was what he meant by the culture of dishonesty, but it also explained why his exhortations were doomed to fail. The lesser man from Mile End understood the people better. Their complaints pointed to a critical alteration in common culture after 1939. This was the eclipse of the ideal of austerity. In part, that departure reflected the all too natural desire among the potentially doomed for passing pleasure. It also constituted a more permanent change in popular attitudes towards consumption. This shift is often held to be entailed in the very nature of commercial civilization itself.[138] Perhaps so—but for most Britons its first realization was traceable to the seemingly peculiar activities of their own war-time government. For as weekly wages continued to outstrip price inflation, the paucity of goods increasingly appeared as something publicly imposed rather than socially endorsed. This was especially true after 1942, when rationing was applied to clothing as well as to food. Particularly galling was its application to women's clothing. Officialdom from that moment came to define—and indeed to proscribe—what it deemed to be frivolous impersonal attire. Not everyone agreed with authorized opinion. Moreover, fewer still acknowledged its right to pass judgment in such matters. The Civilian Clothing (Restorations) order may have reflected Whitehall's wise conclusions about the number of frills proper on women's knickers, but many women disagreed and were willing to take the risks necessary in order to express that disagreement.[139]

In the wake of such measures, the British generally, and the English especially, came to reject the ideal of abstinence more broadly.

In that way too, popular notions of freedom came within a generation to be associated more with possessing things rather than through control of the self. When the Conservatives campaigned for office in 1951 under the slogan of "setting the people free," they both shrewdly responded to, just as they guilelessly exacerbated, the future force of that Promethean impulse. So they came not only to abolish rationing but to sponsor the Wolfenden Report.[140] In the same way, successive Tory administrations presided over both the inauguration of commercial television and the introduction of premium bonds.[141] All of these social changes were traceable in part to the decline of organized religion in England after 1914: but only in part. All owed something to the diminution of Protestant sectarianism in England after 1914; but again only something. They are more fully explained by the broader social and cultural changes that forged an England in which Puritanism itself was increasingly confined to the wilder Celtic shores and the madder conceits of utopian socialism and, as such, came to be seen both by constitution and convention as something decidedly un-English.[142]

Fall Semester 2003

1. Author unknown; cited in James Ramsden, ed., *George Lyttleton's Commonplace Book* (Gettrington, 2002), p. 72.

2. *The Times*, July 12, 1943.

3. Ibid. This intervention was curiously passed over in Iremonger's official *Life*, published just five years later. See F. A. Iremonger, *William Temple, Archbishop of Canterbury: His Life and Letters* (Oxford, 1948), Ch. 10.

4. Studied, that is, as a people *apart* from mainstream European civilization; a genre inaugurated, perhaps, by Hippolyte Taine in his *Notes on England*, Edward Hyams, trans. (London, 1995); see esp. Chs. 2, 3, and 8. These observations were originally composed between 1860 and 1870. A faint whiff of that tradition survives in François Bédarida, *La Société Anglaise du Milieu du XIXe siècle à nos jours* (Paris, 1990). Note Bédarida's extensive treatment of Puritanism on pp. 80–86, 101–06, 226–30, 349–57, and 444ff.

5. Emile Boutmy, *The English People: A Study of their Political Psychology*, R. English, trans. (London, 1904), p. 52.

6. Wilhelm Dibelius, *England*, Mary Agnes Hamilton, trans. (London, 1930), pp. 399–400. This book was originally published in German in 1922 and was based almost entirely on research carried out *before* the outbreak of the First World War.

7. J. C. C. Davidson to F. S. Jackson, Nov. 18, 1923; reprinted in Robert Rhodes James, ed., *Memoirs of a Conservative: J. C. C. Davidson Memoirs and Papers, 1910–1937* (London, 1969), p. 188.

8. Boutmy, *English People*, pp. xi–xii; James, ed., *Davidson Memoirs*, p. 188.

9. Cited in Ian MacKillop, *F. R. Leavis: A Life in Criticism* (Penguin, 1995), p. 29.

10. J. M. Keynes, "My Early Beliefs," in *The Collected Writings of J. M. Keynes* (30 Vols., Cambridge, 1972), Vol. X, p. 437.

11. Pierre Maillaud, *The English Way* (London, 1945), p. 62.

12. George Orwell, *The English People* (London, 1947), p. 14.

13. Ibid., p. 16.

14. As recalled in Margaret Thatcher, *The Downing Street Years* (London, 1993), pp. 10–12; a more subtle account can be found in John Campbell, *Margaret Thatcher* (London, 2000), Vol. 1, Ch. 1, esp. at pp. 23–25.

15. A. L. Rowse, *A Cornish Childhood* (London, 1942), pp. 156–57.

16. Or did he? For a profound analysis of Rowse's more ambivalent relationship with Puritanism, see Richard Ollard, *A Man of Contradictions: A Life of A. L. Rowse* (London, 1999), esp. pp. 10, 23, 287, and 291–92. Much can also be gleaned from a fascinating account of Rowse's schooldays published in Valerie Jacob, *Tregonissey to Trenaren: A. L. Rowse, the Cornish Years* (St. Austell, 2001), Ch. 2.

17. Ernest Barker, ed., "An Attempt at Perspective," in *The Character of England* (Oxford, 1947), pp. 565–66.

18. John Marlowe, *The Puritan Tradition in English Life* (London, 1956); see esp. Ch. IX, "The Decline of the Puritan Tradition." Note similar conclusions in J. D. Scott, *Life in Britain* (London, 1956), esp. Ch. III, "Religion." All of which perhaps makes sense of the complete absence of religion—even in the index—of T. H. Pear, *English Social Differences* (London, 1955).

19. For a contemporary account, see Douglas Goldring, "The New Morality," in *The Nineteen Twenties: A General Survey and some Personal Memories* (London, 1945), Ch. V.

20. Donald Thomas, *An Underworld at War: Spivs, Deserters, Racketeers and Civilians in the Second World War* (London, 2001), p. 183.

21. Ramsden, ed., *Lyttleton's Commonplace Book*, p. 63.

22. D. E. Butler and A. Sloman, *British Political Facts, 1900–1975* (London, 1975), p. 266. In 1920, there were 3,747 divorces; in 1940, 8,396.

23. Butler and Sloman, *British Political Facts*. For the relevant legal background, see Stephen Cretney, *Family Law in the Twentieth Century* (Oxford, 2003), Chs. 6–8.

24. A. J. P. Taylor, *English History, 1914–1945* (Oxford, 1965), p. 170.

25. Ibid. Also T. O. Lloyd, *English History 1906–1992: Empire, Welfare State and Europe* (Oxford, 1993), p. 149. George V's views on marriage and divorce are outlined in Kenneth Rose, *King George V* (London, 1983), pp. 365–67.

26. Specifically attributed to the force of the "nonconformist conscience" in Cuthbert Headlam's diary for Dec. 2, 1936; see Stuart Ball, ed., *Parliament and Politics in the Age of Churchill and Attlee: The Headlam Diaries, 1935–1951* (Cambridge, 1999), p. 100. For a contrary view, see Susan Williams, *The Peoples' King: The True Story of the Abdication* (London, 2003), Ch. 12. Macmillan's dilemma is carefully chronicled in Alistair Horne, *Macmillan, 1894–1956* (London, 1988), Vol. 1, pp. 84–90. It was passed over in his memoirs. But so too, in truth, was his marriage. See Harold Macmillan, *Winds of Change, 1914–1939* (London, 1966), pp. 116–17.

27. This incident is unmentioned in Eden's Memoirs. None of its three volumes covers any aspect of the years 1945–1951. For details, see David Carlton, *Anthony Eden: A Biography* (London, 1981), pp. 270–71; also D. R. Thorpe, *Eden: The Life and Times of Anthony Eden, First Earl of Avon, 1896–1977* (London, 2003), pp. 338–39.

28. For some of the reasons, see Brian Harrison, *Drink and the Victorians: The Temperance Question in England, 1815–1872* (London, 1971), Ch. 15.

29. See Lilian Lewis Shiman, *The Crusade Against Drink in Victorian England* (Basingstoke, 1988), Ch 9.

30. David Willoughby, "The Public House," in *About It and About: Articles from Everyman* (London, 1920), p. 235. Not that the author approved: see pp. 236–39.

31. Arguments in favor were set out in, among others, James Long in "The Story of Drink," Ch. XVII of *The Coming Englishman* (London, 1909), and countered, with characteristic force, in F. E. Smith, "Licensing Policy," in *Unionist Policy and Other Essays* (London, 1913), p. 219. For a modern assessment, see G. R. Searle, *A New England? Peace and War, 1886–1918* (Oxford, 2004), pp. 362–65.

32. Curiously neglected in the relevant chapter of David Lloyd George, *War Memoirs* (London, 1934), Vol. I, esp. Chs. 7 and 8. For a contemporary commentary on its (lack of) progress, see Asquith's letters to Venetia Stanley for Mar. 25, Apr. 1, 8, and finally 23, in Michael and Eleanor Brock, eds., *H. H. Asquith: Letters to Venetia Stanley* (Oxford, 1982), p. 307–09, 527–28, 530, and 567–68.

33. As recorded in Violet Bonham-Carter's diary, May 22–23, 1915; see Mark Pottle, ed., *Champion Redoubtable: The Diaries and Letters of Violet Bonham-Carter, 1914–1945* (London, 1998), p. 36.

34. Pottle, *Champion Redoubtable*. See also Bentley Brinkerhoff Gilbert, *David Lloyd George, A Political Life* (London, 1992), Vol. 2, pp. 151ff.

35. R. J. Q. Adams, *Bonar Law* (London, 1999), p. 15.

36. For Churchill's attitude to the "drink problem" in 1915, see Paul Addison, *Churchill on the Home Front, 1900–1955* (London, 1992), pp. 176–77. His attitude to drink in general is best brought out in his study of fellow-imbiber F. E. Smith. See Churchill, *Great Contemporaries* (London, 1930), Ch. 11.

37. Cited in Thomas, *Underworld at War*, p. 26.

38. M. J. Quinlan, *Victorian Prelude: A History of English Manners, 1700–1830* (New York, 1941), Ch. II; Harold Perkin, *The Origins of Modern English Society, 1780–1880* (London, 1969), esp. pp. 273–90, and 280.

39. Viscount Simon, *Retrospect* (London, 1952), p. 15.

40. James Knox, *Robert Byron: A Biography* (London, 2003), p. 41; such injunctions and the religious habits they sustained were widely recalled, barely one gen-

eration later, with a kind of amused contempt. See, for instance, Harold Nicolson, "The Edwardian Weekend," in *Small Talk* (London, 1937), pp. 36–37.

41. Clifford Hill, "Memoir of an Agricultural Labourer, Gardener and Chauffeur, 1904–1975," in Thea Thompson, ed., *Edwardian Childhoods* (London, 1981), p. 49.

42. J. H. Thomas, *My Story* (London, 1937), p. 18.

43. Some sense of that decline is captured in R. C. Churchill, *The English Sunday* (London, 1954), Chs. 1 and 2, also 9–11. For a historical analysis, see John Wigley, *The Rise and Fall of the Victorian Sunday* (Manchester, 1980), conclusion.

44. Albeit after much debate; see Harold Macmillan's diary entry for Nov. 27–28, 1950, in Peter Catterall, ed., *The Macmillan Diaries: The Cabinet Years, 1950–1957* (London, 2003), p. 32.

45. Denis Brogan, *The English People* (London, 1943), p. 57.

46. George Dangerfield, *The Strange Death of Liberal England* (London, 1935), *passim*.

47. Davidson, *Memoirs*, p. 188.

48. Matthew Arnold, *Culture and Anarchy*, J. Dover Wilson, ed. (Cambridge, 1969), Ch. 4; see the observation of Clyde Binsfield, *So Down to Prayers: Studies in English Nonconformity, 1780–1920* (London, 1977), Ch. 8; and more broadly, see Dale A. Johnson, *The Changing Shape of English Nonconformity, 1825–1925* (New York, 1999), Part II.

49. David M. Thompson, ed., *Nonconformity in the Nineteenth Century* (London, 1972), Part 4; G. I. T. Machin, *Politics and the Churches in Great Britain, 1869–1921* (Oxford, 1987), Chs. 2 and 4.

50. Clyde Binfield, "Hebrews Hellenized? English Evangelical Non-Conformity and Culture, 1840–1940," in Sheridan Gilley and W. J. Shiels, eds., *A History of Religion in Britain* (Oxford, 1994), p. 322–45; also John Wolffe, *God and Greater Britain: Religion and National Life in Britain and Ireland, 1843–1945* (London, 1994), Ch. 7.

51. As exemplified in Baldwin's collected speeches: *On England and other Addresses* (London, 1926), *Our Inheritance: Speeches and Addresses* (London, 1928), *This Torch of Freedom: Speeches and Addresses* (London, 1935), and *Service of our Lives: Last Speeches as Prime Minister* (London, 1937). See the important interpretation of Baldwin's religion in Philip Williamson, *Stanley Baldwin: Conservative Leadership and National Values* (Cambridge, 1999), Ch. 9.

52. For Macdonald's own idiosyncratic religion, see David Marquand, *Ramsay Macdonald* (London, 1977), pp. 53–55.

53. Baldwin, "Religion and National Life," and "The Contribution of the Baptists," in *This Torch of Freedom*, pp. 77–87 and 100–05; David Cannadine, "The Bourgeois Experience in Political Culture: The Chamberlains of Birmingham," in Mark S. Micale and Robert L. Dietle, eds., *Enlightenment, Passion and Modernity* (Stanford, 2000), pp. 148–64.

54. James Ramsey Macdonald, "A Plea for Puritanism," *Socialist Review*, V, 48 (February 1912), pp. 27–33; Adrian Hastings, *A History of English Christianity, 1920–1985* (London, 1986), p. 129.

55. See, among others, H. H. E. Craster, ed., *Viscount Halifax: Speeches on Foreign Policy* (London, 1940), pp. 102–03, 334, 362, and 368; also Lord Lothian, *The American Speeches of Lord Lothian, July 1939 to December 1940* (London, 1941), pp. 10, 34, 71, and 139; finally, A. J. Toynbee, *Christianity and Civilisation* (London, 1940), pp. 22–27. An extended correspondence in *The Times* on this subject, conducted throughout much of February and March 1940, is sensitively discussed in Keith Robbins, "Britain, 1940 and Christian Civilisation," in *History, Religion and Identity in Modern Britain* (London, 1983), pp. 201–02.

56. Arthur Bryant, *The English Saga, 1840–1940* (London, 1940); esp. Ch. 10, "Way of Redemption," p. 334.

57. W. J. Blyton, *Arrows of Desire* (London, 1938), p. 245.

58. *The Times*, July 12, 1943.

59. A typical example can be found in Arthur Marwick, *Britain in the Century of Total War: War, Peace and Social Change, 1900–1967* (London, 1968), Ch. 6. An exception is G. I. T. Machin, *Churches and Social Issues in Twentieth-Century Britain* (Oxford, 1998), Ch. 4, esp. 122ff.

60. For a recent restatement of the orthodox view, see Kenneth O. Morgan, *The People's Peace: British History 1945–1989* (Oxford, 1990), Chs. 4 and 5; more interesting insights can be gleaned from Peter Vansittart, *The Fifties* (London, 1995), Chs. 9–16. Serious analysis begins with Christie Davies, *The Strange Death of Moral Britain* (New Brunswick, N.J., 2004), Ch. 1.

61. See, among others, A. J. P. Taylor, *English History*, Chs. V and IX; Lloyd, *Empire, Welfare State and Europe*, Chs. 6–8; or, more specifically, Noreen Branson, *Britain in the Nineteen Twenties* (London, 1975), and Noreen Branson and Margot Heinemann, *Britain in the Nineteen Thirties* (London, 1971), *passim*.

62. Ernest Barker, *Britain and the British People* (Oxford, 1942), p. 116.

63. Boutmy, *English People*, p. 109.

64. Above all, Marlowe, *The Puritan Tradition*, Chs. 2, 8, and 9; but see the earlier observations of Leland Devitt Baldwin, *God's Englishmen: The Evolution of the Anglo-Saxon Spirit* (London, 1943), pp. 65–66. For the striking absence of Puritanism in foreign views of English character prior to 1850, see Paul Langford, *Englishness Identified: Manners and Character, 1650–1850* (Oxford, 2000), pp. 129–34.

65. The Rt. Rev. A. T. P. Williams, "Religion," in Barker, ed., *The Character of England*, p. 58.

66. Baldwin, *God's Englishman*, pp. 56–57; Marlowe, *Puritan Tradition*, Ch. 2.

67. Patrick Collinson, *The Elizabethan Puritan Movement* (London, 1967), Parts 2 and 3; Collinson, *Godly People: Essays on English Protestantism and Puritanism* (London, 1983), Chs. 1 and 20.

68. For what little evidence there is, see Langford, *Englishman Identified*, pp. 129–36.

69. As unforgettably described by Raphael Samuel, in his "The Discovery of Puritanism, 1820–1914; A Preliminary Sketch," in Jane Garnett and Colin Matthew, eds., *Revival and Religion Since 1700: Essays for John Walsh* (London, 1993), pp. 201–47.

70. John Walsh, "Origins of Evangelical Revival," in G. V. Bennett and J. D. Walsh, eds., *Essays in Modern English Church History* (London, 1966), pp. 132–36; W. R. Ward, *Religion and Society in England, 1790–1850* (London, 1972), Chs. 2 and 3; Bernard Semmel, *The Methodist Revolution* (London, 1974), Ch. 1.

71. Lord Macaulay, "Southey's Edition of Pilgrim's Progress," in *Critical and Historical Essays* (London, 1873), Vol. I, pp. 408–24.

72. As it was in G. O. Trevelyan, *The Life and Letters of Lord Macaulay* (Oxford, 1876), p. 109; and, in another way, David Masson, *The Life of John Milton* (6 Vols, London, 1859–80); see J. G. Nelson, *The Sublime Puritan: Milton and the Victorians* (Madison, Wisc., 1963), pp. 82ff.

73. Samuel, "Discovery of Puritanism," p. 206.

74. Baldwin, "Religion and National Life," p. 80.

75. I owe this insight to Samuel, "Discovery of Puritanism," p. 208.

76. Thomas Carlyle, *Oliver Cromwell's Letters and Speeches* (London, 1895), esp. Vol. III, pp. 142, 186, and 307; also Vol. IV, pp. 15–77.

77. Boutmy, *English People*, p. 52.

78.　See Samuel Smiles, *Self-Help, with Illustrations of Conduct and Perseverance* (London, 1859), which actually mentions Cobden on pp. 20–21, and Russell on pp. 24 and 450–51; similarly, Smiles, *Life and Labour, or Characteristics of Men of Industry, Culture and Genius* (London, 1887); again, respectively on pp. 46, 199, and 379; also 224 and 316.

79.　Carlyle, *Cromwell's Letters*; cited in Maurice Cowling, *Religion and Public Doctrine in Modern England: Accommodations* (Cambridge, 2001), Vol. III, pp. 4–12.

80.　M. R. D. Foot, ed., *The Gladstone Diaries* (Oxford, 1968), Vol. I, p. 595; entry for Dec. 29, 1832.

81.　Boutmy, *English People*, p. 52.

82.　Maillaud, *English Way*, p. 204.

83.　J. S. Mill, *On Liberty* (London, 1859); for its genesis, see Francis E. Mineka and Dwight M. Lindley, eds., *The Collected Works of John Stuart Mill*, Vols *XIV–XVII*; *The Later Letters of John Stuart Mill, 1849–1873* (Toronto, 1972), Vol. 1, p. 294; also John Stuart Mill, *Autobiography* (London, 1873), pp. 251–56.

84.　See especially Bennett's *Anna of the Five Towns*, Peter Preston, ed. (London, 1997); note Bennett's explanatory comments in "The Potteries: A Sketch," pp. 200–02; "Clay in the Hands of the Potter," pp. 203–08 and "My Religious Experience," pp. 209–11; also his *Sketches for Autobiography*, James Heyburn, ed. (London, 1979), Ch. 1.

85.　Dibelius, *England*, p. 401.

86.　Ibid. For a remarkably similar analysis, albeit indigenously inspired and presented as praise, see W. Macneil Dixon, *The Englishman* (London, 1931), esp. Ch. IV "The English Soul," at pp. 131–33.

87.　Ramsden, ed., *Lyttelton's Commonplace Book*, p. 17.

88.　The Earl of Oxford and Asquith, *Memories and Reflections, 1852–1927* (London, 1928), Vol. 1, Chs. 7 and 9; J. A. Spender and Cyril Asquith, *Life of Herbert Henry Asquith, Lord Oxford and Asquith* (London, 1932), Ch. 3.

89.　John Buchan, *Memory Hold the Door* (London, 1940), p. 16.

90.　Raymond Asquith to H. T. Baker, Apr. 21, 1898, in John Jolliffe, ed., *Raymond Asquith: Life and Letters* (London, 1980), p. 45.

91.　Goronwy Rees, *A Bundle of Sensations* (London, 1960), p. 21.

92.　Rees, *Sensations*, p. 21–22.

93.　Angela Lambert, *Unquiet Souls: The Indian Summer of the British Aristocracy* (London, 1984), pp. 37–38 and 73–74. See also Baldwin, *God's Englishman*, pp. 171–73 for specific criticisms of Dibelius on this matter.

94.　Robert Ogilvie, *Latin and Greek: A History of the Influence of the Classics on English Life from 1600 to 1918* (London, 1969), Chs. 4 and 5; also Frank M. Turner, *The Greek Heritage in Victorian Britain* (New Haven and London, 1981), Ch. 2; and Maurice Bowra, "A Classical Education," in Bowra, *In General and Particular: Essays* (London, 1964), p. 59.

95.　Baldwin, *God's Englishman*, pp. 175–76; for a modern account, see Hugh McLeod, *Religion and Society in England, 1850–1914* (Basingstoke, 1996), Ch. 2 and pp. 164–65, 167, and 170. On the Salvation Army, see K. S. Inglis, *Churches and the Working Classes in Victorian England* (London, 1963), Ch. 4.

96.　For its ironic, contemporary, acknowledgement, see Frank Fox, *The English, 1909–1922* (London, 1923), p. 91.

97.　D. W. Bebbington, *The Nonconformist Conscience: Chapel and Politics, 1870–1914* (London, 1982), Ch. 5; Wolffe, *God and Greater Britain*, pp. 140–53.

98.　T. H. Green, *Lectures on the Principle of Political Obligation*, Paul Harris and John Marrow, eds. (Cambridge, 1986); see esp. "Introduction," pp. 1–12; I. M. Greengarth, *Thomas Hill Green and the Development of Liberal Democratic Thought*

(Toronto, 1981), Ch. 1; cf. Walter Pater, *Plato and Platonism* (London, 1893), Ch. 18; also Pater, *The Renaissance*, Adam Phillips, ed. (Oxford, 1986), esp. pp. vii–xviii. Note the important essay by T. S. Eliot, "Arnold and Pater," in Eliot, *Selected Essays* (London, 1951, 3rd edn.), pp. 430–43.

99. E. R. Norman, *Church and Society in England, 1770–1970* (Oxford, 1976), pp. 188–201 and 269ff; also Machin, *Politics and the Churches of Great Britain*, pp. 305–23.

100. For contemporary observations on economic divergence, see Baldwin, *God's Englishman*, p. 182; for subsequent analysis, Derek Aldcroft, *The Inter-War Economy: Britain, 1919–1939* (London, 1970), Ch. 3; for cultural differentiation, note the remarks in the *Headlam Diaries*, p. 570–71, entry for Feb. 1, 1949; for scholarly corroboration, consult Hastings, *English Christianity*, pp. 271ff.

101. The most easily digestible figures can be found in Peter Brierley, "Religion," in A. H. Halsey, ed., *British Social Trends since 1900: A Guide to the Change of Social Structure of Britain* (London, 1988), Ch. 13, and pp. 521ff.

102. Noted in Rowse, *A Cornish Childhood*, p. 164; celebrated in Taylor, *English History*, p. 169; soberly summarized in Davies, *Strange Death of Moral Britain*, pp. 49–50. On the implications of hedonistic Hellenism see, above all, Martin Green, *Children of the Sun: A Narrative of Decadence in England after 1918* (London, 1977), Ch. 2; also the remarks of Robert Skidelsky, "Oxford in the 1920s," in Skidelsky's *Interests and Observations: Historical Essays* (London, 1993), p. 148–51.

103. Lord Beveridge, *Power and Influence* (London, 1953); compare the force of Chs. I and VIII.

104. Cited in Hastings, *English Christianity*, p. 271.

105. Christie Davies, "Moralization and Demoralization: A Moral Explanation for Changes in Crime, Disorder and Social Problems," in Digby Anderson, ed., *The Loss of Virtue: Moral Confusion and Social Disorder in Britain and America* (London, 1993), p. 11.

106. Davies, *Strange Death*, p. 44.

107. Wigley, *Rise and Fall*, conclusion.

108. S. J. D. Green, *Religion in the Age of Decline: Organisation and Experience in Industrial Yorkshire, 1870–1920* (Cambridge, 1996), pp. 367–79.

109. Hastings, *A History of English Christianity*, pp. 105–06; John D. Gay, *The Geography of Religion in England* (London, 1971), pp. 113–15.

110. Hastings, *English Christianity*, pp. 105–06; Davies, "Moralization and Demoralization," pp. 10–11.

111. Davies, *Strange Death*, p. 46–47.

112. Machin, *Churches and Social Issues*, pp. 54–58.

113. Gerald Barry, ed., *This England: The Englishman in Print* (London, 1933); see esp. "The Heavenly Twins," pp. 39–47.

114. Barry, ed., *This England*, p. 41.

115. Ibid., pp. 39–40. Rhyl is, of course, in Wales.

116. Above all, in the work of B. Seebohm Rowntree. See Asa Briggs, *Social Thought and Social Action: A Study of the Work of Seebohm Rowntree, 1871–1954* (London, 1961), pp. 12–24.

117. Philip, Viscount Snowdon, *An Autobiography* (London, 1934), Vol. 1, p. 22.

118. B. Seebohm Rowntree, *Poverty: A Study of Town Life* (London, 1901), esp. Ch. 1; also his *Poverty and Progress: A Second Social Survey of York* (London, 1941), p. v.

119. Rowntree, *Poverty and Progress*, pp. 363–67.

120. Ibid., pp. 360–69.

121. Ibid., p. 369; see also D. E. Butler and J. Freeman, *British Political Facts, 1900–1960* (London, 1963), p. 326; and the remarks in Lloyd, *English History*, p. 265.

122. George B. Wilson, *Alcohol and the Nation* (London, 1940), pp. 11, 253, and 286.

123. Rowntree, *Poverty and Progress*, pp. 363 and 372.

124. Ibid., p. 370.

125. Ibid., p. 363.

126. Ibid., pp. 370–71; also Thomas, *Underworld at War*, p. 3.

127. G. M. Trevelyan, *English Social History: A Survey of Six Centuries Chaucer to Victoria* (London, 1944), p. 571.

128. Resolution 44; see Norman, *Church and Society*, pp. 374–441.

129. B. Seebohm Rowntree and G. R. Lavers, *English Life and Leisure: A Social Study* (London, 1951), Ch. 2, esp. pp. 147–56. For a modern assessment, see Machin, *Churches and Social Issues*, pp. 118–25.

130. Machin, *Churches and Social Issues*, Ch. 4.

131. *The Times*, July, 12, 1943.

132. Cited in Thomas, *Underworld at War*, p. 16.

133. R. J. Hammond, *Food and Agriculture in Britain, 1939–1945: Aspects of Wartime Control* (Stanford, 1955), Chs. 2–5; W. K. Hancock and M. M. Gowing, *British Economy* (HMSO, London, 1949), Chs. III, V–VI, and XVIII; the experience is described in Juliet Gardiner, *Wartime: Britain, 1939–1945* (London, 2004), pp. 144–62, 487–91, and 506–07.

134. David Reynolds, *Rich Relatives: The American Occupation of Britain, 1942–1945* (London, 1995), Part I.

135. Hancock and Gowing, *British War Economy*, pp. 163–65, 169, 325, 342, 502, and 571.

136. Ibid., Chs. XII and XVII.

137. Thomas, *Underworld at War*, pp. 141ff; Gardiner, *Wartime*, pp. 505–07.

138. David Hume, "Of Commerce," in Hume, *Essays, Moral, Political and Literary*, T. H. Green and T. H. Grose, eds. (2 Vols, London, 1875), Vol. 1, pp. 287–99.

139. Thomas, *Underworld at War*, pp. 139ff.

140. Morgan, *The People's Peace*, pp. 119ff and p. 177; on the significance of the first, see Macmillan's remarks for May 13, 1952, in his *Diaries*, pp. 161–62.

141. Morgan, *People's Peace*, pp. 478ff and p. 146; also, Macmillan, Feb. 27, 1952, Oct. 1, 1955 Apr. 26, 1956, and May 16, 1956 in *Diaries*, pp. 145, 487, 554, and 560.

142. Cf. Scott, *Life in Britain*, p. 69 with Noel Annan, *Our Age: Portrait of a Generation* (London, 1990), p. 189.

12

It Didn't *All* Start in the Sixties

KATHARINE WHITEHORN

Some decades get a glittering label for all time: the Naughty Nineties, the Roaring Twenties and of course the Sixties, which seemed to explode with strobe lights and hope, freedom and flower children, and power to the young—or to descend into lascivious decadence, according to your point of view. By contrast, the Fifties have been left in the shadows, generally thought to be just a bare patch of ground between the battlefield of the Forties and the fairground of the Sixties. Yet it was actually one of the most exciting decades of the century.

We had the Festival of Britain in 1951, with its glorious metal sculpture that shot water from one funnel to another, and the Skylon—a perfectly useless, absolutely enchanting structure. The Festival had exhibitions and displays of new materials and all the exuberance and energy that we were supposed to get from the ill-fated Millennium Dome. Somehow it worked. It let off steam. It was full of optimism. And we all went, often. In 1953 we had the Coronation—a new young Queen, plenty of positive national feeling still abounding, much talk of a new Elizabethan age. That was the year, too, that Konrad Lorenz's *King Solomon's Ring*, published in London, brought the whole world of animal ecology to the general public for the first time, and by the end of the decade Leakey—Mary Leakey, actually—had found the bone in the Olduvai gorge which opened a whole new view of the origins of man.

There were the joyous explosions of American musicals and the Ealing studios were going great guns with films like *Lavender Hill*

Mob, and *Man in a White Suit.* Dreary? Boring? Static? When John Osborne's play *Look Back in Anger* carved the Angry Young Man out of the bedrock of British conformity? How about 1954, when Kingsley Amis's *Lucky Jim,* Iris Murdoch's *Under the Net,* and William Golding's *Lord of the Flies* were all reviewed in a single article in the *Telegraph?* How about one colony after another attaining its freedom from British rule, usually under the wing of a great figure—Nkrumah, for example, who led the Gold Coast to independence? This was the decade when TV first hit British homes. Washing machines became available—imagine what that did to ordinary women's lives. And no-one now remembers that before refrigerators, which were only becoming common in this decade, we all had to eat things up in a day or two, however sick of them we might have been. These years saw the start of green belts around cities, and smokeless zones that made the ghastly pea-soup fogs a thing of the past (great was the rejoicing when the roses in London's Regents Park developed Black Spot—the sulphur in the air had hitherto kept it at bay).

It's perfectly true that the great liberalizations: of abortion law, homosexual law reform, greater candor about sex, less censorship, and the withering—for the time being—of the suffocating grip of the class system came in the Sixties. But the growing climate of openness and indeed optimism of the Fifties laid the foundation, not least the arrival in positions of influence of the bright boys and girls from humble backgrounds who had come up through the grammar school system, and could represent the point of view of the toads beneath the harrow (who know where each stroke of the harrow goes). The butterflies upon the road (who preach contentment to the toads) might still deplore their discontents, but they were never again going to have it all their own way.

It is hard to overestimate the impact of free secondary education in a grammar school for the bright girl or boy from a poor background. When, in the Sixties, we were debating, on the Latey committee, whether the age of majority should come down from 21 to 18—for example with respect to the ability to sign a valid contract—one of the strongest arguments in favor of the change was that, very often, the bright eighteen-year-old had a far better grasp of affairs than his parents who had left school at fourteen, so that making the old folks guarantors for him simply made no sense. I doubt if anyone would now argue that teenagers were better educated than their parents—especially not employers, who despair of the near illiteracy of some of their recruits. There may have been injustices in the system of secondary modern and grammar schools and it is a lasting tragedy that the third type, the technical schools, never materialized; but the availability of free further education opened a door of unbelievable opportunity for the lucky ones.

And we knew it. We were, on the whole, exasperated by our elders droning on about how much better things had been before the war; as Susan Cooper wrote in *The Age of Austerity:* "They forgot that for us it could have been a golden age." In so many ways it was—because everything seemed to be getting *better.* Wartime austerities fell away one by one, oranges were back, rationing ended in 1954. The Health Service seemed perfect (expectations were lower, of course), councils were building houses all over everywhere; we honestly thought that poverty and want were things of the past. When Macmillan said at the end of the decade that we'd never had it so good, we would have agreed with him. It took Jean Colin's book in the Sixties, ironically titled *You've Never Had it so Good,* and pieces like the one Gavin Lyall wrote for the *Sunday Times* about the slums we all thought had been bombed to extinction, to make us realize how much of an illusion it all was.

What was interesting politically was that for almost all the Fifties the Conservatives were in power; yet they were positively pink compared to their successors, let alone the full-blooded Thatcherites. The overwhelming Labour majority of the first post-war election gave way to Conservatism in 1951, but it was a very different Conservatism from the pre-war variety: at that time, all the parties endorsed the welfare state. It was the 1944 Butler Education Act—a Tory bill—that empowered bright poor children; no one had yet thought of selling off council houses, which went on being built. There was much discontented astonishment among the old guard that the poor actually enjoyed having decent housing. Before the war they had been sure that if you installed a bath in housing for the poor the great unwashed would keep coal in it.

For a lot of those who had been left-wing idealists, Suez in 1956 was a crystallization point. To an extent, they had lost their way: the socialist paradise they had expected with the post-war Labour government had not materialized, the forces of death and reaction did not seem to have been routed (the public schools, hesitant and braced for their own extinction at the end of the war, seemed after all to have survived intact); the rising tiresomeness of heavy bureaucratic inefficiency and obstructive trade union power were just beginning to be apparent—in wartime you put up with regulation as you put up with rationing, conscription, and Put That Light Out! In peace, surely, it should have slackened off? And then came the extraordinary blunder of Suez, when Prime Minister Anthony Eden, in retaliation for Nasser's nationalization of the Suez Canal, backed Israel's invasion and started bombing Egyptian villages: here was something we *knew* was wrong. The sheep, for a time, seemed distinguishable from the goats.

In the forefront of this trauma was the Sunday newspaper, the *Observer,* which denounced the invasion and our part in it in no uncertain terms. It had the most extraordinary effect. City firms withdrew their advertising and banned *Observer* reporters from press conferences; true blue Conservatives referred to it as "the traitors' paper" for a decade. Its circulation didn't suffer much, but the event substituted poor young idealists for wealthy establishment figures and the paper has had a hard time making ends meet ever since.

We worried about the atom bomb; we worried about the Russian tanks moving into Budapest; and one reason we got steamed up about Suez was that it reduced the contrast between good "Us" and wicked "Them." But only thoughtful idealists and the preternaturally gloomy worried all that much. When we came off the production line, jobs were easy to come by: if you hated the one you were in, you could always get another one—it wasn't too difficult to change. We, who were young in the Fifties, may have indulged in the world-weary cynicism of the truly privileged—witness Françoise Sagan's novel *Bonjour Tristesse,* the phrase with which she and her under-twenties cronies would greet each other. Their real trouble was that they didn't have any trouble. I remember writing at the time that the reason they were so bored all the time was that they had nothing that they *ought* to have been getting on with.

Different layers of society move at astoundingly different speeds, of course. There were true conservatives genuinely mourning a decline in privilege just as working-class people were rejoicing in low unemployment. And there were still great gulfs in the way that women saw themselves. The educated European girl had a superb time of it, with no pressure to be married by the age of twenty-one, as had her American college counterpart. She lived in a safer world and was allowed her independence—in my twenties I cheerfully hitch-hiked round France by myself for a couple of months, and this was decades before the ubiquitous back-packer trails. A girl had a growing chance of getting a decent job and *not* just secretarial or nursing, though both her less educated sister and her more aristocratic one was probably still under pressure to get married early, pander to her man, certainly to avoid having an illegitimate baby; and in 1952 38 per cent of housewives still cooked—that's to say *cooked*—three meals a day.

But women, who during the war had of course taken over all kinds of traditionally male roles, were securing footholds at all levels: the Fifties saw the first woman Recorder (the first stage of the judiciary); the first woman news reader (no, not Angela Rippon in the Seventies—Nan Winton in the Fifties); the first peeresses were allowed to sit in the House of Lords in 1958; and if Simone de Beauvoir was right in saying that freedom for women "commence à la ventre" it is significant that Family Planning was urged on the Lambeth Conference of the Church of England in the same year. Of course contraception did not begin with the Pill; as G. D. H. Cole in "Songs for Socialists" in the Thirties had it:

> The middle classes—me and you
> Already know a thing or two.
> But Oh! The poor they breed like rabbits
> They have the most disgusting habits.

But weren't we all terribly inhibited about sex? Well, no. I forget which American columnist said that everyone tends to think sex was invented the year they reached puberty; he was sneering at someone who thought sex was invented in 1960 "whereas it was actually invented in 1953." It was certainly not till the early Sixties that the contraceptive pill became widely available, but the idea that everyone before that had led chaste and inhibited lives is nonsense. Everyone knows that in wartime sexual restraint goes by the board; it seems a bit naïve to suppose that with the signing of the Yalta agreement all good girls put a padlock on their pants and a No Entry sign on their doors. Certainly we all talked about it less, and there was a good deal of the pretence of being married if you went on a holiday with your mate. There was probably less promiscuity, too, and you didn't have to have reason to say "No."

It was also in the Fifties that, more than ever before, people began to look abroad—not just either the Empire or those funny froggies across the water. From a world polarized into Friend and Enemy and out of bounds anyway, we became more and more open to intriguing foreign possibilities. Fulbright scholarships and the Marshall Plan were the obvious expressions of American idealism, and America was a far-off El Dorado for a huge number of people, but not many actually got there: visas were hard to come by, mass tourism hadn't really got under way. Europe, though, was a massively vibrant influence on Britain. There was the impact of Elizabeth David's books on food, which banished the memory of dried egg, sugar rationing and a dreaded substance called Snoek; her Italian and French and Greek recipes changed forever the stolid pre-war insistence on meat and two veg, both overcooked. French films of the *nouvelle vague* opened up strange vistas: we all went to see Cocteau's *Orphee* or Simone Signoret in *Casque d'Or*. Monnet started the forerunner of the European Union, the Coal and Steel Community, in 1950, and by 1957 it had become the Common Market with all its possibilities.

We got food; we got cheaper travel; we got films; and we got clothes—which were superb. Before Mary Quant and jeans and street cred, there was elegance. When I first covered the Paris fashion shows for *Picture Post* (not that I knew anything about fashion, but the only other girl had left for the south of France with the outgoing editor Lionel Birch) I remember being bowled over by the sheer beauty of the designs. Dresses by Courèges and Balanciaga, exquisitely made, had the same sort of loveliness as romantic sculpture. I had some of them photographed in the Musée Rodin alongside pieces scarcely more beautiful. What worked its way down to the high street was pretty good, too; it had things like the bust and the waist in more or less the normal places, skirts that could swish or cling, thin nylons—there was much ado about Nylon in the Fifties: I remember the PRO for Bri-Nylon, the British version, was an exuberant ex-Board of Trade civil servant: I asked her once what a PRO for nylon had to *do*—did it mean that if there was a headline "woman strangled with nylon stocking" she had to try and stop it? "No, no, dear" she said. "The technical boys would think it was a great tribute to the tensile strength of the yarn." If the New Look in the Forties had been a reaction against wartime austerity (one of the first Dior dresses had 22 yards of fabric in the skirt), what followed in the Fifties was still designed to be pretty to look at rather than sexy or kooky or startling.

And of course there was a male elegance, too—in the Teddy Boy. It seems laughable now that we thought the Teds so alarming: from time to time a party of a dozen or so would make mild mayhem in a seaside town and it would be Shock! Horror! in the papers. Compared to what we have now it might as well have been the teddy bears' picnic. But the Teds were really the first teenagers to have a sense of themselves as something other than half-formed grown ups—and they looked terrific, with their drainpipe trousers and perfect hair.

Maybe you have to remember a world without air travel and nylon, without refrigerators and free secondary education, a world before "kitchen sink" drama, where all the actors had to speak like gentlemen, a world where mothers told their children not to *dare* to be ill because they couldn't afford a doctor, where BBC radio was the only medium other than newspapers and not even the first sputnik had entered space, to appreciate the 1950s. Perhaps only a few of us would say, as Wordsworth said of the French Revolution, "Bliss was it in that dawn to be alive / But to be young was very heaven!" But overall it was a mixed, fascinating, confusing decade, throbbing with possibilities.

Spring Semester 2005

13

Herbert Butterfield:
The Historian as Non-Moralist

GERTRUDE HIMMELFARB

There was a time, a few generations back (as generations are counted in the academy), when every self-respecting graduate program in history had as a prerequisite a course in Historical Methods. One of the texts in that course, and far the most memorable one, was a little book by the English historian Herbert Butterfield, *The Whig Interpretation of History,* originally published in England in 1931 and reprinted repeatedly in the United States as well as in England. Aspiring historians became adept at discovering, in works of history that had nothing to do with Whigs, the tell-tale signs of the "Whig interp," as it was familiarly known: reading the past in terms of the present, and seeing history as the inevitable progress toward liberty and modernity. That interpretation, in turn, was based upon the "Whig fallacy," passing moral judgments on characters and events in the past.

Today, *The Whig Interpretation of History,* once the staple of historical criticism, is virtually unknown among students and dismissed or belittled by many historians. Yet it raises fundamental issues which are ignored at some peril by those who would reconstruct history to accord with their own ideological agenda, or who would deconstruct it on the theory that the past has no reality apart from the present. The Whig interpretation is alive and well, in ways Butterfield may not have anticipated but would surely have deplored.

The problem is that Butterfield himself, who died in 1979, is hardly a sure guide through the thickets of history, let alone through the ongoing history that we call the present. A reappraisal of his own life and work suggest that there are worse fallacies than the Whig fallacy.[1] Those of an older generation, who not only read Butterfield seriously but also knew him personally, may be distressed to find aspects of him, both as an historian and as a public figure—a "public intellectual," as we now say—that we were ignorant of or, perhaps, have generously forgotten. We are also brought back to an England very different from the Churchillian England of fond memory. If we are now obliged to reconsider Butterfield, we may need to reconsider the academic milieu in which he lived and thrived, and the larger world that received him so hospitably and honored him so amply.

The Whig Interpretation of History was not, as one might think from its assured yet casual tone, the work of a mature scholar reflecting upon his craft. It appeared in 1931 when Butterfield was thirty years old, a Fellow at Peterhouse, Cambridge. His only publications before that were a prize essay written as a student on the set topic of the historical novel, a brief article in the *Cambridge Historical Journal* previewing the book he was then writing, and the book itself, *The Peace Tactics of Napoleon, 1806–08,* published in 1929. This monograph, the equivalent of a doctoral dissertation (like most of his contemporaries in Britain, Butterfield did not actually take that degree) was the only full-length scholarly book he was to produce in the following two decades. Covering a period of eighteen months and based largely on published documents with very little archival research, it came as close as anything he was later to write to being the "scientific," "technical" history that he espoused. It was this book that earned him an appointment as university lecturer in 1930. It was also his credential, so to speak, for the provocative work that he published the following year.

The Whig Interpretation of History, a 130-page essay, boldly challenged what Butterfield took to be the prevailing mode of historical discourse: "the tendency in many [British] historians to write on the side of Protestants and Whigs, to praise revolutions provided they have been successful, to emphasize certain principles of progress in the past, and to produce a story which is the ratification if not the glorification of the present."[2] History, in this view, was a linear, incremental process, a victory of light over darkness, a search for origins leading to an end, and above all an occasion for moral judgments. An alternative, non-Whig history would provide not an "explanation" of what happened but rather a detailed narrative account of what did happen. This more modest aim had its own drama, "the romance of historical research."

> The historian's passion for manuscripts and sources is not the de-
> sire to correct facts and dates . . . but the desire to bring himself
> into genuine relationship with the actual, with all the particulari-
> ties of chance and change. . . . The true historical fervour is the
> love of the past for the sake of the past. . . . The true historical fer-
> vour is that of the man for whom the exercise of historical imagi-
> nation brings its own reward, in those inklings of a deeper under-
> standing, those glimpses of a new interpretative truth, which are
> the historian's achievement and his aesthetic delight.[3]

The book received mixed reviews at the time and later, critics faulting it for being rambling and repetitive, consisting of assertions rather than arguments, with no footnotes and few quotations to support the assertions, and sometimes lapsing into moral judgments of its own. Some historians have been even more disparaging. J. H. Plumb described it as "a very short book—short enough to hold the attention of a moderately industrious sixth-former" preparing for his scholarship examination.[4] David Cannadine has dismissed it as "slight, confused, repetitive and superficial."[5] And E. H. Carr found it remarkable because it denounced the Whig interpretation without naming "a single Whig except Fox, who was no historian, or a single historian save Acton, who was no Whig."[6]

In Cambridge, what made the book food for gossip was its implicit attack on George Trevelyan, the Regius Professor of Modern History and the most eminent historian in England. Butterfield protested that his book was directed not against Trevelyan but against the long dead Lord Acton. His description, however, early in the book, of the Whig historian as "Protestant, progressive & whig, and the very model of the nineteenth century gentleman" surely described Trevelyan and not Acton, who was neither Protestant nor a Whig, nor, in many respects, "progressive."[7] It is a tribute to Trevelyan, to his good nature and generosity, that he encouraged Butterfield to write the biography of Charles James Fox, the leader of the liberal faction in Parliament in the late eighteenth century, that he himself had planned to write, and gave him a trove of Fox letters in his possession. That project, the Fox biography, remained the center of Butterfield's scholarly ambitions for twenty years and would have provided a test case for a non-Whig interpretation of history. Like so many other of his undertakings, this one remained unwritten. In 1951, after publishing his only other long book, *George III, Lord North, and the People* (which covered a very short period in Fox's life), and realizing that he would never write that biography, Butterfield, on Trevelyan's urging, turned over the Fox manuscripts to the British Museum.[8]

THERE WAS MUCH TO DISTRACT BUTTERFIELD: his lectures, of course, but also the political ambience of that time and place. Cambridge in the 1930s is remembered today as a hive of Communist theorists, activists, and, not least, spies. Butterfield did not belong to these circles, but he was not impervious to them either. Maurice Dobb, the founding father of British Marxism and a charter member of the British Communist Party, was at Trinity College for the whole of the time that Butterfield was at Peterhouse. It was from Dobb (and not from Marx, whom he gave no indication of having read) that Butterfield gained what knowledge he had of Marxism, and perhaps the sympathy reflected in his essay on Marxist history in 1933. He himself did not subscribe to the Marxist interpretation of the course of history, Butterfield explained, but he did commend it as a valuable method for the study of history, its "structural" analysis of the economic and material conditions of society being more faithful to the complexity of history than the individualistic narrative account of the Whig historian. Returning to the subject in 1949 and again in 1951, he praised Marxism as a corrective to the "linear" view of history and as more profound than "ordinary political narrative"[9]— an odd commentary on his own two works of history, which were linear, political narratives. Maurice Cowling (who was later a colleague at Peterhouse) interpreted the 1933 essay as an "unconscious compact" Butterfield made with those of his pupils who were sympathetic to Marxism.[10] This explanation would also account for his later essays, when Marxism was still more popular in the university. (By then, Dobb had produced an entire school of Marxist historians and Communist Party members, including Eric Hobsbawm and E. P. Thompson.)

Butterfield himself was not a Marxist, let alone a Communist, but he was very much a part of another political disposition prevalent in Cambridge in the 1930s: appeasement. Oxford is more often associated with that tendency, thanks to the famous motion passed by the Oxford Union, one month after Hitler came to power, "not to fight for King and Country." All Souls, perhaps the most prestigious of the Oxford colleges, had among its fellows Geoffrey Dawson, the editor of *The Times,* Lord Halifax, the Chancellor of the University and Foreign Secretary under Chamberlain, and other prominent spokesmen for appeasement. But Cambridge, too, had its share of appeasers, some of whom had the privilege of belonging to the exclusive secret (or not so secret) undergraduate society known as the Apostles, which included such public Communists as Hobsbawm and Thompson, and such covert ones as Anthony Blunt and Guy Burgess. Trevelyan, an Apostle of an earlier generation, defended the policy of appeasement on purely prudential grounds, combining it, as others did not, with a vigorous denunciation of Hitler, support of a strong rearmament program, and, after the outbreak of war, a strong commitment to the war and a public acknowledgment that Churchill had been right and he and his fellow appeasers had been "blind and foolish."[11] (Trevelyan also helped found, in 1933, an organization to assist Jewish émigré scholars in England.)

Butterfield's appeasement was very different, based not on the practical realities of the situation but rather on what he took to be the proper historical attitude. "I do not defend the Fascists for being violent," a diary entry of 1936 reads, "but I wish that the enemies of the Fascists could be more gentle. Though we may regard a certain doctrine as working to corrupt and degrade the world, it is our duty to understand that doctrine, and to give sympathy and imagination to those people who have been seduced by it."[12] In this spirit of "sympathy and imagination" Butterfield accepted an invitation, in December 1938 (after the Nazi invasions of Austria and Czechoslovakia), to lecture at four German universities. His host in Berlin was an historian, Hans Galinsky, who had earlier visited England for the express purpose of recruiting English scholars to the Nazi cause. After the war, when Galinsky was removed from his position at the University of Strasbourg, Butterfield wrote references for him for appointments in Germany. He disapproved of Galinsky's views on Nazism, Butterfield explained, but he could understand how he had arrived at them. "I always thought that his case was one that could be humanly explained. . . . I did not think him unreasonable in his love of his own country. . . . If I thought he had, perhaps, an excessive love of his country, I don't think he had more of it than many men of other countries, including our own."[13]

This note of moral equivalence—equating the Nazi's "love of his country," even "excessive love of his country," with the Englishman's—was Butterfield's characteristic response to Germany before, during, and after the war. "Fight the Germans—yes, certainly, if we have to," a diary entry in 1940 reads. "Fight to save human beings from oppression or even to save the homeland from being invaded by foreigners, however virtuous. But do not think of them or treat them as sub-human. . . . Let us say rather: 'What did we do wrong? What could we have done to prevent the Germans from feeling that they must turn to Hitler?'"[14] Among his colleagues Butterfield had the reputation of having "fascist tendencies" and being "soft on Nazis."[15] Jack Plumb, who was a fellow at Cambridge at the time, remembered him as "critical of the Spanish Republicans, sympathetic, very, to Franco, . . . [and] completely neutral to Hitler."[16]

Butterfield was the only one of four Fellows in Peterhouse to remain in Cambridge throughout the war without doing any kind of military or government service. When another historian proposed to leave Newnham College for a government post, he strongly advised her not to and never forgave her when she did. And when he felt called upon to organize two conferences of refugee historians at Peterhouse in 1942 and 1943, he was annoyed to find that the refugees were more interested in combating the Germans than in taking the properly neutral "academic view," and he cancelled the conference scheduled for the following year. In 1943, he was reported as favoring a separate negotiated settlement with Hitler. Visiting Dublin that year as an external examiner at the university, he saw nothing amiss in going to parties at the German consulate (Ireland having been neutral during the war).[17]

A LITTLE BOOK PUBLISHED BY BUTTERFIELD in 1944 seemed to suggest something like a conversion on his part. *The Englishman and His History,* an essay about the same length as the *Whig Interpretation,* acquired something of the same notoriety as the earlier one, if only because it appeared to contradict it. *"Das Herbert Butterfield Problem,"* the historian J. G. A. Pocock has dubbed it (echoing *"Das Adam Smith Problem,"* the famous Germanic rendition of the supposed inconsistency between Smith's two major works).[18] E. H. Carr (who was himself a staunch appeaser, first of Nazism and then of Stalinism), mocked the emergence of a "deutero-Butterfield" in place of the "proto-Butterfield" of the earlier book.[19] Where the *Whig Interpretation* had posited a break between past and present, so that the past could be understood entirely in its own terms, Butterfield now portrayed the past as thoroughly imbued with the present: a past "coiled up inside the present," a past "used to assist our purposes," an "alliance" or "marriage" of past and present. He reconciled the two books by distinguishing between Whig statesmen and Whig historians, the former "always so much greater" than the latter. By his own account, however, it was the Whig interpretation itself that helped create the England he was now celebrating. And that interpretation was not invented by historians but was part of the English mind and the very "landscape" of English life. "We are all of us exultant and unrepentant whigs," including those, he added ruefully, who, "perhaps, in the misguided austerity of youth," had tried to drive out that Whig history.[20]

Yet there were still echoes of the "proto-Butterfield" in the "deutero-Butterfield." The argument against moral judgments now took the form of an argument for Providence. Providence had appeared in the *Whig Interpretation* as well, although less insistently (and not capitalized). Now it was invoked (capitalized) as a major force in history. With it there emerged the religious theme that was to occupy Butterfield more and more in later years: the relationship between Christianity and history.

Much has been made, and properly so, of Butterfield's Methodist upbringing and convictions. Raised in a Yorkshire working-class family with strong ties to the chapel, he became a lay preacher at the age of sixteen and continued to do occasional preaching on the Cambridge circuit, first as a student and then as a fellow and university lecturer. He ceased preaching in 1936—except, one might say, in the guise of historian. Toward the end of his life he confessed in his journal that, "the desire to 'preach the Gospel,' though it has been submerged on occasion, has perhaps been my most constant motor."[21] Certainly, the rhetoric and passion of the preacher were evident in his repeated invocation of Providence as a rebuke to those self-righteous, moralizing men who tried to interfere with the natural, organic, historical process that was the genius of the English (and, as he now saw it, the Whig) tradition.

It was this providential view that governed Butterfield's attitude toward politics as much as history, reflected in his policy of appeasement and in his persistently conciliatory attitude to Hitler. In one of only two passing references to Hitler in *The Englishman and His History* (this in the middle of the war), Butterfield linked him with Napoleon as one of the "new men" who think that they can become "monarchs and masters of the course of things."[22] But it was not only such new men who were especially "prone to this form of presumption." So were those Englishmen "presumptuous" enough to think that they could usurp the role of Providence by imposing their own moral judgments and trying to "re-model the world to their hearts' desire."[23]

A quarter of a century later, in the preface to a reprint of *The Englishman and His History*, Butterfield said that the excessiveness of his patriotism in that book struck him as "comic."[24] He was apparently beginning to find it excessive almost immediately, to judge by the inaugural lecture delivered only a few months later, in November 1944, on his appointment as Professor of Modern History at Cambridge. The appointment itself was remarkable, considering the paucity of his scholarly writings. (Unlike the American plenitude of professorships, that exalted title is relatively rare in an English university.) More remarkable were some of his observations in that lecture. With the war still in a precarious state, he took the opportunity, while criticizing Nazi and Fascist totalitarianism, to urge his countrymen to extend an "imaginative sympathy" not only to Nazis, whose loyalty to Germany, he said, resembled the patriotism of Englishmen (including himself), but also to those who "for some reason have fallen in love with a foreign power"—presumably German sympathizers in England.[25] It is no wonder that he won the reputation in Cambridge of being "pro-German" or "Germanophile."[26]

What is extraordinary is that this tolerant view of the enemy should have been received, after the war as well, not only with equanimity but with apparent enthusiasm by the English public. His lectures on Christianity and history, delivered in Cambridge in 1948, were broadcast the following year on the BBC, printed in the *Listener,* and published as a book. Citing repeatedly the precept, "all men are sinners," with "self-righteousness" being the worst sin, Butterfield again warned against the presumptuousness of passing moral judgments on the actors of history or trying to control the course of history. Men, nations, and political systems were all equal before God, and equal in their potentiality for sin. Hitler and Stalin, like all political leaders, were confronted not with a choice between good and evil but with a series of "predicaments," and those predicaments, not the will, the intentions, or the ideas of men, determined the course of history. "Providence" and "Predicaments"—these now emerged as Butterfield's watchwords. From this neutral perspective, he found the differences between the pro-Munich and anti-Munich factions like "the quarrels of Tweedledum and Tweedledee." The book concluded with the simple dictum: "Hold to Christ, and for the rest be totally uncommitted."[27] It was an oddly passive, quietistic message for a country that had won the war as a result of the conscious, resolute actions of its leaders and people.

In another lecture about the same time, Butterfield extended this spirit of Christian forbearance to the writing of biographies. Thus the life of "the worst of murderers" could be written in such a way as to make him the "hero" of the story, so that "our pity and sympathy would be around him as we followed him up from childhood." Such a biography, by "a person who did not hate him too much," would enable the reader to see how "a lump of human nature (how a boy playing in a field) could ever have come to be *like that.*"[28] Almost two decades later, in one of Butterfield's last lectures, the country boy was transformed into a city boy: "It would be good if a historian could explain to us how a boy of ten, playing in a city street, could have come to be like that—the historian behaving like a mother who sadly has to observe how a son of hers is going wrong."[29]

BY MID-CENTURY (AND BY THE AGE OF FIFTY), Butterfield had become something of a celebrity. In the single month of October 1949,

three of his books were published: *Christianity and History: The Origins of Modern Science, 1300–1800,* and *George III, Lord North, and the People, 1779–1780.* The book on science, like so many of his others, was based on a series of lectures and had some of the characteristics of that genre; it was repetitive, imprecise, loosely constructed. The dates are deceptive; the focus is on the period between 1550 and the 1680s, rather than the larger scope suggested. Critics have faulted it for its superficial generalizations and lack of original and up-to-date scholarship, and readers of the *Whig Interpretation* may find in it the typical symptoms of the Whig fallacy: foreshadowings, anticipations, and other present-minded evocations of the scientific revolution. The public response was favorable, however, and it became, and still remains (in the revised edition published in 1957), a standard work in the new discipline of the history of science that Butterfield helped create and popularize.

George III, Lord North, and the People is an entirely different kind of book. It was Butterfield's only long scholarly work apart from *The Peace Tactics of Napoleon* twenty years earlier. Like the earlier book, it had a narrow focus, eight months (or eighteen, if the background material is included). Within that focus, it did bear out Butterfield's thesis: liberty was not the result of the intentions or the policies of the protagonists, but rather the unwitting outcome of the struggle between the king and the aristocracy. The reviews were generally unfavorable, complaining, once again, of a lack of knowledge of current literature and research.

These scholarly works were almost interludes in a career that depended not on scholarship but on larger, amorphous reflections in which history provided the context—or, it sometimes seemed, the pretext—for pronouncements about public affairs. Butterfield's status as a "public intellectual" was secure, even as historians carped about his history. His books were reissued in England and America and some were translated into half a dozen languages (*Christianity and History* into Chinese). And he was a frequent lecturer abroad as well as at home. On a lecture tour in Germany in 1950 (his first visit after the war), he repeated his standard message: the most universal and the most dangerous sin was "human presumption and particularly intellectual arrogance." Instead of exhorting his audiences to learn from history, as another historian might have done, he told them that all people must "unlearn" much of their history so that they would not be "frozen" in the past, a comforting thought for Germans who would have liked to forget their own recent Nazi past.[30] In lectures at home, he was less comforting to his own countrymen, blaming them, as much as the Germans, for both world wars. He recalled that one of his students, a conscientious objector

exempted from military service, was so appalled by Hitler's invasion of Norway in 1940 that he enlisted and died in naval service. "I have wondered sometimes," Butterfield reflected, "what his reaction would had been if he had lived to know that Great Britain had had a prior intention of invading Norway—and this even irrespective of the desire to help Finland—and that Hitler, initially unwilling to undertake the adventure, had decided to forestall us."[31] Later, endorsing A. J. P. Taylor's view that Hitler did not start World War II (at least not when it did start), he told an interviewer: "The fact that Taylor fails to condemn Hitler doesn't worry me; it sounds priggish but I don't think passing judgment is in the province of a technical historian. I think that's God's job, that's God's history—though I don't personally like the term."[32]

Some commentators have suggested that Butterfield was "soft" on Hitler and Nazism because he regarded Stalin and communism as the greater enemy.[33] In fact, he applied the same principles of political neutrality and moral equivalence to both. In *Christianity and History,* he praised Stalin for reclaiming Marxism from "the laboratories of the sociologists and economists" and restoring it to the narrative of real history, "a narrative about people—even about national heroes." Communism, he granted, was associated with "unbelief, atrocities, persecution and aggression," but so was democracy in the period of the French Revolution. From a diplomatic point of view, the Soviet Union was not very different from what it would have been if the regime were a Tsarist one or a democracy, because "the general predicament would have been much the same." Butterfield could even imagine himself "a Stalin feeling that the other party, or that the whole predicament, has goaded me into blockading Berlin."[34]

By this time the Cold War was well under way, and Butterfield's argument against anti-communism became a major theme of his lectures not only in England but in the United States (where it was welcomed by the American Left), and in the Soviet Union (where it must have been equally pleasing to communists). *Christianity, Diplomacy and War,* in 1953, was his most extensive criticism of this latest "war of righteousness." After 1940, he said, the British had "produced a situation in which Hitler could not consolidate himself or restore normality, but had to be forever on the move." Now that situation was being repeated in respect to Russia (as he generally referred to the Soviet Union), with ideology—anti-communist ideology, now—once again threatening to undermine the "international order." Just as "anti-Nazis become too much like Nazis," so "anti-communists [become] too like communists, in their angers and

hatreds and indignations." Many of the evils seen in the Russian system had nothing to do with the communist ideal but were rather "organic to the phenomenon of revolution as such." Moreover, that ideal—egalitarianism and a classless society—was itself a Christian and Western product, and was already contributing to the "Westernization" of the world. In any case, once the revolutionary stage of communism was passed, in other countries as well as in Russia, communism itself would be as normal and legitimate a part of the international order as Anglo-Saxon democracy.[35]

Here too Butterfield displayed a nice sense of equivalence—this time being equally tolerant of Communism and Nazism. If he sometimes sounded "like an apologist for the Soviets," he also occasionally sounded like an apologist for the Nazis.[36] In 1953, it might be argued, the enormity of Stalin's dictatorship had not yet fully emerged (or been acknowledged). One could hardly say the same of Hitler's. By then the nature of Nazi totalitarianism and the facts of the Holocaust had been dramatically exposed, so that Butterfield's suggestion that Hitler should have been given an opportunity to "consolidate himself or restore normality" could only have meant a consolidation of his tyranny and the restoration of the "normality" of genocide. (In *Christianity, Diplomacy and War,* the word "Holocaust" appeared only once, referring not to the fate of the Jews but rather to a war against communism that would be "a mere holocaust."[37]) Butterfield was no less conciliatory toward the Soviet Union—this as late as 1960, well after Khrushchev's speech denouncing Stalin, after the suppression of the uprisings in Poland and Hungary, and after many prominent English communists, E. P. Thompson among them, had left the Party in protest.

WHEN BUTTERFIELD ASSUMED THE MANTLE OF HISTORIAN during these years, it was not history proper that occupied him but historiography. *Man on His Past,* published in 1955 (again, a series of lectures repeated as radio talks), is impressively erudite on such subjects as the German historical school of the late eighteenth century and Ranke and Acton in the nineteenth. The book also has the distinction of being one of his few footnoted works. Yet it, too, received mixed reviews, critics complaining of its repetitiousness, lack of focus even within a single essay let alone in the book as a whole, and assertions about "technical," or "scientific" history which were vague and unsubstantiated. It did, however, have the effect of reminding Butterfield's colleagues, and the public, that even as he made the rounds of the lecture circuit and delivered his radio talks, he did so with the authority of the professional historian.

Another book on historiography that appeared two years later, *George III and the Historians,* was less successful in confirming Butterfield's reputation as an historian. A pastiche of lectures and reviews, it was memorable mainly because of its attack on Lewis Namier, the foremost historian of eighteenth-century parliamentary history, thus Butterfield's rival on that subject. It is ironic to read his criticism of Namier's concept of the "structure" of politics, when one recalls his own essays praising Marxism for a "structural" analysis that was preferable to conventional narrative history. Now he found the idea of structure faulty precisely because it displaced narrative history. He also criticized Namier and his followers for belittling the "ideas and purposes" of politicians—which is what he himself did when he made "Providence" and "Predicaments," rather than ideas and purposes, the determinant forces of history.[38]

The reviews of *George III and the Historians* were almost uniformly critical, some very sharply so. Even more damaging than the charges of inaccuracy and inconsistency was the evidence of serious misquotations, one of which Butterfield had to acknowledge publicly in the *Times Literary Supplement.* Privately he confessed that he had "made more howlers than I knew about."[39] Yet once again he emerged if not quite intact, at least not seriously wounded. Called upon by the BBC in 1960 to deliver not one but two obituaries of Namier, he took the occasion, after some dutiful expressions of praise, to repeat his earlier criticisms and to suggest that Namier had misspent his professional life by directing the kind of parliamentary research he did. The historian John Kenyon observed of one of these obituaries: "It was a typical Butterfield performance, each paragraph cancelling out the one before."[40]

In retrospect, it would seem that Butterfield had an enchanted career. By the usual standards of historical scholarship, he produced no great work of history, certainly nothing like the "technical," "scientific" history that he acclaimed as the only true kind of history. "He was a man," Kenyon said, "with a reputation rather like an inverted cone, his wide-ranging prestige balanced on a tiny platform of achievement."[41] In addition to being the Professor of Modern History at Cambridge, he became Master of Peterhouse in 1954 ("If I die tonight," he told his assistant, "I shall have been Master of my college"),[42] President of the Historical Association that same year, Vice-Chancellor of the university in 1959, and reached the height of his profession in 1963 as the Regius Professor of Modern History. (He had been disappointed when he failed to receive that appointment earlier.) The final social seal of approval came with his knighthood in 1968, at which time Sir Herbert resigned both as Master of Peterhouse and as Regius Professor.

And yet, and yet . . . Butterfield deserves still to be remembered as the author of *The Whig Interpretation of History*. This book remains, for all its flaws, a valuable corrective to some of the dominant modes of history today. A generation initiated by it into the discipline of history read it as an exhortation to try to recapture the past in all its concreteness, complexity, contingency, and particularity—a "past-ness" as free from the taint of present-mindedness as is humanly possible. It did not occur to us that this could mean belittling the moral facts of the past—the events, the policies, and the ideas that defined the moral character of a person, a regime, or a period, and which were as surely as much the reality of history as politics, economics, geography, demography, or whatever other facts the historian might think pertinent. We were fully aware of how difficult it would be to meet this challenge without falling into the "Whig fallacy." What we did not then realize was how little Butterfield himself faced up to that challenge.

Perhaps what is needed today is not the revival of a "proto-Butterfield," who was so suspicious of moral judgments as to ignore or belie the moral facts of history, nor a "deutero-Butterfield," who all too fleetingly, and regretfully, lapsed into an occasional moral sentiment or judgment, but a "neo-Butterfield," who can truly appreciate the "romance" of history—which is to say, the moral as well as political "predicaments" confronting statesmen, peoples, and historians as well.

Spring Semester 2005

1. I was inspired to reread yet again *The Whig Interpretation of History,* this time in the context of Butterfield's other work, by the fine biography by C. T. McIntire, *Herbert Butterfield: Historian as Dissenter* (New Haven, 2004). If not an authorized biography (McIntire had lengthy interviews with Butterfield in the years before his death and had access to all his papers), this is certainly an authoritative one, and although generally sympathetic, is not at all hagiographic. A version of the present essay appeared as a review of this book in the *New Republic,* Oct. 11, 2004.

2. Herbert Butterfield, *The Whig Interpretation of History* (London, 1959 [1st ed., 1931]), p. v.

3. Ibid., pp. 72–73, 92, 96.

4. J. H. Plumb, *The Making of an Historian* (Athens, Georgia, 1988), p. 254.

5. David Cannadine, *G. M. Trevelyan: A Life in History* (New York, 1992), p. 208.

6. E. H. Carr, *What is History?* (New York, 1962), p. 50. David Hackett Fischer corrected Carr: "Hallam is mentioned on page four, and Hallam was a historian and a Whig, though he was both just barely." See Fischer, *Historians' Fallacies: Toward a Logic of Historical Thought* (New York, 1970), p. 281.

7. Butterfield, *Whig Interpretation,* pp. 3–4. Although Butterfield, here and elsewhere, cited Acton as a prime example of the Whig fallacy, in this book Acton appears only toward the end in the chapter on moral judgments in history. Most of the book centers on the Whig interpretation of the Protestant Reformation as the central event in the progress of liberty.

8. Late in life, invited to give a lecture at the British Academy, he returned to this subject, trying to compress forty years of research and a vast quantity of notes into twenty-four published pages. He focused on two years of Fox's life to determine whether Fox was "sincere" in pursuing parliamentary reform. When he prepared the lecture for publication in the *Proceedings of the British Academy,* which required footnotes, he made so many errors that he had to send an embarrassed letter to the Secretary of the Academy correcting them.

9. Herbert Butterfield, "Marxist History," in *History and Human Relations* (London, 1951), p. 79. See also "The Christian and the Marxian Interpretation of History" (1949) in C. T. McIntire, ed., *Herbert Butterfield: Writings on Christianity and History* (New York, 1979), pp. 198 and *passim.*

10. Maurice Cowling, *Religion and Public Doctrine in Modern England* (Cambridge, England, 1980), p. 224.

11. Cannadine, *Trevelyan,* pp. 128–36.

12. McIntire, *Historian as Dissenter,* p. 105.

13. Ibid., p. 108.

14. Ibid., p. 112.

15. Ibid., p. 108.

16. Plumb, *Making of an Historian,* p. 7. See also Cannadine, who described Butterfield's attitude toward Hitler (during the war as well as before) as "a neutrality bordering on indifference," *Trevelyan,* p. 208.

17. See Noel Annan, *The Dons: Mentors, Eccentrics, and Geniuses* (London, 1999), p. 246; by the same author, *Our Age: Portrait of a Generation* (London, 1990), pp. 392–93.

18. Keith C. Sewell, "The 'Herbert Butterfield Problem' and its Resolution," *Journal of the History of Ideas* (2004), p. 599. Sewell is quoting J. G. A. Pocock, *Virtue, Commerce, and History* (Cambridge, 1976). Pocock's term is *"Das Herbert Butterfield Problem."*

19. Carr, *What is History?* p. 51. Offended by these epithets, Butterfield told an interviewer, Ved Mehta, that the passage cited by Carr as evidence of the change

had been written not in 1944 but in a lecture in 1938. See Mehta, *Fly and the Fly-Bottle: Encounters with British Intellectuals* (Boston, 1962), pp. 256–57. In fact, while a good part of this book, the historical part, was based on that earlier series of lectures, this particular passage and others on the contemporary situation were unique to this book and quite different, in tone and substance, from the earlier lectures. See Sewell, "The 'Herbert Butterfield Problem,'" p. 602.

20. Butterfield, *The Englishman and His History* (Cambridge, 1944), pp. v–vii, 3–5.

21. McIntire, *Historian as Dissenter,* p. 408.

22. Butterfield, *Englishman and His History,* p. vi.

23. Ibid., p. 135.

24. McIntire, *Historian as Dissenter,* p. 117.

25. Ibid., p. 137 (quoting Butterfield).

26. Ibid., pp. 166, 308.

27. Butterfield, *Christianity and History* (New York, 1950), pp. 141, 146. On "Providence" and "Predicaments," see also pp. 29, 37, 40, 42, 45.

28. Butterfield, "Moral Judgments in History," in *History and Human Relations,* p. 111 (emphasis in original).

29. Butterfield, "Does Belief in Christianity Validly Affect the Modern Historian?" (1969), in McIntire, ed., *Butterfield: Writings on Christianity and History,* p. 149.

30. Butterfield, "The Dangers of History," in *History and Human Relations,* pp.169, 172.

31. Butterfield, *Christianity, Diplomacy and War* (London, 1953), pp. 32–33. (See also p. 62.)

32. Mehta, *Fly and the Fly-Bottle,* p. 251.

33. For example, Plumb, *Making of an Historian,* p. 7; Annan, *Dons,* p. 246.

34. Butterfield, *Christianity and History,* pp. 27, 134, 142, 44–45.

35. Butterfield, *Christianity, Diplomacy, and War,* pp. 65, 107–08, 121.

36. McIntire, *Historian as Dissenter,* p. 245.

37. Butterfield, *Christianity, Diplomacy, and War,* p. 63.

38. Herbert Butterfield, *George III and the Historians* (London, 1957), p. 290.

39. McIntire, *Historian as Dissenter,* p. 287. McIntire pronounced the episode a "disaster," and a "debacle" (pp. 291–92).

40. John Kenyon, *The History Men* (London, 1983), p. 266. See also Annan, *Dons,* p. 264; Annan, *Our Age,* p. 270; Cannadine, *Trevelyan,* p. 210.

41. Kenyon, *History Men,* p. 261.

42. McIntire, *Historian as Dissenter,* p. 271.

14

Gallagher's Empire

JOHN DARWIN

John Gallagher (1919–1980), known to everyone as "Jack," sometimes in partnership with Ronald Robinson, was the most brilliant and original historian of modern imperialism. This is not to
compare him with John A. Hobson or Lenin, whose writing on imperialism was polemic, not history. It is to claim that of all those who
have written historically on the British and other colonial empires
since the time when their archival study became possible, his influence has been the most seminal, far-reaching, and profound.

An important part of Gallagher's influence sprang from an exceptional felicity in both speaking and writing. He could capture the
dilemmas of empire in a phrase: pithy, witty, and memorable. Once
the British Empire became worldwide, he once remarked, the sun
never set on its crises. For the British as a world power, security, like
love affairs or solvency, was here today and gone tomorrow. Colonialism, he observed in 1962 (this was after a visit to the Congo), was
not the form of government hardest to endure, but the form of government safest to attack.[1] In a review of a half-dozen pages, or a short
conference paper (like one delivered in Delhi in 1961), he could
deftly sketch great tracts of modern world history and illuminate
their meaning.[2] This was the fruit of a legendary breadth of reading
and intellectual curiosity. Indeed, Gallagher insisted on studying
empire as part of world history and no region lay beyond his imperial frontier. In the same way, he insisted that the history of a colony
was comprehensible only in the larger frame of its imperial and
global connections. You cannot study the affairs of a colony, he liked

to say, as if they were the annals of a parish. Most of all, Gallagher's was an ironic, detached, and unsentimental view of the British Empire as a world system. It was not a cause to defend or a grievance to denounce but a passing historical phenomenon. The history of empire as Gallagher and Robinson conceived it in the early 1950s was thus already a history for the post-colonial age.

Historical writing, like other forms of creativity, is shaped by the intellect and artistry of the individual but also by the public culture of its time and place. The period in which Gallagher was most active (the 1940s through the 1970s) was exceptional in the cultural history of modern Britain. Its academic and literary culture was remarkable for its range, depth, seriousness, and ambition. Looking back from the blasted heath of the contemporary British scene, it has some of the aura of a golden age. But it was not accidental. The energy that flowed into historical and other forms of writing was generated by the distinctive moral and intellectual climate of post-war Britain—a phase which lasted into the 1960s. Much of the heat and some of the light came from the clash of two competing cultural systems: one still grounded in the ethos of aristocracy, empire, established religion, and the class system; the other repudiating these as the bases of social order and national identity. Post-war Britain might have become a welfare state and espoused meritocracy, but it was still Churchill's Britain: a military and imperial power whose prestige was at stake in Cyprus, Central Africa, Southeast Asia—and Suez. The shape of Britain's future (and hence the meaning of its past) were debated with an intensity that has no parallel today.

This was partly because the contesting parties were so certain that it mattered. This was perhaps the last period in which intellectual life in Britain could be based on the assumption that Britain, and British history, had a global importance. Britain had ruled—and still ruled—large parts of the world. British institutions, vindicated by victory, were the model for parliamentary democracy and representative government. Britain had pioneered the industrial revolution, so its economic, like its constitutional history, seemed of universal significance. With Europe in eclipse and America adjusting to the colossal burdens of its new world role, British opinion and British ideas retained a large sphere of influence, not least in the Commonwealth. This sense of importance and cultural centrality was a powerful stimulant in intellectual life. It was supercharged by the third dynamic element in post-war British society: the well-spring of new intellectual talent thrown up by the war and its social fall-out. Mobilization had jerked millions from their peacetime routines. The enforced mobility of war brought new opportunities and awoke new ambitions. The war meant exotic travel and the chance to gain skills and knowledge unimaginable for most in pre-war Britain. It burst the parochial bounds of life at home and energized a generation. A new public emerged to be entertained, informed, and educated. After 1945, the expansion of secondary schooling opened up academic education to thousands for whom it would otherwise have been prohibitively expensive. Grammar school boys (and some girls) invaded the old universities and formed the main demand for the new universities set up in the 1950s and 1960s. This widening of educational opportunity, and the new audience it created, coincided with—and stimulated—the rapid growth of the newer disciplines in the arts and social sciences: sociology, political science, economic and social history, social anthropology.

It is in this wider setting that we must place the historiographical revolution in the study of empire which Gallagher achieved in partnership with Ronald Robinson. Without this dynamic intellectual climate their ideas would scarcely have been so influential and might not have been formulated at all. As it was they were able to seize the initiative in a subject still largely stuck in its old groove. They did so by asking a series of deceptively simple questions. What sense could be made of Britain's colossal expansion in the nineteenth-century world? Why did the Victorians show no desire to rule many regions of obvious economic value, while scrambling for others that looked more like liabilities than assets? What motives lay behind their late-century rush to annex vast hinterlands in tropical Africa? These were questions that the old tradition of empire history was ill-equipped to answer. Many of its practitioners were less concerned to explain than to justify or condemn. They emphasized moral purpose (the civilizing mission) or material greed (economic imperialism). Their arguments were monocausal and Eurocentric. Their objects were more often political than academic. Partly as a result of this, by the time of Gallagher and Robinson's intervention a neo-Marxist account of British imperial expansion seemed to offer the most sophisticated explanation. It connected the economic revolution in British society with the pattern of its activity abroad. It saw the need for markets, raw materials, and outlets for surplus capital as the driving force in colonial annexation and viewed the late-Victorians' scramble for Africa—the apparent climax of their empire-building—as the consequence of the industrial competition between Britain and the new industrial powers of Europe. It drew a sharp contrast between the indifference to imperialism (defined as territorial occupation or annexation) in the mid-Victorian era of liberalism and free trade and the jingoist, protectionist instincts behind the late-Victorian mania for colonies.

Gallagher and Robinson ridiculed this chronology and the definition of imperialism on which it depended. They acknowledged that the motive for British expansion was fundamentally economic. British industrialization had meant a search for customers. The British had opened their domestic market to the world's raw materials in the hope that non-industrial countries would buy British goods in return. Free trade was the means to integrate new regions into the expanding economy—the commercial economy centered on Britain. But far from being confined to those regions annexed as colonies, British economic ambition was worldwide. In the totality of British expansion, they insisted (in a famous phrase) that the formal empire of colonies was merely the visible part of the iceberg, whose larger portion was, in constitutional terms, invisible. Why, then, were some regions annexed, and others left in varying degrees of independence? The answer, they said, had nothing to do with their economic promise and all to do with the chances of cooperation with the local regime. Where free (or free-ish) trade and the open door could be agreed upon without forcible intervention, mid-Victorian governments gladly avoided the trouble and expense of occupation and rule. Where more forceful action was needed to persuade local rulers to oblige, gunboats were dispatched, expeditions landed, and unequal treaties (most famously in China) imposed at the point of the bayonet. Only if, as in India, it seemed that the whole extent of imperial government were needed to secure the British interest, did London bite the bullet and rule. Of course, this general model left many squares on the imperial chessboard unexplained. Why annex regions without a shadow of economic promise or where, on any reckoning, the costs would far outweigh the benefits? Because, said Gallagher and Robinson, such places had a strategic value in the grand scheme of global expansion. They were the guard posts for the trade routes, communication, and frontiers of the zones where British expansion was really profitable.

It is difficult to overstate the revolutionary impact of the ideas packed into this short essay on the "Imperialism of Free Trade," published in the *Economic History Review* in 1953.[3] In this new interpretation, the novelty of late-Victorian imperialism was sturdily rebutted. The British had been expanding their diplomatic and commercial influence by any means at hand since the 1830s. The wave of tropical annexations after 1880 was not the product of new economic appetites, but sprang from the late Victorians' need to protect their established spheres of interest and influence against the interference of other powers. Annexation was a symptom of weakness and pessimism, not of aggression or over-confidence. The great discontinuity of Victorian imperialism—the supposed indifference to empire in the middle years of the century and the sudden lust for soil in the later—was a myth. The reality was continuous expansion, modified by changes of technique—from informal influence to formal control—when and where cooperation through trade or diplomacy broke down and vital interests were at risk.

This was a startling reversal of historiographical orthodoxy but it carried even more radical implications. Firstly, Gallagher and Robinson had propounded the first systematic account of Victorian imperialism. They had shown not only why some regions were subjected to rule and others left unannexed, but also how the seemingly random nature of British intervention, occupation, and control contained an inner logic—what they called the imperialism of free trade. No case of British expansion could henceforth be studied in isolation because its vital characteristics were determined by its place in the overall advance of British power. Here was the crucial argument for the unitary study of British imperial history and against the adequacy of mere area studies. Secondly, and no less controversially, the variations in British dealings with different regions and states, and in the nature of the colonial regime, when and where it was imposed, were to be accounted for not by the whims, fashions, and fancies of British opinion, but by the extent to which British interlopers could secure the cooperation (collaboration was their term) of local elites. Indeed, the history of imperialism was now to be understood not so much as the blind imposition of external control on resistant populations, but as the fashioning of a bargain between local leaders (usually oblivious to the ethos of nationalism) and imperial outsiders offering benefits that were politically, commercially, or culturally irresistible. On the eve of decolonization, this was a striking, not to say provocative, suggestion.

When this path-breaking article was written in 1953, Jack Gallagher was a young historian of thirty-four: Ronald Robinson, his co-author, was a year younger. Both were junior lecturers on the History Faculty at Cambridge University. Neither was a member of the old upper or middle class. Both had had their view of the world profoundly reshaped by the experience of war. Jack Gallagher's career in particular offers a fascinating glimpse into the interplay of social origins and intellectual outlook. He was the only child of parents who were perched on the bottom-most rung of the respectable working class. His father was a railway-checker, responsible for counting the number of "foreign" wagons that passed over the tracks of the railway company for which he worked.[4] Jack was sent to a nearby elementary school but at the age of eleven won a scholarship to the Birkenhead Institute, a secondary school founded by a group of local businessmen at the end of the nineteenth century. Here he thrived, excelling in history and English literature, becoming editor of the school magazine and head prefect.[5] In 1936 he won one of the handful of state studentships (perhaps 80 in all for England and Wales) that would pay for three years study at a university.[6] Still more remarkably, he gained a major scholarship that would take him to Trinity College, Cambridge, the grandest and wealthiest of Cambridge colleges, and then the powerhouse of British science and philosophy. From the humblest of backgrounds, he had reached the seminary of the social and intellectual elite, by dint of extraordinary academic talent. For Jack was always, as a Cambridge contemporary put it, very, very, very clever.[7]

Like many young men of his age, Jack found his education disrupted by war, and when he returned to finish his degree and then to embark on a dissertation, the influence of his origins was dramatically reasserted. Jack came from Birkenhead, which lay opposite Liverpool on the Mersey. Birkenhead was a Victorian growth, and much of its population, like Jack's own father, were Irish immigrants. As an offshoot of Liverpool, its principal industry was ship-building. Its commercial prosperity, like Liverpool's, was tied up with the vast enlargement of British trade in the nineteenth century. In the 1930s, as that trade contracted, it suffered the scourge of unemployment and poverty, as Gallagher knew at first hand. Liverpool had been the premier port for the Atlantic trade, especially in raw cotton from the American South. It had, however, an older and less respectable career as the center of Britain's slave trade. It was this that had made Liverpool the commercial metropolis of the West African coast, dispatching cotton cloth and metal goods in exchange for slaves, and, when the slave trade was outlawed in 1807, for whatever commodities West Africa could supply. In the struggle to find some substitute for slaves, Liverpool merchants were caught up in the schemes of the 1830s and 1840s to open up the West African interior to legitimate commerce—an enterprise in which the leading Birkenhead ship owner and builder, Macgregor Laird, was to play a leading part.

It was, then, no coincidence that Gallagher chose to write his dissertation on "The British Penetration of West Africa between 1830 and 1865."[8] Nor was the approach he took merely whimsical. Gallagher came from a city (if we consider Birkenhead as part of Greater Liverpool) of merchant princes. He could look across the

Mersey at the monuments to their patrician taste, not least the classical magnificence of the Picton Library, where some of his early research was pursued. Even in the 1930s, Liverpool was still the real capital of British West Africa. No one from Merseyside was likely to underestimate the ruthlessness of mercantile imperialism. So the main protagonists of Gallagher's thesis were not Colonial Office officials or government ministers. They were the palm oil ruffians: the rough and ready traders who took their chance on the West African coast, armed with Liverpool wares and Liverpool credit. They engaged in the long-drawn-out struggle to break the monopoly of the coastal Africans over the trade paths that led to the interior forests. What Gallagher noticed, in this story, was the ambivalence of the London government towards this enterprise, its readiness to let the traders get on with it, the uncertainty of its response to local upsets, and the practical limits to the authority of its agents on the spot. Here was a vital ingredient in the intellectual cocktail that became the imperialism of free trade. Even in the 1820s, noted Gallagher, British governments preferred informal empire to its cumbersome alternative: if possible, they wanted trade without rule. Commercial interests, sometimes with the help of evangelicals and humanitarians, made the running. West Africa was thus a variation on the British pattern in Argentina and China, both studied by Gallagher's near contemporaries at Cambridge, Harry Ferns and Michael Greenberg. In each case, the process at work was a form of imperialism induced by Britain's industrialization but modified by the particularities of the local arena. Here, and in the later formulation of the imperialism of free trade, we can see the subtle influence of the Marxism so prevalent in pre-war Cambridge.[9] This was not Marxism as a political doctrine, but Marxism as an account of world history. It connected Europe's industrial revolution to the great changes in the extra-European world. Intellectually, the crucial medium through which this Marxist history was transmitted was Lenin's reinterpretation of Marx to explain how imperialism had postponed the collapse of capitalism. For in *Imperialism: The Highest Stage of Capitalism* (1916), Lenin had insisted that imperialism was not a matter of colonies, but of imposing economic domination under a variety of political conditions. Empire was not only, or simply, a land-grab. From this to the concept of informal empire was no more than a skip and a jump. And though much of Gallagher's work was designed to refute simple, economistic accounts of British imperialism, Lenin's famous tract long remained the negative pole of his intellectual compass.

Gallagher's college dissertation, submitted in the nick of time (the last chapters were hand-written in haste) was his entry-ticket into an academic career. He was elected to a Fellowship at Trinity and shortly afterwards appointed University lecturer in colonial studies. Even as he embarked on a long career as a teacher, he was already much more interesting than just a smart young academic on the way up. His dissertation, written at breakneck speed after six years in the army, showed an astonishing intellectual assurance. The characters who filled its pages—palm oil ruffians, explorers, missionaries, humanitarians, freed slaves from Sierra Leone, soldiers, sailors, consuls, governors, chiefs, kings, and warlords—revealed his fascination with the gallery of human types. If Gallagher's intellectual introduction to imperialism owed a good deal to Lenin, his imaginative grasp of the human condition showed a considerable debt to Dickens. The Europeans in West Africa in the nineteenth century were nothing if not eccentric: just to be there was a prima facie sign of oddness. In his depiction of their plans, dreams, foibles, errors, and ends, Gallagher gave full rein to his Dickensian penchant for the invariable mismatch of human aims and capacities. All his life, Gallagher delighted in the comic spectacle of overweening ambition and inflated vanity—just as the tragic consequences of failure in love or fortune appealed deeply to his imagination.

"When I find a well-drawn character in fiction or biography," wrote Mark Twain in *Life on the Mississippi* (1883), "I generally take a warm personal interest in them, for the reason that I have met him before—met him on the river." For Jack Gallagher (as for a host of British writers), the part of the river was played by the army in which he served as a tank soldier for six years. It seems likely that wartime service in the army (he refused a commission) also sharpened the dislike for pomp, piety, and self-importance that became so characteristic in later life. Gallagher was not against order, tradition, and civility. Far from it. But he mistrusted those who claimed authority and saved his most acid phrases for the ostentatious parade of high principle or fine feeling. "As often happens in English life," he once remarked of the home-grown critics of empire, "some of the denunciators have been those whose private lives lie in ruins and who therefore set forth to rebuild the state."[10] It was a very Dickensian attitude. Bureaucratic bumbledom was another obvious target. "Chuck them in the bin, Bert," he would tell the college porter at Balliol when the accumulated mountain of brown envelopes was presented to him at the beginning of a term.[11] For his pupils, the combination of this lack of deference with wide culture, unlimited curiosity, historical omniscience, personal charm, and ready wit, could be overwhelming. To be taught by Gallagher was not simply to discuss an essay or learn some facts. It was to enter a world in which language, attitudes, and style (in its widest sense) were as much a part of the syllabus as the dramatic widening of intellectual horizons, or the invocation of Chinese, Russian, or American history (as well as Indian or African) to prove a point or draw a parallel. Gallagher imparted an approach to the past that was deadly serious in its professionalism and rigor, but a view of life that was angular, irreverent, and skeptical.

"The Imperialism of Free Trade" had been the opening salvo of Gallagher's academic career (his Trinity dissertation was never published and he abandoned his doctoral thesis). Thereafter he was to be engaged in three great historical enterprises, the basis for his reputation. The first was the partnership with Ronald Robinson in *Africa and the Victorians* (1961), their joint study of the Scramble for Africa. In "The Imperialism of Free Trade" they had denounced the view that European competition for its economic resources had been the cause of Africa's partition. Now they were equally scathing of the notion (favored by some diplomatic historians) that its origins lay in the need to defuse the tensions of the European balance of power. They ridiculed the idea that colonial expansion was meant to be a vote winner in Britain. They constructed instead a bold new hypothesis, predicated on their original claim that late-Victorian empire-building had little intrinsic value but had been undertaken to protect the older and more valuable gains of mid-Victorian imperialism, above all in India. The rapid partition of tropical Africa was thus really the outgrowth of crisis in two African regions lying across the routes to India: Egypt and South Africa. In both, British predominance was threatened after 1880 by the side-effects of economic change: Egypt's descent into the chaos of bankruptcy and the Transvaal's rise from backveld republic into gold-rich state. Fear of an anti-Western nationalist regime in Egypt led to a unilateral British occupation in 1882. Fear of an all-powerful but anti-British Transvaal drew London into the struggle to squeeze the Boers into submission as part of a British South Africa and step by step towards the South African War of 1899–1902. Both these forward movements alarmed and infuriated the European powers who had hitherto regarded their African interests with cool indifference. The result was a furious rivalry for the tropical hinterlands whose value had so recently seemed—at least to governments in London, Paris, and Berlin—almost negligible.

Three key concepts dominated this grand historiographical revision. First, in keeping with their original emphasis on the importance of conditions on the ground, Gallagher and Robinson insisted that the root cause of Africa's sudden division was not a change of heart in Europe, but a local crisis in Africa—or, more accurately, a fusillade of local crises sparked by the events in Egypt and South Africa. The terms of political collaboration there had been changed in ways that threatened British interests and upset the wider equilibrium in tropical Africa. The British had had to decide whether to risk the collapse of their political stake, or to intervene forcibly to restore the balance in the local arena. Second, in rejecting the claim that economic motives had been uppermost in the British interventions in Egypt, South Africa, and the tropical interiors, Gallagher and Robinson invoked instead the primacy of the "official mind" in the framing of policy. The official mind was a brilliant invention. It stood for the routine assumptions, preferences, and calculations on which officials in the Foreign, India, and Colonial Offices drew when proffering advice to ministers. It embodied the "Cold rules for national safety" handed down from one official generation to the next.[12] It was largely impervious to commercial logic except as adjuncts to its political concerns. Its outlook owed much to a certain aristocratic—or platonic—disdain for the vulgarity of mere business. Above all, argued Gallagher and Robinson (and this was their most telling point), the private archives of the official mind, the correspondence through which options were debated and decisions reached, showed no trace of economic motives, whatever ministers sometimes said in public. Perversely (as we might think), far from hiding their commercial aims behind a screen of statecraft, the politicians were so fearful of public opposition to the unrequited costs of empire that they did the exact reverse.

The third key to their new interpretation was the overriding importance in British policy of grand strategy: the defense of mid-Victorian primacy in the extra-European world against the rivalries and instabilities of the late-Victorian scene. It was the global structure of British power that preoccupied ministers, not the petty game of trade in African backwaters. Pre-emptive annexation was tiresome, but where imperial communications were at risk, it was the only means of averting the future attrition of British world power. What this boiled down to in practice, they argued, was the defense of India and the sea routes that carried trade and troops between Britain and her grandest colony. India was the secret of British power in Asia, and the second center of British expansion. Seen in this light, the partition of Africa was not the grand climax of British or European imperialism, but a side-show to the real drama being played out elsewhere. Gallagher and Robinson summed it up in a mischievous and memorable phrase: the African partition was a gigantic footnote to Britain's conquest of India.

Africa and the Victorians, published in 1961, confirmed the reputations of both its authors as the most original and creative historians of modern imperialism. Within a year, Gallagher had been elected Professor of Commonwealth History at Oxford, a post in which Robinson succeeded him a decade later when Gallagher returned to Trinity and Cambridge. However, the book marked the end of an academic partnership without which neither it nor the ideas that underpinned it would have taken the shape they did, or perhaps any shape at all. Each man had brought distinctive gifts, as well as a shared iconoclasm, to the project. Robinson's was an acute, generalizing mind that searched constantly for the simplest and strongest version of the central argument. Robinson had briefly been a Colonial Office official, and a protégé of one of its most influential postwar policy-makers, Sir Andrew Cohen. He had seen the official mind at close quarters and it may have been his influence that turned their joint attention towards the origins of policy-making as the central problem of the partition. It also seems likely that it was the husband-and-wife team of Robinson and Alice Denny (whose name appears on the title page) that drove the book to a timely completion. Jack Gallagher, Robinson once complained, never got up before midday. Gallagher's contribution is perhaps less obvious but subtle and pervasive nonetheless. The prose of the book, an important part of its lasting appeal and influence, bore his mark in its elegance, wit, and imagery. The deft evocation of personality and character—one of the delights of the book—was an echo of his dissertation, but perhaps his greatest influence may be seen in the alchemy with which a powerful conceptual framework was enriched with an intense historical imagination to create the literary and intellectual fusion on which most great books, historical or other, ultimately depend.

Gallagher's second great enterprise sprang almost naturally from the first. The African partition had revealed the primacy of India in the British system: it was to India that Gallagher now turned his attention. The central problem in the rise, and especially the fall, of the British Empire now seemed to be the fate of the British Raj. What lay behind the rise of Indian nationalism, and the gradual retreat of British rule? What passed for explanation at the end of the 1950s attributed the main cause to the reformist spirit of British policy with its liberal program of constitutional concession and to the irresistible force of Indian nationalism under the inspirational leadership of Gandhi and Nehru. Such high-minded history was bound to provoke Gallagher's skepticism. Worse still, to conceive of British and Indian motives in the clichés of Western politics seemed naïve at best to an historian who had watched decolonization unfold on the banks of the Congo in 1960. "Looking in from the outside is the occupational vice which bedevils Western students of African or Asian history," he wrote in 1962, "even if the road to ethnocentricity is paved with the best of intentions."[13] If the mystery of Indian politics were to be solved, Indian politicians would have to be studied on their own terms, and, ideally, from their own sources. From about 1960, Gallagher began to work systematically on this huge new project, recruiting fresh collaborators and pupils along the way. The vast archives of the British Raj in London and New Delhi had to be broached. The great apparatus of Indian administration had to be reconceived as a system not so much of rule as of collaboration. The provincial and even the district level of government had to be opened up for the clues they might give to the terms of Anglo-Indian cooperation.

By the late 1960s, a whole team of young Cambridge historians was hard at work on the provincial politics of colonial India, on Muslim politics, and on the political economy that colonialism had made. By the early 1970s, this work had thrown up a new version of Indian history to which the label "Cambridge school" was quickly attached.[14] Like the imperialism of free trade, it was more than a little iconoclastic. The Indian politicians now appeared less like the champions of national freedom than skilled and ruthless practitioners in a complex game of faction and patronage. The alliances of provincial bosses that gave the British so much trouble after 1920 were cobbled together in smoke-filled rooms in an acrid atmosphere of mutual mistrust. Gandhi's ideas, however appealing to the wider masses, were treated with bemusement or contempt by many hard-nosed Congressmen. The real core of the Cambridge theory was the claim that Indian nationalism could not be understood as the spontaneous response to colonial oppression, or to the embrace of imported liberal ideals. This developed out of the ways in which Indian interests interacted with the institutions of colonial rule. It was British determination to modernize their government, to regulate society, and develop the economy, which provoked the new kinds of political association that fused eventually into the Indian National Congress. As the British intervened more and taxed more, Indians banded together to defend their interests. As the provincial and central administration of the Raj loomed larger in the localities, and old district bargains were nullified by the *fiat* of higher authority, Indians formed provincial and then All-India associations to shadow, influence, and (if they could) hobble, their colonial masters. The British devolved power downwards to the district and province in order to widen the circle of their Indian allies. Their aim was not so much concession as the mobilization of new clients and partners in the business of rule. Imperialism and nationalism thus marched in parallel, and much of the conflict between them, so Gallagher and his colleagues implied, was really a form of shadow-boxing. Both sides depended on their shaky alliances. Neither dared risk a fight to the finish. Until, that was, the British had used up their political credit and could no longer elicit the minimum of collaboration that they needed for control of the commanding heights of their Indian Empire. When that moment came, the Raj, and the Empire, were finished.

Gallagher himself had intended to write a history of Indian politics that would have run from the First World War to the end of the 1930s. For obscure reasons this was left undone: certainly by the early 1970s his health had begun to decline. In the meantime, he had turned back to write a more synoptic account of the British Empire in its closing phase, dealing mainly with the inter-war years and the Second World War. This was delivered as the Ford Lectures in English History at Oxford and published posthumously in 1982 as *The Decline, Revival, and Fall of the British Empire.* In this third and last of his historical enterprises, he brought together the ideas which he and Ronald Robinson had devised to explain the origins of British expansion with the fruits of his unfinished work on the last years of the Indian Raj. The struggle to defend Britain's imperial power—what Gallagher called the British world-system—was traced in the political and strategic calculations of the policy-makers in Whitehall. What bulked large in the story was the grim reversal of the favorable conditions on which British leaders had relied before 1914. Depression and the rise of Hitler, which had overshadowed Gallagher's own youth, were the agents of imperial decline. Depression accentuated the introversion of the British electorate, its indifference to empire and hostility to its cost, on which Gallagher and Robinson had laid such emphasis in *Africa and the Victorians.* It sharpened the irritation against British rule in every colony. It bled the revenues that were needed for defense, at the very moment when the Hitlerian revolution turned Europe once more into a cockpit. When Hitler allied with Mussolini, and Japan became, to all intents, the third great member of this coalition for upheaval, the strains on the British world-system became almost unbearable. This was where India came in. For British rule in India was designed above all to harness its resources, men, and money to the defense, not just of India, but the whole of the British *imperium* east (and sometimes even west) of Suez. But by the 1920s and 1930s, the need to appease some Indian politicians and divide the rest forced the British to cut down the imperial dividend they collected from India, not least because the Indian economy was badly affected by recession. Just when the British needed it most, the old Anglo-Indian foundation of imperial defense was cracking under the strain of internal change and external pressure.

Yet the end of empire was a paradox: for Gallagher it could be nothing less. In the Second World War, the British were able to reunite their decentralized empire in the fight for survival. They raised a huge volunteer army in India and turned the sub-continent into an armed camp for the war against Japan. When, at Gandhi's instigation, the Indian National Congress rebelled in 1942, the revolt was crushed and its leaders imprisoned. Under the stress of war, British imperialism had revived. The appearance of power was deceptive, however. Mobilizing for war in India had antagonized its political elite, destabilized society, and smashed the basis for Anglo-Indian collaboration in normal times. The war's side effect on Britain was just as crippling. It exhausted the British economy, the old engine-room of imperial expansion. The collapse of the Raj in 1947 and the virtual collapse of the British economy at the same time showed that the backbone of British world power had been snapped. It only remained to divide the spoils.

With the delivery of the Ford Lectures in 1974, the creative period of Gallagher's career was largely complete. Ill-health, perfectionism, the heavy burden of administrative duty that he assumed on his return to Cambridge (where he soon became Vice-Master of Trinity, the uncrowned king of the college), and perhaps a degree of intellectual exhaustion, delayed and then aborted the writing-up of much of his work over the previous decade. In 1980 he died prematurely at the age of sixty.

Today it is customary to measure academic influence and reputation almost entirely on the basis of published work. By that criterion, Gallagher's accomplishment was slim, almost meager: a handful of articles, a half-share in a book, a series of lectures unpublished in his lifetime. In this case, as I hope I have shown, so mechanical a judgment would be grossly misleading. The influence of Gallagher's ideas, especially those jointly conceived with Ronald Robinson, was astonishingly wide. Academic citations of their original essay of 1953 can be counted by the thousands. The concepts they fashioned have been deployed by political scientists, sociologists, and students of international relations, as well as by every variety of historian. The effects of their great revision of British imperial history can be traced in scores of books published since 1960 on French, German, American, and Japanese imperialism, as well as

British. The idea of informal empire (which Gallagher had used—but not originated—in his 1948 dissertation) and of the official mind entered the vocabulary of almost every historian concerned with empire. The historiographical revolution that Gallagher inspired in the study of modern India has aroused much controversy but has yet to be reversed. His analysis of Britain's imperial fall remains, after twenty years, the most powerful, sophisticated, and entrancingly written study of the subject.

That might be enough for a permanent memorial. Still, something else should be added. If Gallagher was slow and reluctant to publish, it was partly because so much of his time and energy—in profligate quantities—was devoted to teaching and the supervision of doctoral research. In Oxford, he supervised at times up to twenty dissertations over a vast range of subjects and continents. It was perhaps in teaching—in the personal communication of ideas, ways of thinking, ways of writing—and in supplying the imaginative stimulus that left the young researcher believing that his was the most important and fascinating subject in the world, that Gallagher realized himself most completely. It was here that all his extraordinary gifts were combined most fully. It was for this that so large a company of the later generation remember him. Through them his influence will continue to be felt for many years to come.

Fall Semester 2002

1. From his review of Lewis Gann and Peter Duignan, "White Settlers in Tropical Africa," *Historical Journal,* V, 1 (1962), p. 198.

2. John Gallagher, "Imperialism and Nationalism in Asia," in Krishna Lal, ed., *Studies in Asian History* (New Delhi, 1969), pp. 393–98.

3. John Gallagher and Ronald Robinson, "The Imperialism of Free Trade," *Economic History Review,* 2nd series, VI, 1 (1953).

4. Admission records of Birkenhead Institute, held at Birkenhead Reference Library.

5. The school magazine was the *Vizor.* Copies in Birkenhead Institute Collection, Birkenhead Reference Library.

6. See *Birkenhead Advertiser,* Sept. 26, 1936.

7. Private information.

8. John Gallagher, "British Penetration of West Africa, between 1830 and 1865," Trinity College Fellowship Dissertation, 1948.

9. See V. H. Kiernan, "Herbert Norman's Cambridge," in R. W. Bowen, ed., *E. H. Norman: His Life and His Scholarship* (Toronto, 1984); H. S. Ferns, *Reading from Left to Right* (Toronto, 1983), pp. 74–83.

10. Review of Gann and Duignan, "White Settlers," p. 198.

11. See Richard Cobb, "Jack Gallagher in Oxford," *Cambridge Review,* Nov. 7, 1980, p. 21.

12. Ronald Robinson and John Gallagher, *Africa and the Victorians* (London, 1961), p. 463.

13. Review of Gann and Duignan, "White Settlers," p. 198.

14. It is best represented in the essays collected in John Gallagher, Gordon Johnson, and Anil Seal, eds., *Locality, Province and Nation* (Cambridge, 1973).

15

The Balfour Declaration
And its Consequences

AVI SHLAIM

Occasionally there are topics that have been written about at such length that it helps to clear the air, or to establish the vantage point from which I intend to consider my subject. My aim therefore is to take a fresh look at the Balfour Declaration in the light of recent scholarship. What I propose to do is to focus on the Declaration itself, on the motives behind it, on the way it was implemented, on the conflicts to which it gave rise, and on its consequences for Britain's position as the paramount Western power in the Middle East. I begin with a note on background.

British imperialism in the Middle East in World War I was intricate, to use a British understatement. In 1915 the British promised Hussein, the Sharif of Mecca, that they would support an independent Arab kingdom under his rule in return for his mounting an Arab revolt against the Ottoman Empire, Germany's ally in the war. The promise was contained in a letter dated October 24, 1915 from Sir Henry McMahon, the British High Commissioner in Egypt, to the Sharif of Mecca in what later became known as the McMahon-Hussein correspondence. The Sharif of Mecca assumed that the promise included Palestine. In 1916 Britain reached a secret agreement with France to divide the Middle East into spheres of influence in the event of an allied victory. Under the terms of the Sykes-Picot agreement, Palestine was to be placed under international control. In 1917 Britain issued the Balfour Declaration, promising to support the establishment of a national home for the Jewish people in Palestine.

Thus, by a stroke of the imperial pen, the Promised Land became twice-promised. Even by the standards of Perfidious Albion, this was an extraordinary tale of double-dealing and betrayal, a tale that continued to haunt Britain throughout the thirty years of its rule in Palestine. Of the three wartime pledges, the most curious, and certainly the most controversial was the Balfour Declaration. Here, wrote Arthur Koestler, was one nation promising another nation the land of a third nation. Koestler dismissed the Declaration as an impossible notion, an unnatural graft, a "white Negro." C. P. Scott, the ardently pro-Zionist editor of the *Manchester Guardian,* played a significant part in persuading the British government to issue the Declaration. In an editorial article, Scott hailed the Declaration as an act of imaginative generosity. "It is at once the fulfilment of aspiration, the signpost of destiny."[1] Elizabeth Monroe in *Britain's Moment in the Middle East* conceded that to the Jews who went to Palestine, the Declaration signified fulfilment and salvation. But she also notes that to the British the Declaration brought much ill will, and complications that sapped their strength. "Measured by British interests alone," argued Monroe, "it is one of the greatest mistakes in our imperial history."[2]

On November 2, 1917, Arthur Balfour, Britain's Secretary of State for Foreign Affairs, addressed a letter to Lord Rothschild, one of the leaders of the British Jews, as follows:

> I have much pleasure in conveying to you, on behalf of His Majesty's Government, the following declaration of sympathy which has been submitted to and approved by the Cabinet: His Majesty's Government view with favour the establishment in Palestine of a national home for the Jewish people, and will use their best endeavours to facilitate the achievement of this object, it being clearly understood that nothing shall be done which may prejudice the civil and religious rights of existing non-Jewish communities in Palestine, or the rights and political status enjoyed by Jews in any other country.

The statement was exceedingly brief, consisting of a mere sixty-seven words, but its consequences were both profound and pervasive, and its impact on the subsequent history of the Middle East was nothing less than revolutionary. It completely transformed the position of the fledgling Zionist movement *vis-à-vis* the Arabs of Palestine, and it provided a protective umbrella that enabled the Zionists to proceed steadily towards their ultimate goal of establishing an independent Jewish state in Palestine. Rarely in the annals of the British Empire has such a short document produced such far-reaching consequences.

IN VIEW OF ITS POLITICAL IMPACT, IT IS NOT SURPRISING that the Balfour Declaration has attracted so much attention from historians of the Middle East. Nor is it surprising that, almost a century later, it remains such a contentious and controversial subject. There are several bones of contention in this debate, all of them revolving around the question of compatibility between the three war-time agreements. On the question of conflict between Britain's promise to Sharif Hussein and to the French the most definitive study is by Elie Kedourie. Kedourie was the first scholar to bring together all the available evidence from British, French, and Arabic sources to elucidate the meaning of the McMahon-Hussein correspondence and to examine its impact on British policy between the wars. His principal conclusion is that the Sykes-Picot agreement did not violate the commitments contained in the McMahon-Hussein correspondence. The Balfour Declaration, however, is only mentioned by Kedourie in passing because it falls outside the scope of his study.[3]

In 1916 the Sharif of Mecca proclaimed himself "King of the Arab Countries," but the Allies recognized him only as King of the Hijaz. On the relationship between Britain's commitments to the Zionists and to King Hussein, the most recent study is *Palestine: A Twice-Promised Land?* by Isaiah Friedman.[4] Friedman's answer to the question posed in the title is that Palestine was not twice-promised in as much as McMahon's offer to recognize and uphold Arab independence after the war was conditional and non-binding and that, in any case, it did not include Palestine. Friedman argues not only that Sir Henry had definitely excluded Palestine from the prospective Arab kingdom but that this was understood by the Hashemite leader at the time. Hussein's silence following the publication of the Balfour Declaration is seen by Friedman as indicative of his attitude. Another piece of evidence cited by Friedman comes from the famous book by George Antonius, the spokesman and chronicler of the Arab national movement. From Antonius we learn that King Hussein "ordered his sons to do what they could to allay the apprehensions caused by the Balfour Declaration among their followers [and] despatched an emissary to Faisal at Aqaba with similar instructions."[5]

Friedman's conclusion is that the charges of fraudulence and deception levelled against the British after the war were largely groundless. Groundless or not, these charges acquired the status of dogma not only in the eyes of Arab nationalists but, more surprisingly, in the eyes of most British officials as well. In the case of King Hussein it is necessary to distinguish much more clearly than Friedman does between his initial response to the Balfour Declaration and his subsequent attitude. When news of the Declaration reached

Hussein he was greatly disturbed by it and he asked Britain to clarify its meaning. Whitehall met this request by the despatch of Commander D. G. Hogarth, one of the heads of the Arab Bureau in Cairo, who arrived in Jedda in the first week of January 1918 for a series of interviews with King Hussein. "Hogarth's Message," as it came to be known, reaffirmed the Entente's determination that "the Arab race shall be given full opportunity of once again forming a nation in the world." So far as Palestine was concerned, Britain was "determined that no people shall be subject to another." Britain noted and supported the aspiration of the Jews to return to Palestine but only in so far as this was compatible with "the freedom of the existing population, both economic and political." Hussein voiced no disagreement with this policy though we may be skeptical of Hogarth's report that he "agreed enthusiastically" with it.[6]

Hogarth's Message is crucial for understanding King Hussein's attitude to the Balfour Declaration. Following the meetings in Jedda, Hussein thought that he had Britain's assurance that the settlement of the Jews in Palestine would not conflict with Arab independence in that country. This explains his initial silence in public and his private efforts to allay the anxieties of his sons. Hussein had great respect for the Jews, seeing them, following the Koran, as "the People of the Book," meaning the Bible. He was not opposed to the settlement of Jews in Palestine and even welcomed it on religious and on humanitarian grounds. He was, however, emphatically opposed to a Zionist takeover of the country. Hogarth gave him a solemn pledge that Britain would respect not only the economic but also the political freedom of the Arab population. When Britain subsequently refused to recognize Arab independence in Palestine, Hussein felt betrayed and accused Britain of breach of faith.[7]

If the disenchantment of Sharif Hussein and his sons with Britain was gradual, the hostility of the Arab nationalists towards Britain on account of the Balfour Declaration was immediate and unremitting. One valuable Arabic source on this period is the diary of Auni Abd al-Hadi. Abd al-Hadi was a Palestinian politician who served as one of Amir Faisal's secretaries at the Paris Peace Conference and during his short-lived administration in Damascus in 1920. He then served Amir Abdullah, Faisal's elder brother, in Transjordan. In 1924 he returned to Palestine and became one of the chief spokesmen of the Palestinian national movement. Abd Al-Hadi's impression was that Faisal resented the Zionist intrusion into Palestine but was wary of upsetting the British. Faisal was also influenced, according to Abd al-Hadi, by the reassuring letters that he received from his father in the early months of 1918 in his camp in Aqaba on the subject of the Balfour Declaration.[8]

For his part, Abd al-Hadi did not believe in the possibility of co-operation with the Zionists in Palestine. He was therefore very critical in his diary of Faisal for signing an agreement on Arab-Jewish co-operation with Dr. Chaim Weizmann at their meeting in Aqaba on June 4, 1919. Abd al-Hadi notes that Faisal signed the agreement without understanding its implications because it was in English, a language he did not know. But he also notes that Faisal added a hand-written codicil making the implementation of the agreement conditional on his demands concerning Arab independence being fulfilled.[9] As these conditions were not fulfilled, the agreement became null and void.

There are a number of other references to the Balfour Declaration in Auni Abd al-Hadi's diary, all of them highly critical of the British and of their Jewish protégés. His basic view, repeated on several occasions, was that the Declaration was made by an English foreigner who had no ownership of Palestine to a foreign Jew who had no right to it.[10] Palestine thus faced a double danger: from the British Mandate and from the Zionist movement. In December 1920 Abd al-Hadi participated in the Third Palestinian Congress in Haifa. The Congress denounced the actions of the British government and its plans for realizing the Zionist goals. It also rejected Balfour's promise of a national home for the Jews in Palestine as a violation of international law, of wartime Allied commitments, and of the natural rights of the inhabitants of the country.[11] In 1932 Abd al-Hadi founded the Palestinian branch of the Pan-Arab Independence Party whose manifesto called for the cancellation of the Mandate and of the Balfour Declaration.[12] Arab hostility to the Balfour Declaration, as exemplified by Auni Abd al-Hadi, could have been predicted from the beginning. So why was the Declaration issued?

There are two main schools of thought on the origins of the Balfour Declaration, one represented by Leonard Stein, the other by Mayir Vereté. What later became the conventional wisdom on the subject was first laid out by Leonard Stein in 1961 in his masterly survey *The Balfour Declaration*.[13] This book provides a careful, detailed, and subtle account of the decision-making process that led Britain to issue the Declaration, but it does not reach any clear-cut conclusions. The conclusion implicit in the narrative, however, is that it was the activity and the skill of the Zionists, and in particular of Dr. Chaim Weizmann, that induced Britain to issue this famous statement of support for the Zionist cause.

Leonard Stein's book was subjected to an extended critique by Mayir Vereté of the Hebrew University of Jerusalem in a notable article he published in 1970 on "The Balfour Declaration and its Makers."[14] According to Vereté the Declaration was the work of hard-headed pragmatists, primarily motivated by British imperial interests in the Middle East. Far from the Zionists seeking British support, it was British officials who took the initiative in approaching the Zionists.

The definition of British interests in the Middle East began in 1915. This process led to the Sykes-Picot agreement which reconciled Britain's interests with those of France, with a compromise over Palestine. On further reflection, however, the British felt that control over Palestine was necessary in order to keep France and Russia from the approaches to Egypt and the Suez Canal. In Vereté's account, it was the desire to exclude France from Palestine, rather than sympathy for the Zionist cause, that prompted Britain to sponsor a national home for the Jewish people in Palestine. It was also thought that a Declaration favorable to the ideals of Zionism was likely to enlist the support of the Jews of America and Russia for the war effort against Germany. Finally, rumor that Germany was courting the Zionists accelerated the pace at which Britain moved towards its dramatic overture. In contrast to Stein, Vereté concludes that Zionist lobbying played a negligible part in drawing Britain towards Palestine.

A similar though not identical argument was advanced by Jon Kimche in *The Unromantics: The Great Powers and the Balfour Declaration*. As the title suggests, the author believes that the driving force behind the Declaration was not sentimentality but hard-headed realism. Kimche, however, attributes this realism not only to the British but to the Zionists as well. Indeed, he maintains that the interests of the two sides were identical, and that by working for a Jewish Palestine they were working at the same time for a British Palestine. The Declaration provided the stepping stones: each of the partners used the same stones but later each went his own way. "This," argues Kimche, "was the basic realism with which Balfour and Weizmann approached their compact; they understood that they would have to go together part of the way, but that a time would come when they would have to part."[15] What is beyond question, as Kimche himself points out, is that there was little room for such sophistication in the heated politics of wartime Britain and post-war Zionism.[16]

The historiography of the Balfour Declaration took a step forward in 2000 with the publication of Tom Segev's book on the British Mandate in Palestine.[17] Segev's contribution lies in the revisionist interpretation he develops of the origins of British rule in Palestine. His "revisionist account" is based on new source material as well as a new synthesis of earlier studies on the subject. In Segev's account, the prime movers behind the Balfour Declaration were neither the

Zionist leaders not the British imperial planners, but Prime Minister David Lloyd George. In his memoirs, written some twenty years after the event, Lloyd George explained his support for the Zionist movement during the First World War as an alliance with a hugely influential political organization whose goodwill was worth paying for. The common wisdom in Britain at the time Lloyd George published his account was that the country had erred in supporting the Zionists and he was probably trying to justify his wartime policy.

Segev will have none of it. Lloyd George's support for Zionism, he argues, was based not on British interests but on ignorance and prejudice. In his own way Lloyd George despised the Jews, but he also feared them, and he proceeded on the basis of an absurdly inflated notion of the power and influence of the Zionists. In aligning Britain with the Zionists, he acted in the mistaken—and anti-Semitic— view that the Jews turned the wheels of history. In fact, as Segev shows, the Jews were helpless, with nothing to offer—no influence other than the myth of clandestine power. As for the Zionists, they could not even speak in the name of world Jewry for they were a minority within a minority.

Lloyd George's misconceptions about the Jews were widely shared in the ruling class in Britain, as was his antipathy towards the French. In Segev's summary, the British entered Palestine to defeat the Turks; they stayed there to keep it from the French; then they gave it to the Zionists because they loved "the Jews" even as they loathed them, at once admiring and despising them. The British were not guided by strategic considerations and there was no orderly decision-making process. The Balfour Declaration "was the product of neither military nor diplomatic interests but of prejudice, faith, and sleight of hand. The men who sired it were Christian and Zionist and, in many cases, anti-Semitic. They believed the Jews controlled the world."[18] Britain's belief in the mystical power of "the Jews" overrode reality, and it was on the basis of such spurious considerations that Britain took the momentous decision to sponsor the Zionist cause.[19]

On one point there is a broad consensus among admirers as well as critics of the Balfour Declaration: it was a considered statement of policy, issued after prolonged deliberations, painstaking drafting and redrafting, and careful wording. Before the British government gave the Declaration to the world, it closely examined every word, and incorporated in the text countless changes and corrections. All these efforts, however, did not result in a clear or coherent text. On the contrary, they compounded the opaqueness, ambiguity, and, worst of all, the internal contradictions.

The greatest contradiction lay in supporting, however vaguely, a right to national self-determination of a minority of the inhabitants of Palestine, while implicitly denying it to the majority. At the time that the proposed statement was under discussion in the War Cabinet, the population of Palestine was in the neighborhood of 670,000. Of these, the Jews numbered some 60,000. The Arabs thus constituted roughly 91 per cent of the population, while the Jews accounted for 9 per cent. The proviso that "nothing shall be done which may prejudice the civil and religious rights of existing non-Jewish communities in Palestine" implied that, in British eyes, the Arab majority had no political rights.

Part of the explanation for this peculiar phraseology is that the majority of the ministers did not recognize the Palestinians as a people with legitimate national aspirations, but viewed them as a backward, Oriental, inert mass. Arthur Balfour was typical of the Gentile Zionists in this respect. "Zionism, be it right or wrong, good or bad," he wrote in 1922, is "of far profounder import than the desires and prejudices of the 700,000 Arabs who now inhabit that ancient land."[20] The most charitable explanation that may be offered for this curious claim is that in an age of colonialism everyone was in some sense implicated in its ideology. Balfour may appear today like an extreme example of the colonial mentality, but he was not untypical of his era.

Yet Balfour's specific proposal to come out in favor of the establishment of a Jewish homeland in Palestine did not enjoy unanimous support round the Cabinet table. Edwin Montagu, the Secretary of State for India and the only Jewish member of the government, considered Zionism a threat to the Jews of Britain and other countries. He denounced Zionism as a "mischievous political creed, untenable by any patriotic citizen of the United Kingdom."[21] Montagu rejected the idea of the Jews as a nation and argued that the demand for recognition as a separate nation put at risk their struggle to become citizens with equal rights in the countries in which they lived.[22]

Lord Curzon, a member of the War Cabinet, was more troubled by the implications of the proposed move for the rights of the Arabs of Palestine. "How was it proposed," he asked his Cabinet colleagues, "to get rid of the existing majority of Mussulman inhabitants and to introduce the Jews in their place?" In a paper to the Cabinet he returned to the theme:

> What is to become of the people of the country? . . . [The Arabs] and their forefathers have occupied the country for the best part of 1,500 years, and they own the soil. . . . They profess the

Mohammedan faith. They will not be content either to be expropriated for Jewish immigrants or to act merely as hewers of wood and drawers of water for the latter.[23]

Montagu and Curzon were overruled. The three most powerful men in the Cabinet, Lloyd George, Balfour, and Lord Milner, threw their weight behind the proposal. At the crucial meeting, on October 31, 1917, the Cabinet approved the final wording of the declaration of sympathy for a national home for the Jews in Palestine. Curzon restated his misgivings and his pessimism about the future of Palestine. Largely in deference to his anxieties, the final version of the Declaration contained the caveat about protecting the civil and religious rights of the non-Jewish communities in Palestine.[24] Chaim Weizmann was waiting outside the room where the War Cabinet met. In the early afternoon, Sir Mark Sykes emerged, calling "Dr. Weizmann, it's a boy!"

While Chaim Weizmann's part in procuring the Balfour Declaration may have been exaggerated, his role in keeping Britain to her rash wartime promise was of critical importance. To the peace conference that convened at Versailles in January 1919, Weizmann went as the head of the Zionist delegation. His aim was to ensure that the British would remain in Palestine. At the conference he pleaded for the international ratification of the Balfour Declaration. But at the San Remo conference, in April 1920, the French representative objected to the inclusion of the language of the Balfour Declaration in the text of the mandate over Palestine. It took strong British pressure to persuade the League of Nations to incorporate the commitment to establish a Jewish national home in the terms of Britain's mandate to govern Palestine.[25]

Even before the international ratification of the Balfour Declaration, violent protests broke out in Palestine against Britain's pro-Zionist policy and against Zionist activities. The Arabs emphatically refused to recognize the Declaration and anything done in its name, seeing it as the thin end of the wedge of an Anglo-Jewish plot to take over their country. Arab resentment towards the British and their protégées culminated in the Nebi Musa riots of April 1920. A court of inquiry appointed to investigate the riots noted that the Balfour Declaration "is undoubtedly the starting point of the whole trouble." The court also reached the conclusion that Arab fears were not unfounded.[26] The Nebi Musa riots were the first intrusion of mass violence into the Arab-Jewish conflict. The riots did nothing to advance the political aims of the Arab nationalists but they also bode ill for the Zionists' expectation of achieving their ends peacefully.

The riots and their aftermath, in the words of Bernard Wasserstein, "created a gangrene of suspicion and mistrust in the British-Zionist relationship in Palestine which was to subsist throughout the three decades of British rule."[27]

Throughout these three decades Britain was subjected to repeated criticism from Zionist quarters for reneging, or at least backsliding, on its wartime pledge to the Jews. In self-defense the British pointed out that the Balfour Declaration committed them to support a national home for the Jews in Palestine, not a Jewish state. Not all British officials, however, adhered to this interpretation. Balfour and Lloyd George, for example, admitted in 1922 at a meeting with Winston Churchill and Chaim Weizmann, that the Balfour Declaration "had always meant a Jewish State."[28]

The troubled and tangled history of the British Mandate in Palestine has been told many times before, recently among others by Joshua Sherman and Naomi Shepherd.[29] Most historians of this period attribute to British policy a pro-Arab bias. Some Zionist writers go further: they accuse Britain not only of persistent partiality towards the Arabs, but of going back on its original promise to the Jews.

Tom Segev makes a major contribution to the existing literature on this issue by putting Britain's record as a mandatory power under an uncompromising lens. His verdict is that British actions considerably favored the Zionist position and thus helped to ensure the establishment of a Jewish state. The evidence he presents of British support for the Zionist position is both rich and compelling. So is the evidence he adduces for the proposition that once the Zionist movement came to Palestine with the intention of creating a Jewish state with a Jewish majority, war was inevitable. From the start there were only two possibilities: that the Zionists would defeat the Arabs or that the Arabs would defeat the Zionists. British actions tended to weaken the Arabs and to strengthen the Zionists as the two national movements moved inexorably towards the final showdown. The Arab nationalists in Palestine, under the leadership of Haj Amin al-Husseini, despaired of Britain and eventually threw in their lot with Nazi Germany. The Zionists, under the leadership of Chaim Weizmann, hitched a lift with the British Empire, advancing under its sponsorship to the verge of independence. The Zionists were not slow to grasp the importance for a weak national liberation movement of securing the sponsorship and support of a great power. Indeed, ensuring the support of the paramount Western power of the day remains to this day a basic tenet of Zionist foreign policy.

From the start, the central problem facing British officials in Palestine was that of reconciling an angry and hostile Arab majority to the implementation of the pro-Zionist policy that was publicly proclaimed on November 2, 1917. In general, British officials in Palestine had much more sympathy for the Arabs than the policy-makers in London. Many of these officials had an uneasy conscience, even a feeling of guilt, as a result of the decision of their political masters to honor Britain's wartime promise to the Jews while breaking its promise to the Arabs. Some suggested a revision of the policy because, in their opinion, it involved an injustice to the Arabs. But they constantly ran up against the argument that the Declaration constituted a binding commitment. Even Lord Curzon, who had originally opposed the Balfour Declaration, concluded in 1923 that the commitment to the Zionists could not be ignored "without sub-stantial sacrifice of consistency and self-respect, if not of honour." [30]

Arab resentment and riots in Palestine persuaded the Lloyd George government to replace the military government with a civil administration, but not to reverse its pro-Zionist policy. And once the government resolved to continue to support a Jewish homeland in Palestine, it could not have chosen a more suitable man for the post of High Commissioner than Sir Herbert Samuel. Samuel's as-sociation with Zionism was intimate and his attachment to the Zion-ist cause was perhaps the one passionate commitment of his entire political career. [31] Samuel was sent to Palestine not because of—or even despite—his Jewishness, but because he was a Zionist. The ap-pointment pleased the Zionists but it destroyed the last vestiges of Arab faith in Britain's integrity and impartiality. Before Samuel took over from the military government, the chief administrative officer asked him to sign what became one of the most quoted documents in Zionist history: "Received from Major General Sir Louis Bols, KCB—One Palestine, complete." Samuel signed. [32]

Traditional British historians have tended to regard Herbert Samuel as an impartial administrator in the emerging conflict between Palestinian Arabs and Zionists. Sahar Huneidi, an Arab scholar living in London, challenges this claim in a major revisionist study of the early period of the Mandate. She argues that most of the measures Samuel took during his tenure in Palestine—in the polit-ical, economic, and administrative spheres—were designed to pre-pare the ground not just for a Jewish national home but for a fully-fledged Jewish state. Using a wide range of primary sources, both English and Arabic, Huneidi charts Samuel's career in Palestine against the complex background of British policy in the region. [33]

Huneidi argues convincingly that during Samuel's five years as High Commissioner in Palestine, from 1920 to 1925, he remained an ardent supporter of Zionism. But under the impact of fierce anti-Jewish riots, he began to doubt the practicality of a policy which seemed, as he put it, to be a recipe for "a second Ireland." He therefore devised endless schemes to draw the Arab notables into the political community of Palestine. All these schemes, however, proved inadequate to the task of reconciling the Arabs of Palestine to Zionism.[34]

The failure of his attempts to bring together Arabs and Jews within a unified political framework led Samuel to try to satisfy each community separately. His preferred method was the devolution of power to the increasingly separate communal institutions of the Arabs and the Jews. This policy encouraged the trend towards the internal partition of Palestine. Under Samuel's successors this trend gathered further momentum. While alleviating the inter-communal conflict in the short run, this process exacerbated the problem in the long run by driving Arabs and Jews further and further apart. As the two communities built up the institutional strength required for the struggle ahead, the Government of Palestine became little more than an umpire.[35]

Isaiah Berlin, an Anglo-Jewish supporter of Zionism and a prescient observer, was moved to compare the Palestine Mandate to a minor English public school:

> There was the headmaster, the high commissioner, trying to be firm and impartial: but the assistant masters favoured the sporting stupid boarders (Arabs) against the clever swot dayboys (Jews) who had the deplorable habit of writing home to their parents on the slightest provocation to complain about the quality of the teaching, the food, and so on.[36]

The role of umpire became increasingly difficult to sustain with the passage of time. High Commissioners came and went but their hands were tied by the pledge of November 2, 1917. Shortly after his arrival in Palestine, in December 1928, Sir John Chancellor reached the conclusion that the Balfour Declaration had been a "colossal blunder," unfair to the Arabs and detrimental to the interests of the British Empire. In January 1930 he sent a long memorandum to London. He wanted to extricate Britain from the Balfour Declaration and to deal a blow to Zionism. His ideas were given a respectful hearing in London and the King asked for a copy.[37]

On learning that the King would like to hear from him directly about the state of affairs in Palestine, Chancellor obliged with a 16-page letter explaining why, in Chancellor's view, Britain's national home policy in Palestine was misguided, unjust, and impossible to carry out. It also repeated his earlier proposals for restricting Jewish immigration and land purchases in Palestine. The Jews took the view that the Arabs of Palestine were free to go to any part of Arabia and that they should be induced to move to Transjordan. Chancellor was strongly opposed to any such action on the grounds that it would be inconsistent with the part of the Balfour Declaration which laid down that in the establishment of a Jewish national home, nothing should be done to prejudice the rights of the non-Jewish communities in Palestine. Chancellor portrayed the Jews as an emotional people:

> What makes them difficult to deal with is that they are, regardless of the rights and feelings of others, very exacting in pressing their own claims. Even as a minority of the population of Palestine the Jews adopt towards the Arabs an attitude of arrogant superiority, which is hotly resented by the Arabs with their traditions of courtesy and good manners.[38]

Nor did the Jews cherish genuine sentiments of loyalty towards Britain. In spite of what they said on public occasions when it was in their interest to proclaim their devotion, "the bulk of the Jewish population of Palestine have little feeling of gratitude or loyalty towards Great Britain for what she has done for the establishment of the Jewish National Home."[39]

Having delivered his tirade against the Jews, Chancellor returned to the basic problem facing Britain and made a concrete proposal for dealing with it:

> The facts of the situation are that in the dire straits of the war, the British Government made promises to the Arabs and promises to the Jews which are inconsistent with one another and are incapable of fulfilment.
>
> The honest course is to admit our difficulty and to say to the Jews that, in accordance with the Balfour Declaration, we *have* favoured the establishment of a Jewish National Home in Palestine and that a Jewish National Home *in* Palestine has in fact been established and will be maintained and that, without violating the other part of the Balfour Declaration, without prejudicing the interests of the Arabs, we cannot do more than we have done.[40]

Chancellor's memoranda, and a number of other reports that also underlined the gravity of the situation in Palestine, contributed to a reformulation of the official line in London. In October 1930, after several discussions in Cabinet, Colonial Secretary Lord Passfield issued a White Paper. The premise and the principal innovation of the White Paper was that the Balfour Declaration imposed on Britain a binary and equal obligation towards both Jews and Arabs. Accordingly, Jewish immigration to Palestine was linked to the Arab as well as the Jewish economy. In the past, Jewish immigration quotas were determined by the absorptive capacity of the Palestine economy. From this point on, Jews were to be allowed into the country only at a rate that would not put Arabs out of jobs. In the spirit of Chancellor's proposals, the White Paper assumed that the Jews would remain a minority. Chancellor and his officials were pleased by this redefinition of official policy, but their success was short-lived. Dr. Weizmann succeeded in getting the new policy reversed within a few months. Once again the Zionists had won and the Arabs failed in London.[41]

As Chancellor had predicted, unrestricted Jewish immigration and land purchases in Palestine produced further unrest and periodic outbreaks of violence. The fundamental contradiction between Arab nationalist aspirations and Britain's 1917 undertakings to the Jews continued to render the Mandate inoperable. The influx of German Jews to Palestine following the Nazi rise to power in 1933 provoked deep anxieties among the Arabs. In 1936 the Arab Higher Committee declared a general strike with the aim of halting Jewish immigration, banning the sale of land to Jews, and establishing an independent national government. The general strike snowballed into a full-scale revolt that was to last three years. The British government's belated response to the outbreak of the Arab Rebellion consisted of appointing a Royal Commission, with Earl Peel as chairman, to investigate the underlying causes of the disturbances. The Peel Commission's report went to the heart of the problem:

> Under the stress of the World War the British Government made promises to Arabs and Jews in order to obtain their support. On the strength of those promises both parties formed certain expectations. . . . An irrepressible conflict has arisen between two national communities within the narrow bounds of one small country. . . . There is no common ground between them. . . . This conflict was inherent in the situation from the outset. . . . We cannot—in Palestine as it is now—both concede the Arab claim of self-government and secure the establishment of the Jewish National Home. . . . This conflict between the two obligations is all the more unfortunate because each of them, taken separately, accords with British sentiment and British interests.[42]

The Peel Commission proposed the partition of Palestine. The logic behind partition was unassailable. It was the only solution then and it remains the only solution today to the tragic conflict between the two national movements. In 1937 the Jews accepted partition but the Arabs rejected it; so the conflict continued and the violence escalated.

The Arab Rebellion of 1936–39 demonstrated once again that there could be no compromise between the two rival communities in Palestine: only war could decide the issue. The Jewish community was militarily weak and vulnerable. It would have been easily defeated had Britain not intervened to restore law and order. The Jewish national home, in the last resort, had to be defended by British bayonets.

In November 1938 Major General Bernard Montgomery arrived in Palestine. His task was to crush the revolt. "Monty" was a short-tempered professional soldier with no inclination to study the details of the conflict in Palestine. He gave his men simple orders on how to handle the rebels: kill them. This is what his men did, and in the process they broke the backbone of the Arab national movement. When the struggle for Palestine entered its most crucial phase, in the aftermath of World War II, the Jews were ready to do battle whereas the Arabs were still licking their wounds.

The costs of the British presence in Palestine were considerable and the benefits remained persistently elusive. Palestine was not a strategic asset: it was not a source of power but of weakness. Field Marshal Sir Henry Wilson, the highest ranking British soldier in the Middle East in the early 1920s, kept repeating that the British had no business being in Palestine, and the sooner they left, the better. "The problem of Palestine is exactly the same . . . as the problem of Ireland," he wrote, "namely, two peoples living in a small country hating each other like hell." Wilson castigated the civilians—he called them the "frocks"—for failing to understand that the Empire could not afford the luxury of spreading itself too thin. Again and again, he demanded that Palestine, or "Jewland" as he called it, be abandoned.[43]

The logic of this position became irresistible after India's independence was declared in 1947. For if India was the jewel in the Empire's crown, Palestine was hardly more than an anemone in the King's buttonhole. Economic considerations reinforced the strategic arguments for withdrawal from Palestine. Hugh Dalton, the Chancellor of the Exchequer, deployed both arguments in a letter to Prime Minister Clement Attlee. "The present state of affairs is not only costly to us in manpower and money," wrote Dalton, "but is . . . of no real value from the strategic point of view—you cannot in any case have a secure base on top of a wasps' nest—and it is exposing our young men, for no good purpose, to abominable experiences and is breeding anti-Semites at a most shocking speed."[44]

In February 1947 the Labour government decided to hand the Mandate over Palestine to the United Nations, the League of Nations' successor. The Mandate was relinquished because it was unworkable. All of Britain's attempts to find a formula for reconciling peacefully the rival claims of Arabs and Jews to the country had finally failed. On November 29, 1947 the UN General Assembly voted for the partition of mandatory Palestine into two independent states, one Arab and one Jewish. The Arabs of Palestine, the Arab states, and the Arab League, rejected partition as illegal, immoral, and impractical. The passage of the resolution was thus the signal for the outbreak of a vicious civil war between the two communities in Palestine, a war which was to end in a Jewish triumph and an Arab tragedy.

Britain refused to assume responsibility for implementing the UN partition resolution. It set a firm date for the end of the Mandate— May 14, 1948. As the Mandate approached its inglorious end, both sides felt let down by the British, accusing them of duplicity and betrayal. The manner in which the Mandate ended was the worst blot on Britain's entire record as the mandatory power. Britain left Palestine without an orderly transfer of power to a legitimate government. In this respect, the end of the Palestine Mandate has the dubious distinction of being unique in the annals of the British Empire.

The consequences of the Balfour Declaration were not confined to Palestine. The Declaration engendered anger towards Britain throughout the Arab world and at all levels of Arab society from the intellectual elites to the masses. Together with the Sykes-Picot agreement, Balfour's Declaration became a central point of reference for Arab intellectuals after the First World War. Edward Said, for example, in *The Question of Palestine* dwells at great length on the unspoken assumptions behind the Declaration. For him it is a prime example of the moral epistemology of imperialism. The Declaration, he writes, was made:

> (a) by a European power, (b) about a non-European territory, (c) in flat disregard of both the presence and the wishes of the native majority resident in the territory, and (d) it took the form of a promise about this same territory to another foreign group, so that this foreign group might, quite literally, *make* this territory a national home for the Jewish people.[45]

At the other end of the spectrum there were popular demonstrations against the Balfour Declaration in the inter-war period by people whose grasp of its meaning was tenuous at best. One amusing example was a demonstration organized in al-Karak by Sulayman An-Nabulsi, a schoolteacher who was later to become prime minister of Jordan:

> On the anniversary of the Balfour Declaration, he led his class into the streets, with the cry: *"Falyasqut wa'd Balfour!"*, which, figura-

tively translated, means: "Down with the Balfour Declaration!".
The crowd in the streets was ignorant of its meaning, so started
yelling: *"Falyasqut Karkur!"* ("Down with Karkur!"). Karkur was a
local Armenian shoemaker and he ran out into the crowd, cry-
ing, "Balfour, oh people, Balfour". Others yelled *"Falyasqut wahid
balkun!"* ("Down with a balcony!") and *"Falyasqut wahid min fawq!"*
(Down with one from the top!").[46]

In Britain itself opinions about the Balfour Declaration remained
sharply divided long after the end of the Palestine Mandate. Richard
Crossman argued passionately that Balfour, Lloyd George, and Milner all felt under an obligation, in the moment of Allied victory,
to do something for oppressed world Jewry. Strategic calculations,
Crossman believed, were at most secondary factors.[47] The opposite
interpretation was advanced with equal passion and partisanship by
Arnold Toynbee. Toynbee believed that Balfour and his colleagues
understood the consequences for the Arabs of fostering the equivalent of a white settler community but went ahead all the same for the
sake of sustaining British influence in the eastern Mediterranean.[48]
"I will say straight out," Toynbee told an interviewer in 1973, "Balfour
was a wicked man." He was wicked because he used the League of Nations mandate to rob the Arabs of their right to self-determination.
"The Arabs had no political experience," Toynbee stated, "and they
were thrown into the most subtle and intricate political situation you
can imagine. They were clearly unprepared for it. This is part of the
monstrosity of the whole affair."[49]

Britain's failure in Palestine can be at least partly attributed to the
Balfour Declaration for that was the original sin. In Arabic there is
a saying that something that starts crooked, remains crooked. The
Balfour Declaration was not just crooked; it was a contradiction in
terms. The national home it promised to the Jews was never clearly
defined and there was no precedent for it in international law. On
the other hand, it was arrogant, dismissive, and even racist, to refer
to 90 per cent of the population as "the non-Jewish communities in
Palestine." And it was the worst kind of imperial double standard,
implying that there was one law for the Jews, and another law for
everybody else.

With such a singularly inauspicious and murky beginning, British
rule in Palestine was predestined to fail, as in a Greek tragedy. It was
not just a policy failure, but an egregious moral failure. Britain had
no moral right to promise national rights for a tiny Jewish minority
in a predominantly Arab country. It did so not for altruistic reasons
but for selfish, if misguided reasons. At no stage in this long saga did
the Jews feel that they were getting from their great power sponsor

the support to which they felt entitled by virtue of the Balfour Declaration, and the end of the Mandate was accompanied by the most bitter recriminations. The Arabs were violently opposed to the Balfour Declaration from the start. They held Britain responsible for the loss of their patrimony to the Jewish intruders. By the end of the Mandate, there was no gratitude and no goodwill left towards Britain on either side of the Arab-Jewish divide. I can only agree with Sir John Chancellor that the Balfour Declaration was a colossal blunder. It has proved to be a catastrophe for the Palestinians and it has given rise to one of the most intense, bitter, and protracted conflicts of modern times.

Spring Semester 2003

1. Quoted in Daphna Baram, *Disenchantment: The Guardian and Israel* (London, 2004), p. 43.

2. Elizabeth Monroe, *Britain's Moment in the Middle East, 1914–71* (London, 1981), p. 43.

3. Elie Kedourie, *In the Anglo-Arab Labyrith: The McMahon-Husayn Correspondence and its Interpretations, 1914–1939* (Cambridge, 1976).

4. Isaiah Friedman, *Palestine: A Twice-Promised Land? The British, the Arabs and Zionism, 1915–1920* (New Brunswick, N.J., 2000), Vol. 1.

5. Ibid., p. xlvii; George Antonius, *The Arab Awakening: The Story of the Arab National Movement* (Beirut, 1938), p. 269.

6. Timothy J. Paris, *Britain, the Hashemites and Arab Rule, 1920–1925: The Sherifian Solution* (London, 2003), p. 44.

7. Antonius, *The Arab Awakening*, pp. 267–69 and 331–32.

8. Auni Abd al-Hadi, *Mudhakkirat Auni Abd al-Hadi (The Memoirs of Auni Abd al-Hadi)*, Introduction and research by Khairieh Kasmieh (Beirut, 2002), pp. 56–57 and 292.

9. Ibid., p. 57.

10. Ibid., pp. 141 and 164.

11. Ibid., p. 139.

12. Ibid., p. 161.

13. Leonard Stein, *The Balfour Declaration* (London, 1961).

14. Mayir Vereté, "The Balfour Declaration and its Makers," *Middle Eastern Studies*, 6, 1 (January 1970).

15. Jon Kimche, *The Unromantics: The Great Powers and the Balfour Declaration* (London, 1968), p. 69.

16. Ibid.

17. Tom Segev, *One Palestine, Complete: Jews and Arabs under the British Mandate* (London, 2000).

18. Ibid., p. 33.

19. Ibid., p. 43.

20. Ibid., p. 45.

21. Quoted in Margaret McMillan, *Peacemakers: The Paris Conference of 1919 and Its Attempt to End War* (London, 2001), p. 427.

22. Segev, *One Palestine, Complete*, p. 47.

23. Quoted in David Gilmour, "The Unregarded Prophet: Lord Curzon and the Palestine Question," *Journal of Palestine Studies*, 25, 3 (Spring 1996), p. 64.

24. Ibid.

25. Segev, *One Palestine, Complete*, pp. 116 and 142.

26. Ibid., p. 141.

27. Bernard Wasserstein, *The British in Palestine: The Mandatory Government and the Arab-Jewish Conflict, 1917–1929* (Oxford, 1991, 2nd edn.), p. 71.

28. Gilmour, "Unregarded Prophet."

29. A. J. Sherman, *Mandate Days: British Lives in Palestine, 1918–1948* (London, 1997); and Naomi Shepherd, *Ploughing Sand: British Rule in Palestine* (London, 1999).

30. Wasserstein, *The British in Palestine*, p. 16.

31. Bernard Wasserstein, *Herbert Samuel: A Political Life* (Oxford, 1992), p. 204.

32. Segev, *One Palestine, Complete*, p. 155.

33. Sahar Huneidi, *A Broken Trust: Herbert Samuel, Zionism and the Palestinians, 1920–1925* (London, 2001).

34. Wasserstein, *The British in Palestine*, pp. 16–17.

35. Ibid., p. 17.

36. Quoted in Avi Shlaim, *The Politics of Partition: King Abdullah, the Zionists, and Palestine, 1921–1951* (Oxford, 1990), p. 54.

37. Segev, *One Palestine, Complete,* pp. 334–35.

38. Sir John R. Chancellor to Lord Stamfordham, May 27, 1930, Middle East Archive, St. Antony's College, Oxford.

39. Ibid.

40. Ibid.

41. Segev, *One Palestine, Complete,* pp. 335–38.

42. Palestine Royal Commission, *Report,* Cmd. 5479, p. 370.

43. Segev, *One Palestine, Complete,* p. 147.

44. Ibid., p. 495.

45. Edward W. Said, *The Palestine Question* (New York, 1979), pp. 15–16.

46. Peter Gubser, *Politics and Change in Al-Karak, Jordan: A Study of a Small Arab Town in its District* (London, 1973), p. 22.

47. Richard Crossman, *A Nation Reborn: The Israel of Weizmann, Bevin and Ben-Gurion* (London, 1960), pp. 31–32.

48. Wm. Roger Louis, *The British Empire in the Middle East: Arab Nationalism, The United States, and Postwar Imperialism, 1945–1951* (Oxford, 1984), p. 39.

49. Arnold Toynbee, "Arnold Toynbee on the Arab-Israeli Conflict," *Journal of Palestine Studies,* 2, 3, (Spring 1973).

16

The "Wilsonian Moment" in India And the Crisis of Empire in 1919

EREZ MANELA

The immediate wake of the Great War saw the emergence of the United States as a dominant global power, and with it the Wilsonian vision of a world order composed of self-determining nation-states. The forces unleashed by the American intervention in the international arena during this period helped to shape and to energize anti-colonial national movements among non-European peoples. By examining the Indian responses to 1919 within the broader international contexts, this lecture hopes to shed some light on the role of the "Wilsonian moment" in the process that led to the emergence of colonial peoples as independent actors in international affairs, a process that defines a central transformation in twentieth-century international history: the shift from an imperial to a post-colonial international order.

In the heady months following the armistice in November 1918, President Woodrow Wilson loomed large in the minds of countless war-weary Europeans. He inspired optimism. When he landed on European shores in December 1918 he was met with an ecstatic reception as the harbinger of a new era of peace and justice in world affairs. H. G. Wells later wrote that, "for a brief interval, Wilson stood alone for mankind. And in that brief interval there was a very extraordinary and significant wave of response to him throughout the earth. . . . He ceased to be a common statesman; he became a Messiah."[1] John Maynard Keynes, probably the best known and most influential of Wilson's post-war critics, was equally dramatic, recalling how the President's "bold and measured words carried to the peoples of Europe above and beyond the voices of their own politicians." Though one can detect a disillusioned tone here, because he wrote after the event, Keynes caught the spirit of the time:

> Never had a philosopher held such weapons wherewith to bind the princes of this world. How the crowds of the European capitals pressed about the carriage of the President! . . . What a place the president held in the hearts and hopes of the world when he sailed to us in the *George Washington!* What a great man came to Europe in those early days of our victory! [2]

Similar hopes and perceptions were common far beyond Europe. Across the colonial world, in Asia, Africa, and the Middle East, many looked to Wilson to champion their dignity and independence, and adopted as their own his oft-cited principle of the right to self-determination. India was an outstanding example. Nationalists across the subcontinent waited in excitement and anticipation for the post-war order championed by Wilson. The prominent liberal V. S. Srinivasa Sastri, wrote:

> The words of the message [of Woodrow Wilson] have an appeal to the Eastern as well as to the Western hemisphere. . . . His appearance in London was hailed with unparalleled demonstration. Imagination fails to picture the wild delirium of joy with which he would have been welcomed in Asiatic capitals. It would have been as though one of the great teachers of humanity, Christ or Buddha, had come back to his home, crowned with the glory that the centuries had brought him since he last walked the earth. [3]

Woodrow Wilson as an ancient Asian sage—a striking image indeed! And Sastri's appraisal was not an isolated one. Indian nationalists recognized the significance of Wilsonian rhetoric of self-determination and appropriated it in redefining the goals of their movement. They made concerted efforts to take advantage of the new opportunities and forums in the international arena to advance those goals.

THE INDIAN NATIONAL MOVEMENT HAD EMERGED among Western-educated Indians in the last quarter of the nineteenth century. It had assumed institutional form with the establishment of the Indian National Congress in Bombay in 1885. Though Congress represented an all-India national identity, before 1914 it was hardly an anti-colonial body since its activities were aimed at securing rights for Indians within the Empire, rather than challenging the legitimacy of imperial rule itself. In their customary addresses at the annual December gatherings, Congress politicians often criticized the government of the Raj for inefficiency and misrule, but at the same time typically reaffirmed India's loyalty to Britain. The demands for reform went little beyond calling for a measure of self-government for India within the framework of the Empire: more freedom for Indians, but freedom as British subjects, not as an independent nation.[4] As late as 1911, the Delhi Durbar, where George V held audience for his Indian subjects, was considered a spectacular success as a highpoint of British imperial authority in India. By 1914, one historian of British India has written, "India was proceeding, if not in growing trust between government and popular leaders, at least in increasing prosperity, and in gaining self-confidence."[5] The British Raj, it seemed to most contemporaries, English and Indian alike, might last for a thousand years.

The outbreak of the First World War initially gave little reason to revise this assessment. Despite the wholesale transfer of troops from India to distant battlefields—for a time, only 15,000 British troops remained in the country—few Indians seized the opportunity of the Empire's military vulnerability to revolt. In fact, at the Indian National Congress session in Madras in December 1914 the gathered dignitaries resolved to convey to the King and people of England India's "profound devotion to the throne, its unswerving allegiance to the British connection, and its firm resolve to stand by the empire at all hazards and at all costs."[6]

Pronouncements of loyalty to Britain were matched by the actual Indian contributions to the war effort in both men and materiel; a total of 1.2 million Indian men fought in Europe and the Near East, 800,000 of them in combat units.[7] Even erstwhile "Extremists," who had split from Congress in 1907 charging excessive timidity in demanding Indian self-rule, supported the war effort. The pre-eminent Extremist leader, the fierce Marathi journalist and scholar Bal Gangadhar Tilak, fresh out of Mandalay prison after serving a six-year sentence for sedition, saw the large-scale recruitment of Indians into the military as an opportunity to establish the equality of Indians as citizens of the Empire. He expressed great satisfaction at the intention of the government to enroll Indians in the Defence of India Force, and urged the masses to respond whole-heartedly to this call to the defense of the Empire.[8]

As the war drew on and the death toll mounted, both statesmen and the public in Europe and elsewhere attached to the bloodshed ever-broader meanings and purpose, nothing less, in fact, than a creation of a more just and peaceful world. As the idea spread that the end of the war would bring a transformation in international relations, Indians increasingly came to expect that their loyalty and sacrifice would be rewarded by a greater voice in their own government. If in the initial years of the war few in India speculated on its aftermath, by the end of 1916 one prominent Congressman, Surendranath Banerjee, opined that the world was "on the eve of a great reconstruction," of which Britain and India would both be part. Others echoed that sentiment, noting that significant advances toward Indian self-government must come soon. "The war," observed one Indian nationalist, "has put the clock . . . fifty years forward."[9]

Sensing the swelling anticipation among the Indian political elite on whose co-operation the Raj depended, the British government became increasingly concerned with preserving the stability of the imperial bond with India. British military weakness in India, coupled with wartime economic and social hardships, could provide fertile ground for political discontent. In the summer of 1917, therefore, the British War Cabinet, after considerable debate, moved to consolidate Indian loyalty to the Empire through an appeal to nationalist opinion. E. S. Montagu, the recently appointed Secretary of State for India, announced the government's intention to move India toward colonial self-government after the war, declaring that the British aim was to effect "the increasing association of Indians in every branch of the administration and the gradual development of self-governing institutions with a view to the progressive realization of responsible government in India as an integral part of the British Empire."[10]

The Montagu Declaration, though carefully hedged, went far beyond any previous official overtures to Indian nationalists, and it was received with some enthusiasm by many of them. At the same time, however, the entry of the United States into the war in April 1917 further shifted the debate about the post-war international order, and with it the expectations of Indians and other colonial peoples of the post-war settlement. The United States joined the war, President Wilson had declared, so "that every people has a right to choose the sovereignty under which they shall live." Governments, he said, must rule by the consent of the governed; this principle would be the only basis for international legitimacy, and would be enforced through a "common covenant" among nations, an institutional framework that would reflect the "brotherhood of mankind."[11]

There is little doubt that Wilson was thinking of Europe, rather than the colonial world, when he uttered those words. But the intentions behind spoken words need not, and often do not, match their impact on audiences. The American President articulated his vision in terms that implied universal applicability. After the United States joined the war, Wilsonian rhetoric spread rapidly in India through news agency reports, nationalist newspapers, and everywhere politics was discussed. By the last weeks of the war, the *New York Times* reported that the President's rhetoric was widely known all across India, with the President's principles for a new world order even "being quoted by villagers in the remotest part of India." Wilson's words, the report enthused, had spread among the largely illiterate populace "almost entirely by word of mouth," and they "have gripped their hearts as nothing else has done since the war began."[12] It is, of course, impossible to determine the actual proportion of Indians who had some knowledge of Wilson and his speeches, or to gauge directly any impact that they may have had on the thinking and expectations of the Indian masses beyond the scope of the political elite and the press. It is clear, however, that the spread of Wilsonian rhetoric at a moment of international flux encouraged politically aware Indians to envision a post-war reconstruction of international affairs based on the principles of self-determination and the equality of nations, and the emergence of a post-imperial international society in which India would have a place as a self-determining nation.

Indian activists living abroad were among the first to realize the potential implications of Wilsonian rhetoric for India. One of the most prominent among them was the Punjab native Lala Lajpat Rai, a leading nationalist figure in the pre-war years and one of the Lal-Bal-Pal trio of "Extremist" leaders—the other two were Bal Tilak and Bipin Chandra Pal—who led the battle against the partition of Bengal in 1905 and the split from the Moderate-controlled Congress in 1907. After their movement was suppressed and Tilak jailed for sedition, Lajpat Rai left India and in 1914 arrived in the United States, where he remained throughout the war. He soon began to propagate the cause of Indian nationalism in the United States, penning opinion pieces in publications such as the *Nation* and the *New York Times*. He also published a book on the nationalist movement in India in which he argued that Indian nationalism was not merely an anti-British movement, but part of an international resurgence of subject peoples striving for liberation.[13] In October 1917, buoyed by Wilsonian rhetoric, Lajpat Rai established the India Home Rule League of America for the purpose of spreading "correct knowledge of Indian affairs in America," and began publishing a journal, *Young India,* under its auspices.[14]

Lajpat Rai recognized the United States as a major new actor in the world arena, whose actions bore directly on the Indian situation. In February 1918, a month after Wilson made his famous Fourteen Points address, he wrote in an editorial that the President's utterances "were bound to help all the subject peoples of the world in their fight for the right of self-determination." Wilson's views, in Lajpat Rai's enthusiastic view, represented the best kind of leadership; reading the President's messages with their lofty principles, "one begins to wish that the whole world could be constituted into a single republic, with President Wilson as its head."[15] Reviewing the recent Montagu Declaration in the light of Wilsonian principles, Lajpat Rai welcomed British willingness to move India toward self-government but rejected its claim that the British government alone would determine the nature and pace of political progress in India. That could not stand since it was in direct contradiction to Wilson's insistence that every people must be free to determine its own government.

The following month, after the American President declared that the war "had its roots in the disregard of the rights of all peoples to determine their political life," Lajpat Rai cabled to thank him personally for his words. They were bound, he wrote to Wilson, to "thrill the millions of the world's 'subject races'" and constitute "a new charter of world's freedom." In a *Young India* editorial, Lajpat Rai stated that Wilson had "put the whole thing in a nut shell" and that the future of the world depended on the implementation his principles.[16] Arguing against skeptics who thought that Wilson's advocacy of self-determination applied to Europe alone, Lajpat Rai wrote that nothing in the President's words suggested that limitation, and that the discussion among the Allies of applying the principle to the German colonies in Africa suggested its validity outside Europe. Moreover, the force of universal principles could not for long be confined to certain regions, whatever the intent of their author. Wilson's words would be the "war cry of all small and subject and oppressed nationalities," and constitute "a new charter of democracy and liberty," which the people of Asia would use as much as, if not even more than, those of America and Europe.[17] American participation in the war had overshadowed the contribution of the imperial powers of Europe, he concluded. They now had little choice but to support Wilson's plan for the post-war international order.

Such excitement about the possibilities of the post-war world was mirrored among leaders within India as well, and as they appropriated and adapted the Wilsonian rhetoric of self-determination their expectations and demands were swiftly transformed. This was apparent in the summer of 1918, when the British government moved to implement the Montagu Declaration with the publication of the Montagu-Chelmsford Report, a reform plan that proposed to transfer some areas of responsibility in provincial governments to ministers who would answer to popularly elected legislators. Such concessions, which might have been considered far-reaching only a few years earlier, were now seen as woefully behind the times. Tilak, back at the center of national politics, condemned the report as "inadequate, unsatisfactory and disappointing." Nationalist politicians and press now called for "the immediate grant of self-determination to India."[18]

In its discussions about the possibilities of the post-war settlement, the nationalist press often speculated on the significance of the recent ascendancy of the United States in world affairs. If Wilson's principles were the basis for the peace conference, then Britain would have "to frame her policy of governing India in accordance with them." Another dominant idea in Indian newspapers was that the end of the war meant nothing less than "the freedom of nations, their right of self-determination." A window of opportunity was open for political action in the international arena. India had to stake its claims: "We should put forward our demands," declared one writer. "It will be a sin if India does not lay her ailments before Dr. Wilson."[19]

In December 1918, the Indian National Congress, convened in Delhi for its annual session, adopted a resolution that directly called for the application of the principle of self-determination to India. The session urged that India be represented at the peace table by elected delegates, and designated Tilak along with Gandhi and the prominent leader Muslim Syed Hasan Imam as its representatives to the conference.[20] British officials, however, were not prepared to yield to calls for Indian self-determination. As was the case in Egypt, the British intention was to move towards gradual reforms whose pace would be strictly controlled by London. The India Office was determined to avoid any discussion of Indian issues at the peace table. Even Montagu, whose private papers reflect genuine intentions to move India toward self-government, essentially ignored the demands of the Delhi Congress that India be represented in Paris by elected representatives.[21] In Delhi, he wrote, there was no longer a significant difference between Moderates and Extremists, since both wished to go far beyond what the British were willing to concede. Now, he concluded, there were only "Extremists and super-Extremists."[22]

India was in fact represented at the peace conference when the delegates convened in January, but it was not by the men elected by Congress. Like the self-governing Dominions—Canada, South Africa, Australia and New Zealand—the Government of India was invited to send a delegation to Paris which, the powers agreed, would be admitted to deliberations that touched upon Indian interests. The delegation, however, represented the Raj, not the nationalist movement. It was headed by Secretary Montagu, and its two Indian members—Sir S. P. Sinha and Ganga Singh, the Maharaja of Bikaner—were hand-picked by the British authorities. Bikaner, Montagu reported with some relish, distinguished himself at the conference by securing for India separate representation in the new League of Nations, winning the point and "even bearding and obtaining the necessary answer from the great President Wilson himself." The Maharaja capped his triumph by inviting the French Premier Clemenceau—widely known as "the Tiger"—on a tiger hunt: "That amazing septuagenarian has that one ambition, and you may find him in your jungles next cold weather," Montagu wrote to the Viceroy. "The whole proceeding appears to have concluded by Bikaner displaying to the Big Five the tiger tattooed on his arm, which was inspected and approved not only by Clemenceau, but by Orlando and Wilson. Thus, we make peace with Germany!"[23]

Despite the unrepresentative nature of the Indian delegation, which was roundly condemned by the nationalist press in India, Montagu recognized that the presence in an international forum of a separate delegation for India was unprecedented and symbolically significant. It meant, he warned, that India's international status had "soared far more rapidly than could have been accomplished by any of our reforms," and could therefore disrupt its relationship to the Empire.[24] The separate representation of India in the international arena, even if only pro forma, would ultimately render untenable the British insistence on denying India self-determination domestically. In May 1919 he informed the Viceroy that it had been decided that India would become a "State Member of the League of Nations," adding:

> My dear Friend, I wonder whether I over-rate the importance of this sort of occurrence. We are trying to make the English think about internal political reforms in India, but the constitutional position which she has achieved for herself in the last few months is amazing and is wholly inconsistent with an attitude of ascendancy on our part, either economic or governmental."[25]

It was precisely this tension that had emerged between the international and the imperial status of India, the growing gap between avowed principles and actual policies, that allowed, even propelled, Indian nationalists to redefine their movement—its goals, its means, and its timetable. They sought to liberate their battle from the strait-jacket of British policy and take it into the international arena, with Tilak, the old Extremist, leading the charge.

BY THE TIME HE WAS ELECTED BY THE DELHI CONGRESS as a representative to the peace conference, Tilak was already in London working to internationalize India's demand for self-determination. He was much encouraged when it was decided in the preliminary discussions that India would have a separate representation at the peace talks. The decision signaled London's willingness, he believed, to have the Indian nationalist view put before the conference and presented an opportunity that should be fully exploited. In reality, of course, the decision was the result of imperial politics—the demands of the Dominions and the Government of India for a voice in the proceedings—and, as soon became clear, did not reflect any readiness on Whitehall's part to have the voices of Indian nationalists heard at the conference. Nevertheless, throughout the month of January 1919 the letters and reports that arrived in India from Tilak and his entourage in London were optimistic about the possibility of advancing the Indian cause in Paris.[26]

To put pressure on London, Tilak and his supporters orchestrated a broad campaign, with numerous organizations at the local and provincial levels in India—branches of home rule leagues, provincial committees of the Indian National Congress—dispatching petitions addressed to the peace conference and its principals. All carried a similar message, co-ordinated by the nationalist leadership: India wanted self-determination in accordance with President Wilson's principles.[27] Tilak also appealed to Wilson directly: "the world's hope for peace and justice is centered in you as the author of the great principle of self-determination," he wrote, asking the President to ensure that his "principles of right and justice" were applied to India. The only reply, however, came in the form of a terse note from Wilson's personal secretary: "the matter of self-determination for India," it read, was "a question which will be taken up in due time by the proper authorities."[28] As was the case with other colonial movements at the time, Wilson's general sympathy for claims of self-determination did not translate into the realm of policy. The European settlement consumed all of the President's energies in Paris; the rest, he assumed, would be sorted out in due course by the League of Nations.[29] His impotence on this issue was well recognized by the British, and on receiving news of Wilson's acknowledgement of Tilak's letter, a Foreign Office official wrote: "Not much attention need be paid to Pres. Wilson's acknowledgement."[30]

Initially, Tilak believed that the Lloyd George government would be sympathetic to the cause of Indian home rule, and intended his campaign to aid the Prime Minister domestically in bringing India's case before the conference. Lloyd George, however, soon proved unsympathetic to Indian nationalist demands, and they were ignored by British officials both in Paris and London. Indian petitions to the peace conference were simply filed away into archival oblivion, never to come under discussion. When Tilak, citing his appointment by the Delhi Congress as a delegate to the peace conference, applied for a passport to travel from London to Paris, his request was denied. "The idea of our going to Peace Conference is not relishable to them," he noted, "and any deputation coming here after the Peace Conference is over will be . . . not of much use."[31]

By April, the failure of the efforts to bring the case for Indian self-determination before the peace conference was clear, but Tilak remained convinced of the importance of action in the international arena for advancing the Indian nationalist cause. "We must keep knocking at its doors, every now and then, on one pretext or another," he wrote of the emerging League of Nations, "in order to build world opinion in our favour."[32] During his stay in England, he and his supporters wrote a series of pamphlets, including one entitled "Self Determination for India," designed to enlist British and international opinion in their cause. The pamphlets were distributed in England, as well as in India and in the United States. Praising the work of Lajpat Rai's Home Rule League in America, Tilak urged the Indian National Congress to set up permanent propaganda missions in England, France, America, Germany, and Japan. "A favourable opinion of the civilised world towards Indian aspirations," he wrote, "is a valuable asset in our struggle for freedom. We cannot afford to neglect world opinion except at our peril."[33] Such faith in the important role of "world opinion," a staple concept in the Wilsonian worldview, represents yet another facet of the influence of the "Wilsonian moment" on the Indian national movement.

The public mood within India, optimistic in the immediate wake of the armistice, quickly soured. Heady hopes for a transformation of international affairs dissipated into a combustible mix of disillusionment and frustration. The explosion came when Parliament passed the Rowlatt Bills, which were intended to stem the rising agitation for home rule by extending the Government of India's wartime powers of arrest and internment without trial. Gandhi, who had been rising gradually in Indian politics since his return from South Africa in 1914, now emerged as a figure of national stature, leading the movement to oppose these "Black Acts." Though he had been a staunch supporter of the Empire throughout the war, he now concluded that his hopes of achieving equality for Indians were in vain. Calling the Rowlatt Bills a "symptom of deep-seated disease among the ruling class" of the Empire, Gandhi declared a nationwide *hartal,* or general strike, in protest.[34] The British response was brutal, most infamously with the massacre on April 13, 1919 of nearly four hundred unarmed protesters gathered in Jallianwala Bagh, in the city of Amritsar. That bloody episode, its horror compounded in Indian eyes by the reluctance of the authorities to punish those responsible, came to symbolize the oppressive nature of British control and mark a new era of resistance to imperial rule. It dealt a severe blow to the Indians' faith in British intentions to move India expeditiously toward home rule, and the early promise of the "Wilsonian moment" made their disillusionment all the more bitter. In this light it is perhaps ironic that Wilson himself, several months later, cited the case of India as one of the achievements of the peace conference. In the very last speech of his public campaign for the Treaty against Senate opponents, he declared that India's membership in the League of Nations gave "that great and voiceless multitude . . . a voice among the nations of the world."[35]

Tilak returned to India in November 1919, having remained in England for more than a year in an effort to promote the Indian cause. Despite the failure to gain a hearing for Indian demands in Paris, he continued to exhort Congress to make use of the international arena in its fight against British rule. One Tilakite newspaper declared in December that "the most important" task before the upcoming Indian National Congress session was to arrange to put the case for Indian self-determination before the League of Nations. India's position, it argued, was "hopelessly anomalous": like the self-governing British Dominions, India had been admitted into the League as a member, and as such could vote on the appeals of others to self-determination. At the same time, it was prevented from applying that principle to itself. The paper again condemned the notion, contained in the Montagu Declaration of 1917, that the time and manner of India's progress toward self-government could only be determined by Parliament: this was "just the opposite of self-determination" and was now exposed as illegitimate, since "President Wilson has plainly said . . . that all claims to self-determination" can be brought before the League of Nations. India's international rights and status, then, would trump imperial policy and allow for the expression of an independent Indian nationhood.[36]

Tilak himself was unable to continue the fight much longer; he died in Bombay of pneumonia on August 1, 1920, at the age of sixty-four. By that time, Gandhi had emerged as the pre-eminent figure of the Indian national movement, leading a redefinition of its goals and means in a direction far more radical than even the Extremists would have imagined only a few years before. With the adoption of Gandhi's policy of non-co-operation in 1920, the Indian National Congress officially abandoned its long-time posture as a "loyal opposition," and now sought to coerce the government, albeit through passive resistance, rather than appeal to it by constitutional means. The pro-Empire Moderates, who as late as 1915 had been in control of the movement, were now insignificant as a political force.[37] The newfound contempt for the Empire among Indians was apparent in the widespread protests that met the visiting Prince of Wales in 1921, in striking contrast to the spectacle of imperial loyalty that had greeted George V in Delhi only a decade before. Debates and dissention in Congress about goals and means did continue in subsequent years.[38] But the spring of 1919 marked a crucial watershed in the transformation of Congress from a colonial institution aimed at self-government within the Empire into an anti-colonial movement dedicated to severing India from the Empire.

In the thirty-fourth annual session of Congress, held in December 1919 in Amritsar in a show of solidarity with the victims of the Jallianwala Bagh massacre, Pandit Motilal Nehru, presiding, recounted before the assembled delegates the disappointments and disillusionments of the year that was just ending:

> Last year when we met at Delhi the great war had ended and we were all looking forward, full of hope, to the great peace which would endure and which would bring the blessings of freedom to all nationalities. The time had come for the fulfillment of the many pledges made to us and, in accordance with the principles laid down by statesmen in Europe and America, this Congress demanded self-determination for our country. Peace has now come, partially at least, but it has brought little comfort even to the victors. The pledges of statesmen have proved but empty words, the principles for which the War was fought have been forgotten and the famous fourteen points are dead and gone.[39]

The recent reforms, Motilal emphasized, were "inadequate, unsatisfactory and disappointing," and Parliament had to move quickly to establish "full Responsible Government in India in accordance with the principle of self-determination."[40]

A few months before Motilal's address in Amritsar, his son, the twenty-nine-year-old Cambridge-educated Jawaharlal, penned a review of the philosopher Bertrand Russell's 1918 book, *Roads to Freedom*. It gave the young Nehru a chance to reflect on world affairs:

> Much was expected of the war. It was to have revolutionized the fabric of human affairs, but it has ended without bringing any solace or hope of permanent peace or betterment. President Wilson's brave words have remained but words, and the "fourteen points," where are they? We have sorrowfully to recognize that "the Millennium" is not for our time. The great moment has passed and for ourselves it is again the distant hope that must inspire us, not the immediate breathless looking for deliverance.[41]

The Fourteen Points were perhaps dead, but the debate about self-determination was very much alive. As a language of legitimacy, a vision of an international order of independent nation-states, it was now absorbed into the Indian movement and would henceforth define and guide it. A decade later, Jawaharlal, now himself presiding over the Lahore Congress of 1929, officially announced the Indian demand for *purna swaraj*, or complete independence. "The brief day of European domination is already approaching its end," he declared. "The future lies with America and Asia. . . . India today is part of a world movement."[42]

And so it was: a movement away from empire and toward self-determining nations as the organizing, legitimating principle of international community. Though Indian demands for self-determination were rejected by the British and ignored at the peace conference—ignored indeed by Wilson himself—their legitimacy was now firmly established, not least among Indian nationalists. Alternatives that had seemed mainstream and plausible just a few years earlier, such as gradual self-rule leading to Dominion status, were no longer viable within the nationalist movement. Thus, the "Wilsonian moment" served as the indispensable catalyst (not only in India, but in Egypt and Ireland as well) for the imperial crisis of 1919. In this light, international history appears, alongside imperial and national histories, as a crucial framework for illuminating the process of decolonization and the dissipation of empire in the twentieth century—not only the British Empire but also "empire" more generally as an organizing principle of international affairs.

Summer Semester 2004

Note on the Historiography of Wilsonianism

Though the influence of Wilsonianism in the colonial world has largely remained unexplored, there is voluminous literature on virtually all other aspects of the topic. Writing on Wilson and his international role began immediately after Versailles. A few of these accounts defended Wilson and his diplomacy, but the vast majority portrayed the United States President and his project as a tragic failure. The two early accounts that have best stood the test of time are both by British authors. John Maynard Keynes, *The Economic Consequences of the Peace* (London, 1919), is no doubt the better known, but Harold Nicolson, *Peacemaking 1919* (London, 1933), is perhaps richer and more interesting for the engaging first-hand account it provides of the Peace Conference from the perspective of a disillusioned British Wilsonian.

Post-1945 scholarship on Wilsonianism was framed largely by the rival and highly influential views presented in George F. Kennan, *American Diplomacy, 1900–1950* (New York, 1951) and William Appleman Williams, *The Tragedy of American Diplomacy* (Cleveland, 1959). In Kennan's "realist" critique, Wilsonianism epitomized America's naïve idealism on the world stage; Williams' "new left" approach posited Wilson as a ruthless practitioner of the "Open Door imperialism" that defined US foreign policy in the twentieth century. Though their respective accounts of Wilsonianism now seem monochromatic and somewhat dated, they have been immensely influential, inspiring numerous scholars to produce more nuanced versions of these interpretations. Lloyd C. Gardner, *Safe for Democracy: Anglo-American Response to Revolution, 1913–1923* (New York, 1984) is a notable work on Wilson in the New Left tradition, while the writings of Lloyd E. Ambrosius, most recently *Wilsonianism: Woodrow Wilson and His Legacy in American Foreign Relations* (New York, 2002), offer a sophisticated critique of Wilsonianism from a realist perspective.

If both Kennan and Williams wrote in the tradition of the historiography of US foreign relations, Arno J. Mayer's influential contributions examined the emergence and impact of Wilsonianism within the context of European diplomacy. Mayer's two-part *magnum opus, Political Origins of the New Diplomacy, 1917–1918* (Cleveland, 1959), and *Politics and Diplomacy of Peacemaking: Containment and Counterrevolution at Versailles, 1918–1919* (New York, 1967), charts the rise and fall of Wilsonianism in the wake of the Great War within the framework of the clash between revolutionary "forces of movement," led by the Russian Bolsheviks, and reactionary "forces of order," the imperialist-capitalist powers of Western Europe. Wilsonianism, in this view, was designed to neutralize Bolshevism by co-opting it; it was a doomed effort to chart a middle way between revolution and reaction, and to promote international change while preserving order.

Another type of tension within Wilson's world role, between theory and practice, or rhetoric and policy, is perceptively analyzed in N. Gordon Levin, *Woodrow Wilson and World Politics: America's Response to War and Revolution* (New York, 1968). No account of the literature on Wilson can be complete without mentioning the work of Arthur S. Link, who devoted his entire prolific career to the study of Wilson. In addition to his 69-volume edition of *The Papers of Woodrow Wilson* (Princeton, N.J., 1966–1993), an indispensable resource for research on Wilsonianism, a number of his works are still useful for understanding Wilson's foreign policies, including *Wilson the Diplomatist: A Look at His Major Foreign Policies* (New York, 1957), and the relevant essays in *The Higher Realism of Woodrow Wilson, and Other Essays* (Nashville, 1971).

Of the more recent literature, two works in particular stand out. Thomas J. Knock, *To End All Wars: Woodrow Wilson and the Quest for a New World Order* (New York, 1992), seamlessly combines several strands of history—intellectual and political, domestic and international—to present a compelling account of Wilson's worldview and the reactions to it both at home and abroad, with a focus on the left-progressive sources and supporters of the Wilsonian project. Frank Ninkovich, *The Wilsonian Century: U. S. Foreign Policy since 1900* (Chicago, 1999), on the other hand, reconceptualizes the intellectual underpinnings of United States foreign policy in the last century around his definition of Wilsonianism as "crisis internationalism": an essentially "realist" program designed to meet the challenges of a dangerous, unstable international environment by constructing international institutions and promoting an active American role in world affairs.

1. H. G. Wells, *The Shape of Things to Come* (New York, 1933), p. 82.

2. Keynes, *The Economic Consequences of the Peace* (London, 1919), pp. 34–35. Keynes' book was one of the earliest and most influential critics of Wilson's performance at Paris. For more on him see Robert Skidelsky, *John Maynard Keynes: A Biography* (London, 1983).

3. Cited in D. V. Gundappa, "Liberalism in India," *Confluence*, 5, 3 (1956), p. 217.

4. Presidential Address of Dadabhai Naoroji, Twenty-second Session of the Indian National Congress, Calcutta, Dec. 1906, in A. M. Zaidi, ed., *Congress Presidential Addresses* (New Delhi, 1986), Vol. 2, pp. 294–97; see also D. G. Karve and D. V. Ambekar, eds., *Speeches and Writings of Gopal Krishna Gokhale* (Bombay, 1966), Vol. 2, p. 201,

5. Percival Spear, *The Oxford History of Modern India, 1740–1975* (Delhi, 1978, 2nd edn.), p. 333–34.

6. S. R. Bakshi, *Home Rule Movement* (New Delhi, 1984), p. 9, citing the Report of the Indian National Congress, Madras, 1914.

7. Spear, *Modern India,* p. 335.

8. Poona District Congress Committee Papers, file no. 5, "Resolutions of the Bombay Provincial Congresses, 1916–1920," p. 99, Manuscript Division of the Nehru Memorial Museum and Library, New Delhi (NMML).

9. Speech by Surendranath Banerjee at the 1916 Congress, quoted in M. R. Jayakar, *The Story of My Life* (Bombay, 1958), Vol. I, p. 156; Speech by Madan Mohan Malaviya in the Imperial Legislative Council, Mar. 23, 1917, cited in Judith M. Brown, *Modern India: The Origins of an Asian Democracy* (Oxford, 1994, 2nd edn.), p. 198.

10. Frederick Madden and John Darwin, eds., *Selected Documents on the Constitutional History of the British Empire and Commonwealth* (Westport, Conn., 1993), Vol. VI, pp. 678–79; see also Judith M. Brown, "War and the Colonial Relationship: Britain, India, and the War of 1914–18," in DeWitt C. Ellinwood and S. D. Pradhan, eds., *India and World War I* (New Delhi, 1978), pp. 19–43.

11. An Address in Washington to the League to Enforce Peace, May 27, 1916, in Arthur Link and others, eds., *The Papers of Woodrow Wilson (PWW)* (69 Vols., Princeton, N.J., 1966–1993), Vol. 37, pp. 113–17; an address to the Senate, Jan. 22, 1917, *PWW,* Vol. 40, p. 536–39; message delivered to the Provisional Government of Russia on May 26, 1917 and made public on June 9, *PWW,* Vol. 42, p. 365–67.

12. "Wilson's Words in India," *New York Times,* Oct. 5, 1918.

13. *Hindi Brahman Samachar* (Jagadhri, Hindu), in "Punjab Press Abstract 1918," Mar. 18, 1918, Oriental and India Office Collection, London (OIOC), L/R/5/200, p. 181; Lajpat Rai, *Young India: An Interpretation and a History of the Nationalist Movement from Within* (New York, 1916), pp. 222–23.

14. See Alan Raucher, "American Anti-Imperialists and the Pro-India Movement, 1900–1932," *Pacific Historical Review,* 43 (1974), pp. 94–100.

15. "India and the World War," *Young India,* 1, 2 (February 1918), pp. 2 and 11.

16. *Young India,* 1, 3 (March 1918), pp. 1–3.

17. Ibid., 1, 2 (February 1918), pp. 2–3.

18. Vasant D. Rao, "Tilak's Attitude towards the Montagu-Chelmsford Reforms," *Journal of Indian History,* 56 (1978), pp. 172–73; *Observer* (Lahore), May 11, 1918, OIOC, L/R/5/200, 277.

19. *Mahrátta,* "Bombay Press Abstract," Oct. 6, 1918, OIOC, L/R/5/174, p. 19; *Hindi Brahmin Samachar,* Nov. 25, 1918; *Tribune* (Lahore), Dec. 20, 1918, "Punjab Press Abstract, 1919," OIOC, L/R/5/201, p. 3; *Kesari* (Poona), n.d., OIOC, L/R/5/200, p. 596.

20. Thirty-third Indian National Congress session, Delhi, Dec. 1918, NMML, All-India Congress Committee (AICC), File 1, Part II, p. 347.

21. Montagu to Chelmsford, Jan. 11, 1919, NMML, Chelmsford Papers, Roll 4.

22. Montagu to Chelmsford, Nov. 28, 1918, National Archives of India, New Delhi (NAI), Montagu Papers, Roll 1.

23. Ibid., Feb. 18, 1919.

24. Ibid., Jan. 22, 1919.

25. Ibid., May 1, 1919.

26. Memorandum, London, Dec. 11, 1918, enc. in Tilak's letter to Khaparde, Dec. 18, 1918, NAI, G. S. Khaparde Papers (KP), File 1, pp. 1–2; Tilak to Khaparde, London, Jan. 16, 1919, NAI, KP, File 2, p. 110; Tilak to D. W. Gokhale, London, Jan. 23, 1919, NAI, KP, File 1, pp. 4–7.

27. Burma Provincial Congress Committee (PCC) to Sec. of AICC, Jan. 15, 1919, NMML, AICC Papers, File 7, pp. 3–5; Sec. of Bihar & Orissa PCC to Sec. of AICC, Feb. 1, 1919, ibid., File 6, p. 171; Sec. of Bengal PCC to Sec. of AICC, Feb. 7, 1919, ibid., File 6, p. 183; Sec. of Madras PCC to AICC, Feb. 13, 1919, ibid., File 6, p. 193.

28. Close to Tilak, Jan. 14, 1919, quoted in T. V. Parvate, *Bal Gangadhar Tilak: A Narrative and Interpretive Review of His Life, Career and Contemporary Events* (Ahmedabad, 1958), p. 463.

29. Wilson to Tumulty, June 27, 1919, in Link and others, eds., *PWW,* Vol. 61, p. 291.

30. Foreign Office memo, Feb. 12, 1919, Public Record Office, London, PRO FO 608/211, fol. pp. 124–25.

31. Tilak to Sir Maurice Hankey, Secretary of the British Delegation, Feb. 22, 1919; and Hankey to Dutasta, Feb. 28, 1919, PRO FO 608/211, fol. pp. 128–37; Tilak to D. W. Gokhale, London, Jan. 23, 1919, NAI, KP, File 1, pp. 4–7; also Rau, "Tilak's Attitude," pp. 174–75.

32. Tilak to D. W. Gokhale, London, Feb. 6, 1919, NAI, KP, File 1, p. 10; unsigned memorandum entitled "How We Get On II," enc. in Tilak's letter from London, Mar. 20, 1919, NAI, KP, File 1, pp. 13–14; Parvate, *Bal Gangadhar Tilak,* pp. 489–90.

33. Manisha Dikholkar, *The History of India's Freedom Struggle in Britain: British Reaction and Responses, 1885–1920* (Bombay, 1996), pp. 192–94; also Rao, "Tilak's Attitude," p. 175.

34. Gandhi to Chelmsford, Feb. 24, 1919 and Mar. 11, 1919, NMML, Chelmsford Papers, Roll 10.

35. An Address in the City Auditorium at Pueblo, Colorado, Sept. 25, 1919, Link and others, eds., *PWW,* Vol. 63, p. 505.

36. *Mahrátta,* Dec.14, 1919, in Parvate, *Bal Gangadhar Tilak,* pp. 463–64.

37. Ainslie T. Embree, "The Function of Gandhi in Indian Nationalism," in Paul F. Power, ed., *The Meanings of Gandhi* (Manoa, 1971), p. 67; Peter Heehs, *India's Freedom Struggle, 1857–1947: A Short History* (Delhi, 1988), pp. 90–94.

38. See Ravinder Kumar, "From Swaraj to Purna Swaraj: Nationalist Politics in the City of Bombay, 1920–32," in D. A. Low, ed., *Congress and the Raj: Facets of the Indian Struggle, 1917–1947* (London, 1977).

39. Amritsar Congress, Presidential Address, Dec. 23, 1919, NMML, Motilal Nehru Papers, Part III, Speeches and Writings, File 2.

40. Amritsar session of Congress, presidential address, NMML, AICC Papers, File 1, Part I, p. 109.

41. Incomplete and unpublished review of Bertrand Russell's *Roads to Freedom* (1918), written sometime after April 1919, NMML, Jawaharlal Nehru Papers, Writings & Speeches, Serial No. 21.

42. Gopal, ed., *Selected Works of Jawaharlal Nehru* (14 Vols., New Delhi, 1972–1981), Vol. 4, p. 185.

17

Ireland and the Empire-Commonwealth, 1918–1972

DEIRDRE McMAHON

In the British general election of December 1918 the Irish revolutionary party, Sinn Féin, won seventy-three seats and annihilated the Irish Parliamentary Party which had represented nationalist Ireland in Parliament since the 1880s. In January 1919, in line with Sinn Féin's policy of abstention from Westminster, those Sinn Féin MPs who were not in jail or on the run gathered in Dublin to set up their own assembly, Dáil Éireann. The *Irish Times* described these proceedings as "a solemn act of defiance of the British Empire by a body of young men who have not the slightest idea of that Empire's power and resources."[1] More thoughtful observers considered Sinn Féin to be a more potent threat than their ineffectual predecessors. How did the Sinn Féin leaders regard the Empire? The Irish guerilla leader Michael Collins had vivid childhood memories of the Boer War and greatly admired the Boer leader de Wet. In his various journals Arthur Griffith, founder of Sinn Féin, devoted considerable space to Indian affairs although he was lukewarm about Gandhi. The American-born de Valera, on the other hand, who spent eighteen turbulent months in the United States raising funds for the Dáil, was more interested in American parallels.

The establishment of the Dáil was followed by guerilla war that lasted for two and a half years. During that war there was a pervasive belief in British political and military circles that the trouble was being caused by a minority of malcontents and that once they were under control, the cowed moderate majority would emerge. It was to be an enduring theme in later colonial wars. In 1956 the Governor of Cyprus, Sir John Harding, told a House of Commons committee that the EOKA terrorists consisted of about "fifty wild men" whom he hoped to eliminate by the end of the year. Listening skeptically to Harding was the former Labour Prime Minister, Clement Attlee, who recalled being told in 1920 that Irish and Indian nationalism were "artificial movements engineered by a handful of agitators."[2]

WHEN LLOYD GEORGE SUCCEEDED ASQUITH as Prime Minister in December 1916 it was hoped that he would give a greater impetus to the search for a settlement. However, careful scrutiny of Lloyd George's career would have revealed that he had had reservations about Irish Home Rule. In a speech in Belfast in February 1907 he warned against the dangers of separatism and said that the schism of Ireland from the Empire was "unthinkable." He never displayed any insight into Irish affairs and on various occasions displayed anti-Catholic prejudice, particularly during the 1918 conscription crisis which he blamed on the Catholic clergy. There is no evidence that Lloyd George was forced by his Conservative colleagues in the coalition government to take a hard line on Ireland: this was his own clear preference.

The Colonial Secretary, the veteran southern Irish unionist Walter Long, had twice been invited by Lloyd George to take on the Chief Secretaryship (a post he had held briefly in 1905) but Long refused. He became instead in April 1918 chairman of the Cabinet's Irish Committee which was drafting a new Government of Ireland Bill and from then until the end of 1920 he was effectively the Cabinet's enforcer on Ireland. Long had by now become a convert to federalism; he dismissed Sinn Féin and thought that if only the government was "Firm. Firm. Firm" then it would fade away. He regarded Dominion Home Rule, which was now being widely canvassed as a possible solution, as "blather."[3] Lloyd George concurred. The war fostered Lloyd George's imperial consciousness and he was, moreover, surrounded by imperialist prophets such as the South African leader, J. C. Smuts, and Sir Alfred Milner, as well as leading members of the Round Table group like Philip Kerr, W. G. S. Adams, Edward Grigg and L. S. Amery who had joined the Cabinet secretariat after 1916. As peace returned, Dominion Home Rule for Ireland did not accord with Lloyd George's vision for the post-war world.

For Kerr, one of the Prime Minister's closest advisers, Ireland was part of a more cosmic threat: "There is really an attack going on everywhere on Government as such," he wrote to Lloyd George in September 1920. "It is obvious in Ireland, in Egypt, in Mesopotamia, and in India, and we have reached such a stage that in all these places the revolutionaries are on the verge of success . . . I would turn your whole attention to the problems of Great Britain and the British Empire."[4] Kerr saw the American Irish as the sinister manipulators of events who had linked up with "Indians, Egyptians, Bolshies, and all the haters of England in France, Germany, etc. . . . . If they can secure a republic for Ireland, either by bamboozlement, or because they can tire England by murder and outrage, they know that they can create a precisely similar movement in India, Egypt, etc."[5] Throughout 1919, 1920, and 1921 the gloomy quartet of Ireland, Egypt, Mesopotamia, and India appeared with monotonous regularity on the Cabinet agenda. The fear of a domino effect in each theater of imperial unrest gripped British ministers as they thrashed around for a solution.

By the end of 1920 Lloyd George was coming under increasing pressure from Commonwealth leaders to do something about Ireland, which was causing unrest in Irish communities in Australia, New Zealand, and Canada and, most prominently, America. But Long was adamant that Dominion Home Rule was "impossible to grant unless we are prepared to go the whole length and accept the inevitable conclusion, namely practical, if not legal independence . . . sooner or later, Ireland would demand complete Dominion status . . . and this England could never concede."[6] But there was no satisfactory definition of what Dominion Home Rule or Dominion status actually meant. At the Imperial Conference which assembled in London in June 1921 Smuts tried to seek such a definition and warned, prophetically, that the delay in reaching a satisfactory solution "which the example of Ireland gives to the whole Commonwealth, is one which we only neglect at our peril."[7] Dominion status was offered to the Irish while the Imperial Conference was sitting but apart from Smuts none of the Dominion leaders were consulted about it. No definition of Dominion status emerged from the seven weeks of the Conference deliberations.

Following the truce that came into operation on July 11, 1921, Irish and British representatives, led by Eamon de Valera and Lloyd George respectively, spent a grueling summer arguing about what sort of relationship Ireland would have with the Empire-Commonwealth. After de Valera's return from America in December 1920 Erskine Childers had become his principal constitutional adviser and played a significant role in shaping the policy of external association which was to be the basis of the Irish negotiating position: Ireland would be associated with, but not be a member of, the British Empire. De Valera and Childers both believed that for reasons of geography and self-interest Britain would never treat Ireland on the same basis as the overseas Dominions like Canada and Australia. This point was underlined when Smuts visited Dublin early in July 1921 to try and persuade de Valera to accept Dominion status, urging him not to press for a republic. When de Valera replied that the choice was for the Irish people to make, Smuts replied "the British people will never give you this choice. You are next door to them."[8] On July 20 Lloyd George made his first offer: Dominion status involving membership of the Empire and an oath of allegiance to the Crown, as well as a defense agreement. De Valera replied on August 10 asserting Ireland's indefeasible right to realize her own destiny. Dominion status for Ireland would be illusory, he argued, because the freedom enjoyed by the other Dominions was due to geography and not to legal enactments. He expressed his willingness to enter into a treaty of free association with the British Commonwealth, the basis of his idea of external association. After further exchanges both sides agreed to enter negotiations without preconditions. The reaction of the other Dominion leaders was one of profound relief though the New Zealand premier, W. F. Massey, who had an Ulster background, urged Lloyd George not to coerce Ulster: "Any move in that direction will mean very serious trouble all over the Empire. . . . People who are loyal [must] be treated fairly and justly."[9]

DURING THE NEGOTIATIONS WHICH STARTED in October 1921 allegiance to the Crown, membership of the Empire and defense guarantees were the core of the British demands. But throughout, Dominion status was never defined and neither was de Valera's alternative of external association which was being constantly developed as the negotiations proceeded. In the end, under threat of immediate and terrible war, the Irish delegates were forced to concede to the British demands. The Anglo-Irish treaty signed on December 6, 1921 established the Irish Free State as a self-governing Dominion within the British Empire. The Free State would have the same constitutional status as Canada; the Crown would be represented by a Governor-General; and members of the Free State parliament would take an oath of allegiance. The terms created an immediate split which led directly to the Irish civil war six months later.

The signing of the Anglo-Irish Treaty had profound repercussions in the wider imperial sphere. To the relief of the other Dominions, Irish agitation subsided and following the outbreak of the civil war in June 1922 there was a great revulsion among Irish communities in the diaspora who were horrified by it. But the Irish Treaty had more immediate consequences in the case of both Egypt and India. In the autumn of 1921 British ministers faced negotiations not only with the Irish but with the Egyptians led by the Egyptian Prime Minister Adli Pasha. Philip Kerr spoke with Adli at the end of October 1921 and urged Lloyd George to "screw him up to going back and fighting for a reasonable settlement. If he doesn't Zaghlul [the radical nationalist leader] will go Sinn Féin, and though we can put him down, Zaghlul will begin to create a Pan-Islamic-Sinn Féin machine making mischief everywhere."[10] In both sets of negotiations the problem was similar: how far could nationalist demands be met in Ireland and Egypt? British ministers were well aware that hostile sections of the British Conservative party were monitoring both sets of negotiations in case unacceptable concessions were made. Zaghlul was deported to the Seychelles in December 1921.

For India the Irish negotiations and their aftermath had equally paralyzing consequences. Just the week after the start of the Irish negotiations Lloyd George telegraphed to the Viceroy, Lord Reading, in forthright terms: "Our course in India is being watched in many other quarters, and we cannot afford to be misunderstood. The British Empire is passing through a very critical phase, and it will not survive unless it shows now in the most unmistakable fashion that it has the will and the power to stand by its policies and to deal conclusively with any who challenge its authority."[11] In December 1921, when the question of whether to start negotiations with Gandhi was under consideration, although the Secretary of State for India, Edwin Montagu, was in favor of talks with Gandhi, the rest of the British Cabinet was not. Pressure to arrest Gandhi increased from Conservative MPs who were emphatic that the surrender to Sinn Féin must not be repeated with the Indian Congress Party led by Gandhi. Gandhi was arrested in March 1922 just as the Irish Treaty was going through the British parliament.

BY THE WAVE OF A CONSTITUTIONAL WAND which harked back to the first Home Rule debates in 1886, Ireland was given the same constitutional status as Canada. But as critics had pointed out then, Canada was too distant and too big to prevent it seceding from the Empire. The Canadian analogy was based on a profound misconception: Ireland, unlike Canada, was a Dominion by revolution not evolution. Furthermore the Dominion settlement suffered from fatal flaws: as a concept Dominion status was still in the process of evolution; the Irish had never asked for it; it came too late; it was imposed; and it was accompanied by partition and civil war. The surprise is that it lasted as long as it did.

The Cosgrave government, with able ministers such as Kevin O'Higgins, Desmond FitzGerald, and Patrick McGilligan, played a major role in expanding the constitutional independence of the

Commonwealth at the various imperial conferences in 1926, 1929, and 1930. The 1926 conference led to the Balfour Report which at last produced the elusive definition of Dominion status. Following the 1930 conference the Statute of Westminster was passed which repealed the right of the British Parliament to legislate for the Dominions. But the nature of these advances demonstrated that for the new Irish Free State Commonwealth membership resembled the chafing of an ill-fitting shoe. Allegiance to the Crown, insisted upon by the British negotiators in 1921 and underlined in the 1922 Constitution and the Balfour Report four years later, carried a weight of historical baggage which ensured that the Crown could never be the same focus of loyalty as it was for Australia, Canada, and New Zealand. In 1921 British negotiators complained bitterly that the Irish were living in some fantasyland in their demand for a republic; Lionel Curtis, constitutional adviser to the British delegation and later head of the Irish Branch at the Colonial Office, criticized their obsession with American models and ideas. But the Irish were the realists: what they wanted, then as later, was precision; what they were to get consistently from British ministers and officials until Ireland finally left the Commonwealth in 1948 was a lot of pious waffle about indivisible crowns and indissoluble unity. Even if the Cosgrave administration had succeeded in eliminating the more objectionable aspects of the Treaty (and it is now known that it was considering some of the measures that de Valera later implemented), it is likely that the Commonwealth would have become a cul-de-sac for the Irish. As a forum for articulating Irish sovereignty, the League of Nations represented both an escape from the constitutional navel-gazing of the imperial conferences and more exciting opportunities for a new, small state anxious to make an impression on the world stage.

When de Valera came to power in March 1932, it was barely eight years since he had been released from jail at the end of the Irish civil war, which had been fought over the terms of the Treaty and which had claimed the life of his friend Erskine Childers in one of the first executions of the civil war. These painful memories made de Valera's innate wariness towards the Commonwealth understandable. He was also wary initially about the League of Nations but became an enthusiastic and active participant in its proceedings for the rest of the decade. America was the place outside Ireland that de Valera knew best and apart from Britain he did not visit any other part of the Commonwealth until after he left office in 1948. Nor did he have an extensive acquaintance with Commonwealth statesmen since he did not attend any of the imperial conferences in the 1930s. Within days of taking office de Valera introduced a bill to abolish the oath of allegiance and disputed several substantial payments that were due to Britain. Over the next four years he introduced further bills designed to chip away at the powers of the Crown in the internal affairs of the Free State. These moves led to a six-year dispute with Britain during which the British government was forced to make a fundamental reassessment of the Commonwealth.

If de Valera had opted for Irish secession from the Commonwealth, it would have made the British position clearer if not easier. The problem for all the sixteen years he was in office was that he never did. When drafting his new constitution in 1936, he told the British Dominions Secretary, Malcolm MacDonald, that his proposals, which were a variant of external association, were perfectly consistent with staying in the Commonwealth and that if the British government thought otherwise then it "would have to turn them out." At the end of that year, during the Abdication crisis, de Valera rushed the External Relations Act through the Dáil. The Act recognized the King as the symbol of the cooperation of the Commonwealth and confirmed certain of his functions in external affairs. In July 1937 de Valera's new constitution, which was republican in all but name, was passed by referendum. After consultation with the other Dominions the British government stated that the new constitution did not affect Irish membership of the Commonwealth. This evasion had the merit of papering over the immediate cracks in the Commonwealth at a time of worsening international tension. The dispute with Britain came to an end in April 1938 in an agreement which, among other things, returned the Irish ports retained under the 1921 Treaty. This made Irish neutrality possible the following year when the Second World War broke out. Ireland was the only Commonwealth state to remain neutral; by the end of the war the Irish relationship with the Commonwealth was almost invisible.

IRELAND AND INDIA HAD BEEN LINKED TOGETHER in the minds of British ministers and officials even before the first Home Rule Bill in 1886. However, popular nationalism and imperialism were not in direct competition with each other until much later and serving in the British colonial administration helped Irish people to take advantage of the British connection at a time when opportunities at home were severely restricted. Many leading post-1916 nationalists had close links with the Indian Civil Service (ICS). The brother of Eoin MacNeill, founder of the Gaelic League and the Irish Volunteers, was in the ICS, as was the brother of Patrick McGilligan who served as a key minister in Cumann na nGaedheal/Fine Gael administrations up to the 1950s. Cearbhall Ó Dálaigh, the former Chief Justice and President of Ireland from 1974 to 1976, also had family connections with the ICS.

There were long-established links between Irish and Indian nationalism. Two of the most active Irish MPs on India were Frank Hugh O'Donnell and Michael Davitt. O'Donnell believed three things: that Irishmen were specially qualified to prescribe cures for imperial disorders; that Home Rulers were the natural parliamentary allies of the unenfranchised Empire; and that nationalists in Ireland should form an alliance with nationalists in Asia and Africa to achieve self-government.[12] O'Donnell was one of the first proponents of the idea to transform the Empire into a Commonwealth of partners admitted to membership on the basis of equality. O'Donnell sensed that when the British came face to face with the challenge of extended nationalism, they would surrender gracefully and salvage what they could. However, some historians have taken the view that the close alliance between Indian and Irish nationalists was detrimental to Indian interests.[13] Most MPs were exhausted by the endless and debilitating debates on Ireland and this made them less ready to turn to the long-term problems of nationalism elsewhere in the Empire and less willing to examine British rule in India. O'Donnell was influential in the setting up of the Congress Party in India in 1885. The rising, urban middle-classes who were to join Congress were much influenced by Irish nationalism. One Indian journal declared in 1905: "We have only to follow the example of the Irish. We want a common object to move us; we want a leader to direct us; we want the sinews of war to strengthen us."[14]

When the First World War broke out, the Indian Congress Party, like the Irish Parliamentary Party, supported the war effort. But by 1916, as in Ireland, there was disillusion with the war and anger at Indian losses suffered in Mesopotamia. There was also an armed movement, the Ghadr, organized by the Sikhs and based in the Punjab. The Governor of the Punjab was General Sir Michael O'Dwyer from Barronstown in Co. Tipperary and O'Dwyer was to say in his memoirs that in suppressing the Ghadr he had the example of the 1916 Easter Rising firmly in his mind. In fact, the Director of Criminal Intelligence in India was receiving reports in the months before the rising that Indian students in Dublin (one of whom was V. V. Giri, a future President of India) were in touch with "Irish nationalists of doubtful loyalty" and were even writing for seditious journals like *Nationality*.[15]

When the First World War ended, the disillusionment evident in the middle of war was even more marked because nationalist opinion believed that India had been poorly rewarded for its help. Instead, as in Ireland, there was coercion in the form of the anti-terrorist Rowlatt Acts. The number of demonstrations escalated and in Amritsar on April 13, 1919 Brigadier General Reginald Dyer ordered his forces to fire on demonstrators. Nearly 400 people were killed and many more injured. Amritsar had far-reaching effects. Moderate Indian nationalists lost faith in British rule and Gandhi became leader of the Congress Party as a result of the massacre. Dyer's immediate superior, Sir Michael O'Dwyer, defended him but Dyer was dismissed by the Secretary of State for India.[16]

In Parliament Dyer's strongest support came from such prominent Ulster Unionists as Sir Edward Carson and Sir Henry Wilson. Most of the votes cast in his favor in the House of Commons came from Ulster Unionist MPs. The Irish War of Independence was at its height as the Amritsar debate was in progress and the parallels with what was happening in Ireland were all too clear. The Liberal newspaper, the *Manchester Guardian,* commented that "General Dyer's more thorough supporters by no means intend to stop at India. . . . After India, Ireland. After Ireland, British workmen."[17]

In 1929, eight years after Ireland, Dominion status became the goal of British policy in India. There was considerable reluctance to concede Dominion status to India. Lord Birkenhead, Secretary for India and one of the signatories of the Irish Treaty in 1921, stated his belief in 1924 that it "was frankly inconceivable that India will ever be fit for Dominion self-government."[18] In the early 1930s, when the British government was preparing a new Government of India Bill, there was a revolt by die-hard Conservative MPs, notably Winston Churchill (another signatory of the 1921 Treaty), who were implacably opposed to any further measure of self-government for India. The shadow of Ireland loomed over this debate as these MPs frequently cited what they called "the surrender" to Sinn Féin as an argument against concessions to Gandhi and the Congress Party. Conservative MPs also pointed to de Valera's election in 1932 as another warning of what might happen in India if radical nationalism was not suppressed. In India the Irish example was so sensitive that *My Fight for Irish Freedom,* the memoirs of the IRA leader, Dan Breen, was banned.[19] It was, in the words of a Calcutta Special Branch officer, "something in the nature of a bible" to the Bengal terrorists and furnished them with "a detailed description of how to run successfully a terrorist campaign."[20]

The Government of India Act was finally passed in 1935. The Congress Party won most of the seats in the provincial elections of 1937 but their political rivals, the Muslim League, were starting to consolidate their support among the predominantly Muslim states of India. When the Second World War broke out in 1939, the Viceroy, Lord Linlithgow, declared war on behalf of India but did not consult any Indian politicians from either Congress or the Muslim League. Congress withdrew from the provincial legislatures. In March 1940 the Muslim League, led by Mohammed Ali Jinnah, made its first formal demand for a separate Muslim state, to be called Pakistan. The parallels with Ulster struck many observers at the time. The Congress Party, like Sinn Féin between 1919 and 1921, paid no attention to this demand and believed, again like Sinn Féin, that as a collection of Muslim states divided between India's eastern and western borders, Pakistan was simply unviable.

In 1942 Congress embarked on a "Quit India" movement which led to its leaders being arrested and interned for the rest of the war. Although several attempts were made to try and secure a settlement with Congress during the war, they were half-hearted particularly since Churchill, the British Prime Minister, was hostile to any advance in Indian independence. In February 1945 the Secretary of State for India, L. S. Amery, presented a memorandum to the Cabinet's India Committee which examined the shape of a future treaty with India once it was decided to transfer power. It examined the precedents that might guide British ministers and officials, specifically the 1921 Irish Treaty. In the twenty-three years since the signing of that instrument, this was the most comprehensive postmortem ever undertaken by the British government and it was carried out in the context of what to do about India. Ireland was a deeply dispiriting precedent. Nearly every article of the 1921 Treaty was relevant to an Indian treaty but "the subsequent history of the relations between Great Britain and Southern Ireland has not been a very happy one. [The Treaty's] ratification was carried by a majority of 64 to 57, and the party opposed to it, the Fíanna Fáil, continued to work for its practical nullification."[21] Amery concluded that while none of the signatories expected the Treaty to have a long shelf life (an erroneous assumption, as Churchill could have pointed out), they doubtless hoped that it would last longer than it did.

By the end of the war, time was running out for British rule in India. Throughout 1946 and 1947 there was an intense debate in London over whether India and Burma should stay in the Commonwealth. Officials responsible for India and Burma considered that some form of allegiance to the Crown was essential although

Ireland was, again, seen as an unfortunate precedent. The new Indian Viceroy, Lord Mountbatten, was determined that India would remain in the Commonwealth and in May 1947 Congress leaders agreed to accept Dominion status until the draft constitution was ready. With the transfer of power now scheduled for August 1947, the Prime Minister, Clement Attlee, was warned by his Cabinet Secretary that urgent consideration should be given to some new form of Commonwealth association other than Dominion status. The discussions which took place in Whitehall make depressing reading as they revealed the same obsession with allegiance to the Crown and the same reluctance to envisage any new form of Commonwealth membership for countries like Ireland and now India which had very different political and historical backgrounds. In India's case there was also the issue of race.

In February 1948 de Valera was defeated in the general election and was succeeded as Taoiseach by John A. Costello who presided over a heterogeneous coalition of five parties. Costello had always disliked the External Relations Act, as did his new Minister for External Affairs, Seán MacBride. De Valera had considered repealing the Act after the war but he stayed his hand, waiting to see what would happen with India. The Indian government had sent a delegation to Dublin at the end of 1947 to consult de Valera about their future constitutional status. He urged them to consider some form of external association. In September 1948, during a visit to Canada, Costello announced that the External Relations Act would be repealed *and* that Ireland would be leaving the Commonwealth. In view of the discussions taking place over India, secession from the Commonwealth did not necessarily follow from the repeal of the Act, something that Costello never apparently considered. Ironically, British officials were at this time actually suggesting to the Indians that they use the External Relations Act as a basis for staying in the Commonwealth. Following talks in October-November 1948 between Irish, British, and other Commonwealth ministers, it was agreed that reciprocal arrangements regarding trade and citizenship rights were the best solution for the new Irish position. British ministers, resentful at the precipitate way Costello had announced the repeal of the Act, wanted to take a harder line with the Irish but found that the other Commonwealth leaders were opposed; they hoped that an informal relationship between Ireland and the Commonwealth might evolve, and even that the Irish might rejoin the Commonwealth.

After a winter of further argument and debate over what to do about Ireland and India, the British government finally threw in the towel and agreed on April 8, that the best solution would be for

India to recognize the King as head of the Commonwealth and as the symbol of the free association of Commonwealth peoples: in effect this enshrined de Valera's concept of external association. Events moved swiftly after this. On April 18, Ireland left the Commonwealth and became the Republic of Ireland. Nine days later, at the Commonwealth Prime Ministers' Conference in London, India affirmed its desire to remain in the Commonwealth and to accept the King as the "symbol of the free association of its independent member nations." On May 3, the British government published its Ireland Bill, which revealed a bitter sting in the tail in the shape of the clause stipulating that in no event would Northern Ireland or any part of it cease to be part of the United Kingdom "without the consent of the Parliament of Northern Ireland."[22]

IN SEPTEMBER 1949 A BRITISH LABOUR MP, A. L. Ungoed-Thomas, met de Valera at the Council of Europe in Strasbourg and reported their conversation to the Commonwealth Relations Office in London. De Valera "emphasised that he had always been most careful to state that he did not wish to leave the Commonwealth so long as it was understood that no allegiance to the Crown of England was involved. The Indian Commonwealth solution would have exactly met his position, and he was clearly angry at Mr Costello's action."[23] British ministers and officials were very encouraged by these comments and the British Ambassador in Dublin, Sir Gilbert Laithwaite, observed that if Southern Ireland was prepared "not only to come back into the Commonwealth on the same basis as India, but in addition to accept allegiance to The King, then it might no doubt be possible to devise some system under which, subject to adequate guarantees to the North and to the agreement of the Northern Ireland Parliament, there could be an all-Ireland Parliamentary Body."[24] But he doubted whether, "even if Southern Ireland came back into the Commonwealth on the Indian basis, the North would be prepared to whittle away its relation to The King or be satisfied with [his] position merely as 'Head of the Commonwealth.'"[25]

The contraction of Ireland's international role after 1948 was clear. It had left the Commonwealth and was still excluded from the United Nations by a Soviet veto that was eventually lifted in 1955. When Ireland joined the UN it had diplomatic relations with only twenty countries but the UN, like the League of Nations before it, provided the Irish with valuable diplomatic contacts around the world. Even before the departure from the Commonwealth, formal diplomatic links had been established with Australia in 1946 and, before the Second World War, with Canada in 1939. India opened an embassy in Dublin in 1949 and the first Irish embassy in Africa was opened in Nigeria in 1960. The civil war that erupted in Nigeria in 1967 provoked an Irish response to a foreign conflict not seen since the Spanish civil war. There were hundreds of Irish missionaries working in Nigeria and many had long-established connections with the eastern Igbo tribe who seceded to form the new state of Biafra. Despite enormous domestic pressure, the Irish government refused to recognize the new state and was considerably influenced by the parallels with Northern Ireland. It had great sympathy for Nigerian attempts to maintain the unity of their newly independent state and Frank Aiken, Minister for External Affairs, argued that if self-determination was conceded to the Igbos this would be an unfortunate precedent for other tribes. The Nigerians were also assured that the Irish would not raise the matter at the United Nations.

As at the League of Nations, the Irish were strong defenders at the UN of small nations like Hungary and Tibet which had been invaded by more powerful neighbours. They also took a strong line on apartheid in South Africa, which was criticized by a number of Irish people in South Africa. Replying to one such letter in December 1957 de Valera stated that the Irish government "was far too keenly aware, from our history, of the meaning of class segregation and the supremacy of one race over another, not to feel sympathy for those who are now treated as "second-class" citizens in their own country."[26] During Frank Aiken's long tenure as Minister for External Affairs (1957–69), he took a particular interest in decolonization and told the French bluntly that they were doing a disservice to western civilization by denying independence to Algeria. Ireland, he told the General Assembly in 1960, "has a memory which gives us a sense of brotherhood with the newly emerging peoples of today. . . . We stand unequivocally for the swift and orderly ending of colonial rule and other forms of foreign domination."[27]

UN membership did not diminish Irish interest in the Commonwealth. The possibility that Ireland might rejoin the Commonwealth was discussed in 1957–58, during de Valera's last term as Taoiseach. In February 1957 Cardinal D'Alton of Armagh (who had known de Valera since their schooldays) gave an interview to the journalist Douglas Hyde and proposed, *inter alia*, that a reunited Ireland should rejoin the Commonwealth "on the same basis as India." D'Alton's statement was well received in the Irish and British press and by his fellow bishops though official reactions in Dublin, Belfast, and London were cool. The British Ambassador in Dublin, Sir Alexander Clutterbuck, thought D'Alton's proposals "courageous and sensible" but doubted if any Irish political party would support rejoining the Commonwealth, particularly with a general election campaign under way.[28] The former Labour minister and historian of the 1921 Treaty, Lord Pakenham (later Lord Longford), discussed the matter with de Valera in September 1957 but de Valera made it clear that rejoining the Commonwealth was dependent on the ending of partition. Neither Lord Home, the Commonwealth Secretary, nor the British Prime Minister, Harold Macmillan, exactly radiated enthusiasm at the prospect of the Irish rejoining the Commonwealth. Macmillan did not think that: "a united Ireland—with de Valera as a sort of Irish Nehru—would do us much good. Let us stand by our friends."[29] Home thought they were well rid of the Irish, who had been such a disruptive force in the Commonwealth before 1949.

The issue emerged again in March 1958 when, during a visit to London, de Valera and Frank Aiken proposed to Lord Home that: "Northern Ireland should surrender its direct allegiance to the Queen in return for a United Republic of Ireland within the Commonwealth, which would recognise the Queen as its head."[30] But the British response was negative. This proposal surfaced once more in November 1959 just after Sean Lemass succeeded de Valera as Taoiseach. Lemass was sure that a relationship between a reunited Ireland and the Commonwealth could be worked out but doubted if the Northern Ireland government would consider it. A few years later, however, it was reported that the liberal Ulster Unionist MP, Henry Clark, had asked Paul Keating, counsellor at the Irish embassy in London, when the Irish would rejoin the Commonwealth adding that Lemass "would make a great impression at the Commonwealth Conference."[31] In July 1965, Sir Joe Garner, Permanent Under-Secretary at the Commonwealth Relations Office (CRO), told the Irish Ambassador in London, J. G. Molloy, that he would like to see Ireland back in the Commonwealth.[32] But Europe was already beckoning; the first Irish application to join the Common Market was in 1961 and Ireland eventually joined in 1973. The question of Irish sovereignty had been a major issue for Irish officials and historical parallels were unavoidable, as the Irish Ambassador in Rome wrote in 1970: "our entry into the EEC with all the rights of a member state is hardly on all fours with the act of Union of 1800 which has proved so difficult for Ireland to reverse."[33]

Until the relevant archives are released, we do not know whether rejoining the Commonwealth was seriously discussed by the two governments during the Northern Ireland Troubles although it surfaced in the press from time to time. It received more attention immediately before and after the 1998 Belfast Agreement. Before she left office in 1997 the Irish President, Mary Robinson (whose family had close links with the British colonial service), suggested that the Irish government should seriously consider the idea.[34] The Taoiseach, Bertie Ahern, seemed willing to consider rejoining but did not subsequently expand on this in any detail. In an article in the *Irish Times* in November 2001, a Canadian law professor, Robert Martin, urged the Irish to rejoin, pointing out that all but one of the priority recipient countries for Irish overseas aid were members of the Commonwealth. The Commonwealth, he wrote, "is not, as many Irish people imagine it to be, the British Empire in drag; it is not the resurrected cadaver of empire. It's over half a century since Ireland left the Commonwealth. It's time for the Irish to take another look."[35]

Spring Semester 2005

Bibliographical Note

The study of Ireland's relations with the British Empire-Commonwealth has been transformed over the last quarter century. This is particularly evident in the area of Irish involvement in imperial wars, especially the Boer War, the First World War and the Second World War. For the Boer War there has been the pioneering work of Donal McCracken[36] and Donal Lowry.[37] For decades after Irish independence, Irish involvement in the First World War was shrouded in silence although many thousands of Irishmen fought and died in the war. This historical neglect began to change in the 1980s with the research of David Fitzpatrick,[38] Keith Jeffery,[39] Patrick Callan,[40] and Terence Denman.[41] There is now considerable interest in the First World War in Ireland, as testified by the revival of Irish regimental associations, such as those of the Royal Dublin Fusiliers and the Royal Munster Fusiliers. Irish involvement in the Second World War has recently been discussed in a illuminating volume of essays edited by Brian Girvin and Geoffrey Roberts.[42]

The richness of the Irish Diaspora experience, for too long dominated by stereotypes from the United States, has been chronicled in major studies by D. H. Akenson, David Fitzpatrick, and Andy Bielenberg.[43] Irish missionaries, Protestant and Catholic, who were a consequence of the Diaspora, are now attracting scholarly attention in the Irish Missionary History Project which is based at the National University of Ireland, Maynooth. Irish links with, and influence on Indian revolutionary nationalism have been explored by Richard P. Davis[44] and Howard Brasted[45] while Scott B. Cook has studied the Irish role in the Indian Civil Service.[46]

Regarding Irish relations with the Commonwealth, the release of Irish government records and major private collections such as those of Eamon de Valera, as well as the publication of *Documents on Irish Foreign Policy*,[47] have meant that Irish scholars are no longer so dependent on British sources. This is particularly evident in recent studies of Ireland's international role outside the Commonwealth in the League of Nations and later the United Nations.[48]

Two volumes of essays published over the last decade, *"An Irish Empire"? Aspects of Ireland and the British Empire*,[49] and *Ireland and the British Empire*,[50] encapsulate much of the new research that has been carried out since the early 1980s.

1. *Irish Times,* Jan. 23, 1919.

2. Harold Nicolson, *Diaries and Letters, 1945–62* (London, 1968), p. 303.

3. John Kendle, *Walter Long, Ireland and the Union, 1905–20* (Dublin, 1992), pp. 46–51.

4. Kerr to Lloyd George, Sept. 2, 1920, House of Lords, Lloyd George Papers, F/90/1/18.

5. Ibid., Sept. 14, 1921.

6. Long to Lloyd George, Sept. 26, 1920, Lloyd George Papers, F/34/1/46.

7. "The Constitution of the British Commonwealth," 1921, British Library (BL), Balfour Papers, Add. MSS. 49775.

8. Thomas Jones, *A Whitehall Diary: Ireland, 1918–25,* Keith Middlemas, ed. (Oxford, 1971), Vol. III, p. 83.

9. Jellicoe to Colonial Office, Nov. 11, 1921, Lloyd George Papers, F/10/1/44.

10. Kerr to Lloyd George, Oct. 28, 1921, Lloyd George Papers, F/34/2/9.

11. Lloyd George to Reading, Oct. 21, 1921, Lloyd George Papers, F/41/1/30.

12. Howard Brasted, "Indian Nationalist Development and the Influence of Irish Home Rule, 1870–1886," *Modern Asian Studies,* 14 (1980), pp. 42–65; Brasted, "Irish Nationalism and the British Empire in the Late Nineteenth Century," in Oliver MacDonagh, W. F. Mandle, & Pauric Travers, eds., *Irish Culture and Nationalism, 1750–1950* (London, 1983), pp. 84–95.

13. Mary Cumpston, "Some Early Indian Nationalists and their Allies in the British Parliament, 1851–1906," *English Historical Review,* 76 (1961), pp. 279–97.

14. *Amrita Bazar Patrika,* Nov. 4, 1905, quoted in Brasted, "Indian Nationalist Development," p. 63.

15. Weekly report by the Director of Criminal Intelligence, May 2, 1916, National Archives of India, Home (Political) 577–80, Part B.

16. Michael O'Dwyer, *India as I Knew It* (London, 1925).

17. Derek Sayer, "British Reaction to the Amritsar Massacre, 1919–20," *Past & Present,* 131 (1991), pp. 130–64.

18. Anthony Read & David Fisher, *The Proudest Day: India's Long Road to Independence* (London, 1998), p. 205.

19. Report, Sept. 10, 1935, National Archives of India, Home (Political) 41/6/35.

20. Ibid.

21. Memorandum by Amery, Feb. 1, 1945, *India: The Transfer of Power* (HMSO, London, 1970–83), V, pp. 503–16.

22. Ireland Act (12 & 13 Geo. VI, c. 41).

23. Memorandum by Ungoed-Thomas, Sept. 5, 1949, PRO DO 35/3941.

24. Ibid., minute by Laithwaite, Nov. 2, 1949.

25. Ibid.

26. Quoted by Joseph Morrison Skelly, *Irish Diplomacy at the United Nations, 1945–65: National Interests and the International Order* (Dublin, 1997), p. 190.

27. Ibid., pp. 21–22.

28. Clutterbuck to Commonwealth Relations Office, Mar. 7, 1957, PRO DO 35/7845.

29. Home to Macmillan, Aug. 1957, PRO DO 35/7891.

30. Ibid., memorandum by Home, Mar. 18, 1958.

31. Quoted by John Horgan, "Irish Foreign Policy, Northern Ireland, Neutrality and the Commonwealth: The Historical Roots of a Current Controversy," *Irish Studies in International Affairs,* 10 (1999), pp. 146–47.

32. Quoted by Daithi Ó Corráin, "'Rendering to God and Caesar': The Irish Churches and the Two States in Ireland, 1949–73," (University of Dublin Ph.D. Thesis, 2004), p. 82. Garner had been dealing with Irish affairs since the 1930s and in *The Commonwealth Office, 1925–68* (London, 1978) wrote sympathetically about Irish relations with the CRO, formerly the Dominions Office.

33. Quoted by Gary Murphy, "'A Measurement of the Extent of our Sovereignty at the Moment': Sovereignty and the Question of Irish Entry to the EEC, New Evidence from the Archives," *Irish Studies in International Affairs,* 12 (2001), p. 202.

34. *Independent,* June 4, 1997.

35. *Irish Times,* Nov. 23, 2001.

36. Donal P. McCracken, *The Irish Pro-Boers* (Johannesburg, 1989).

37. Donal Lowry, *The South African War Reappraised* (Manchester, 2000).

38. David Fitzpatrick, ed., *Ireland and the First World War* (Mullingar, Ireland, 1988).

39. Keith Jeffery, *Ireland and the Great War* (Cambridge, 2000).

40. Patrick Callan, "Recruiting for the British Army in Ireland during the First World War," *Irish Sword,* XXI (1987).

41. Terence Denman, *Ireland's Unknown Soldiers: The 10th (Irish) Division in the Great War* (Dublin, 1992).

42. Brian Girvin and Geoffrey Roberts, eds., *Ireland and the Second World War: Politics, Society and Remembrance* (Dublin, 2000).

43. David Fitzpatrick, *Irish Emigration 1801–1921* (Dublin, 1984); D. H. Akenson, *The Irish Diaspora: A Primer* (Belfast, 1994); Andy Bielenberg, ed., *The Irish Diaspora* (Harlow, England, 2000).

44. Richard P. Davis, "India in Irish Revolutionary Propaganda, 1905–22," *Journal of the Asiatic Society of Bangladesh,* 22, 1 (1977).

45. Howard Brasted, "Irish Models and the Indian Nationalist Congress, 1870–1922," *South Asia,* VIII (1985).

46. Scott B. Cook, "The Irish Raj: The Social Careers and Origins of Irishmen in the Indian Civil Service, 1855–1914," *Journal of Social History,* XX (1986–87).

47. Volume IV, which deals with the period 1932–1936, was published in 2004.

48. Michael Kennedy, *Ireland and the League of Nations, 1919–46* (Dublin, 1996); Joseph Morrison Skelly, *Irish Diplomacy at the United Nations, 1945–65* (Dublin, 1997).

49. Keith Jeffery, ed., *"An Irish Empire"? Aspects of Ireland and the British Empire* (Manchester, 1996).

50. Kevin Kenny, ed., *Ireland and the British Empire* (Oxford, 2004).

18

British Intellectuals and East Asia In the Inter-war Years

ANTONY BEST

For the majority of British intellectuals in the inter-war years, East Asia was a world away both literally and metaphorically and, in an age when the concept of "national character" predominated, knowledge of the region was often expressed in the form of clichés that had been handed down from the previous century. Thus the Japanese were characterized as disciplined and ambitious but hampered by a lack of originality in thinking, while the Chinese were industrious but inept at governance. Reinforcing these impressions were the two major sources of information on the region: journalists and travel writers. Both tended not to possess any knowledge of East Asian languages, and the result of this limited ability to understand the culture and politics of China and Japan was that they often fell back on the stereotypes that were familiar to their readers.[1] Politicians and publicists therefore frequently pontificated on what was best for the region from a position of little real knowledge.

Some members of the educated elite in Britain did have more direct experience. One notable group was those from the artistic world whose interest in the rich cultural legacy of the region led to a desire to experience its atmosphere and see its treasures at first hand. Thus, figures such as Harold Acton took up teaching posts allowing a long exposure to Asian culture, while others such as Osbert Sitwell paid more fleeting visits. The inter-war period also saw new attempts to encourage a wider appreciation of Chinese and Japanese art and literature. This was, for example, a time enriched by Arthur Waley's translations of Chinese and Japanese poetry and, most celebrated of all, the peerless exhibition of Chinese art at the Royal Academy in London in 1935–36, which attracted around 400,000 visitors.[2] The flow of culture was not, however, just in the one direction, for these years also saw Laurence Binyon's lectures in Japan on British watercolor painting in 1929, and an exhibition of British modern art in Tokyo in 1931.

It was not only the past that led to interest in East Asia, for in addition the region presented a fascinating laboratory for studying the effects of modernity. This, after all, was an area of the world that was widely perceived as having only just emerged from feudalism. It included one country, Japan, that appeared to have reacted very ably to the sudden arrival of the West and which was creating a hybrid state and society that combined qualities from both Asian and European civilizations. It was, however, questioned whether this progress was all to the good, for Japan contained a strain of militarism that augured ill for the future and led some to label it as the "Prussia of the East." Its neighbor, China, was even more of a problem. Due to its immense size and the sheer weight of its past, China was merely stumbling towards modernity, but the very fact that its course was so uncertain made it a subject of great interest, for the fate of its 400,000,000 people was something that the world could not ignore. Moreover, the existence of the treaty ports and China's potential as a market meant that there was a direct British interest in assessing the country's progress.

The result of China's unpredictability and the questions about Japan's trajectory meant that the region's problems came to be seen by politically inclined intellectuals as having wider application, for they seemed to go to the heart of the dilemmas of the modern world. As a result, there was a regular flow of opinion-makers and intellectuals to East Asia; some looking for an interesting vacation, others involved in academic and political business. These years saw visits by philosophers and writers such as Bertrand Russell and George Bernard Shaw in order to observe local conditions. Meanwhile, the leading thinkers on international affairs from the Round Table and Chatham House (the Royal Institution of International Affairs), such as Lionel Curtis, Charles Webster, Arnold Toynbee, and Sir Frederick Whyte came to the region to attend the conferences of the Institute of Pacific Relations. These journeys not only made them more familiar with political, economic, and social conditions in the region, but also led to acquaintances being developed and correspondence begun with local intellectuals. However, whether these students of modernity fully understood the region is a different matter, for on the whole their visits were brief and they too did not speak any local languages.

To assess what difference this elite interest in East Asia made to British policy, I would like to concentrate on the political interest in the region rather than the purely cultural. I will start by looking at the stance of progressive intellectuals and then map out the conservative perspective. By the early 1920s the enthusiasm for Japanese modernization that had been expressed by people such as the Webbs in the period immediately before the Great War had died away.[3] Many now saw Japan as anachronistic; it remained wedded to the politics of imperialism and militarism just as the world was moving towards "new diplomacy." But while British enthusiasm for Japan waned, a growing interest developed in China in the early decades of the twentieth century. This had its roots in the belief that this once great civilization, which had fallen into disrepair in the anarchy of the warlord years, was beginning to drag itself into the modern world. The internationalists approved of this rebirth and argued that Britain should do its utmost to nurture the "new China." An article in the *Round Table* in December 1922 argued that:

> A solution of China's problem is a solution of our problem too. To work with China, for China, without asking for any direct reward is not mere idealism. It implies a recognition of the fact that the world is economically one, and that in helping China we help ourselves.[4]

As this comment implies, the prize in prospect was that China could be won for the Western world. This would be good for the long-term interests of British trade and, it was hoped, for the future of peace and stability in the region. Moreover, it was held that the likely alternative, if the West did not prove welcoming, was that the "new China" might be seduced by the confrontational creeds of pan-Asianism or Bolshevism.

China began to impinge even more on the British consciousness with the May Thirtieth incident in 1925 and the start of the sixteen-month long strike that brought Hong Kong to its knees. This clash with British interests led to debate about whether China's grievances were justified and whether the main nationalist vehicle, the Kuomintang (KMT), could form an effective government. Progressive intellectuals and politicians answered both questions in the affirmative. For example, Labour MPs declaimed passionately about the appalling working conditions that existed in Western-owned factories in Shanghai, while both liberals and socialists hailed the KMT as the personification of Chinese nationalism and as a progressive, anti-imperial force that would awaken China from its slumbers. As such it was seen as leading a political movement that Britain should not disdain but welcome.

Support for the Kuomintang and for its "new China" thus became a progressive cause in Britain, as indeed it did in the United States. One important factor that encouraged this identification with China was the conviviality of the articulate, young Western-educated men and women who gained positions in the nationalist government. For example, after his first visit to China the civil servant Sir Arthur Salter observed: "I feel no 'colour' sense in China—with their Western-educated people I often talk with less consciousness of difference of race than with many Europeans."[5] Reinforcing this was their propensity, as noted above, to engage in correspondence with British contacts and to demonstrate enthusiasm for internationalism. This contrasted with the intellectuals in Japan, who, as one writer observed, surprised Europeans by "judging universal questions by strictly Japanese standards."[6]

Also important was that the problems raised by China, such as the treatment of labor and the future of imperialism, were central political issues at the time. The Chinese example could be used as a case study to reinforce abstract arguments about the nature of capitalism, the role of the state, and the future of international politics. However, it is worth noting that this support for China was not unconditional. With the failure of the KMT in the late 1920s to bring civil strife to an end, many progressive thinkers began to have doubts about whether the party could live up to their expectations. In 1930 a writer in the *Round Table,* probably Lionel Curtis, observed that: "Disappointment, not to say disillusionment, is the keynote."[7]

The attitudes taken up in the late 1920s naturally came into even sharper focus with the deepening of Sino-Japanese tensions in the 1930s: first in the Manchurian crisis of 1931–33 and then in the opening of full-scale hostilities in July 1937. This period has, of course, been studied intensively, and I will not rehearse the intricate diplomacy of the period.[8] What is more important for my purpose is the way in which the crisis in East Asia helped to solidify opinion on the Left to the extent that China became a symbol of opposition to fascism thus echoing the appeal of Republican Spain.

For progressives, concern for the future of collective security was probably more significant than the lingering sympathy for China. They saw Japan's actions as a direct challenge to the authority of the League of Nations that had to be resisted. For example, following the publication of the Lytton Report in October 1932 the publicist Henry Wickham Steed observed the crisis constituted the most dangerous time since the end of the war and that there was only a slim chance of avoiding "the utter breakdown of everything we care for."[9] Linked to this sense that Japan must not be allowed to triumph was a perception that its apparent interest in territorial aggrandizement and its militarism represented unwelcome throwbacks to the dark days of "old diplomacy." As one National Liberal MP declared in February 1933, Japan was engaged in "blatant imperialism at a time when imperialism should be dead."[10] Japan therefore had to be shown that its selfishness was anachronistic and that it would not prevail. Another angle to this issue was that opposition to Japan was seen as a necessary precursor to a deeply held liberal cause, namely closer relations with the United States. Thus, while the prominent internationalist, Lord Lothian, supported appeasement of Germany, he consistently advocated Anglo-American collaboration to contain Japanese aggression. Indeed, in the autumn of 1934, concerned at reports in the press that the National Government favored a *rapprochement* with Japan, both he and General J. C. Smuts used public speeches and newspaper articles as an opportunity to denounce any such move.[11]

Reinforcing the opposition to Japanese aggression was the fact that in its military campaigns Japan engaged in a brutal new mode of warfare that was guaranteed to provoke a hostile reaction from the British public, namely the use of force against civilians. The first provocative act came in February 1932, when Japan unleashed its bombers against Chapei, one of the Chinese areas of Shanghai. Worse was to come in the Sino-Japanese War, for when that escalated into full-scale conflict in August 1937 the bombers returned to the skies targeting civilian areas in Shanghai, Nanking, and Canton. In the wake of similar events in Spain, including the destruction at Guernica, this campaign prompted the most vociferous criticisms of Japan yet heard. One of these outraged individuals was the Liberal social reformer Violet Markham, who wrote:

> This China business fills me with utter horror. Is the whole civilised world impotent to restrain those devils in Japan? . . . I feel to sit back quietly and watch those people massacred by the thousand is a disgrace to the manhood and womanhood of the civilized world. I feel desperately about it all but how to stop it is beyond me for that means war. Still—. . .[12]

Implicit in this protest was the sense that Japan itself had turned its back on civilization, but others were more explicit. The classicist and League enthusiast Gilbert Murray observed in print that the Japanese were "a people fallen back into barbarism," and even Beatrice

Webb had to forget her past Japanophilia and was forced to con-
clude that Japan had "'lost her head' and I think her soul."[13]

Adding further fuel to the fire was the fact that Japan was con-
sciously ranging itself alongside the Fascist Powers in Europe. This
made it easy to draw parallels between the violent methods of the
three right-wing revisionist states and present them as a concerted
threat to civilized values. Thus Spain and China could be presented
as being on the frontline of the war to protect democracy from fascism. However to argue this case convincingly was not easy, for it required a rose-tinted view of Chiang Kai-shek's China. For example,
Harold Laski's assertion in 1938 that Japan's "militarist autocracy"
was trying to "stifle a nascent Chinese democracy" ignored the fact
that Japan was still probably more pluralist than China and that the
KMT's "Blue Shirts" had clearly modeled themselves on similarly
appareled individuals in Italy and Germany.[14]

The Left's answer to the problems of East Asia was to lobby the
government to support moral and economic sanctions against Japan
and to do all it could to assist Chinese resistance and reconstruction.
This pressure for action rose to a crescendo in the autumn of 1937,
when John Maynard Keynes wrote to *The Times* demanding a cessation of trade and the issue became one of the dominant themes in
the debate in the House of Commons on the King's Speech.[15] Again
East Asia was not seen in isolation. One argument used to stress
the necessity of action was that Japan was a weak link in the Anti-
Comintern Pact. Lord Robert Cecil, among others, contended that
pressure on Japan would help to "make the dictators of Europe more
reasonable."[16] In addition, progressives began a number of private
initiatives to assist the Chinese cause. A China Campaign Committee
was established which tried to sponsor a boycott of Japanese goods.[17]
A book of essays, *China Body and Soul,* to which—interestingly—
both Arthur Waley and Laurence Binyon contributed, was published
and its proceeds given to Chinese refugees.[18] Some went even further: the Labour MP Philip Noel-Baker involved himself in a wild
scheme to establish an international volunteer air force to defend
Chinese cities against Japanese bombers.[19]

It is worth noting that this opposition to Japan was largely based
on disapproval of that country's methods and did not contain any
racial aspect. Moreover, there was a degree of sympathy in regard to
the forces that were driving Japan towards expansion. Ever since the
1920s all sides of the political spectrum had recognized that Japan
faced a terrible dilemma due to its rapidly increasing population
and the impossibility of emigration to the United States, Canada, or
Australia. The only satisfactory answer to this problem, it was held,

was for Japan to follow a policy of rapid industrialization.[20] Therefore, in the wake of the Manchurian crisis in 1931, the idea developed on the Left that Japan's sudden shift from liberalism to imperial expansion was directly linked to the descent of the world economy into depression and protectionism. As early as January 1934 Arnold Toynbee warned that Japan's aggression in Manchuria had arisen from economic causes and that "this act is certain to be followed by others unless the rest of the world offers Japan . . . a reasonable remedy for her pressing ills."[21] This explanation for Japan's aggression was interesting because, of course, it tallied with the general belief among progressive intellectuals that protectionism was the root of all evil and that the best way to return the world to stability was the revival of Britain's liberal trading regime. Thus once again attention was focused on East Asia because its affairs were seen as acting as a commentary on debates closer to home.

It must be remembered, however, that, while the liberal Left might have dominated the intellectual life of Britain in the 1930s, the center ground of politics was held by the Conservative Party, which was by far the most significant player in the National Government. It is therefore vital to look at how right-wing politicians and commentators viewed Japan and China. Among the conservative ranks in British society there tended to be greater sympathy for Japan than for China. The former was seen as a country that had taken a gradual, constitutional route towards good governance. It stood for patriotism, thrift, and law and order, and, moreover, possessed that one institution guaranteed to bring stability—a monarchy. As the Duke of Atholl once noted, it was "a great Island, which in some respects resembles Britain."[22]

China, in contrast, was seen as being mired in anarchy. Conservatives argued that the Chinese people had not yet acquired the ability to run a modern state and that until they did China was unfit to take up a position of equality in the civilized world. In regard to the events of the 1920s, from the first the KMT's challenge to British treaty rights was dismissed as entirely unwarranted and illegal, and it was believed that the nationalists should be met with force—the one language that "Orientals" understood. Underlying this tough attitude was the conviction that the KMT was entirely in the hands of its Soviet advisers. Indeed, even after the KMT split with the Russians in mid-1927, some still suspected that a lingering affiliation to communism remained. Moreover, echoing the attitude of the "Shanghai-landers," the Right expressed great skepticism about whether the KMT would ever be capable of effective government. Prejudice against the Chinese existed at the highest levels. Lord Birkenhead, the Secretary of State for India, may have been jesting when he observed that the Chinese could not object to British forces in Shanghai being equipped with gas, as this "ought not to be unacceptable to an opium-addicted people," but this cruel quip is, nevertheless, revealing.[23] It is also interesting that, when Japanese interests in north China had been threatened by the KMT in May 1928, Winston Churchill tellingly called for assistance to Japan on the grounds that it was "on the side of civilization against barbarism and brutality."[24]

Considering the conservative stance in the late 1920s it is no surprise that during the Manchurian crisis right-wing sympathy was reserved almost exclusively for Japan. The common refrain by this point was that China had become no more than a geographical expression, for the KMT had failed to restore unity or to rule effectively. Indeed, instead of concentrating on governing, the KMT was seen as having engaged in endless anti-foreign provocations in its illegitimate crusade against the unequal treaties. The Japanese decision to strike back was therefore perceived as both an understandable loss of patience and an attempt to bring order to chaos. As one anonymous conservative commentator noted in the spring of 1932:

> We are informed that a state of war exists between Japan and China, but this is absurd, for China as an entity does not exist. The China of to-day only exists on paper; it is a unit only on the map. Japan is, therefore, not fighting China but anarchy and all the -isms so closely connected with Soviet Russia.[25]

Crucial to this image was that the main focus of attention was Manchuria. This was an area where the KMT had never held sway and where the Japanese control of the Kwantung lease had, as the journalist J. O. P. Bland put it, "made . . . a flourishing oasis in the howling desert of Chinese misrule."[26] Accordingly, the right drew a parallel between Japan's efforts to bring order to Manchuria in 1931 and Britain's own past when it had been forced to occupy Egypt in 1882. Japan's behavior was thus recognized as being imperialistic, but this was not seen as a bad thing. Moreover, it was noted that the Japanese presence in Manchuria would make a valuable bulwark against the expansion of Soviet influence in East Asia.

Thus, as far as right-wing opinion was concerned, Japan's actions were understandable and did not seem in any way to threaten British interests. Indeed, to them the contrary appeared more likely, for Japan would bring prosperity to Manchukuo and so create a new, stable market for British trade. Therefore the idea that Britain should oppose Japan because the latter's behavior contravened the principles of the Covenant of the League of Nations appeared to some Tories as utter cant and nonsense. In February 1933 Winston Churchill made a speech at a meeting of the Anti-Socialist and Anti-Communist Union stating that the League would be well advised to concentrate on Europe where it could be of service. Leo Amery went even further by using the occasion of the House of Commons debate on the Lytton report to attack the "worship of unrealities at Geneva."[27] Moreover, on the grounds that the certainties of "old diplomacy" were more reliable than the abstraction of collective security, some now argued that the abrogation of the alliance had been a dire error of judgment. Thus, just as much as the Left, the Right used events in the East as an illustration of all that they felt was wrong with the world.

The idea that Japan was entirely justified in its actions was, however, subject to modification over time. Three reasons existed for this change of opinion: trade competition, global strategy, and Christian morality. Of these the first to have a significant effect on the Conservative Party was the rise from 1932 of Japanese trade competition. The flood of cheap exported goods such as cotton textiles, ceramics, and woollens into British imperial markets seriously affected a number of regions in Britain, with the result that local MPs began to campaign for the introduction of higher tariffs and quotas. The scale of the challenge and the need to be seen to act often led to the use of provocative language. Indeed, one of the more extreme anti-Japanese commentators, Samuel Hammersley, the MP for Stockport, went so far as to describe Japan's trade competition as "a new and extremely grave menace to the civilization of Western Europe."[28] The "yellow peril" had returned with a vengeance.

By impinging directly on British interests, Japanese trade pushed some in the Conservative Party to take a much more critical attitude towards the erstwhile ally. Others drifted in this direction out of concern for Britain's strategic position and due to moral qualms about Japan. The most prominent of these was Churchill. As noted above, in the early 1930s Churchill had taken a relaxed view of Japanese aggression, but once the government in Tokyo began to move towards Germany's orbit his attitude abruptly changed. In a number of his newspaper articles from 1936 onwards he outlined the parallels between the political violence and worship of war that appeared to be endemic in both countries, and drew attention to the need to contain Japan. By the autumn of 1937 he, like Keynes and Cecil, appears to have believed that economic sanctions were necessary to curb Japanese aggression.[29] If so he was not alone, for in August and

September 1937 three Cabinet ministers wrote to the Foreign Secretary, Anthony Eden, calling for pressure to be brought to bear on
Japan. One of these was the deeply religious Lord Halifax who observed that Japan's indiscriminate bombing of civilians appeared to
him to be "the worst thing—for morality and civilization—that we
have yet seen."[30] Thus for some Conservatives the brutal behavior of
Japan raised the same qualms about the future of civilized values as
it had done on the left.

The situation therefore was that by the time the Sino-Japanese
War had developed into a full-scale conflict, it was hard to find
many opinion-makers who would defend Japan's actions. Japan was
now viewed by almost the whole range of the political spectrum as
an aggressor state unworthy of sympathy. The only exceptions were
"die-hard" conservative journals, such as the *English Review* and the
National Review, which continued to use Britain's alienation from
Japan as an excuse to attack the tenets of "new diplomacy."

What role did the public debate about East Asia have on government policy? The only period in which its influence has been acknowledged is that of the Manchurian crisis, where both Bassett
and Thorne have shown how the government attempted the impossible task of conciliating both the pro-League and pro-Japanese
lobbies.[31] Regrettably, their lead has not been followed up, but
surely the period after 1933 is just as worthy of such of an approach,
for at every twist and turn of the story the government's freedom of
movement was constrained by its desire not to alienate significant
segments of public opinion.

Following the Manchurian crisis, the rise of security concerns
in Europe led some in the Cabinet, such as the Chancellor of the
Exchequer, Neville Chamberlain, to propose the appeasement of
Japan. However, the direction of public debate in Britain about
East Asia made this a difficult policy to pursue. One aspect of any
such policy of conciliation had to be recognition of the state of
Manchukuo. This would have been in line with the British self-image
of always taking a pragmatic line in foreign policy and of recogniz-
ing realities. The problem, however, was that any such policy would
have been construed as an overt rejection of the League and would
therefore have created a political storm that might have outweighed
the benefits. Here it is important to recall that the government's
overt commitment to adhere to the principles enshrined in the
League's Covenant was publicly proclaimed in every King's Speech
to Parliament until 1937. Another possible aspect of this policy,
namely the economic appeasement of Japan, was unattractive, for it
would almost inevitably have led to considerable opposition from

Conservative back-benchers. Put simply the problem, as one diplomat noted in January 1937, was that:

> Japan has intentions in the East which conflict with "public opinion" here, which is now more vocal than it was and influences Houses of Commons and Governments much more easily (c.f. Manchukuo and Abyssinia). This would be a real difficulty in the East.[32]

At the same time outright support for China, as desired by the progressives, was not a viable alternative, not just on strategic grounds, but also because of conservative doubts about the fiscal probity and administrative efficiency of the Chinese government. The parameters of the cautious policy followed by the government thus need to be seen as having been shaped both by strategic realities and by the nature of contemporary political debate.

What emerges from this brief study of how opinion-makers viewed events in East Asia in the inter-war period is that diplomacy was not merely left to a government that dreamt up policy cocooned from outside pressure. It was rather the case that the educated elite was interested in the region and lobbied actively for particular policies to be pursued. Almost inevitably this lobbying split into ideologically based factions, with progressives favoring China and conservatives backing Japan. This in part reflected the day-to-day politics of the region and the arguments about the best way in the circumstances of perpetuating British interests, but more important perhaps was the way in which these two countries came to be seen as exemplars of particular approaches towards politics. For example, while the immediate issue in the face of the initial rise of Chinese nationalism was the future of the treaty-port system, it is also clear that the debate was framed in a way that reflected the influence of the key issues that dominated British politics. Thus the Right-Left divide over subjects such as working conditions and the right to strike, and what attitude to take towards imperialism, were played out in the context of discussing China's problems. Later on the complex nature of Sino-Japanese tensions also fell victim to this reductionism, being viewed largely through the prism of the debate about internationalism and the role it should play in Britain's foreign policy.

None of this should be a surprise. After all, how else would we expect British intellectuals to react to events in a distant region of which they had little real experience but by filtering them through their own ideology and preoccupations? My point, though, is that while British statesmen tried to forward their state's interests in a supposedly objective manner, they were forced to take note of arguments that did not necessarily reflect regional realities but which, for domestic political reasons, they could not ignore. Matters of principle and the awareness that certain acts might take on symbolic importance thus complicated British statecraft and narrowed the range of options.

Fall Semester 2004

1. Nicholas Clifford, *"A Truthful Impression of the Country": British and American Travel Writing in China, 1880–1949* (Ann Arbor, 2001).
2. *The Times*, Mar. 3, 1936.
3. Colin Holmes, "Sidney Webb and Beatrice Webb and Japan," in Hugh Cortazzi and Gordon Daniels, eds., *Britain and Japan, 1859–1991: Themes and Personalities* (London, 1991), pp. 166–76.
4. "The Malady of China," *Round Table* (December 1922), p. 128.
5. Salter to Markham, May 12 [1931], Markham papers, British Library of Political and Economic Science, London, file 25/73.
6. "The Problem of Japan," *Round Table* (June 1930), p. 534.
7. "China in 1930," *Round Table* (September 1930), p. 799.
8. See, for example, Wm. Roger Louis, *British Strategy in the Far East, 1919–1939* (Oxford, 1971).
9. Wickham Steed to Gooch, Oct. 26, 1932, Wickham Steed Papers, British Library (BL), Add. MSS, 74129.
10. *Parliamentary Debates* (Commons), Feb. 27, 1933, col. 87.
11. See, for example, J. C. Smuts, "The Present International Situation," and Lord Lothian, "The Crisis in the Pacific," *International Affairs* (January 1935), pp. 1–19 and pp. 157–75.
12. Markham to Jones, Sept. 23, 1937, in T. Jones, *A Diary With Letters 1931–1950* (London, 1954), p. 364.
13. Gilbert Murray, "Introduction," in E. R. Hughes, ed., *China Body and Soul* (London, 1938), p. 15, and Holmes, in Cortazzi and Daniels, eds., *Britain and Japan*, p. 172.
14. Harold Laski, "China and Democracy," in Hughes, ed., *China Body and Soul*, p. 82.
15. Keynes to Editor, *The Times*, Sept. 29, 1937.
16. Cecil to Cadogan, Apr. 24, 1939, Cecil Papers, BL, Add. MSS. 51089.
17. Takao Matsumura, "Anglo-Japanese Trade Union Relations Between the Wars," in Gordon Daniels and Chushichi Tsuzuki, eds., *The History of Anglo-Japanese Relations: The Cultural and Social Dimension 1600–2000* (New York, 2000), Vol. 5, p. 275.
18. See Hughes, ed., *China Body and Soul*.
19. Minutes of meeting, July 15, 1938, Noel-Baker papers, Churchill College Archive Centre, Cambridge, NBKR 4/66.
20. See, for example, "The Problem of Japan," *Round Table* (June 1930), pp. 524–35.
21. A. J. Toynbee, "The Next War—Europe or Asia?" *Pacific Affairs* (March 1934), pp. 3–13. See also C. K. Webster, "Japan and China," *Contemporary Review* (June 1934), pp. 650–56.
22. *Parliamentary Debates* (Lords), vol. 96, c. 534.
23. Irwin papers, Asian, Pacific and African Collections, BL, Mss.Eur.C152/3 Birkenhead to Irwin, Jan. 27, 1927.
24. Churchill to A. Chamberlain, May 8, 1928, in M. Gilbert, ed., *Winston S. Churchill, Companion,* (London, 1979), Vol. V, Part 1, p. 1281.
25. Orient, "Practical Politics in the Far East," *Empire Review* (April 1932), p. 212.
26. Bland to Editor, *The Times*, Oct. 19, 1931.
27. *Parliamentary Debates* (Commons), Feb. 27, 1933, col. 83. For Churchill's speech of Feb. 17, 1933, see R. Rhodes James, ed., *Winston S. Churchill: His Complete Speeches 1897–1963* (New York, 1974), Vol. V, pp. 5219–20.

28. *Parliamentary Debates* (Commons), July 4, 1933, col. 271.

29. Owen, undated note [Oct. 1937], Beaverbrook papers, House of Lords Library, BBK/C/86.

30. Halifax to Eden, Sept. 27, 1937, Avon papers, Birmingham University Library, AP20/5/28.

31. R. Bassett, *Democracy and Foreign Policy: A Case History, the Sino-Japanese Dispute, 1931–1933* (London, 1952), and C. Thorne, *The Limits of Foreign Policy: The West, the League and the Far Eastern Crisis of 1931–1933* (London, 1972).

32. Vansittart to Chatfield, Jan. 1, 1937, Public Record Office (now the National Archives), FO 800/395.

19

Anglo-American "Liberal" Imperialism, British Guiana, 1953–64, And the World Since September 11

RICHARD DRAYTON

In the front court of St Catharine's College, Cambridge, there is an old bronze bell which calls a few to prayer at six in the evening, and more to dinner at seven-thirty. One might assume that it is an ancient part of the college. But the bell only reached England in the 1960s. It came from Demerara, the central province of British Guiana, where it had regulated the rhythms of the Versailles sugar plantation two hundred years earlier, calling slaves to the fields, to shifts at the mill, to public punishments, or announcing their deaths. The missionary John Smith, "the Demerara Martyr," hanged by the planters in 1823 wrote: "At about six in the morning the ringing of a bell, or the sounding of a horn, is the signal for them to turn out to work. No sooner is the signal made than the black drivers, loudly smacking their whips, visit the Negro houses to turn out the reluctant inmates."[1] The bell, now exerting a more benevolent discipline, belongs perhaps in the fiction of the Guyanese novelist Wilson Harris, where particular individuals, objects, and practices often provide secret channels connecting two seemingly very separate places and historical moments. In the carnival of world history, we might argue, old players similarly often return to the stage hidden behind new masks.

British Guiana, it is likely, sits in a hazy region of your mind, one part El Dorado, another Demerara sugar, a third suicide by "Kool-Aid." Only perhaps a vague memory of Chapman's reverie on:

> Guiana, whose feete are mines of gold
> Whose forehead knockes against the roof of stares

Stands on her tip-toes at faire England looking
Kissing her hand, bowing her mighty breast
And every sign of all submission making,
To be her sister . . .

And surreal twin sister of a kind she is: her capital is Georgetown, where the Anglican cathedral is St. George's, and two competing whorehouses are called The Oxford and The Cambridge.

British Guiana is also the crux of an unsavory Anglo-American family secret. In the middle of the twentieth century, Britain and the United States repeatedly interfered in the politics of this colony. Britain, first, removed from power by armed force the democratically elected Cheddi Jagan government. It then sought to destroy the socialist political party at the core of the Guyanese national movement. When this only partly succeeded, Britain allowed the United States to run a program of covert action, including the use of terrorist bombings, to destabilize the local government. When this failed, Britain imposed a constitutional change, and imprisoned key operatives. By 1964 they succeeded, to the extent that the "anti-communist" Forbes Burnham replaced Jagan as Premier. But Burnham's party gravitated towards the Soviet Union within less than a decade. Moreover, Burnham ruled Guyana tyrannically and corruptly for the next thirty years. The West's intervention both failed to secure its cold war interests, and created a social tragedy from which Guyana has yet to emerge.[2]

The parable of British Guiana deserves to be more widely known. It offers many lessons for our age, a period in which some in Britain and the United States appear so supremely confident that they know what is best for the world.

IN NOVEMBER 2003, GEORGE W. BUSH PAID the first formal state visit of a President of the United States to the United Kingdom. In a speech delivered in the Banqueting House of Whitehall Palace, Bush declared that the British and American peoples were united in an "alliance of values," and that they shared "a mission in the world."[3] Here as elsewhere, his speechwriters cunningly echoed Tony Blair's Atlanticist speeches. Blair had intoned at Blackpool in 2002 in the ramp-up to the Iraq War that, "the basic values of America are our values too," while in 1997, and on many occasions after, he promised that "when Britain and America work together, there is little we cannot achieve."[4] Neither Bush nor Blair had any doubt that either the "mission," or the "achievement," was for the greater human good.

Bush's speech made a fascinating appeal to the British historical unconscious. The image in the mirror with which he conjured was the old Whig idea of Britain as the diffuser of Liberty and Progress to the world. There are two key symbols of this heroic vision of Britain. The first and principal one is the Second World War, the prototype of the "good war," a perennial figure of Atlanticist rhetoric, and the Churchillian moment formed the climax of Bush's speech. The second icon, usually concealed in the more private chambers of the British heart, is a certain idea of the British Empire as both the summit of national greatness and a force, more or less, in the end, for good. Invoking the example of "the righteous courage of Wilberforce, and the firm determination of the Royal Navy over the decades to fight and end the trade in slaves," Bush's speechwriter pointed delicately at a tradition through which he (and Blair) would like us to understand the current age of Anglo-American imperialism. Antislavery, of course, from the Victorian era onwards, stood as the emblem of the British Imperial marriage of brute force and emancipatory virtue. Palmerston's proclamation in 1841 that "Our duty, our Vocation . . . is not to enslave but to set free," found easy echoes in the promises of General Maude to the people of Mesopotamia in 1917 that "Our armies do not come into your cities and lands as conquerors or enemies, but as liberators," and in the somewhat less resonant cant which surrounded "Operation Iraqi Freedom" of 2003.

Until a few years ago, only historians talked about "Liberal Imperialism." We used it to explain the British Empire from perhaps the 1830s. From that time the British, having spent two centuries exterminating American Indians, trading and torturing slaves, and excluding other nations from its colonial trade, came to favor, at least in principle, free trade, free labor, antislavery, and protecting aborigines. Liberal Imperialism excuses its violence with the promise of the democratic institutions and economic prosperity it will eventually bestow on the conquered. Its most important intellectual was John Stuart Mill, who in *On Liberty* justified Britain's Indian tyranny on the grounds that the overlords were in the position of parents supervising the development of children, concluding "Despotism is a legitimate mode of government when dealing with barbarians, if the end be their improvement."[5] This British Empire offered the eventual possibility of constitutional equality, although, we must remember, it was not imagined, before the Second World War, that darker-skinned colonials would be "ready" for such privileges for many decades. Meanwhile, governors appointed by the Crown could maintain the liberal order by limiting the local right to free speech and free association, banning books and newspapers, and, in crises, imprisoning dissidents without trial. Imperial historians were always aware of the contradictions within the idea of "Liberal Imperialism," and few believed that it had a real life outside small circles in Oxford or London.

Since September 11, 2001, however, the idea of "Liberal Imperialism" found new public life. In early 2002, in the aftermath of the Afghanistan War, Robert Cooper, a Foreign Office mandarin and confidante of Blair, published an essay on "The New Liberal Imperialism" in which he described a global political landscape in which advanced nations needed to accept their right to dominate and direct the backward, through whatever means necessary. In its most chilling paragraph, Cooper writes:

> The challenge to the postmodern world is to get used to the idea of double standards. Among ourselves, we operate on the basis of laws and open cooperative security. But when dealing with more old-fashioned kinds of states outside the postmodern continent of Europe, we need to revert to the rougher methods of an earlier era—force, pre-emptive attack, deception, whatever is necessary to deal with those who still live in the nineteenth century world of every state for itself. Among ourselves, we keep the law but when we are operating in the jungle, we must also use the laws of the jungle.[6]

Presumably, although Cooper never descends from the lofty rhetoric of policy to deal with concretes, this Liberal agenda explains why it was necessary to kill perhaps over three thousand Afghan civilians with Anglo-American bombs,[7] to murder thousands of captured Taliban combatants at Mazar-i-Sharif and in the shipping containers of Kunduz,[8] and to detain without trial and to torture thousands of other people at Bagram air force base, on Diego Garcia, at Guantanamo Bay, or via "renditions" in countries including Jordan, Morocco, Egypt, and Saudi Arabia.[9] Hovering in the background of Cooper's thesis is his presumption that there was, in some undefined age, an old Liberal Imperialism, an era of heroic Victorian liberal expansion.

The historian Niall Ferguson rapidly stepped forward to paint this backdrop. In *Empire* (2002), a popular book which accompanied a television series, Ferguson proclaimed that after about 1800, something called "Liberal Imperialism" emerged in the British Empire, characterized by free labor, free trade, good government, justice, and protection of aborigines, and this ultimately evolved towards decolonization which, he implies, may not have been such a good thing. No professional historian of the British Empire shared Ferguson's simple and sunny view of its later history, but it was sweetly in tune with the British historical unconscious. The Second World War, naturally, bulked large: for Ferguson, it was a magical ethical bath, the great moment when the British Empire, in its victory over the Nazis, washed away its historical sins. And the modern Whig pyramid was completed with a celebration of the contemporary moment: in *Empire*'s concluding section, Ferguson chimed in with the vision of the Project for a New American Century, and proclaimed that it was now the responsibility and right of the United States to stand over a new global Liberal Imperial order.[10]

These comforting myths of Anglo-American virtue survive because those who invoke them scissor away uncomfortable historical facts. They quietly airbrush out of the heroic family portrait of the Second World War those prominent Anglo-Americans who lent aid and comfort to the Nazi regime, even into the 1940s—including President Bush's grandfather and Queen Elizabeth II's uncle. That Russia, not the United States, stood first as Britain's ally, and defeated the best troops of the Wehrmacht, is long forgotten. Absent, too, from the confected memory are the atrocities committed by Anglo-American airpower in Dresden, Hamburg, Hiroshima, and Nagasaki. The destructive impact of British and American imperialism is similarly consigned to the memory hole. That Britain and America can be a force for horror and evil, as well as good, is too unpleasant to contemplate.

Of course, in November 2003, parallel to Bush's visit, there was a very different expression of Anglo-American solidarity. Led by a contingent of several hundred American expatriates, who massed behind a sign that read, "Proud of my country, Ashamed of President Bush," some 200,000 people (according to *The Times*) marched through London to Trafalgar Square. While this was one tenth of the epic protest against the impending attack on Iraq that filled Hyde Park on February 15, 2003, it was still the largest weekday demonstration in British history, and it was accompanied by events in over one hundred towns and cities across Britain, including Sheffield, Edinburgh, Cardiff, Glasgow, Swindon, Nottingham, Norwich, York, Oxford, and even Calderdale in West Yorkshire. In the shadow of Nelson's Column, speakers denounced the betrayal of the real values of the Anglo-American community by Bush and Blair, and appealed to the memory of such transatlantic icons as Tom Paine, Frederick Douglass, the Pankhursts, and Paul Robeson. On a giant video screen behind the podium flashed images of cowering detainees at Guantanamo Bay, the "shock and awe" destruction of entire urban neighborhoods, and maimed children. One sequence traced the history of American foreign policy since 1945, with slides flashing by for Iran (1953), Guatemala (1953), via Brazil (1964) and Indonesia (1965), to Chile (1973) and Panama (1989). For about twenty seconds, in the midst of this, the crowd could see an image that declared: "British Guiana, 1961–64." But it is likely that few, even there, understood its meaning.

> THIS IS THE DARK TIME, MY LOVE
> All round the land brown beetles crawl about.
> The shining sun is hidden in the sky
> Red flowers bend their heads in awful sorrow.
>
> This is the dark time, my love.
> It is the season of oppression, dark metal, and tears.
> It is the festival of guns, the carnival of misery.
> . . . .
>
> Who comes walking in the dark night time?
> Whose boot of steel tramps down the slender grass?
> It is the man of death, my love, the strange invader
> Watching you sleep and aiming at your dream.[11]

The dark time WAS 1953. In April of that year, just a month or so before the birth in England of one Anthony Blair, the People's Progressive Party (PPP) came to power in the first elections ever held under universal suffrage in British Guiana, winning 51 per cent of the popular vote, and eighteen of twenty-four constituencies. One hundred and thirty-three days later, on October 9, Governor Savage suspended the constitution, and sent British troops to arrest and imprison the leaders of the PPP. The poem with which this section begins was written by one of these political prisoners, a man called Martin Carter, now Guyana's national poet.

The British government published the official reasons for its removal from power of the PPP in a White Paper.[12] They claimed that Jagan and his ministers intended to foment civil disorder, and "to turn British Guiana into a totalitarian state subordinate to Moscow."[13] No evidence was provided then, or indeed later, for this. The brisk cablese of a memorandum from the British Mission to the United Nations sent to the Colonial Office in late September helps us understand what lay behind this accusation:

> If our action can be presented as firm step taken to prevent attempt by communist elements to sabotage new and progressive constitution, it will be welcomed by American public and accepted by most United Nations opinion. If on the other hand it is allowed to appear as just another attempt by Britain to stifle a popular nationalist movement . . . effect can only be bad.[14]

The British in Guiana, like the Americans a year later in Guatemala, found "anti-communism" to be a useful mask behind which to hide other interests. To the Cabinet, Oliver Lyttleton was more candid: the PPP had "destroyed the confidence of the business community."[15]

How had Jagan's government offended the businessmen? The first of the PPP's sins was its proposal to raise the rent at which the Crown leased land to the sugar planters, in order to force them either to use it or release it for peasant cultivation. This was indeed a radical shift, since the colonial state for almost a hundred years had let most of the arable land of the colony to British investors at peppercorn rents, allowing them to let it stand idle, in order to suppress wages which would have been forced upwards had more workers had the option to become peasant cultivators. As the West India Royal Commission of 1887 noted, "What suited [the planters] best was a large supply of labourers, entirely dependent on being able to find work on the estates, and consequently, subject to their control and willing to work at low rates of wages." By "planters" in 1953, we do not mean single entrepreneurs: the colony's agricultural economy was in the hands of three large English-registered agribusiness conglomerates. Booker Brothers McConnell and Co. (which later whitewashed its past with the Booker Prize) was the largest of these. So extensive were its interests, encompassing 70 per cent of sugar production and some fifty subsidiary companies, that the colony's initials, "BG," were humorously translated as "Booker's Guiana." The malnourished workers of Demerara underpinned its global interests. Bookers had another complaint: the PPP was supporting the demand of the Guyana Agricultural Workers Union (GAWU) for recognition as the representative of the sugar workers in place of a corrupt company union. A GAWU strike in August and September 1953, which brought sugar production to a halt, had the public support of the PPP government. In September 1953, Henry Seaford, who ran Bookers' Liverpool shipping line from London wrote angrily to the Colonial Office that something needed to be done about the PPP: "Unless something drastic is done, Bookers will cease to exist as a large firm in five years. I consider that the future of Bookers is at stake."[16] Agrarian reform and trade union rights were clearly, in the eyes of London, secondary in importance to the rights of businessmen to maximize profits.

Jagan also had acquired enemies in the colony's other main business sector: bauxite mining. Demerara has the most valuable bauxite deposits in the world (with the highest alumina to silicate and titanate impurity ratio). So valuable were they that in 1916 the United States had threatened to hold up munitions shipments to Britain until it allowed Alcoa's Canadian subsidiary to control the mines.

ALCAN (the Aluminium Company of Canada) controlled DEMBA (the Demerara Bauxite Company), which produced most of the colony's output, the rest coming from the smaller holding of the American company Reynolds. British Guiana, with its neighbor Surinam, had provided two-thirds of American bauxite imports by the end of the Second World War, while in the 1950s it supplied most of the raw material for Canada's aluminum smelters, which in turn represented the main source of that metal for British aircraft production. DEMBA paid no royalties on ore produced on its own lands, while Reynolds paid no taxes on profits. As a consequence, in the four years prior to 1953, DEMBA made about £1 million pounds a year profit annually, remitting the larger part of this as dividends to its shareholders. While British Guiana through its resources and cheap labor subsidized the standard of living of people in Canada, Britain, and the United States, infant mortality among its poorest citizens reached close to 200 in every 1000 live births and it provided no option to continue to secondary education for 99 per cent of its elementary school children. Another of Jagan's crimes had been his demand that taxes and royalties rise significantly so that more of the value of British Guiana's mineral product remain in the colony.

Of course, Jagan was foolhardy to think he could change overnight the colonial state's role in forcing down wages, crushing trade unions, and minimizing the social rent paid by capital. His attempt to revise a century-old tradition was particularly unwelcome at a time when British economic recovery after the Second World War was so highly leveraged on the dollars and cheap raw materials which the Sterling Bloc secured from the colonies' exports of rubber, tin, cocoa, bauxite, and sugar. He was equally imprudent to demand that civil service and private sector jobs should go to Guyanese nationals before they went to others, and in particular should go to people who were not white. For stacking the political deck to keep whites on top was as central a tradition of "Liberal Imperialism" as manipulating the labor, land, and tax structure to the benefit of business. This had been originally done simply via property: the franchise had required wealth and income, so that in 1850 of the 150,000 inhabitants of British Guiana, only 1,000 were electors, while in 1900 only 11,000 out of 300,000 people could vote. When in 1928, the black and brown middle class had become sufficiently large and prosperous to take control of the colonial legislature, the British promptly imposed Crown Colony government, in which the elected members of the new Legislative Council were fewer than the nominated and ex-officio members, and restricted the franchise

more tightly by imposing income, property, and literacy qualifi-
cations. (This, of course, was only a belated echo of the use of Crown
Colony government in Trinidad and Jamaica in the previous century
to prevent black majority parliamentary rule.) The Wilson-Snell
Commission frankly admitted its racial agenda: it sought to prevent
"the loss to public life . . . of the small but important European class
which still controls the principal agricultural and commercial activities in this colony." Jagan's complaint that, even in 1950, the most
senior positions in the Colonial Secretariat were still occupied by
people of British or "White dominion" extraction, was viewed as
racial rabblerousing. Another justification for the British intervention in 1953 was that the PPP intended to shut whites out of civic life.

There was little in the PPP's program that was revolutionary. At
no point did it commit itself to nationalizing the commanding
heights of the economy. Jagan was a nationalist who spoke a Marxist language, and saw no reason to fear a socialist future. His record
in power in 1953 and after showed that he was far too shy of using
the power of the state or extra-parliamentary force to achieve political ends. He was moreover personally incorruptible. None of this
saved him.

FROM 1953 UNTIL 1956, THERE WAS A DECLARED "state of emergency,"
and the Governor and his nominees ruled British Guiana directly
until 1957, when they chanced another election. During that period they did not prosecute Jagan or any other PPP minister for the
many alleged criminal conspiracies with which the Colonial Office
had justified the 1953 invasion.[17] But the colonial officials had not
been still. Their strategy, as the Colonial Office minute of Rogers to
Lloyd of October 16, 1953 put it, was "to go hard at [the PPP] and
smash it."[18] Their target was the inter-ethnic alliance that the PPP
had forged between the mainly rural Indian sugar and rice workers,
and the mainly urban African city and bauxite workers. The symbols of these communities were the leaders Cheddi Jagan, an Indian dentist, and Forbes Burnham, a black lawyer. The Special
Branch report of May 1953 on the PPP had characterized Jagan as
the leader of "Communist Section" of the PPP, and Burnham of the
"Non-Communist 'self-government' section."[19] A determined campaign to encourage tensions within the party and to woo Burnham
ensued. The rock against which they aimed the chisel was the threat
that with Jagan as leader, the hopes of the Guyanese for self-government would be permanently frustrated: on this theme Oliver
Lyttleton, the Conservative Colonial Secretary, mused in the House
of Commons that there were territories which might never become

independent, while the Robertson Commission on British Guiana of
1954 concluded, "so long as the present leadership and policies continue, there is no way in which any real measure of self-government
can be restored." Burnham, a brilliant orator—he had won the prize
for public speaking while at the London School of Economics—and
an observant Methodist with a taste for good living and a transparent
ambition, seemed a good candidate for co-option. A choir of voices
began to call him out of the crowd: the Robertson Commission report echoed the earlier Special Branch report, identifying him as the
right kind of nationalist, while the local newspapers and the Rev. Dr.
Soper, a visiting Methodist clergyman, pronounced him the coming
man. In June 1955, Governor Savage wrote to Lennox-Boyd, the
Colonial Secretary: "I would have hoped that in the months ahead,
the PPP split would have been made almost irrevocable."[20] By the
end of 1955 Burnham did split the PPP, forming by 1957 a new political party later called the People's National Congress (PNC). It was
to this body that the hopes of the Colonial Office, and of Sir Patrick
Renison, the new Governor, turned. But to their disappointment,
even though they redrew the constituency boundaries to favor Burnham, the PPP won nine of the fourteen seats in the general election
of August 1957.

Jagan, looking at the decolonization of India and Pakistan a generation earlier, at Bandung in 1955, at the British debacle in Suez in
1956, at the independence of Ghana in 1957, and his own continued electoral strength, assumed that the British had learned to do
business with him, and that his destiny was to lead his country to political sovereignty. He wholly misunderstood the environment in
which he was operating. Most strikingly, he took the decision in
April 1960 to make an official visit to Cuba without seeking British
approval, and to make public his wish for British Guiana, before and
after independence, to have close relations with Cuba, and to learn
from the agrarian reform program of the Cuban Revolution. From
Jagan's naïve perspective, nothing should be more natural than that
one socialist Caribbean country might learn from another, but
those who gazed from the North saw this, and his visit, and the orbit
of policy of which it appeared to be a part, as a clear indicator of
what Jagan might do were he at the helm of a sovereign Guyana. The
British strategy at this moment at the end of the 1950s was to court
Jagan, and to delay the path to independence just long enough for
a political alternative to emerge. But after 1960, there were others
who were less patient.

The quiet Americans began to take a direct interest. Earlier they
had been content merely to support British action. The Eisenhower

administration in 1953 had lobbied Latin American governments to ensure that they raised no complaints about the British intervention in British Guiana either in the councils of the Organization of American States or the United Nations.[21] In the late 1950s, possibly without formally consulting the British, they began to work through the labor unions. Perhaps the earliest dimension of American Cold War action in the British West Indies had concerned trade unions. By the early 1950s, the British and American unions with the help, it is likely, of some skillfully placed cash gifts had succeeded in persuading almost all the Anglophone Caribbean labor movement to switch its international affiliation from the World Federation of Trade Unions (WFTU) to the anti-communist ICFTU (International Confederation of Free Trade Unions). In the process, an important network, nourished with substantial CIA participation, now linked the AFL-CIO in Washington to trade unions throughout the region. While the British Guianese trade union linked to Jagan's PPP remained loyal to the WFTU, the leaders of the other Guyanese unions were already in communication with the ICFTU. The CIA, via American unions and the AFL-CIO, formed direct connections with key figures in British Guiana, as throughout the hemisphere.[22] By 1962, these liaisons would be given an institutional center in the American Institute for Free Labor Development (AIFLD). Serafino Ramauldi (ICFTU representative), William Doherty (later President of AIFLD from 1966 to 1996), and William McCabe (AFL-CIO representative), who we now know were CIA employees, directed substantial funds to anti-Jagan unions and unionists, building up ties to an urban Afro-Guyanese labor base around Burnham.[23]

The next general election was to be held in August 1961, and since Macmillan's "wind of change" speech, these appeared to be the last polls before British Guiana became independent. Believing he might win, Burnham declared that his PNC would support the demand for independence by whatever party won the election. The Americans were equally keen on this outcome: in the wake of the Bay of Pigs fiasco, the Kennedy administration was determined that no self-declared Marxist such as Jagan would take British Guiana to independence. The Americans appear to have urged the British to "take action to influence the results of the election," but Home at the Foreign Office declared that the methods proposed—which are not explicitly described in the declassified documents—were not feasible.[24] What the British did allow was a major propaganda effort on Burnham's behalf. During the election campaign, the United States Information Service (an arm of the State Department) projected films at Georgetown street corners depicting the horrors of

Bolshevism in Eastern Europe and Cuba, while the Christian Anti-Communist Crusade distributed pamphlets and comic books. Money also began to appear mysteriously: within Georgetown, opposing Jagan became a kind of career in a community with high unemployment. The constituency boundaries were redrawn to give maximum advantage to Burnham's PNC. The PPP still won comfortably, taking a crushing twenty of the thirty-five parliamentary seats contested.

This was a devastating result, and it led the Americans to seek a rather more muscular kind of engagement. By late August 1961, just after the election, Arthur Schlesinger urged President Kennedy to approve a full "covert program" in British Guiana which would include "anti-Communist clandestine capabilities."[25] He was aware that the British, whose analysis of the situation remained rather more nuanced, would hesitate, and Dean Rusk encouraged his Ambassador in London to play up "the intelligence gathering aspect of covert activity" and to "play down covert political action."[26] He was successful, and by September 1961 an agreement was in place on Anglo-American intelligence cooperation in British Guiana. Governor Grey alluded in a secret memorandum to "the joint US-UK-Canadian operation" and to "the difficulties [he and the American Consul Melby had] of keeping Jagan in play without him becoming suspicious."[27]

The irony is that it was Grey, and the Colonial Office, who were being adroitly kept in play. By late 1961, Washington had a clear objective in British Guiana, which it would prosecute with determination over the next three years. It wanted Britain to delay independence for British Guiana until Burnham was in power. This appeared a feasible goal, since the silver lining to the cloud of the election result was that the PPP had only won 43 per cent of the popular vote, a mere 2 per cent above the share of the PNC. Burnham himself, reneging on his earlier promise to respect the result of the election, urged that only an election on the basis of proportional representation could provide effective democratic representation for the Guianese people. But the first step was to ensure that the British would not allow Jagan to take the country to independence. For the wheels of British and American policy on British Guiana were not yet in alignment. In late January 1962, Home warned Rusk that, with or without Jagan, Britain would probably give independence to the colony within the next two years.[28] The American response to this in February 1962 took two forms, one reply came on the streets of Georgetown, the capital of British Guiana, another came wearing the high collar and tails of a diplomatic communication.

On what became known as "Black Friday" in February 1962, a riot took place in Georgetown in which parts of the city were put to flame while official and unofficial strikes brought work to a halt.[29] These were fomented by Burnham, and the official investigations afterwards noted that there had been significant visits from American trade unionists before, during, and after the disturbances. It has been suggested to me that officers of the British Secret Intelligence Service knew was going on, but there was a clear effort at "plausible deniability" and many ministers of Her Majesty's Government, and indeed some American officials, appear to have been in the dark. Reginald Maudling, the Colonial Secretary, rather innocently asked Arthur Schlesinger, the Harvard historian who was Kennedy's "fixer," whether the CIA had played a role in stimulating the recent riots. A similar question was put in Washington by Hugh Fraser, the Parliamentary Under-Secretary at the Colonial Office, to John McCone, who Kennedy had appointed as Director of the CIA only a few months earlier after the Bay of Pigs debacle. The Americans both coolly denied any involvement.[30] Adlai Stevenson, then United States representative at the United Nations, appears also to have been out of the loop: when he protested to Rusk that American meddling in British Guiana would damage the reputation of the United States among African and Asian nations, he was informed that the CIA was "in no way involved in the recent disturbances in Georgetown."[31] A week later the State Department did however admit that perhaps "private American citizens" appeared to be taking an interest in the affairs of British Guiana.[32] The reality was that a CIA covert operation was in motion.

It is quite possible that the State Department, and perhaps even McCone, were not fully in control of the British Guiana operation. Rusk, in a cable sent from Geneva to Washington, and "Repeated to London eyes only for the Ambassador and Wisner" in March 1962 insisted: "For present I do not believe covert action with or without British is indicated. . . . Dept please have Wisner advised not to pressure matter for time being."[33] Wisner, of course, is the man most responsible for creating the covert action capabilities of the CIA during the Cold War. In 1948, Wisner, a veteran of the wartime Office of Strategic Services and Wall Street lawyer, had organized the CIA's semi-detached "Office for Policy Coordination," which was charged with "propaganda, economic warfare, preventive direct action, including sabotage, antisabotage, demolition and evacuation procedures; subversion against hostile states, including assistance to underground resistance groups, and support of indigenous anti-communist elements in threatened countries of the free world." As

Deputy Director for Plans of the CIA, a post he held until 1958, he was at the center of the creation of the CIA's global "black ops" capacity.[34] He had worked particularly closely with organized labor—including the infamous Jay Lovestone—to create the International Confederation of Free Trade Unions, through which his influence extended into Africa and the Caribbean.[35] He appears to have been a key figure in Operation Mockingbird—the CIA campaign to create a network of sympathetic journalists in the print and mass media, whose success can still be measured today—and in some of the more mysterious MKULTRA psychological experiments. He was Head of the CIA Station in London in the early 1960s, with responsibilities which included the remaining British colonies, as well as his old specialty of Western Europe. The trade union route of CIA intervention, which was so central to the 1962–64 period, and in particular to the riots of 1962, resembles Wisner's mobilization of anticommunist trade union activity in France and Italy a decade earlier. The use of terrorist bombings and civil disorder to create space for a political "Third Force" in British Guiana, on the other hand, was remarkably similar to the kind of campaign organized by Wisner and his collaborators in South Vietnam from 1952 onwards. Wisner belonged to the earlier, free-wheeling culture of covert action with McCone was attempting to rein in, and indeed in late 1962, he was suddenly forced to retire from the CIA.

A different kind of American pressure came via the crisp linen stationary of the State Department. In February 1962, a week after the riots, Dean Rusk wrote Alec Douglas-Home a remarkable letter: "I must tell you now that I have reached the conclusion that it is not possible for us to put up with an independent British Guiana under Jagan. . . . It seems clear to me that new elections should now be scheduled, and I hope we can agree that Jagan should not accede to power again."[36] The initial responses of Harold Macmillan and Home did them some credit, even if their high-mindedness was a little rich coming from Home, who two years earlier had agreed with the Americans that Patrice Lumumba, the President of the Congo, should perhaps "fall into a river of crocodiles." Macmillan, in a private memorandum to Home, described Rusk's letter as "pure Machiavellianism," exposing a "degree of cynicism" which he did not expect from Rusk who was "after all . . . not an Irishman . . . nor a millionaire."[37] Home penned a sharp reply to Rusk, beginning with a pointed allusion to earlier American policy:

> It was [the United States's] historic role to have been for long years the crusader and the prime mover in urging colonial emancipation. The communists are now in the van. Why? Amongst

other things because premature independence is a gift for them. . . . [Now] I do not think it is possible to beat them by canceling the ticket for independence and particularly if this is only to be done in the single instance of British Guiana. You say that it is not possible for you "to put up with an independent British Guiana under Jagan" and that "Jagan should not be allowed to accede to power again." How would you suggest that this can be done in a democracy? And even if a device could be found, it would almost certainly be transparent. . . . [I]t will be very hard to provide a reasonable prospect that any successor regime will be more stable or more mature.[38]

The Americans, however, cared less about the stability or maturity of any future regime than about the removal of Jagan. Impotent to dislodge Castro in Cuba, the Kennedy administration appeared determined not to allow others to claim that it had allowed a communist regime to emerge on the mainland of South America. As Schlesinger noted in a memorandum to Kennedy in March 1962, "a firm decision has been taken to get rid of the Jagan government."[39] Home and Rusk, meeting in Geneva on other business on April 13, 1962, agreed that the two powers would work closely on the situation, and by April 28, Sir Norman Brook, Her Majesty's representative in Washington, advised McGeorge Bundy, the President's National Security Adviser, that American requests for "greater intelligence gathering facilities in British Guiana" would be sympathetically considered.[40] The British, from Home's reply to Rusk in February, appear to have sought two favors in exchange: American pressure on Guatemala with respect to the British Honduras boundary dispute, and tolerance for British maneuvers in Central Africa. (The precise issues at stake were not made explicit in the documents, but probably concerned the Central African Federation and Southern Rhodesia crises.) Some deal was done, and the tactic of forcing a new election under proportional representation before independence became British policy.

And so initially with only the hesitant toleration of the British, but ultimately with their protection and participation, the CIA launched between 1962 and 1964 a successful campaign to destabilize the Jagan government. American trade unions provided the salaries, training, tactical advice, and well over $1 million in strike pay that sustained repeated trade union disturbances, culminating in 1963 in an eighty-day general strike, the longest in world history, which ruined the economy and public finance. At the same time, the Americans organized a campaign of terrorism, as they had in Vietnam a decade earlier, supplying the PNC and a small right-wing party called the United Front, with guns, ammunition, and bomb making chemicals, and fomenting riots. When the Special Branch of the British Guiana police force attempted to prosecute those involved in creating violence and disorder, the British colonial government suppressed its investigations. Peter Owen, the Assistant Commissioner of Police, investigated nineteen events between June 8, 1963 and July 21, 1963, which included the blowing up of the Transport and Harbours Department, arson at the Georgetown ferry, explosives at the Ministries of Home Affairs, Health and Housing, at schools, shops, and cinemas, and by December 1963 had identified those responsible, who included Burnham and his closest allies in the PNC.[41] The Special Branch investigated further and reported that the plan to cause civil disorder called "X13" was financed by an American called Gerald O'Keefe, who had entered the colony on three occasions from February 1962 to August 1963.[42] (O'Keefe, parenthetically, was one of the key CIA meddlers in the international labor movement: he was active in the supporting the mining and bus strikes which destabilized the Allende regime in Chile in 1973, and was active also in Australia and New Zealand. Doubtless, his son is now licking his wounds after a season in Venezuela.) The Governor, Sir Ralph Grey, and his successor, Sir Richard Luyt, suppressed these police reports and did not prosecute any of the named conspirators. Owen himself was ordered to leave British Guiana to take up the post of Commissioner of Police in Aden.

In 1964 the Colonial government took the decision to use its emergency powers to detain political activists, and of the forty-one people it chose, thirty-seven of these were PPP members. The British by this swift move denied the PPP its parliamentary majority (since many of those detained were legislators), and, most strikingly, incarcerated all of its prominent Afro-Guyanese leaders, including Brindley Benn, the Deputy Premier. This was an interesting moment for the Governor to deprive Jagan of black colleagues and spokesmen, for the PNC had been busy stoking racial violence across the country, denouncing the PPP as the "coolie party." It is difficult not to think that a clear objective of British policy in Guiana was to encourage those ethnic cleavages. Whether or not this was policy, the colonial power stood by while a wave of communal violence unfolded across the country in 1962–64 in which perhaps two hundred people died. Its nadir was the horrific Wismar incident of May 1964, in which Indians were subjected to a day and night of arson, plunder, beatings, rape, mutilation, and murder, while the police force and the British Army kept at a distance. Racial self-segregation became the order of the day: across the country, what had been multi-ethnic communities became Indian or African villages or neighborhoods, and the PPP and the PNC became almost exclusively identified with a single ethnic community. To the amusement of the Governor, the PPP ministers in Georgetown now depended on British troops for their own safety.[43]

While the terrorist offensive was in full swing, Kennedy, Rusk, Bundy, Macmillan, Home, and the new Colonial Secretary Duncan Sandys spent a day on British Guiana at a weekend conference at Birch Grove at the end of June 1963.[44] By July 1963, Macmillan wrote to Kennedy to assure him that the British "had come to the conclusion that the right thing to do is to impose a system of proportional representation without a referendum," but for "presentational reasons" would wait until the November 1963 Lancaster House conference to show their hand.[45] The one possible problem, Macmillan noted to Kennedy, was if Jagan and Burnham somehow found some agreement before that meeting, but he assumed that "your people would be doing what they can to discourage any joint moves."[46] At the Constitutional Conference, Jagan made it easy for them, agreeing to leave the choice of electoral model to Duncan Sandys, the Secretary of State for the Colonies. Sandys, with much earnest talk of the best interests of the colony, imposed proportional representation.[47] The CIA then made sure, with the help of Governors Grey and Lyte, that 1964 was a year of turmoil for Guyana and stress for the PPP. Still, in the elections of December 1964, the PPP again won the most votes, but Burnham in alliance with the United Front, by virtue of proportional representation, held a narrow parliamentary majority. The British, now that their man was in the saddle, granted independence less than eighteen months later in May 1966.

For this Anglo-American victory, the Guyanese people would pay for the next thirty years, and they are still paying. Burnham remained in power, through rigged elections, corruption, and terror, until his death in 1986. Predictably, as an American diplomat admitted in 1990, a clandestine American operation in 1968 had taught Burnham how to rig the election (some of the tactics, including forcing people off electoral rolls, and the use of overseas and proxy votes, are not unknown in American domestic elections).[48] The irony was that by the 1970s Burnham announced that Guyana was on the "road to socialism," nationalized the bauxite and sugar industries at home, and formed friendly ties with the Eastern Bloc. He indeed provided facilities for Cuban planes to refuel on their way to supply their troops in Angola. Burnham ruined the economy and civic life of Guyana, and turned the country into the highest per capita exporter of migrants in the world. Only in 1992 would fair elections predictably return the weary Cheddi Jagan to power. But the legacy of the trauma of 1953 to 1964 continues to poison the political culture of Guyana. Inter-ethnic African vs. Indian violence is an everyday part of Guyanese life today: it was not in 1953. In 2004, the leader of the African Cultural and Development Association, a black community group, warned former President Carter, who was visiting Guyana en route to observe the elections in Venezuela: "this place is getting ready to go to a civil war."[49] While a formal civil war seems unlikely, what is certain is that distrust and fear will remain part of Guyanese civic life for at least another generation. It is said that a contrite Schlesinger burst into tears and apologized to Jagan when he met him again in 1990. But tears cannot wash away the horror that the arrogance of imperial elites imposes on the world.

BRITISH GUIANA WAS CLEARLY NOT THE WORST CASE of either British or American involvement. The suppression of Mau Mau in Kenya was infinitely more brutal: Caroline Elkins and David Anderson have exposed how hundreds were shot on the spot, thousands hung after minimal trials, and some half a million Kenyans were detained in a system of over 100 prison camps where over 100,000 human beings were tortured and starved to death.[50] There are no photographs from British Guiana, as there were from Malaya, of British troops posing with the decapitated heads of insurgents. Compared also to the murder and torture of hundreds of thousands which followed other CIA adventures in Iran and Guatemala in the 1950s, Brazil and Indonesia in the 1960s, or Chile in the 1970s, British Guiana was a mere bagatelle. It is, nonetheless, an instructive example of how Britain and America in close alliance are not always a force for good.

The British Guiana story is a revelatory episode in the histories of the cold war, of Anglo-American cooperation, and of what Ronald Robinson and Wm. Roger Louis called "the imperialism of decolonization."[51] In no other British colony was the United States allowed such direct agency, nor in any other, except in the case of Malaya, was decolonization so explicitly linked to fear of Communism. It is a textbook case, in Chalmers Johnson's expression, of "blowback." What this "fear of Communism" really meant in the colonial world deserves closer examination.

In the rhetoric of the time, and for conservative historians looking back, anti-communism was about the defense of freedom against totalitarianism. If however, one looks more closely, the West's priority in what, from 1955, became known as the "The Third World," was not liberty, but the protection of the world created by nineteenth- and early twentieth-century imperialism. Economic interests did matter: it was oil in Iran that led, in 1953, to the Anglo-American overthrow of Musaddiq's government; it was bananas and land reform in Guatemala that led to the CIA's overthrow of the Arbenz government in 1954 and the installation of a military tyranny which would last thirty years; and it was oil in Iraq that led the Americans and the British to plot the murder of President Quassim, recruiting a young Iraqi exile in Egypt called Saddam Hussein as a CIA agent, and to engineer the coup in 1963 which brought first the Ba'athist Party, and ultimately Saddam Hussein, to power. In British Guiana, sugar and bauxite mattered in the span from 1953 to 1964. But it was never resources alone, although they decided the level of intervention. What mattered was the regime of power for its own sake—that people who seemed like oneself, or people one controlled or patronized, were in control.

Joseph Schumpeter was partly right when he wrote in 1918:

> For it is always a question, when one speaks of imperialism, of the assertion of an aggressiveness whose real basis does not lie in the aims followed at the moment but an aggressiveness in itself. And actually history shows us people and classes who desire expansion for the sake of expanding, war for the sake of fighting, domination for the sake of dominating. It values conquest not so much because of the advantages it brings, which are often more than doubtful, as because it is conquest, success, activity.[52]

This desire was for him "an atavism," modern imperialism just a relic of an age of feudalism, monarchical absolutism, and export monopolies, at odds with the logic of capitalism which sought peace and free exchange, which would ultimately prevail. This taste for dominance was produced in history, a vestige of forgotten inequality. What Schumpeter did not understand was that the moderns knew how to make inequality as well as the ancients, and that capitalism—national and global—could itself be a theater of dominance, a space in which there were symbolic and psychological rewards, and not just material advantages, for those on top. He did not see the very modern role of violence in making and defending, or in dramatizing, socio-economic privilege and subordination, nor even its displacement into violent forms of paternalism.

It may be worth inspecting more closely the line of descent which connects the "Liberal Imperialism" of the nineteenth century, that of the "cold war," and the imperialism of that thing we call the "war on terror." We may argue that they draw on the same cultural reservoir: that peculiar complex of Christianity, its displacements into political economy, and racism. By racism I do not mean attitudes which we may choose to opt in or out of: racism is not ultimately a question of the individual conscience, it is a fact of social relations, located in the fabric of how we organize labor, exchange, politics, criminal justice, war and peace. Four centuries of European imperialism created a world in which dark skins were associated with cheap labor, with powerlessness, with bodies which were assumed not to feel pain like those of whites and which might be mistreated with impunity. Racism, as a set of personal attitudes, merely came in the train of these social relations: *"Proprium ingenii humanii odisse quem laeseris,"* in Tacitus's phrase—"it is in the nature of men to hate whom we hurt." The West's agenda in the Third World during the cold war was to preserve as much of that world made by nineteenth-century imperialism as possible, and the word "communist" was often merely a twentieth-century word for those, like Nelson Mandela or Martin Luther King or Cheddi Jagan, who sought to turn it upside down. We must be wary that the word "terrorist" is not similarly used with such criminal ignorance and dishonesty, and that more terror is not unleashed upon the world in the name of a "liberal" order.

In the Anglo-American relationship, the British in 1962 should have continued to resist American pressure for abrupt action. There may be similar lessons to be learned from later moments of British capitulation. It is certainly time for British and American policymakers to take stock of their capacity for evil.

Fall Semester 2004

1. On John Smith and the 1823 Rebellion see Emilia Viotti da Costa, *Crowns of Glory, Tears of Blood: The Demerara Slave Rebellion of 1823* (New York, 1994).

2. For the British Guiana experience see Cheddi Jagan, *Forbidden Freedom: The Story of British Guiana* (London, 1954), and *The West on Trial* (London, 1966); Phil Reno, *The Ordeal of British Guiana* (New York, 1964); Latin American Bureau, *Guyana: Fraudulent Revolution* (London, 1984); Thomas Spinner, *A Political and Social History of Guyana, 1945–83* (Boulder, 1984); Jane Sillery, "Salvaging Democracy? The United States and Britain in British Guiana, 1961–64" (unpublished D. Phil. Thesis, Oxford, 1996); Cary Fraser, "The New Frontier of Empire in the Caribbean: The Transfer of Power in British Guiana, 1961–1964," *International History Review*, XXII, 3 (2000); Mark Curtis, *Web of Deceit: Britain's Real Role in the World* (London, 2003).

3. "President Bush Discusses Iraq Policy at Whitehall Palace in London," at http://www.whitehouse.gov/news/releases/2003/11/20031119-1.html

4. "Speech by Prime Minister Tony Blair to Labour Party Conference, Blackpool," Oct. 1, 2002, at http://www.britemb.org.il/News/blair011002.html; "Speech by the Prime Minister Tony Blair at Lord Mayor's banquet," Nov. 10, 1997, at http://www.number-10.gov.uk/output/Page1070.asp.

5. John Stuart Mill, *On Liberty* (London, 1982 edn.), p. 69.

6. Robert Cooper, "The New Liberal Imperialism," Apr. 7, 2002, at http://www.observer.co.uk/Print/0,3858,4388912,00.html. A revised version of the essay is published in Cooper, *The Breaking of Nations: Order and Chaos in the Twenty-First Century* (London, 2004).

7. Marc Herold, "A Dossier on Civilian Victims of United States' Aerial Bombing of Afghanistan: A Comprehensive Accounting" (unpublished essay, University of New Hampshire, 2001).

8. Physicians for Human Rights, "Preliminary Assessment of Alleged Mass Gravesites in the Area of Mazar-I-Sharif, Afghanistan" (Boston, 2002); Jamie Doran, director and producer, "Afghan Massacre: The Convoy of Death" (2002).

9. "US Decries Abuse but Defends Interrogations," *Washington Post*, Dec. 26, 2002.

10. In *Colossus: The Price of America's Empire* (London, 2004), Ferguson expanded this vision of the United States as liberal hegemon (while regretting that he considered it unlikely to fulfil its mission).

11. Martin Carter, *Poems of Resistance* (London, 1954).

12. *Report on the Suspension of the Constitution of British Guiana, Parliamentary Papers*, 1952–53, XXIII (8980); PRO CO 1031/343.

13. "British Guiana: Suspension of the Constitution," Oct. 9, 1953, PRO CO 1031/1003.

14. Curtis, *Web of Deceit* (London, 2003), p. 352; Memorandum to the Colonial Secretary, Sept. 30, 1953, PRO PREM 11/827.

15. "British Guiana," Sept. 25, 2003, PRO PREM 11/827.

16. H. Seaford to J. Campbell, Sept. 8, 1953, PRO CO 1031/121.

17. *Report on the Suspension of the Constitution of British Guiana.*

18. Rogers to Lloyd, Oct. 16, 1953, PRO CO 1031/1171.

19. "British Guiana: Intelligence Report for April 1953 by W. A. Orrett on the general election and the prospects for internal security," PRO CO 1031/128, no 22.

20. Savage to Lennox-Boyd, June 1, 1955, PRO CO 1031/143.

21. *FRUS*, 1952–54, II (1), p. 562, "National Intelligence Estimate": "Communist penetration of British Guiana has posed a new problem in the Caribbean area"; for mediation with Latin American governments on behalf of Britain see *FRUS*, 1952–54, IV, pp. 29–30 and 37–38.

22. Ronald Radosh, *American Labor and United States Foreign Policy* (New York, 1969).

23. Ashton Chase, *History of Trade Unions in British Guiana* (Georgetown, 1964).

24. Home to Rusk, Aug. 18, 1961, *FRUS*, 1961–63, XX, doc. 246.

25. See, among others, Schlesinger to Kennedy, Aug. 30, 1961, *FRUS*, 1961–63, XII, pp. 524–25.

26. Rusk telegram, Sept. 5, 1961, *FRUS*, 1961–63, XII, doc. 254.

27. Grey to Ambler-Thomas, Sept. 29, 1961, PRO CO 1031/4176; for reference to the U.S.-U.K. agreement see Memorandum on Washington talks, Apr. 28, 1962, PRO CAB 133/246.

28. Memorandum of Jan. 22, 1962, PRO CO 1031/4176.

29. Report of a Commission of Enquiry into Disturbances in British Guiana (London, 1962).

30. See Schlesinger to Bruce, Mar. 1, 1962, *FRUS*, 1961–63, XII, p. 550; Fraser to Maudling, Mar. 20, 1962, *FRUS*, 1961–63, XII, p. 491–92.

31. Stevenson to Rusk, Feb. 26, 1962 and Cleveland to Stevenson, Mar. 9, 1962, in *FRUS* XII.

32. Memorandum of Mar. 15, 1962, *FRUS*, XII. doc. 272.

33. Rusk to the Department of State Geneva, Mar. 13, 1962, *FRUS*, 1961–63, XII, doc. 270.

34. David F. Rudgers, "The Origins of 'Covert Action,'" *Journal of Contemporary History*, 35, 2 (April 2000), pp. 249–62.

35. Anthony Carew, "The American Labour Movement in Fizzland: The Free Trade Union Committee and the CIA," in *Labour History*, 1998, pp. 25–42; Opoku Agyeman, *The Failure of Grassroots Pan-Africanism: The Case of the All-African Trade Union Federation* (Lanham, 2003).

36. Dean Rusk to Lord Home, Feb. 19, 1962, *FRUS*, 1961–63, XII, pp. 544–45.

37. Macmillan minute to Rusk to Home, Feb. 19, 1962, PRO PREM 11/3666.

38. Home to Rusk, Feb. 26, 1962, PRO PREM 11/3666.

39. Schlesinger to Kennedy, Mar. 8, 1962, *FRUS*, XII.

40. Memorandum on White House Meeting of Apr. 28, 1962, PRO CAB 133/300.

41. Report of Dec. 11, 1963 quoted by J. Silverman, MP for Birmingham-Aston, *Parliamentary Debates* (Commons), Apr. 27, 1966, c. 1133–34.

42. "Research Paper on the People's National Congress Terrorist Organization," Superintendent P. Britton of the Special Branch, Aug. 14, 1963.

43. See for example Sir Ralph Grey to Sir Hilton Poynton, Feb. 18, 1962, PRO CO 1031/3181.

44. "FO Record of a Meeting Between Mr. Macmillan and President Kennedy at Birch Grove House on the current situation in British Guiana," PRO PREM 11/4586, ff. 33–36; the American equivalent is less full, *FRUS*, 1961–63, XII, pp. 607–09.

45. Macmillan to Kennedy, July 18, 1963, PRO PREM 11/4593.

46. Macmillan to Kennedy, Sept. 28, 1963, PRO PREM 11/4593.

47. "British Guiana conference, 1963," PRO CAB 133/157, BG 4(63) 2 & 3.

48. Paul Kattenberg, quoted in Sillery, "Salvaging Democracy?"

49. Quoted in *Barbados Advocate*, July 15, 2004.

50. Caroline Elkins, *Britian's Gulag: The Brutal End of Empire in Kenya* (London, 2005); David Anderson, *Histories of the Hanged: Britian's Dirty War in Kenya and the End of Empire* (London, 2004).

51. Ronald Robinson and Wm. Roger Louis, "The Imperialism of Decolonization," *Journal of Imperial and Commonwealth History*, XXII, 3 (September 1994); for the cold war as explanation see Jagan, *The West on Trial;* Sillery, "Salvaging Democracy?"; and John Lewis Gaddis, *We Now Know: Rethinking Cold War History* (Oxford, 1997).

52. Joseph Schumpeter, *The Psychology of Imperialism* (New York, 1918).

20

Africa Writes Back:
Publishing the African Writers Series
At Heinemann

JAMES CURREY

The African Writers Series was started in 1962, almost exactly twenty-five years after the foundation of Penguin books. The paperback series was to become to Africans in its first quarter-century what Penguin Books had been to British readers for twenty-five years. It provided good serious reading at affordable prices for the professional classes that were emerging rapidly as countries in Asia and Africa became independent. The choice of color—orange—for the novels was shamelessly copied from Penguin. By the time of the tenth anniversary in 1972 it had become known in Africa as the "orange series" and its volumes were stacked high in the key positions inside the entrances of the university campus bookshops from one side of Africa to the other. The writer and critic Edward Blishen said at the time of the tenth anniversary: "I shall tell my grandchildren that I owe most of what education I have to Penguins and that through the African Writers Series I saw a new, potentially great, world literature coming into being."[1]

I have called this lecture "Africa Writes Back" because I have seen over a much longer period—forty years, now—how Africans achieved the confidence to write back in novels, plays, and poetry about what was happening to them. English was not only the language of authority in the countries of the former British Empire; it was also the language in which the subject peoples reacted to the imposition of power. Writers in India, the Caribbean, and Africa came to take advantage of the language that they shared, but they had to have publishing opportunities. To begin with those opportunities were almost all in London. By 1962 quite a lot of work by Caribbean writers had been published there. Some Indian writers were also fairly well established on London lists. But practically no creative work by Africans had appeared. Seeing books published by Africans in England showed other writers in Africa that they too might get published.

The crucial factor in paperback publishing is marketing. How do you build up sales so that the unit cost is driven so low that you can increase your print runs and put the books onto more economic web printing machines? It was the received wisdom in British publishing in the early 1960s that the only books that could be sold in Africa were school textbooks. There was not what is called "a general market"—that is, an "average reader" going into a bookstore to buy a specific title and coming out with one or two other inexpensive paperbacks bought on impulse. The colonial authorities saw books as having a purpose—the education of a new elite. Books for enjoyment, books which might enhance understanding of other Africans' ways of love and death, were not on their agenda. Alan Hill, the founder of Heinemann Educational Books, was described to me recently by the former head of the Longmans African division as "an inspired madman" because he did the things that other British publishers thought were a waste of time. A grandson of missionaries, he grew up knowing something about Africa. On his first visit to Nigeria in 1959 he was proud of the fact that William Heinemann had the previous year published a novel called *Things Fall Apart* in hardback. Nobody knew anything about it. At the elite University College in Ibadan, the expatriate staff refused to believe that a recent graduate could have had a novel published by a prestigious London publishing house. Chinua Achebe has said that as a student he read Joyce Cary's *Mister Johnson,* which is set in Nigeria. Achebe thought, "If this man can get such a bad book about Nigeria published, why don't I have a go?"[2] A clear case, I believe, of an African writing back.

Alan Hill, in the heady atmosphere of the independence years (Ghana in 1957; Nigeria in 1960), saw the need to make serious general books by Africans available in a paperback series like Penguin. It was an inspired choice to make Chinua Achebe the Editorial Adviser to the series. The first four titles included Achebe's *Things Fall Apart* and its sequel *No Longer at Ease.* First printings were about 2,500. It was a cautious start. Chinua Achebe's name became a magnet for new writing. The photograph of the author on the back of the paperback reinforced the idea that Africans might get published.

If people in the United States have read any single novel by an African author it is most likely to have been *Things Fall Apart* as it is often assigned for literature courses. Heinemann now claims sales of nine million but I think they have lost count. There have been translations into many other languages not included in Heinemann's total. Neither Penguin nor Pan, the two paperback series in Britain in 1958, bought rights. It now appears in Penguin Modern Classics. The publishing success of this novel can be attributed to its having been brought to the attention of the reading public by appearing in paperback as the first title in the African Writers Series.

A big problem from the outset for the series was that paperbacks are mostly reprints. But what was there to reprint when so few novels by Africans had been published in hardback by British or American publishers? Chinua Achebe, at the very start of the African Writers Series in 1962, was at a conference on African writing at Makerere University College in Uganda in East Africa. He heard a knock at the door of his guest house one evening and found a student standing there who offered him the manuscripts of two novels. The name of the Kenyan student was Ngugi (then James Ngugi, now Ngugi wa Thiong'o). The two novels, *Weep Not, Child* and *The River Between,* were to be the first *new* titles in the series. That was the moment of take off, when Heinemann Educational Books took on the role that was at that time almost exclusively performed in London by general hardback publishers—for the first time publishing new creative writing whether novels, plays, or poetry. There was also the stiffening thread of political works by people with names such as Mandela, Mboya, or Kaunda.

Ngugi got the idea of writing novels from the Caribbean. A range of writers from the West Indies were being accepted from the 1950s onwards by established literary hardback publishers in London. Henry Swanzy's BBC Colonial Service program "Caribbean Voices" gave hope to Derek Walcott, V. S. Naipaul, and many other writers. Africans needed hope as well. Ngugi tells in *Homecoming* of the impact the Barbadian George Lamming's novel, *In the Castle of My Skin,* had on him: "He evoked for me, an unforgettable picture of a peasant revolt in a white dominated world. And suddenly I knew that the novel could speak to me, could, with a compelling urgency, touch cords deep down in me."[3]

We take it for granted that there are multiple outlets—books, journals, newspapers, broadcasters—which are accepting creative writing all the time. We also take it for granted that there are literary agents to place work. And we know that, once a book is published, there is an industry of reviewing, promotions, and feature-writing. Although this had long been the case in Britain and in America, forty years ago what we needed was to get that industry to take writing by Africans seriously.

Another problem was that paperbacks were not reviewed in newspapers. Novels had to be published in hardback to be noticed. We needed to get the work of African writers into the reviewing columns along with the regular output from the hardback literary publishers. Reviews were necessary in order to get orders from public libraries, which, at that time, were the main patrons of new writing. The father firm William Heinemann agreed, reluctantly, to publish Ngugi's novels in hardback first. Heinemann Educational Books later published many of the writers in hardback under the imprint "Heinemann." Only gradually did enterprising reviewers come to realize that there was a new vitality in the writing from Africa and they started looking to the orange paperbacks for something special.

Keith Sambrook was the director at Heinemann Educational Books who was in charge of the rapid expansion of offices in what we were then coming to call the "Third World." Keith Sambrook, with Chinua Achebe's active encouragement, built on the success of the initial four titles with a canny sense of originality. There were anthologies of poetry, prose, short stories, and plays. There were some translations from African languages and there were translations from the French of novels by Mongo Beti and Ferdinand Oyono. (The Parisian publishers had been much more enterprising in the 1950s). Some other publishers with educational lists in Africa were also starting paperback series of writers from Africa. Rex Collings, who had started his publishing life at Penguin, had persuaded Oxford University Press to start the "Three Crowns Series." The plays of Wole Soyinka stood out, and he was to be the first African winner of the Nobel Prize for Literature. In 1965 Rex Collings left Penguin, taking Soyinka to Methuen, which had one of the most distinguished drama lists. In 1967, when I joined Keith Sambrook at Heinemann, the first thirty titles in the African Writers Series had already gone a long way towards establishing a new canon of African literature.

The central problem at Heinemann Educational Books was it was an educational company that needed the educational system to build up the sale of its paperbacks to keep the prices down. We did not know that the new examination boards would be so enterprising in prescribing texts by Africans. In fact the examination boards and the universities and schools were delighted to use contemporary books by young African writers. The British firms—Oxford University Press, Longman, Macmillan, Evans, Nelson—dominated the educational textbook market in Africa in the early 1960s. Heinemann Educational Books came later but made such a success of the African Writers Series that it helped us get a lot of textbook contracts.

My more cautious colleagues were concerned that sex, religion, and politics might keep the books out of schools. The inhibitions that concerned an educational publisher a few years after the Lady Chatterley obscenity trial did not worry Chinua Achebe, who wanted the African Writers Series to reflect all the richness and variety of an emerging Africa. He was concerned with the widest literary criteria. Nevertheless, all school textbooks had to be approved for publication by a formal committee of directors and editors sitting round a table beneath the chandeliers of the ballroom of a house in Mayfair which had belonged to Lord Randolph Churchill and his wife Jenny. After the discussion had gone on for some time about whether schools would find the subject matter objectionable, the Chairman, Alan Hill, would say "Well, James, what did the old Chinua say?" He knew—everyone knew—that if I had brought the proposal to the meeting, then young Chinua Achebe would already have said "yes" (even if it was on the telephone while passing through London from the Uli airstrip in Biafra to raise funds in America). So Alan Hill would say "Right, James. You want to do it? Go ahead and do it!" Thanks to the imaginative support of Chinua Achebe, Heinemann established with the first hundred titles in the series that there was a general as well as an educational market in Africa.

I visited Chinua and Christie Achebe at the University of Nigeria at Nsukka during the civil war of 1967. The house was a shell. The walls were black. There was no electricity. Achebe gave me the manuscript of his short stories called *Girls at War,* which became No. 100 in the Series when published in 1972. He said that the time had come to hand over his role as Editorial Adviser to another African writer and he and I agreed that nobody could be more appropriate than Ngugi, now a writer of acclaim not only in Kenya but throughout the world. Ngugi immediately accepted but then decided after six weeks that the duties would interfere with his own writing. But we took a positive decision to widen the African input into the series. By the tenth anniversary of the series, Heinemann had active editorial offices in both Ibadan and Nairobi. We decided that we would replace the Editorial Adviser of the series with a triangular system of consultation among the publishing editors in Ibadan, Nairobi, and London. In Nairobi, Henry Chakava, Simon Gikandi, and Laban Erapu were all significant figures. Aig Higo, a poet, kept us in touch with the active Nigerian literary scene. Chinua Achebe and Ngugi continued to give reports and recommend new manuscripts. Central to the policy was enthusiasm. Nobody had a veto. All three offices usually came to an agreement over novels. Selection of poetry tended to be a much more individual choice. The anthologies of plays tried to represent work from across the continent and from different traditions.

Heinemann had built an active international network of choice in Africa. Consultation was not without considerable effort and expense. Again and again one was reminded that telephoning was expensive and unreliable. Cables were the text messages of the time and just as likely to be ambiguous. Photocopying the wide range of hopeful manuscripts to share among three offices was still relatively expensive. Air fares were still high. (In 1959 it had cost Oxford University Press the equivalent of my annual salary to fly me to South Africa.) I was only able to justify the heavy costs of travel by going to see the educational authorities about textbook adoptions during the working day; in the evenings I and my African colleagues could drink and eat with the writers or go to their plays. It would never have been cost effective to go round Africa only to see the writers.

We could accept a fraction of the manuscripts received by the three offices—I would guess the number was one in thirty or forty. We spent a lot of money on reports. If the first response were positive, I would get a second report. If both the reports were good and offered suggestions for rewriting, I would send them to the writer even if we were rejecting the manuscript. We felt that it was constructive to pass on the reactions of our readers. Writing is a lonely business and some advice is better than a cold rejection slip. We invested this effort in order to bring on new writers. Increasingly there were publishers in the larger African countries encouraged by the growing market for creative writing, although the African Writers Series was so dominant that most writers offered their work to us first.

It has often been said that it was inappropriate for the African Writers Series to be published in the old imperial capital of London. Individuals, usually European or American, have accusingly said to me "a series of African writers should be published in Africa." The writers wanted to be published in London, and the common hope was that they would be treated as "writers" rather than "African writers." With Heinemann the most outstanding writers could often have it both ways. From a London base we were able to make the literary contacts that introduced these writers to readers not only in Britain and America but also in places as distant as Canada, India, and Australia, and we sold translation rights in the major languages of Europe and Asia. At the same time, through the medium of English, we often introduced African writers in Portuguese and French to a larger audience than they were able to reach in the original language. Sembene Ousmane is one example of this. The Egyptian publishing industry was the largest in Africa. Colloquial Arabic was used in the modern novel in spite of religious opposition. The first publication of English translations of the novelist Naguib Mahfouz appeared in the African Writers Series as well as in our parallel Arab Authors. He was the second African winner of the Nobel Prize for Literature. Heinemann published work by each of the first three African Nobel Laureates years before they received the prize

The correspondence files of the African Writers Series are now held in the University of Reading library, where Mike Bott has persuaded several of the leading British publishers to lodge their archives. That collection, like the Harry Ransom Center, is an important resource for anybody studying twentieth-century writing and publishing. It has been fascinating for me to re-examine my publishing correspondence with some of the most outstanding authors we published in the series, particularly three writers—Bessie Head, Nuruddin Farah, and Ngugi—who now have gained international recognition.

THERE ARE SOME QUESTIONS ABOUT THE African Writers Series that people ask again and again about areas of recurrent interest. I hope from my answers will emerge the extraordinary experience of being deeply involved in the formation of a new, potentially great, world literature. Intrinsic to our handling of African writers was the need to build bridges: to literary agents, to hardback publishers who would get reviews and library sales, to broadcasters, to United States publishers, and to publishers in foreign languages. It was exciting to create this international network. We knew a great deal about the literary industry in London and New York and we took great pride in getting the outstanding African writers known in the literary circles in those publishing centers.

At Heinemann Educational Books in London we wanted to show off the best work from Africa and at the same time to show up the disdainful attitudes of the well-established literary imprints to whom we offered hardback rights. If the Caribbean writers were now established in London then recognition of the African writers must follow. I was disappointed that the Zimbabwean writer Dambudzo Marechera's first book *The House of Hunger* did not get a review in the influential liberal newspaper the *Guardian,* though this was probably because it had only been published in paperback. I had given a copy to Doris Lessing and she reviewed it enthusiastically in *Books and Bookmen.* I sent the review to Bill Webb, literary editor of the *Guardian,* and he belatedly got it reviewed. He rang me up a few months later and said it had been chosen as a joint winner of the *Guardian* fiction prize, which was at the time the most prestigious award for new writing. I always found a more adventurous response among New York publishing editors—in particular from Tom Engelhardt at Pantheon. He accepted *The House of Hunger* for American publication even before it won the prize.

One of the challenges we faced was getting books recognized that "literary publishers" had turned down. Bessie Head's first two novels were published by Simon and Schuster in New York and Gollancz in London, so she had had far more literary acceptance than most African writers. She also had a posh agent, Hilary Rubinstein, who had spoken for Penguin in the Lady Chatterley obscenity trial, but he had failed to place *A Question of Power*. Simon and Schuster, Gollancz, Chatto, and Cape all said it needed substantial rewriting. Bessie refused. She felt personally insulted because *Power* was largely autobiographical.

I was sent the much rejected manuscript by Randolph Vigne, one of her South African friends who was in exile in London. I had worked with him when he was the covert editor of the political and literary journal the *New African* in Cape Town in the crisis-torn early 1960s. We had already published some of Head's early work. This manuscript proved to be the most shocking portrayal of schizophrenia I had ever read. Bessie Head had been born in Fort Napier Mental Institution, Pietermaritzburg, where her mother was confined. Was her mother mad, or was she just considered mad by South African society because she had an affair with her parents' Zulu stable boy? Bessie was worried she was following her mother into insanity. Here is the blast she gave Rubinstein on June 16, 1972:

> Patronage galls me. I see that you are waiting patiently and hopefully for another book. Please do not bother. This letter is intended to end whatever business relationship we had. If you cannot wait for another agent to come and collect my affairs from A. P. Watt you are free to throw the whole bloody lot out of the window. . . . I don't need your patronage Hilary. You are not my type. You know what would happen with the fourth book: "Poor dear, she's a loony." I am supposed to write books that are rejected by you. I prefer to be rejected by both Gollancz and McCalls then see what I do next. This is goodbye.[4]

The novelist Richard Lister responded to the novel on September 27:

> I feel very strongly opposed to the idea that the author should be asked to do any re-writing. The thing is superb as it is. . . . I do feel that it could be made slightly more accessible to the reader, but all that I think is necessary—or, I think desirable—for this is a fair

number of very trifling editorial amendments. These are very small points indeed mostly, in fact, a matter of punctuation. Sometimes a sentence pulls one up and has to be re-read to grasp the meaning. Sometimes this is because it expresses something that is complex or demands a pause for thought; but it is often because the comma is in the wrong place.[5]

By the time we received Lister's report I had already written to her, on August 14, 1972, accepting the book:

> *A Question of Power* numbs me. I go back and back to it. . . . It is big. You throw the lot at us and I really can feel, feel, feel though I cannot always understand. I know you have laid the inside of your head on the paper and I think we are asking you to do the impossible. . . . The book will never be easy. But it has to be slightly more accessible. It is a public exposure of a very private thing. Having gone so far with your public exposure can you go a little further? Can you go back to it? Can you stand outside it?[6]

I told Bessie Head that she did not need to change a word, a comma. Acceptance transformed her and she immediately set to work and made the book much more accessible. The African Writers Series was doing so well that I was able to get it accepted. General market titles were selling in Africa. It did not matter that it might not sell in schools. Without the series her most remarkable piece of work might not have appeared.

Another problem we encountered was attempts to impose "metropolitan" standards on African writers. What in fact happened was that, through the African Writers Series, writers from Africa were showing new directions to a worldwide audience. The most ambitious writers insisted on being judged by international standards. Nuruddin Farah told me early on: "I am nothing but a nomad."[7] Over the years, as he has lived in India, Nigeria, Italy, Britain, Russia, the United States, and now South Africa, he has continued to reveal the realities of life in his native Somalia. I was so gripped by the manuscript of his first novel, *From a Crooked Rib,* that I took it to bed, to the dismay of my wife, Clare, who complained that I rustled the pages. Farah was amused when I asked in my letter of acceptance if the author was a woman because I felt the manuscript contained a perceptive description of a woman in a Muslim society. Ebla does not see why, while her husband is away training in Rome, she should not take a second husband as a man in a Muslim society might take a second wife.

Second novels often present problems for author and publisher. It took four years of revisions before Farah's next work, *A Naked*

Needle, was published. Farah had been studying James Joyce, and the obscurity of his new manuscript put off two British readers who were themselves both practicing novelists. At that time Farah lived in Trieste, drawing on the colonial Italian of his native land and, an outsider like Joyce, poised on the outer edge of the English imagination. Omalara Leslie, at the University of Ibadan, wrote in October 1974 that "it is one of the few really genuinely global and non-parochial African novels in which the contemporary African experience is a felt and living reality."[8]

Simon Gikandi, in 1981 just out of the University of Nairobi and working for Henry Chakava (Gikandi is now teaching at Princeton), reported on *Sardines,* the second of Nuruddin Farah's trio "Variations on the themes of an African dictatorship":

> I honestly think that Farah will become one of the great masters of the African novel. For me *Sardines* came as a pleasant surprise. I left off Farah after reading *From a Crooked Rib* and *The Naked Needle* which were not so strong in comparison with other urban novels, but I seem to have missed the potential that was evident in them. In *Sardines,* Farah brings to the African novel complexity and consciousness of style unrivalled, except by the Soyinkan creation *The Interpreters.*[9]

These reports were immensely important, as I could only get books approved by the editorial meetings in London with reports from Africa. Our readers made comparisons across the world of literature. Simon Gikandi in one report managed to include references to Infante Cabrera, Wole Soyinka, Carlos Fuentes, James Baldwin, Dambudzo Marechera, and John Williams. My colleagues deserved to be impressed.

Understandably authors wanted to be read beyond the ghetto of the African Writers Series. After we had published the first two books in paperback of Nuruddin Farah's trilogy about the dictatorship of Siyad Barre in his native Somalia, it was produced in hardback by the enterprising Allison and Busby and sub-contracted to the African Writers Series. Farah has continued to publish regularly in New York and London—the international network.

We always made a point at the series of not reinforcing colonial ideologies by selecting only material acceptable to a metropolitan publisher. Ngugi set his own agenda in Kenya, publishing three novels and a play by the time he was thirty. His books were, like those by Lamming and Conrad, in a great tradition. He was on his way. Heinemann had been selling phenomenal numbers, for example 50,000 copies of *Weep Not, Child* in one month in Nigeria. Despite his success, he was becoming something of an enigma to his publishers. Keith Sambrook said to a colleague in Nairobi in 1973:

> I am a bit puzzled by Ngugi; he seems to have come to a full stop. The short stories are good but, in confidence, I don't think they show any advance on his previous, admittedly high, standard of writing. He is full of ideas, young, famous—what serious writing is he doing or planning?[10]

The seriousness of the next stage was to overwhelm everyone and especially the ruling elite of Kenya. Mwai Kibaki had been elected as a welcome replacement to Moi as President of Kenya. When he was Minister of Economic Affairs under Kenyatta, Kibaki had launched Ngugi's fourth novel, *Petals of Blood,* in the Nairobi City Hall in July 1977: 1000 guests; 500 hardbacks sold. Success! But it was plays, and particularly plays in the Gikuyu language, that were to bring Ngugi into confrontation with the Kenyan ruling elite.

Ngugi and Micere Mugo had found that plays were more effective than novels when they had put on *The Trial of Dedan Kimathi* at the National Theatre in Nairobi in 1975. In it they forcefully put the case that the peasants had led the Mau Mau struggle against the British, but that the independence deal with the British had robbed the peasants. That play was in English. Ngugi wa Thiong'o, and his cousin Ngugi wa Mirii, were asked by the villagers of Kamiriithu to write a play in Gikuyu for the open-air theater they were building. The ruling class allowed him to address the intellectuals in English. But when he talked to the peasants in their own language the authorities were angry. This play, *Ngaahika Ndeenda (I will Marry who I Want),* was banned by the District Commissioner in November 1977. On the last day of the year Ngugi wa Thiong'o was taken in chains to Kamiti maximum security jail to be held without trial until almost the end of 1978. He emerged brandishing the manuscript of a novel written secretly in prison on sheets of toilet paper.

This was his first novel to be written in Gikuyu and it was later translated as *Devil on the Cross.* When it was published with the Kamiriithu play in Nairobi in 1980, Henry Chakava and his colleagues, to avoid government sanctions, got the copies out of the printers, straight into the trunks of their cars and off to the bookshops across Gikuyu country. There were three printings in two months. Ngugi told us, with great delight, of an exciting new phenomenon in Kenyan bar life at this time. A new class of readers emerged. A man would read aloud from the novel until his glass of beer was dry. He would then place the open book face down until the listeners had bought him another beer. Literacy paid. Ngugi had, on entering one bar, been surrounded by people all giving as their own names the names of the characters they had been playing in bar room readings of the Ngugis' play.

Ngugi's duel with the authorities continued. When he wrote a musical play for villagers of Kamiriithu, they booked the National Theatre for the performances. The authorities never even acknowledged applications for a licence to perform. So fifty villagers bussed into Nairobi each day, sang songs in several Kenyan languages on the steps of the National Theatre and then went into rehearsal in a theater on the University of Nairobi campus. After some ten days this was banned and the District Commissioner sent in three truckloads of troops to tear down the theater at Kamiriithu.

By supporting Ngugi, Henry Chakava not only risked his job and the future of Heinemann as a textbook publisher in Kenya: he was attacked by men with pangas. He was threatened on the telephone. Money was demanded of him. His offices were raided when Moi ordered the arrest of Matigari, not realizing that he only existed as a character in an Ngugi novel. Chakava was backed by Keith Sambrook and Alan Hill in his publication of Ngugi. I believe that the directors of any of the other big British textbook publishers with companies in Kenya would have dropped Ngugi. There is a sour footnote to this story. The owners of Heinemann in the late 1980s wanted to re-establish control over Henry Chakava, but he maintained his independence and when they used the ultimate sanction—the withdrawal of the "Heinemann" brand name—he set up EAEP (East African Educational Publishers), which was so successful that Heinemann had to go back later to get themselves effectively represented.

I am often asked if too many books were published in the African Writers Series. Chinua Achebe was also asked this question by an interviewer for the London *Independent* at the time of the thirtieth anniversary in 1992, and I offer his response: "All I can say is, better too many than too few."[11] My aim was to publish as many good books as possible. In one year in the late 1970s, when the commodity price boom was favoring Nigeria, Zambia, and Kenya, we published twenty-two titles. That was a lot for a single publisher, but not many for an entire continent. Of course, the accountants wanted winners every time. My colleagues in Africa and I wanted as wide a choice as possible. Some of our selections—to our own surprise—became winners. The overall success of the series gave us the freedom to experiment. We kept books in print. People in the universities and the schools knew that if, at the last minute, they adopted a text for a course it would be available. They never knew when a Penguin title would go out of stock. I met David William Cohen of The Johns Hopkins University in about 1979 and he amazed me by telling how he, an historian, used African novels with his first-year students who had enrolled in a course in African history. That there were enough texts with which to engage his students was because the African Writers Series was being imaginatively marketed from New Hampshire by my old colleagues John Watson and Tom Seavey.

The creation of the African Writers Series was, I think, inspired. Those of us most closely involved in the project made use of the advantages of being in London and being a part of the English-speaking publishing world to stimulate an explosion of creative writing in Africa. In these days of so much pessimism about the present and future of Africa one can nevertheless say that African writing and African music have reached out across the world. One can say with confidence that the Africans have learned to "write back."

Fall Semester 2004

1. Quoted in John St. John, *William Heinemann: Century of Publishing 1890–1990* (London, 1990), p. 519.

2. Chinua Achebe, *Morning Yet on Creation Day* (London, 1975), p. 70.

3. Ngugi wa Thiong'o, *Homecoming* (London, 1975), p. 81.

4. Bessie Head, *A Question of Power*, Reading University Library (hereafter RUL) MS 3221 HEM 13/3.

5. Ibid.

6. Ibid.

7. Nuruddin Farah, *From a Crooked Rib*, RUL MS 3221 HEB 12/13.

8. Nuruddin Farah, *Naked Needle*, RUL MS 3221 HEB 13/8.

9. Nuruddin Farah, *Sardines*, RUL MS 3221 HEB 13/5.

10. Ngugi wa Thiong'o, *Secret Lives*, RUL MS 3221 HEB 12/9.

11. Interview with Chinua Achebe by Jenny Uglow in *Independent on Sunday*, Jan. 3, 1993.

21

"A Bright Shining Mecca": British Culture and Political Warfare In the Cold War and Beyond

SCOTT LUCAS

The world balance of power at the present time depends as much on the ideas in men's minds—in the mind of the Italian civil servant, the Vietnamese peasant, or the London docker—as on the weapons in the hands, or even the money in the pockets.[1]

It has not exactly been front-page news but, in the last five years, scholars have been rewriting the history of American foreign policy in the early cold war. The conflict was a diplomatic, economic, and military struggle with the Soviet Union, but it was more than this. As NSC 68, the US blueprint for a global campaign to vanquish Soviet Communism, stated in September 1950:

> Unwillingly our free society finds itself mortally challenged by the Soviet system. No other value system is so wholly irreconcilable with ours, so implacable in its purpose to destroy ours, so capable of turning to its own uses the most dangerous and divisive trends in our own society, no other so skillfully and powerfully evokes the elements of irrationality in human nature everywhere . . .[2]

This emphasis on the ideological and cultural dimension of "America" has taken history beyond presidents, statesmen, and generals. The United States campaign for freedom relied on a nexus of government and private action. George Kennan, who was not only promoting containment but looking at liberation of peoples behind the Iron Curtain, published "The Inauguration of Organized Political Warfare" in May 1948. The concept of a voluntary movement was central to the strategy: "Throughout our history, private American citizens have banded together to champion the cause of freedom for people suffering under oppression. . . . Our proposal is that this tradition be revived specifically to further American national interests in the present crisis."[3] Having castigated the ideals of Soviet Communism—as previously with National Socialism and Italian Fascism—as little more than the manipulated propaganda of a state-controlled system, Washington had to ensure that its ideological crusade was led by individuals freely speaking of their country's superiority. This State-private network was not controlled by the government of the day—it was established and developed more through negotiation, not only by "official" agencies but also individuals and groups working on a contract or even "unofficial" basis for those agencies—but there was an element of illusion about the "autonomy" of American freedom. While there was overt government support for some aspects of the crusade, much of it was supported through covert funding and guidance.[4]

Yet recent scholarship, even as it offers a comprehensive portrayal of American culture and foreign policy in the cold war, runs the risk of a different limitation. The global conflict is reified as a bipolar contest between blocs led by the United States and the Soviet Union. Washington's closest ally, Britain, if mentioned at all, is reduced to a passive follower of an American lead.

British, rather than American initiatives, helped define the crusade for freedom. Indeed, it was the British who developed the notion of "political warfare" in the Second World War, and it would be the British who would consider the need for a peacetime version as the Grand Alliance with Moscow fell apart. Before Kennan's memorandum proposing an organized campaign, before initiatives such as the Marshall Plan and the rhetoric of the Truman Doctrine, the British were considering a global propaganda effort. Within a year of V-E Day, top Foreign Office advisors were arguing, "We have no choice but immediately to defend ourselves in every possible way and everywhere . . . directing our campaign against Communism as such (which we should frankly expose as totalitarianism) rather than against the policy of the Soviet Government."[5] The Foreign Secretary, Ernest Bevin, stepped in with an important modification: "I am quite sure that the putting over of positive results of British attitudes would be a better corrective."[6]

A study of Britain's mobilization on the cultural front gives depth to the concept of an Anglo-American alliance waging a total battle against a Soviet foe. However, it also takes us beyond simple extensions of the so-called special relationship. The objective of the

British strategy went well beyond supporting United States foreign policy in the cold war. Bevin appealed to his colleagues, "We should seek to make London the Mecca for Social Democrats in Europe."[7] The campaign soon became far more than a positive projection against Communism, directing itself to nationalist movements which posed a different kind of challenge to London's global influence. And, as America's own crusades also looked beyond Europe to different parts of the "developing world," Washington and London could find themselves not only on parallel but divergent paths.

IN THE SPRING OF 1949, GEORGE ORWELL lay in a Gloucestershire sanatorium, seriously ill with tuberculosis. He would be dead within nine months, but lifted by an experimental course of streptomycin, he was receiving visits from old friends. One of these visitors was Celia Kirwan, the sister-in-law of Arthur Koestler and a figure in her own right on the London literary scene, having served as Cyril Connolly's assistant on *Horizon*. After the death of his first wife, Orwell, who had struck up a friendship with Koestler during the war and stayed with him during the winter of 1945–46, was infatuated with Kirwan and proposed marriage to her. She politely declined, but the two stayed in touch.

Kirwan had a motive beyond concern for Orwell's health. She was one of the first employees of the top-secret Information Research Department (IRD), established in January 1948 to co-ordinate and disseminate pro-British and anti-Communist propaganda. She told Orwell of proposed IRD initiatives and reported to her superiors that: "he was glad to learn of them and expressed his wholehearted approval of IRD aims."[8] Orwell said he was too ill to participate himself but he suggested others who might. As she departed, Kirwan left "some material" and promised to send him "photostats of some of his articles on the theme of Soviet repression of the arts, in the hope that he may become inspired when he is better to take them up again."[9]

Orwell's inspiration took a more immediate turn. Since 1945, he had kept a notebook listing 135 "crypto-Communists" including Labour MPs, the future Poet Laureate Cecil Day-Lewis, Orson Welles, Paul Robeson, John Steinbeck, Michael Redgrave, Stephen Spender, J. B. Priestley, Charlie Chaplin, the political economist Harold Laski, and the historians Isaac Deutscher and A. J. P. Taylor. After some thought—"the whole difficulty is to decide where each person stands, & one has to treat each case individually"—Orwell passed thirty-eight names to Kirwan and the IRD.[10]

Orwell is as much an icon as a political writer for the English. The incident of "The List" has thus provoked much agonized comment on whether the author who warned of Big Brother wound up co-operating with him. Such deliberations are simplistic. Orwell's communication with Kirwan was far more than a blacklist. His intervention pointed not only to the depth of the covert State-private network behind Britain's cultural campaign but also the motivation for that network: the belief that there was a moral imperative for anti-Communism and for the projection of an "English way" around the world. Ernest Bevin told Cabinet colleagues, "[We should seek] to oppose the inroads of Communism, by taking the offensive against it, basing ourselves on the standpoint of the position and vital ideas of British Social Democracy and Western civilisation, and to give a lead to our friends abroad and help them in the anti-Communist struggle."[11]

The campaign took in all spheres of activity. Ian Jacob, the BBC's director of external programming, had set the Corporation's autonomy aside in 1946 when he agreed that "the BBC [would] temper its broadcasts to accord with the national interest."[12] Jacob joined the Foreign Office's Russia Committee (the Committee changing its meetings from Tuesdays to Thursday to fit Jacob's schedule) and soon won the praise of the Permanent Under-Secretary, Orme Sargent, "The BBC are over the whole foreign field extremely helpful and cooperative."[13] Denis Healey, who had been a Communist Party member as a student but had returned from the war to become Secretary of the Labour Party, served as a liaison both to "private" outlets who could disseminate Government material and to foreign activists, such as Eastern European writers, who could provide that material.[14] The Trade Unions Congress published a newsletter which was covertly financed by government agencies. Academics such as the Soviet specialist Leonard Schapiro published books and articles, sometimes with publishers such as Bodley Head or Allen and Unwin, sometimes with the British intelligence services' "private" publisher Ampersand, based on "information" passed to them by Government contacts.[15]

The key Cabinet meeting to organize this State-private network took place on January 8, 1948. Bevin prepared a memorandum for ministerial colleagues which set out the need for "a small section in the Foreign Office," linked to British intelligence agencies, to promote the British case overseas. With the proviso that "it was important that in the execution of the policy that too much emphasis should not be laid on its anti-Soviet aspect," the Cabinet established the IRD, to be funded secretly in the same manner as the security and intelligence services.[16]

The significance of the IRD's formation can only be seen, however, in the full context of the Cabinet meeting. Ministers were considering not one but five memoranda, including "Review of Soviet Policy," "Policy in Germany," and "The First Aim of British Foreign Policy." Almost a year before the newly formed National Security Council was setting out a United States global policy to confront the Soviet Union, Britain was stealing a march.

The British vision, in contrast to that of Washington, was of a campaign which moved far beyond anti-Soviet or anti-Communist activity and propaganda. Indeed, Britain was trying to establish a global role distinct from Washington as well as Moscow. Five days before the Cabinet meeting, Prime Minister Clement Attlee described the "Third Force" for a national radio audience:

> At one end of the scale are the Communist countries; at the other end the United States of America stands for individual liberty in the political sphere and for the maintenance of human rights, but its economy is based on capitalism, with all the problems which it presents and with the characteristic extreme inequality of wealth in its citizens . . . .
>
> Great Britain, like the other countries of Western Europe, is placed, geographically and from the point of view of economic and political theory between these two great continental states. . . . Our task is to work out a system of a new and challenging kind, which combines individual freedom with a planned economy, democracy, with social justice.[17]

This dimension of the British campaign was withheld from American colleagues: a British Embassy official reported: "We were, of course, very careful to exclude any controversial points and in particular the need to contrast our own principles not only with those of communism, but also with the 'inefficiency, social injustice and moral weakness of unrestrained capitalism.'"[18]

The far-reaching extent of the Labour Government's objectives was soon obscured by prosaic limitations. Financial restrictions and, following from this, military constraints meant that Bevin's search for an American commitment to Continental defense risked becoming a substitute for British policy rather than a complement to it. Risk became reality soon after the formation of NATO when Britain, having exhausted the loan provided by the United States after the Second World War and beset by a continuing drain on foreign reserves, had no alternative but to devalue the pound and to acquiesce in US conditions for "convertibility" of sterling and the break-up of a British trading zone. The Permanent Under-Secretary's Committee, the key inter-departmental panel advising ministers, concluded in May 1949, "The Commonwealth alone cannot form a Third World

Power equivalent to the United States or the Soviet Union. . . . A weak, neutral Western Europe is undesirable and a strong, independent Western Europe is impracticable."[19]

British ambitions had been checked. Indeed, the collapse of the "Third Force" concept occurred so quickly that some participants rewrote history to claim it never existed. Christopher Mayhew, the Parliamentary Under-Secretary of State at the Foreign Office, insisted that the positive dimension was emphasized merely to win the approval of Labour MPs who were sceptical of an alliance with the United States: "We only dealt with the Third Force idea frankly, or at least I did, because . . . I didn't want Bevin to be defeated and humiliated inside the Labour Party."[20] Some advisors had foreseen conditions upon the Third Force before it was presented for Cabinet approval, the Foreign Office's Christopher Warner noting: "This idea was somewhat misleading since Western Europe could only be built on the Marshall Aid Plan and must be dependent upon American military backing against the Soviet threat." Ministers such as Bevin and Attlee, however, seized upon the response of another official, Gladwyn Jebb, that the Third Force was "put . . . forward as an objective which might eventually be achieved."[21]

More importantly, British political warfare and the cultural efforts supporting it were linked with London's interests outside Europe. The first campaign after the World War was directed at the threat to Britain's position in the Middle East. In March 1948, after the coup in Czechoslovakia consolidated Communist control, the Cabinet was still considering "the weapon of propaganda [to] be used to the full" against "The Threat to Western Civilisation" posed by Soviet policy in Europe.[22] Bevin had already established that British policy was seeking union with "not only the countries of Western Europe but also their Colonial possessions in Africa and the East . . . [to] form a bloc which, both in population and productive capacity, could stand on an equality with the Western hemisphere and Soviet blocs."[23] A special Cabinet committee established for "anti-Communist propaganda" confirmed that "all our propaganda should give a high priority to the British Commonwealth."[24]

Bevin's vision was re-confirmed in July 1949 by the Permanent Under-Secretary's Committee, which established that "this [Russian] expansionist tendency is liable to conflict with British and Western interests, not only by working towards a Russian domination of continental Europe but also by challenging Britain's strategic and economic position in the Middle East and the Far East."[25] The IRD, which had quickly grown from its initial complement of eight officers to take in more than 300 "contract" agents who produced and disseminated material, moved beyond the challenge of the Soviet bloc to confront nationalist oppositions from Malaya to Burma to Kenya to Egypt.[26]

The strategy did not preclude co-operation with US agencies and the American concept of political warfare. On the contrary, the emphasis on anti-Communism in conversations in Washington were valuable for British campaigns against nationalist insurgencies. After the Americans rapidly expanded their State-private network and covert operations under the mandate of NSC 68, the blueprint for a comprehensive global campaign to vanquish the Soviet bloc, high-level Foreign Office representatives visited Washington to agree on "close consultation and cooperation on common objectives" and the British Embassy appointed a liaison officer for psychological operations.[27] The following year, Frank Wisner, the United States intelligence officer masterminding the creation of the "Mighty Wurlitzer" to play overseas propaganda, came to London to discuss the British contribution.[28]

While British "information" services tried to sustain a global position, Anglo-American efforts focused on the battle for European hearts and minds. The United States covertly provided funds and guidance for "private" groups promoting European federalism, such as the American Committee for a United Europe. The leading intellectual movement, the Congress for Cultural Freedom, was based in Europe but it was underpinned by money from the CIA and, to a much lesser extent, MI6 and supervised by the Estonian-born CIA officer Michael Josselson. This combination of political, intellectual, and cultural contacts eventually led to the most famous (and misunderstood) United States-European "network," the Bilderberg group, which first met in Oosterbeek, Holland, in 1954.

The cultural spearhead for this political warfare was the journal *Encounter*. First proposed in the 1951 meetings between Frank Wisner and his British counterparts, the initiative was developed in meetings between Nicolas Nabokov, François Bondy, Malcolm Muggeridge, Tosco Fyvel, and Fredric Warburg, as well as Michael Josselson. They agreed that London would be the center of the venture. The American editor was Irving Kristol, the former assistant editor of *Commentary* and one of the forefathers of anti-Communist "neo-conservatism," and the the British editor was Stephen Spender. Kristol oversaw the "political" dimension of the journal, while Spender was the channel for most of the literary contributions.

Spender was never cognizant, until newspaper revelations in 1966, of the role of United States and British intelligence services in the formation and development of *Encounter*. Kristol has always maintained that he was also "unwitting" about the State involvement; he was equally insistent that he was an "independent" editor. The former assertion appears to be true, despite widespread party chatter about the source of *Encounter*'s budget; the latter is far more debatable. Kristol did clash with Josselson about the content of the journal, particularly the balance between a "cultural" and "political" approach, but the eventual output was usually acceptable to both editor and sponsor. As Kristol framed the crusade that linked him and the CIA, "The elite was us—the 'happy few' who had been chosen by History to guide our fellow creatures toward a secular redemption." [29]

One of the most controversial essays in *Encounter* was "A Postscript to the Rosenberg Case" by Leslie Fiedler, which appeared in the debut number of the journal. Fiedler's attempt to blame the Rosenbergs' plight upon the Communists, rather than the United States Government that sentenced them to death, and his characterization of the couple as "dehumanized" disturbed even supporters of *Encounter,* including Stephen Spender, not to mention subversive European left-wingers. E. M. Forster expressed his resentment of "the contempt and severity with which [the essay] treats Ethel Rosenberg's last days. . . . I wonder how [Fiedler] will act if he is ever condemned to death." [30] Yet it was another contribution by Fiedler in 1954 that may offer more insight into the tensions within the Anglo-American political culture of the cold war. Whereas "A Postscript" was a defensive response to European criticisms, "The Good American" took issue against an alleged European anti-Americanism:

> The self-distrust of the [European] intellectuals, their loss of faith in their function and in the value of their survival, blends with the Marxist dogma that one's own bourgeoisie (if you are a bourgeois, yourself!) is the worst enemy. Conditioned by this principled self-hatred, the European intellectual finds it hard to forgive America for being willing and able to let him live; and even harder to forgive himself for knowing that he could be, in our "McCarthy-ridden" land, if not happy at least unhappy in his customary way. Both these resentments he takes out on a mythicised image of all he hates, which he calls America. [31]

"The Good American" displayed the double edge of the State-private campaign. On the one hand, it set out the necessity for "Europe" to overcome any cultural fears about "America" in the cause of an ideological battle against Communism. On the other hand, Fiedler ran the risk that, by chastising self-hating Europeans, he would alienate them rather than bring them into the fold of the "Free World."

Far from agreeing with such a view of the Good American and the Self-Hating European, British contributors to *Encounter*—not only "intellectuals" but also politicians and officials—tried to negotiate a middle position in this polemical cold war. They used the pages of the journal to consider how European socialism and economic and social policies differed from those of the United States. They reflected on the military and political dynamics of "alliance." Leading Labour politicians such as Hugh Gaitskell, Anthony Crosland, and Richard Crossman contributed to the journal, but they were always careful to uphold their autonomy. As Gaitskell warned at the time of *Encounter*'s inception, it was "quite clear . . . that any politics we published would be suspect through people knowing we had American support."[32]

Such negotiations continued in the spirit of British government directives that, in a cold war which was "a struggle for men's minds . . . a struggle to determine whether the mass of mankind shall look for hope towards the Soviet Union or towards the Western democracies, . . . the United Kingdom [was] by its peculiar combination of cultural prestige and material power best fitted . . . [to be] the highest exemplar of Western civilization."[33] Yet, if London's ideological and cultural campaign developed in the context of British objectives, that campaign would not have been possible without the "global" context of America's political warfare and its development of State-private networks.

That tension was compounded by a gap in resources. British intelligence services and their private allies never had the budgets or access to funds of their American cousins, and never had the scope of operations supported by the CIA's International Organizations Division. When Frank Wisner lectured British colleagues in 1951, "It is essential to secure the cooperation of people with conspicuous access to wealth in their own right," a Foreign Office representative could only quip, "People with conspicuous access to wealth in their own right = rich people."[34] As early as 1953, the British "organisation" behind *Encounter,* the British Society for Cultural Freedom, had become little more than a front for money channeled through the accounts of Lord Victor Rothschild.

After 1967, when the covert dimension of the State-private network was exposed, the British were left far behind. Far from shutting down the covert network, the United States Government sought other hiding places. Richard Bissell, the former Deputy Director of the CIA and a key official in the formation of the network, told the Council on Foreign Relations in 1968: "If the agency is to be effective, it will have to make use of private institutions on an expanding

scale, though those relations which have been 'blown' cannot be resurrected. We need to operate under deeper cover, with increased
attention to the use of 'cut-outs.'"[35]

Some elements of the network were brought into the open, as
with the public establishment of Radios Free Europe and Liberty in
1971. Others, such as the CIA's extensive links with journalists, remained cloaked. Later organizations such as the National Endowment for Democracy, funded by the government but ostensibly "au-
tonomous," would be established after the Reagan administration's
initiatives such as "Project Democracy" and Reagan's declared confrontation with the Soviet "evil empire." When the Berlin Wall came
down in 1989 and Soviet Communism followed two years later, the
National Endowment for Democracy quickly claimed a major role
in the victory; unlike the United States Information Agency, which
struggled for a post-cold war role and was eventually abolished in
1999, the National Endowment for Democracy flourished with
campaigns that moved far beyond the former Soviet bloc.

Meanwhile the British campaign had dwindled away. In part, political warfare followed the contraction of Britain's overseas position;
in part, the campaigns of the Information Research Department
like other government ventures would be vulnerable to the large-
scale budget cuts forced by Britain's economic crises of the 1970s; in
part, the evolution of the new Europe of the European Economic
Community and Ostpolitik raised the prospect of cold war obsoles-
cence for British efforts. There were some ripples from controversial projects such as the Institute for the Study of Conflict but the
abolition of the IRD in 1977, after the British mainstream press
finally blew the Department's cover, was simply the last stage in a
long process.

The demise of Britain's agency for political warfare confirmed
that London had moved beyond any formal Anglo-American
structure. However, one may question whether it ever projected a
suitable notion of "America" on Washington's behalf, for the Brit-
ish-based dimension of the State-private network was never a con-
duit for an agreed perspective. The case of "American Studies" in
Britain is seminal.

In the 1950s the United States network sought the development
of American Studies programs at British universities and helped
create the British Association for American Studies (BAAS). Leading British academics and promising postgraduates who special-
ized in American history and literature were supported through
conferences, overseas tours, research grants, book purchases, and
cataloging of sources. Those academics and postgraduates generally

promoted the vision of "America" as "a mutual understanding between our two democracies who will carry the common burdens of the future."[36] It has been established, however, that this process was far more complex than control or even co-optation of British academics by the US government. The negotiation of support was triangular, with the Rockefeller Foundation playing an essential role not only in serving as the ultimate source of funding but in establishing the scope of "American Studies." There were differences of interest and emphasis—bureaucratic, political, economic, and intellectual—among the three actors.[37] Frank Thistlethwaite, the first Chairman of British Association for American Studies, may have admitted, "It would be a considerable responsibility to turn down the means of getting ourselves so comfortably established," but he and his colleagues also sought "autonomy" from both the United States government and the Rockefeller Foundation in their use of grants.[38]

By the 1960s that autonomy had led to a very different "American Studies." The United States Government now faced the Civil Rights Movement and the Vietnam War, and the role of the foundations had changed with the end of the large-scale Rockefeller grants. British academics portrayed an "America" which was not necessarily one of progress and consensus but of conflict at home and dubious achievement abroad. And, by the 1990s and the end of the cold war, the foundations of the 1950s arrangement were in danger. The locus of United States support for cultural and intellectual initiatives had moved from Western Europe to other parts of the world; however tensions went far beyond shifts in funding. A controversial after-dinner speech in 1995 by the United States Ambassador to Britain, William Crowe, at the BAAS Annual Conference led to a rift between the US Embassy and the Association, including a cessation of Embassy funding to future conferences and to debates over the future of institutions such as the University of London's Institute of US Studies.[39] Some programs began to interrogate the notion of a "constructive anti-Americanism" to the point where at least one was labeled by United States-based critics as a seat of "anti-American Studies."[40]

IN THE POST-SEPTEMBER 11 WORLD, there was a renewed Anglo-American effort at political warfare. The London *Guardian* reported in October 2001 on meetings in Washington for a global communications network "coordinating and magnifying the vital propaganda campaign which the US and Britain are leading against the global terrorist coalition."[41] That effort would soon turn its attention toward Iraq. In March 2002, as Lynne Cheney, the former head of the National Endowment of Humanities, opened a State Department exhibition in London of twenty-eight photographs of the demolished World Trade Center, her husband, Vice-President Dick Cheney, was proposing "regime change" in Baghdad to Prime Minister Tony Blair.[42] The British Government's contribution to the public diplomacy effort would include the September 2002 dossier of Saddam Hussein's supposed stockpile of weapons of mass destruction, including the claim that chemical and biological weapons could be deployed within 45 minutes. [43]

The reality of the British State-private network in support of this political warfare was complex. Certainly "private" voices were raised and pens were wielded in support of American-led operations against the enemy in Afghanistan and then in Iraq. Those assertions took place, however, in the midst of a protracted, heated debate over the wisdom of those operations.[44]

Britain was not entirely an unquestioning ally in the War on Terror. President Bush himself seemed to recognize this in his plea, a week after United States bombs began falling on Afghanistan: "I'm amazed that there is such misunderstanding of what our country is about that people would hate us. I, like most Americans, I just can't believe it, because I know how good we are."[45] Reductionist critiques such as Robert Kagan's "Americans are from Mars, Europeans are from Venus" were a caricature. The United States in fact possessed military hardware and economic resources that Europe did not possess or wish to use.[46]

Throughout the cold war, the ideological and cultural contest was often framed as "us" versus "them" with no room for a middle position such as "neutralism." The expression of that dichotomy has been even more dramatic in recent years, with President Bush's "you are either with us or you are with the terrorists." In this formulation, as well as Kagan's, Venusians who did not make a choice were weak or worse. Yet the British Government, even as it stood fast as the first among American allies, clearly chose the post-war cultural campaign seeking a middle position for a European Mecca. The failure to realize that vision was due not to a shift in ideology or a loss of will but to a grudging recognition of military and economic limitations.

More than fifty years later that issue is still at the heart of British political culture. While Prime Minister Blair and his supporters continued to invoke the "special relationship," others inside and outside the Government have queried the assumption of a fundametal Anglo-American alliance. Kagan's "Europe" is a crude sketch but it does point to an essential development: with the evolution of political, legal, and military structures as well as the formation of the European Union with a single currency, there is an alternate space for negotiation and implementation of foreign policy. Robin Cook, the former Foreign Secretary who resigned from the Blair Cabinet on the eve of the current war in Iraq, has argued, "The single most strategic and historically most remarkable achievement of the Blair administration was to put Britain back at the heart of Europe. We've got to do that all over again, is the short answer."[47] Public intellectuals such as Timothy Garton Ash and Jonathan Freedland have outlined this new European framework and strategy; others such as George Monbiot have gone further in calling for a new global approach to intervention, economics, and "democracy."[48]

American invocations of public diplomacy and Presidential agonizing over "why don't they like us?" will do little to alter this new environment. The cold war, fought as a total conflict, may have fostered institutional links and even structural changes underpinning a British political culture allied with the United States against Soviet Communism. Some of those joint undertakings may have been maintained, for example, under the umbrella of NATO, or renewed in later campaigns such as the interventions in the Balkans and the Middle East. However, the framework of the "special relationship" has never been comprehensive—to put the argument in crude cold war language, it could not contain British political interests which diverged from those of the United States as early as the 1950s. It could not contain economic, cultural, and even ideological shifts that challenged an assumed Anglo-American unity. It could not do so then, and despite the catch-all twenty-first-century framework of the "War on Terror," it cannot do so now.

Summer Semester 2004

1. Christopher Mayhew, "British Foreign Policy since 1945," *International Affairs*, 26, 4 (1950), p. 477.

2. State Department-Department of Defense report (NSC 68), Apr. 7, 1950, *US Declassified Document Reference System*, Retrospective 71D.

3. Policy Planning Staff report, "The Inauguration of Organized Political Warfare," May 4, 1948, *Foreign Relations of the United States, 1945–1950: Emergence of the Intelligence Establishment*, Document 269.

4. Research, analysis, and debate on the State-private network, particularly by scholars based in Europe, have developed rapidly in the last decade. See, for example, the essays in Helen Laville, ed., *The State-Private Network: The United States Government, American Citizen Groups and the Cold War* (London, 2005). Nor is this research and analysis confined to the realm of history. It is also relevant to comprehension of the full extent of America's current wars. A memorandum by Secretary of Defense Donald Rumsfeld, leaked to the press in October 2003, exposed the current State-private network. After posing the general questions, "Are we winning or losing the Global War on Terror? Is the USG changing fast enough?" In response Rumsfeld set out specific ideas such as "Should we create a private foundation to entice radical madrassas to a more moderate course?" (MSNBC News website, "Rumsfeld's Memo on Iraq, Afghanistan," Dec. 5, 2003, msnbc.msn. com/id/3225926/).

5. Kirkpatrick memorandum, May 22, 1946, PRO FO 930/488/P449/1/907.

6. Bevin note, undated, PRO FO 930/488/P449/1/907.

7. "Future Foreign Publicity Policy," Jan. 8, 1948, PRO CAB 129/23, C.P. (48)8.

8. Quoted in Peter Davidson, *The Complete Works of George Orwell* (London, 1998), Vol. XX, p. 319.

9. Ibid.

10. See Scott Lucas, *Orwell* (London, 2003), pp. 105–12.

11. "Future Foreign Publicity Policy," Jan. 8, 1948, PRO CAB 129/23, C.P. (48)8.

12. Mackenzie note, Dec. 7, 1946, PRO FO 371/71632A/N11368/G.

13. Russia Committee minutes, Sept. 24, 1946, PRO FO 371/56886/N12615; Nigel Williamson, "BBC was Party to Anti-Soviet Publicity Campaign," *The Times*, Aug. 18, 1995; Sargent to Peterson, July 28, 1947, PRO FO 371/66370/N8114/271/38. See also Michael Tracey, *A Variety of Lives: A Biography of Sir Hugh Greene* (London, 1983), pp. 119–22.

14. Nicholas Bethell, "Healey Served as Covert Linchpin in War of Words," *The Times*, Aug. 18, 1995; Richard Norton-Taylor, "Labour's Role in Secret Anti-Communist Plan Revealed," *Guardian*, Aug. 18, 1995.

15. Scott Lucas, "The British Ministry of Propaganda," *Independent on Sunday*, Feb. 26, 1995.

16. Offering contrasts and irony, two of the first eight officials of the IRD were Robert Conquest, later prominent as a historian of the Soviet Union, and Guy Burgess, one of the five Cambridge "Ring of Spies" providing information to Moscow.

17. Attlee radio broadcast, reported in *The Times*, Jan. 5, 1948.

18. Quoted in Richard Norton-Taylor, "Labour's Role in Secret Anti-Communist Plan Revealed," Aug. 18, 1995.

19. Permanent Under-Secretary Committee report, PUSC (22) Final, May 5, 1949, PRO FO 371/76384/W3114/3/500G.

20. Quoted in Paul Lashmar and James Oliver, *Britain's Secret Propaganda War 1948–1977* (Stroud, UK, 1998), p. 27.

21. Russia Committee minutes, Dec. 18, 1947, PRO FO 371/66375/N14892/271/38G.

22. Bevin memorandum, "The Threat to Western Civilisation," Mar. 3, 1948, PRO CAB 129/25, C.P. (48) 72. The first major IRD campaign culminated in an assault at the United Nations upon a Soviet "slave system" with "no parallel in history." ("Slave System in Russia Attacked by Britain," *Daily Telegraph & Morning Post,* Oct. 16, 1948; "Soviet 'Slave System': Mr Mayhew's Attack," *The Times,* Oct. 16, 1948.)

23. Cabinet minutes, Jan. 8, 1948, PRO CAB 128/12.

24. Cabinet committee (GEN 231) minutes, July 22, 1948, PRO CAB 130/37.

25. Permanent Under-Secretary Committee report, PUSC (31), July 27, 1949, PRO FO 371/77622/N11007.

26. See Susan Carruthers, *Winning Hearts and Minds: British Governments, the Media and Colonial Counter-Insurgency, 1944–1960* (Leicester, 1995).

27. Circular to Diplomatic Missions, "Regaining the Psychological Initiative," undated [1950], US National Archives, Diplomatic Branch, Lot Files, Lot 53 D 47, Box 12. Adam Watson, the liaison officer in 1950, was the first Deputy Head of IRD.

28. In an irony echoing Guy Burgess's service for IRD, Wisner was accompanied by Kim Philby, the chief MI6 officer in Washington, who was the most important Soviet agent within Whitehall. Frances Stonor Saunders, *Who Paid the Piper? The CIA and the Cultural Cold War* (London, 1999), p. 167.

29. Irving Kristol, "Memoirs of a Trotskyist," 1977, reprinted in *Reflections of a Neoconservative: Looking Back, Looking Ahead* (New York, 1983), p. 5.

30. Quoted in Barbara Sussex, *Encounter: Forming a Euro-American Cultural Bloc?* (M.Phil. Thesis, University of Birmingham, 2002), p. 43.

31. Leslie Fiedler, "The Good American," *Encounter,* 2, 3 (March 1954), p. 54.

32. Quoted in Sussex, *Encounter,* p. 44.

33. See Wesley Wark, "Coming In from the Cold: British Propaganda and Red Army Defectors, 1945–1952," *International History Review,* 9, 1 (1987), pp. 48–72.

34. Quoted in Saunders, *Who Paid the Piper?* p. 167.

35. Bissell is quoted in Richard Cummings, *The Pied Piper: Allard K. Lowenstein and the Liberal Dream* (New York, 1985), reprinted in Bob Feldman, "Time for Ford Foundation and CFR to Divest?" Oct. 8, 2002. See also the report on the CFR discussion in Dillon to Rostow, Nov. 22, 1968, US Declassified Document Reference System, 1989 2326.

36. Quoted in David Reynolds, "Whitehall, Washington, and the Promotion of American Studies in Britain during World War Two," *Journal of American Studies,* 16 (1982), p. 187.

37. See Ali Fisher, "Double Vision, Double Analysis: The Role of Interpretation, Negotiation, and Compromise in the State-Private Network and British American Studies," in Laville, ed., *State-Private Network* (London, 2005); Ali Fisher and Scott Lucas, "Master and Servant? The US Government and the Founding of the British Association for American Studies," *European Journal of American Culture* (2002), pp. 16–25.

38. Quoted in Fisher and Lucas, "Master and Servant?" p. 16.

39. The author was in the audience addressed by Crowe. The fallout from the speech and the audience reaction was described to the author by several knowledgeable sources.

40. W. Scott Lucas, "Revealing the Parameters of Opinion: An Interview with Frances Stonor Saunders," in G. Scott-Smith and H. Krabbendam, *The Cultural Cold War in Western Europe, 1945–1960* (London, 2003), pp. 15–40; John Earl Haynes and Harvey Klehr, *In Denial: Historians, Communism, and Espionage* (San Francisco, 2003), p. 48.

41. Michael White, "Campbell Takes a Spin to White House," *Guardian,* Oct. 29, 2001.

42. See Liam Kennedy, "Remembering September 11: Photography as Cultural Diplomacy," *International Affairs*, 79, 2 (March 2003), pp. 315–26; Julian Borger and others, "'Inaction is Not an Option,'" *Guardian*, Mar. 12, 2002.

43. See Richard Norton-Taylor and Michael White, "Blair Misused Intelligence, Says Ex-Spy Officer," *Guardian*, Oct. 29, 2004.

44. Two days after Sept. 11, 2001, the United States Ambassador to Britain, Philip Lader, was a member of the panel on the BBC's flagship political discussion program, *Question Time*. Lader was greeted by hostile questioning from the audience, including the assertion that aspects of US foreign policy had provoked the attacks. The incident was quickly represented by many outlets as the height of an insensitive, irrational hatred of the US, "disgusting . . . a terrible insult not only to America but also hundreds of British families who have lost relatives." For William Shawcross, "There is just one racism that is tolerated—anti-Americanism. Not just tolerated, but often applauded." Jason Deans, "Question Time Accused of Anti-US Bias," *Guardian*, Sept. 14, 2001; William Shawcross, "Stop This Racism," *Guardian*, Sept. 17, 2001. It could be interpreted, however, as a far from irrational criticism of American foreign policy. As a former British minister wrote, "A mature debate will depend on our ability to separate issues of cause and effect from questions of moral responsibility." David Clark, "To Explain is Not to Excuse," *Guardian*, Sept. 21, 2001. For further description and discussion, see Scott Lucas, *The Betrayal of Dissent: Beyond Orwell, Hitchens, and the New American Century* (London, 2004), pp. 87–115. See John Arlidge, "BBC Apologises to Envoy for Anti-American Abuse," *Guardian*, Sept. 16, 2001.

45. Quoted in CNN, *Late Edition with Wolf Blitzer*, Oct. 14, 2001.

46. See Robert Kagan, *Of Paradise and Power: America and Europe in the New World Order* (New York, 2003).

47. Robin Cook, "We Should Have Said, Sorry, We Cannot Go with You Now," *Observer*, Mar. 23, 2003.

48. See Timothy Garton Ash, *Free World: America, Europe, and the Surprising Future of the West* (London, 2004); Jonathan Freedland, "What Would You Suggest?" *Guardian*, Feb. 19, 2003; George Monbiot, "A Charter to Intervene," *Guardian*, Mar. 23, 2004.

22

British Studies at
The University of Texas, 1975–2005

Fall Semester 1975

Paul Scott (Novelist, London), 'The *Raj Quartet*'

Ian Donaldson (Director, Humanities Research Center, Australian National University), 'Humanistic Studies in Australia'

Fritz Fellner (Professor of History, Salzburg University), 'Britain and the Origins of the First World War'

Roger Louis (UT History), 'Churchill, Roosevelt, and the Future of Dependent Peoples during the Second World War'

Michael Holroyd (Biographer, Dublin), 'Two Biographies: Lytton Strachey and Augustus John'

Max Beloff (former Gladstone Professor of Government, Oxford University, present Principal of Buckingham College), 'Imperial Sunset'

Robin Winks (Professor of History, Yale University), 'British Empire-Commonwealth Studies'

Warren Roberts (Director, HRC), and David Farmer (Assistant Director, HRC), 'The D. H. Lawrence Editorial Project'

Harvey C. Webster (Professor of English, University of Louisville), 'C. P. Snow as Novelist and Philosopher'

Anthony Kirk-Greene (Fellow of St. Antony's College, Oxford), 'The Origins and Aftermath of the Nigerian Civil War'

Spring Semester 1976

Joseph Jones (UT Professor of English), 'World English'

William S. Livingston (UT Professor of Government), 'The British Legacy in Contemporary Indian Politics'

John Higley (UT Associate Professor of Sociology), 'The Recent Political Crisis in Australia'

Elspeth Rostow (UT Dean of General and Comparative Studies), Standish
Meacham (UT Professor of History), and Alain Blayac (Professor
of English, University of Paris), 'Reassessments of Evelyn Waugh'
Jo Grimond (former Leader of the Liberal Party), 'Liberal Democracy in
Britain'
Gaines Post (UT Associate Professor of History), Malcolm Macdonald (UT
Government), and Roger Louis (UT History), 'The Impact of
Hitler on British Politics'
Robert Hardgrave (UT Professor of Government), Gail Minault (UT
Assistant Professor of History), and Chihiro Hosoya (Professor of
History, University of Tokyo), 'Kipling and India'
Kenneth Kirkwood (Rhodes Professor of Race Relations, Oxford Univer-
sity), 'The Future of Southern Africa'
C. P. Snow, 'Elite Education in England'
Hans-Peter Schwarz (Director of the Political Science Institute, Cologne
University, and Visiting Fellow, Woodrow Wilson International
Center for Scholars), 'The Impact of Britain on German Politics
and Society since the Second World War'
B. K. Nehru (Indian High Commissioner, London, and former Ambas-
sador to the United States), 'The Political Crisis in India'
Robert A. Divine (UT Professor of History), Harry J. Middleton (Director,
LBJ Library), and Roger Louis (UT History), 'Declassification
of Secret Documents: The British and American Experiences
Compared'

Fall Semester 1976

John Farrell (UT Associate Professor of English), 'Revolution and Tragedy
in Victorian England'
Anthony Honoré (Regius Professor of Civil Law, Oxford University),
'British Attitudes to Legal Regulation of Sex'
Alan Hill (UT Professor of English), 'Wordsworth and America'
Ian Nish (Professor of Japanese History, London School of Econom-
ics), 'Anglo-American Naval Rivalry and the End of the Anglo-
Japanese Alliance'
Norman Sherry (Professor of English, University of Lancaster), 'Joseph
Conrad and the British Empire'
Peter Edwards (Lecturer, Australian National University), 'Australia
through American Eyes: The Second World War and the Rise of
Australia as a Regional Power'
David Edwards (UT Professor of Government), Steven Baker (UT Assis-
tant Professor of Government), Malcolm Macdonald (UT Gov-
ernment), Bill Livingston (UT Government), and Roger Louis
(UT History), 'Britain and the Future of Europe'
Michael Hurst (Fellow of St. John's College, Oxford), 'The British Empire
in Historical Perspective: The Case of Joseph Chamberlain'
Ronald Grierson (English Banker and former Public Official), 'The
Evolution of the British Economy since 1945'

Marian Kent (Lecturer in History, University of New South Wales), 'British Oil Policy between the World Wars'

Constance Babington-Smith (Fellow of Churchill College, Cambridge), 'The World of Rose Macaulay'

William Todd (UT Kerr Professor of English History and Culture), Walt Rostow (UT Professor of History and Economics), and James McKie (UT Dean of Social and Behavioral Sciences), 'Adam Smith after 200 Years'

Spring Semester 1977

Carin Green (Novelist), and Elspeth Rostow (UT American Studies), 'The Achievement of Virginia Woolf'

Samuel H. Beer (Professor of Government, Harvard University), 'Reflections on British Politics'

David Fieldhouse (Fellow of Nuffield College, Oxford), 'Decolonization and the Multinational Corporations'

Gordon Craig (Wallace Professor of Humanities, Stanford University), 'England and Europe on the Eve of the Second World War'

John Lehmann (British Publisher and Writer), 'Publishing under the Bombs—The Hogarth Press during World War II'

Philip Jones (Director, University of Texas Press), William S. Livingston (UT Christian Professor of British Studies), Michael Mewshaw (UT Assistant Professor of English), David Farmer (Assistant Director, HRC), Roger Louis (UT History), and William Todd (UT History), 'The Author, his Editor and Publisher'

Dick Taverne (former M.P), 'The Mood of Britain: Misplaced Gloom or Blind Complacency?'

James B. Crowley (Professor of History, Yale University), Lloyd C. Gardner (Professor of History, Rutgers University), Akira Iriye (Professor of History, University of Chicago), and Roger Louis (UT History), 'The Origins of World War II in the Pacific'

Rosemary Murray (Vice-Chancellor of Cambridge University), 'Higher Education in England'

Burke Judd (UT Professor of Zoology), and Robert Wagner (UT Professor of Zoology), 'Sir Cyril Burt and the Controversy over the Heritability of IQ'

Sandy Lippucci (UT Government), Roger Louis (UT History), Bill Livingston (UT Government), and Walt Rostow (UT Economics), 'The Wartime Reputations of Churchill and Roosevelt: Overrated or Underrated?'

Fall Semester 1977

Donald L. Weismann (UT University Professor in the Arts), 'British Art in the Nineteenth Century: Turner and Constable—Precursors of French Impressionism'

Standish Meacham (UT Professor of History), 'Social Reform in England'

Joseph Jones, 'Recent Commonwealth Literature'

Lewis Hoffacker (former US Ambassador), 'The Katanga Crisis: British and other Connections'

James M. Treece (UT Professor of Law), Roger Louis (UT History), Warren Roberts, and Bill Todd, (UT History) 'The Copyright Law of 1976'

Charles Heimsath (Visiting Professor of Indian History), Bob Hardgrave (UT Government), Thomasson Jannuzi, (Director, UT Center for Asian Studies), C. P. Andrade (UT Professor of Comparative Studies), and Bill Livingston (UT Government), 'Freedom at Midnight: A Reassessment of Britain and the Partition of India Thirty Years After'

Lord Fraser of Kilmorack (Chairman of the Conservative Party Organization), 'The Tory Tradition of British Politics'

Bernth Lindfors (UT Professor of English), 'Charles Dickens and the Hottentots and Zulus'

Albert Hourani (Director, Middle East Centre, Oxford University), 'The Myth of T. E. Lawrence'

Mark Kinkead-Weekes (Professor of English, University of Kent) and Mara Kalnins (British Writer), 'D. H. Lawrence: Censorship and the Expression of Ideas'

J. D. B. Miller (Professor of International Relations, Australian National University), 'The Collapse of the British Empire'

Peter Green (UT Professor of Classics), Robert King (UT Dean of Social and Behavioral Sciences), Bill Livingston (UT Government), Bob Hardgrave (UT Government), Roger Louis (UT History), and Warren Roberts (Director, HRC), 'The Best and Worst Books of 1977'

Spring Semester 1978

Peter Green (UT Classics), Malcolm Macdonald (UT Government), and Robert Crunden (UT Professor of American Studies), 'British Decadence in the Interwar Years'

Terry Quist (UT Undergraduate), Steve Baker (UT Government), and Roger Louis (UT History), 'R. Emmet Tyrrell's *Social Democracy's Failure in Britain*'

Stephen Koss (Professor of History, Columbia University), 'The British Press: Press Lords, Politicians, and Principles'

John House (Professor of Geography, Oxford University), 'The Rhodesian Crisis'

T. S. Dorsch (Professor of English, Durham University), 'Oxford in the 1930s'

Stephen Spender (English Poet and Writer), 'Britain and the Spanish Civil War'

Okot p'Bitek (Ugandan Poet), 'Idi Amin's Uganda'

David C. Goss (Australian Consul General), 'Wombats and Wivveroos'

Leon Epstein (Professor of Political Science, University of Wisconsin), 'Britain and the Suez Crisis of 1956'

David Schoonover (UT School of Library Science), 'British and American Expatriates in Paris in the 1920s'

Peter Stansky (Professor of History, Stanford University), 'George Orwell and the Spanish Civil War'

Alexander Parker (UT Professor of Spanish), 'Reflections on the Spanish Civil War'

Norman Sherry (Professor of English, Lancaster University), 'Graham Greene and Latin America'

Martin Blumenson (Office of the Chief of Military History, Department of the Army), 'The Ultra Secret'

Fall Semester 1978

W. H. Morris-Jones (Director, Commonwealth Studies Institute, University of London), 'Power and Inequality in Southeast Asia'

Hartley Grattan (UT Emeritus Professor of History), Gilbert Chase (UT Professor of American Studies), Bob Crunden (UT Professor of American Studies), and Roger Louis (UT History), 'The British and the Shaping of the American Critical Mind: A Discussion of *Edmund Wilson's Letters on Literature and Politics*'

James Roach (UT Professor of Government), 'The Indian Emergency and its Aftermath'

Bill Todd, (UT History) 'The Lives of Samuel Johnson'

Lord Hatch (British Labour Politician), 'The Labour Party and Africa'

John Kirkpatrick (HRC Bibliographer), 'Max Beerbohm'

Brian Levack (UT Associate Professor of History), 'Witchcraft in England and Scotland'

M. R. Masani (Indian Writer), 'Gandhi and Gandhism'

A. W. Coates (Economics), 'The Professionalization of the British Civil Service'

John Clive (Professor of History and Literature, Harvard University), 'Great Historians of the Nineteenth Century'

Geoffrey Best (University of Sussex), 'Flightpath to Dresden: British Strategic Bombing in the Second World War'

Kurth Sprague (UT Instructor in English), 'T. H. White's *Once and Future King*'

Gilbert Chase, 'The British Musical Invasion of America'

Spring Semester 1979

Peter Green (UT Professor of Classics), Sandy Lippucci (UT Instructor in Government), and Elspeth Rostow (UT Dean of the LBJ School of Public Affairs), 'P. N. Furbanks's biography of *E. M. Forster*'

Roger Louis (UT History), Bob Hardgrave (UT Government), Gail Minault (UT Professor of History), Peter Gran (UT Assistant

Professor of History), and Bob King (UT Dean of Liberal Arts), 'E. M. Forster and India'

Paul M. Kennedy (East Anglia University, Visiting Professor of History, Institute of Advanced Study, Princeton), 'The Contradiction between British Strategic Policy and Economic Policy in the Twentieth Century'

Richard Rive (Visiting Fulbright Research Fellow from South Africa), 'Olive Schreiner and the South African Nation'

Charles P. Kindleberger (Professor of Economics, Massachusetts Institute of Technology), 'Lord Zuckerman and the Second World War'

John Press (English Poet), 'English Poets and Postwar Society'

Richard Ellmann (Goldsmiths' Professor of English Literature, Oxford University), 'Writing a Biography of Joyce'

Michael Finlayson (Scottish Dramatist), 'Contemporary British Theater'

Lawrence Stone (Professor of History, Institute of Advanced Study, Princeton), 'Family, Sex, and Marriage in England'

C. P. Snow, 'Reflections on the Two Cultures'

Theodore Zeldin (Oxford University), 'Are the British More or Less European than the French?'

David Edwards (UT Professor of Government), 'How United the Kingdom: Greater or Lesser Britain?'

Michael Holroyd (British Biographer), 'George Bernard Shaw'

John Wickman (Director, Eisenhower Library), 'Eisenhower and the British'

Fall Semester 1979

Robert Palter (Philosophy), 'Reflections on British Philosophers: Locke, Hume, and the Utilitarians'

Alfred Gollin (Professor of History, University of California at Santa Barbara), 'Political Biography as Political History: Garvin, Milner, and Balfour'

Edward Steinhart (History), 'The Consequences of British Rule in Uganda'

Paul Sturges (Loughborough University), and Dolores Donnelly (Toronto University), 'History of the National Library of Canada'

Sir Michael Tippett (British Composer), 'Moving into Aquarius'

Steven Baker (UT Assistant Professor of Government), 'Britain and United Nations Emergency Operations'

Maria Okila Dias (Professor of History, University of São Paulo), 'Intellectual Roots of Informal Imperialism: Britain and Brazil'

Alexander Parker (UT Professor of Spanish), 'Reflections on *Brideshead Revisited*'

Barry C. Higman (Professor of History, University of the West Indies), 'West Indian Emigrés and the British Empire'

Gaines Post (UT Associate Professor of History), 'Britain and the Outbreak of the Second World War'

Karen Gould (UT Lecturer in Art), 'Medieval Manuscript Fragments and English 17th Century Collections: New Perspectives from *Fragmenta Manuscripta*'

John Farrell (UT Associate Professor of English), Eric Poole (HRC) and
    James Bieri (UT English): Round Table Discussion of Jeanne
    MacKenzie's new biography, *Dickens: A Life*
Joseph O. Baylen (Regents Professor of History, Georgia State University),
    'British Journalism in the Late Victorian and Edwardian Eras'
Peter T. Flawn (President of UT), 'An Appreciation of Charles Dickens'

Spring Semester 1980

Annette Weiner (UT Assistant Professor of Anthropology), 'Anthropolo-
    gists in New Guinea: British Interpretations and Cultural Rela-
    tivism'
Bernard Richards (Lecturer in English, Oxford University), 'Conservation
    in the Nineteenth Century'
Thomas McGann (UT Professor of History), 'Britain and Argentina: An
    Informal Dominion?'
Mohammad Ali Jazayery (Director, Center for Middle Eastern Studies),
    'The Persian Tradition in English Literature'
C. Hartley Grattan (UT Professor of History) 'Twentieth-Century British
    Novels and the American Critical Mind'
Katherine Whitehorn (London *Observer*), 'An Insider's View of the *Observer*'
Guy Lytle (UT Assistant Professor of History), 'The Oxford University
    Press' *History of Oxford*'
C. P. Snow, 'Reflections on *The Masters*'
Harvey Webster, '*The Masters* and the Two Cultures'
Brian Blakeley (Associate Professor of History, Texas Tech University),
    'Women and the British Empire'
Stephen Koss (Professor of History, Columbia University), 'Asquith, Bal-
    four, Milner, and the First World War'
Tony Smith (Associate Professor of Political Science, Tufts University),
    'The Expansion of England: New Ideas on Controversial Themes
    in British Imperialism'
Stanley Ross (UT Professor of History), 'Britain and the Mexican
    Revolution'
Rowland Smith (Chairman, Department of English, Dalhousie Univer-
    sity), 'The British Intellectual Left and the War 1939–1945'
Richard Ellmann (Goldsmiths' Professor of English, Oxford University),
    'Oscar Wilde: A Reconsideration and Problems of the Literary
    Biographer'
James Bill (UT Professor of Government), 'The United States, Britain, and
    the Iranian Crisis of 1953'

Fall Semester 1980

Decherd Turner (Director, HRHRC), 'The First 1000 Days'
Roger Louis (UT History), 'Britain and Egypt after the Second World War'
Alistair Horne (Visiting Fellow, Woodrow Wilson Center, Washington,
    DC), 'Britain and the Fall of France'

Edward Rhodes (UT Associate Professor of History), Peter Green (UT Classics), William Todd (UT History), and Roger Louis (UT History), 'Literary Fraud: H. R. Trevor-Roper and the Hermit of Peking'

Mark Kinkead-Weekes (Professor of English, Kent University), 'D. H. Lawrence's *Rainbow:* Its Sense of History'

Sir John Crawford (Vice-Chancellor, Australian National University), 'Hartley Grattan: In Memoriam'

John Stubbs (Assistant Professor of History, University of Waterloo), 'The Tory View of Politics and Journalism in the Interwar Years'

Donald L. Weismann (UT University Professor in the Arts), 'British Art in the Nineteenth Century'

Fran Hill (UT Assistant Professor of Government), 'The Legacy of British Colonialism in Tanzania'

R. W. B. Lewis (Professor of English, Yale University), 'What's Wrong with the Teaching of English?'

Charlene Gerry (British Publisher), 'The Revival of Fine Printing in Britain'

Peter Gran (UT Assistant Professor of History), 'The Islamic Response to British Capitalism'

Tina Poole (HRHRC) 'Gilbert and Sullivan's Christmas'

Spring Semester 1981

Bernard N. Darbyshire (Visiting Professor of Government and Economics), 'North Sea Oil and the British Future'

Christopher Hill (Master of Balliol College, Oxford), 'The English Civil War'

Elizabeth Heine (Assistant Professor of English, UT San Antonio), and Roger Louis (UT History), 'A Reassessment of Leonard Woolf'

Bernard Richards (Brasenose College, Oxford), 'D. H. Lawrence and Painting'

Miguel Gonzalez-Gerth (UT Professor of Spanish), 'Poetry Once Removed: The Resonance of English as a Second Language'

John Putnam Chalmers (Librarian, HRHRC), 'English Bookbinding from Caedmon to Le Carré'

Peter Coltman (UT Professor of Architecture), 'The Cultural Landscapes of Britain: 2,000 Years of Blood, Sweat, Toil & Tears to Wrest a Living from this Bloody Mud'

Thomas H. Law (former Regent University of Texas), 'The Gold Coins of the English Sovereigns'

Sidney Weintraub (Rusk Professor of International Affairs, LBJ School), James W. McKie (UT Professor of Economics), and Mary Williams (Canadian Consulate, Dallas), 'Canadian-American Economic Relations'

Amedée Turner (Conservative Member of the European Parliament), 'Integrating Britain into the European Community'

Muriel C. Bradbrook (Fellow of Girton College, Cambridge), 'Two Poets: Kathleen Raine and Seamus Heaney'

Ronald Sampson (Chief of the Industrial Development Department, Aberdeen), 'Scotland—Somewhat of a British Texas?'

Fall Semester 1981

Jerome Bump (UT Professor of English), 'From Texas to England: The Ancestry of our Victorian Architecture'

Lord Fraser of Kilmorack, 'Leadership Styles of Tory Prime Ministers since the Second World War'

William Carr (Professor of History, University of Sheffield), 'A British Interpretation of American, German, and Japanese Foreign Policy 1936–1941'

Iqbal Narain (Professor of Political Science and former Vice-Chancellor, Rajasthan University, Jaipur), 'The Ups and Downs of Indian Academic Life'

Don Etherington (Assistant Director, HRHRC), 'The Florence Flood, 1966: The British Effort—or: Up to our Necks in Mud and Books'

E. V. K. Fitzgerald (Visiting Professor of Economics), 'The British University: Crisis, Confusion, and Stagnation'

Robert Crunden (UT Professor of American Studies), 'A Joshua for Historians: Mordecai Richter and Canadian Cultural Identity'

Bernth Lindfors (UT Professor of English), 'The Hottentot Venus and Other African Attractions in Nineteenth-Century England'

Chris Brookeman (Professor of American Studies, London Polytechnic), 'The British Arts and Society'

Nicholas Pickwoad (Freelance Book Conservator), 'The Libraries of the National Trust'

Kurth Sprague (UT Instructor), 'John Steinbeck, Chase Horton, and the Matter of Britain'

Martin J. Wiener (Professor of History, Rice University), 'Cultural Values and Socio-Economic Behavior in Britain'

Werner Habicht (Professor of English, University of Würzburg), 'Shakespeare in Nineteenth-Century Germany'

Spring Semester 1982

Stevie Bezencenet (Lecturer in Photography, London College of Printing), 'Contemporary Photography in Britain'

Jane Marcus (UT Assistant Professor of English), 'Shakespeare's Sister, Beethoven's Brother: Dame Ethel Smyth and Virginia Woolf'

Wilson Harris (UT Professor of English), and Raja Rao (UT Professor of Philosophy), 'The Quest for Form: Britain and Commonwealth Perspectives'

Al Crosby (UT Professor of American Studies), 'The British Empire as a Product of Continental Drift'

Lord St. Brides (Visiting Scholar, University of Texas), 'The White House and Whitehall: Washington and Westminster'

Elizabeth Fernea (Senior Lecturer in English and President of the Middle East Studies Association), 'British Colonial Literature of the Middle East'

Maurice Evans (Actor and Producer), 'My Early Years in the Theater'

Joan Bassin (Kansas City Art Institute), 'Art and Industry in Nineteenth-Century England'

Eugene N. Borza (Professor of Ancient History, Pennsylvania State University), 'Sentimental British Philhellenism: Images of Greece'

Ralph Willett (American Studies Department, University of Hull), 'The Style and Structure of British Television News'

Roger Louis (UT History), 'Britain and the Creation of the State of Israel'

Peter Russell (Professor of Spanish, Oxford University), 'A British Historian Looks at Portuguese Historiography of the Fifteenth Century'

Rory Coker (UT Professor of Physics), 'Frauds, Hoaxes and Blunders in Science—a British Tradition?'

Ellen DuBois (Professor of History, SUNY Buffalo), 'Anglo-American Perspectives on the Suffragette Movement'

Donald G. Davis, Jr. (UT Professor of Library Science), 'Great Expectations—and a Few Illusions: Reflections on an Exchange Teaching Year in England'

Anthony Rota (Managing Director, Bertram Rota Ltd.), 'The Changing World of the Bookdealer'

Eisig Silberschlag (former President, Hebrew College, Visiting Gale Professor of Judaic Studies), 'The Bible as the Most Popular Book in English'

Fall Semester 1982

Woodruff Smith (Professor of History, UT San Antonio), 'British Overseas Expansion'

The Rt. Hon. George Thomas (Speaker of the House of Commons), 'Parliamentary Democracy'

Nigel Nicolson (English Historian and Biographer), 'The English Country House as an Historical Document'

Lord St. Brides (Visiting Scholar), 'A Late Leaf of Laurel for Evelyn Waugh'

Lt. Col. Jack McNamara, USMC (Ret.), 'The Libel of Evelyn Waugh by the *Daily Express*'

James Wimsatt (UT Professor of English), 'Chaucer and Medieval French Manuscripts'

Christopher Whelan (Visiting Professor, UT Law School), 'Recent Developments in British Labour Law'

Brian Wearing (Senior Lecturer in American Studies, Christchurch, New Zealand), 'New Zealand: In the Pacific, But Of It?'

Robert Hardgrave (UT Professor of Government), 'The United States and India'

James McBath (Professor of Communications, University of Southern California), 'The Evolution of *Hansard*'

Paul Fromm (Professor of Economics, University of Toronto), 'Canadian-United States Relations: Two Solitudes'

John Velz (UT Professor of English), 'When in Disgrace: Ganzel's Attempt to Exculpate John Payne Collier'

Roger Louis (UT History), 'British Origins of the Iranian Revolution'

Spring Semester 1983

Sir Ellis Waterhouse (Slade Professor of Fine Arts, Oxford University), 'A Comparison of British and French Painting in the late Eighteenth Century'

E. J. L. Ride (Australian Consul General), 'Australia's Place in the World and her Relationship with the United States'

Edward Bell (Director of the Royal Botanic Gardens, Kew), 'Kew Gardens in World History'

The Very Rev. Oliver Fiennes (Dean of Lincoln), 'The Care and Feeding of Magna Carta'

C. V. Narasimhan (former Under-Secretary of the United Nations), 'Last Days of the British Raj: A Civil Servant's View'

Warren G. Osmond, 'Sir Frederic Eggleston and the Development of Pacific Consciousness'

Richard Ellmann (Goldsmiths' Professor, Oxford University), 'Henry James among the Aesthetes'

Janet Caulkins (Professor of French, University of Wisconsin at Madison), 'The Poor Reputation of Cornish Knights in Medieval Literature'

Werner Habicht (Professor of English, University of Würzburg), 'Shakespeare and the Third Reich'

Gillian Peele (Fellow of Lady Margaret Hall, Oxford), 'The Changing British Party System'

John Farrell (UT Professor of English), 'Scarlet Ribbons: Memories of Youth and Childhood in Victorian Authors'

Peter Russell (Professor of Spanish, Oxford University), 'A Not So Bashful Stranger: *Don Quixote* in England, 1612–1781'

Sir Zelman Cowen (Provost of Oriel College, Oxford), 'Contemporary Problems in Medicine, Law, and Ethics'

Dennis V. Lindley (Visiting Professor of Mathematics), 'Scientific Thinking in an Unscientific World'

Martin Blumenson (Office of the Chief of Military History, Department of the Army), 'General Mark Clark and the British in the Italian Campaign of World War II'

Fall Semester 1983

Anthony King (Professor of Politics, University of Essex), 'Margaret Thatcher and the Future of British Politics'

Alistair Gillespie (Canadian Minister of Energy, Mines, and Resources), 'Canadian-British Relations: Best and Worst'

Charles A. Owen, Jr. (Professor of English, University of Connecticut), 'The Pre-1400 Manuscripts of the *Canterbury Tales*'

Major-General (Ret.) Richard Clutterbuck (Reader in Political Conflict, University of Exeter), 'Terrorism in Malaya'

Wayne A. Wiegand (Associate Professor of English, University of Kentucky), 'British Propaganda in American Public Libraries during World War I'

Stuart Macintyre (Australian National University, Canberra), 'Australian Trade Unionism between the Wars'

Ram Joshi (Visiting Professor of History, former Vice-Chancellor, University of Bombay), 'Is Gandhi Relevant Today?'

Sir Denis Wright (former British Ambassador in Iran), 'Britain and the Iranian Revolution'

Andrew Horn (Head of the English Department, University of Lesotho), 'Theater and Politics in South Africa'

Philip Davies (Professor of American Government, University of Manchester), 'British Reaction to American Politics: Overt Rejection, Covert Assimilation'

H. K. Singh (Political Secretary, Embassy of India), 'United States-Indian Relations'

Roger Louis (UT Professor of History), Ram Joshi (UT Visiting Professor of History), and J. S. Mehta (UT Professor, LBJ School), 'Two Cheers for Mountbatten: A Reassessment of Lord and Lady Mountbatten and the Partition of India'

Spring Semester 1984

M. S. Venkataramani (Director of International Studies, Jawaharlal Nehru University), 'Winston Churchill and Indian Freedom'

Sir John Thompson (British Ambassador to the United Nations), 'The Falklands and Grenada in the United Nations'

Robert Farrell (Professor of English, Cornell University), 'Medieval Archaelogy'

Allon White (Lecturer in English, University of Sussex), 'The Fiction of Early Modernism'

Peter Green (UT Professor of Classics), Roger Louis (UT Professor of History), Miguel Gonzalez-Gerth (UT Professor of Spanish & Portuguese), Standish Meacham (UT Professor of History), and Sid Monas (UT Professor of Slavic Languages and History): 'Orwell's *1984*'

Uriel Dann (Professor of English History, University of Tel Aviv), 'Hanover and Britain in the Time of George II'

José Ferrater-Mora (Fairbank Professor of Humanities, Bryn Mawr), 'A. M. Turing and his "Universal Turing Machine"'

Rüdiger Ahrens (University of Würzburg), 'Teaching Shakespeare in German Universities'

Michael Brock (Warden of Nuffield College, Oxford), 'H. H. Asquith and
  Venetia Stanley'
Herbert Spiro (Professor of Political Science, Free University of Berlin),
  'What Makes the British and Americans Different from Everybody
  Else: The Adversary Process of the Common Law'
Nigel Bowles (Lecturer in American Government and Politics, University
  of Edinburgh), 'Reflections on Recent Developments in British
  Politics'
Harold Perkin (Mellon Distinguished Visiting Professor, Rice University),
  'The Evolution of Citizenship in Modern Britain'
Christopher Heywood (Senior Lecturer, Sheffield University), '*Jane Eyre*
  and *Wuthering Heights*'
Dave Powers (Curator, Kennedy Library), 'JFK's Trip to Ireland, 1963'
R. W. Coats (Visiting Professor of Economics), 'John Maynard Keynes: The
  Man and the Economist'
David Evans (UT Professor of Astronomy), 'Astronomy as a British Cul-
  tural Export'

Fall Semester 1984

John Henry Faulk, 'Reflections on My Sojourns in the British Middle East'
Lord Fraser of Kilmorack, 'The Thatcher Years—and Beyond'
Michael Phillips (Lecturer in English Literature, University of Edin-
  burgh), 'William Blake and the Rise of the Hot Air Balloon'
Erik Stocker (HRHRC), 'A Bibliographical Detective Story: Reconstruct-
  ing James Joyce's Library'
Amedée Turner (Member of the European Parliament), 'Recent Devel-
  opments in the European Parliament'
Michael Hurst (Fellow of St. John's College, Oxford), 'Scholars versus
  Journalists on the English Social Classes'
Charles Alan Wright (UT William B. Bates Professor of Law), 'Reflections
  on Cambridge'
J. M. Winter (Fellow of Pembroke College, Cambridge), 'Fear of Decline
  in Population in Britain after World War I'
Henk Wesseling (Director of the Centre for the History of European Ex-
  pansion, University of Leiden), 'Dutch Colonialism and the Im-
  pact on British Imperialism'
Celia Morris Eckhardt (Biographer and author of *Fannie Wright*), 'Frances
  Wright and *England as the Civilizer*'
Sir Oliver Wright (British Ambassador to the United States), 'British For-
  eign Policy—1984'
Leonard Thompson (Professor of African History, Yale University), 'Polit-
  ical Mythology and the Racial Order in South Africa'
Flora Nwapa (Nigerian Novelist), 'Women in Civilian and Military Rule in
  Nigeria'
Richard Rose (Professor of Political Science, University of Strathclyde),
  'The Capacity of the Presidency in Comparative Perspective'

Spring Semester 1985

Bernard Hickey (University of Venice), 'Australian Literary Culture: Short Stories, Novels, and "Literary Journalism"'

Kenneth Hafertepe (UT American Studies), 'The British Foundations of the Smithsonian Castle: The Gothic Revival in Britain and America'

Rajeev Dhavan (Visiting Professor, LBJ School and Center for Asian Studies), 'Race Relations in England: Trapped Minorities and their Future'

Sir John Thompson (British Ambassador to the United Nations), 'British Techniques of Statecraft'

Philip Bobbitt (UT Professor of Law), 'Britain, the United States, and Reduction in Strategic Arms'

David Bevington (Drama Critic and Theater Historian), 'Maimed Rites: Interrupted Ceremony in *Hamlet*'

Standish Meacham (UT Professor of History), 'The Impact of the New Left History on British and American Historiography'

Iris Murdoch (Novelist and Philospher), and John O. Bayley (Thomas Warton Professor of English, Oxford University), 'Themes in English Literature and Philosophy'

John P. Chalmers (Librarian, HRHRC), 'Malory Illustrated'

Thomas Metcalf (Professor of History, University of California at Berkeley), 'The Architecture of Empire: The British Raj in India'

Robert H. Wilson (UT Emeritus Professor of English), 'Malory and His Readers'

Lord St. Brides, '*A Passage to India*' Better Film than Novel?'

Derek Pearsall (Medievalist at York University), 'Fire, Flood, and Slaughter: The Tribulations of the Medieval City of York'

E. S. Atieno Odhiambo (University of Nairobi, Visiting Professor, The Johns Hopkins University), 'Britain and Kenya: The Mau Mau, the "Colonial State," and Dependency'

Francis Robinson (Reader in History, University of London), 'Indian Muslim Religious Leadership and Colonial Rule'

Charles B. MacDonald (Deputy Chief Historian, US Army), 'The British in the Battle of the Bulge'

Brian Levack (UT Associate Professor of History), 'The Battle of Bosworth Field'

Kurth Sprague (UT Lecturer in English), 'The Mirrors of Malory'

Fall Semester 1985

A. P. Thornton (Distinguished University Professor, University of Toronto), 'Whatever Happened to the British Commonwealth?'

Michael Garibaldi Hall (UT Professor of History), and Elizabeth Hall (LBJ School), 'Views of Pakistan'

Ronald Steel (Visiting Professor of History), 'Walter Lippmann and the British'

Douglas H. M. Branion (Canadian Consul General), 'Political Controversy and Economic Development in Canada'

Decherd Turner and Dave Oliphant (HRHRC), 'The History of the Publications of the HRHRC'

Robert Fernea (UT Professor of Anthropology), 'The Controversy Over Sex and Orientalism: Charles Doughty's *Arabia Deserta*'

Desley Deacon (Lecturer, UT Department of Government), 'Her Brilliant Career: The Context of Nineteenth-Century Australian Feminism'

John Lamphear (UT Associate Professor of History), 'The British Colonial "Pacification" of Kenya: A View from the Other Side'

Kingsley de Silva (Foundation Professor of Ceylon History at the University of Peradeniya, Sri Lanka), 'British Colonialism and Sri Lankan Independence'

Thomas Hatfield (UT Dean of Continuing Education), 'Colorado on the Cam 1986: From "Ultra" to Archaeology, from Mr. Micawber to Mrs. Thatcher'

Carol Hanbery MacKay (UT Assistant Professor of English), 'The Dickens Theater'

Ronald Brown, Jo Anne Christian, Roger Louis (UT History), Harry Middleton, and Ronald Steel—Panel Discussion: 'The Art of Biography: Philip Ziegler's *Mountbatten*'

Spring Semester 1986

B. J. Fernea (UT English and Middle Eastern Studies), Bernth Lindfors (UT Professor of English), and Roger Louis (UT History), '*Out of Africa:* The Book, the Biography, and the Movie'

Robert Litwak (Woodrow Wilson International Center for Scholars, Washington, DC), 'The Great Game: Russian, British, and American Strategies in Asia'

Gillian Adams Barnes (UT English), and Jane Manaster (UT Geography), 'Humphrey Carpenter's *Secret Gardens* and the Golden Age of Children's Literature'

Laurie Hergenhan (Professor of English, University of Queensland), 'A Yankee in Australia: The Literary and Historical Adventures of C. Hartley Grattan'

Brian Matthews (Flinders University of South Australia), 'Australian Utopianism of the 1880s'

Richard Langhorne (Fellow of St. John's College, Cambridge), 'Apostles and Spies: The Generation of Treason at Cambridge between the Wars'

Ronald Robinson (Beit Professor of the History of the British Empire, Oxford University), 'The Decline and Fall of the British Empire'

William Rodgers (Vice-President, Social Democratic Party), 'Britain's New Three-Party System: A Permanent or Passing Phenomenon?'

John Coetzee (Professor of Literature, University of Cape Town), 'The Farm Novel in South Africa'

Ayesha Jalal, (Fellow, Trinity College, Cambridge), 'Jinnah and the Partition of India'

Andrew Blane (Professor of History, City College of New York), 'Amnesty International: From a British to an International Movement'

Anthony Rota (Antiquarian Bookdealer and Publisher), 'London Pride: 1986'

Elspeth Rostow (Dean, LBJ School), 'The Withering Away of Whose State? Colonel Qaddafi's? Reflections on Nationalism at Home and Abroad, in Britain and in the Middle East'

Ray Daum (Curator, HRHRC), 'Broadway—Piccadilly!'

Fall Semester 1986

Dean Robert King and Members of the '"Unrequired Reading List" Committee—The British Component': Round Table Discussion.

Paul Sturges (Loughborough University), 'Popular Libraries in Eighteenth-Century Britain'

Ian Bickerton (Professor of History, University of Missouri), 'Eisenhower's Middle East Policy and the End of the British Empire'

Marc Ferro (Visiting Professor of History), 'Churchill and Pétain'

David Fitzpatrick (Visiting Professor of History, Queen's University, Kingston, Ontario), 'Religion and Politics in Ireland'

Adam Watson (Center for Advanced Studies, University of Virginia, former British Ambassador to Castro's Cuba), 'Our Man in Havana — or: Britain, Cuba, and the Caribbean'

Norman Rose (Chaim Weizmann Professor of History, Hebrew University), 'Chaim Weizmann, the British, and the Creation of the State of Israel'

Elaine Thompson (Senior Fulbright Scholar, American University), 'Legislatures in Canberra and Washington'

Roger Louis (UT Professor of History), 'Suez Thirty Years After'

Antonia Gransden (Reader in Medieval History, University of Nottingham), 'The Writing of Chronicles in Medieval England'

Hilary Spurling (British Biographer and Critic), 'Paul Scott's *Raj Quartet:* The Novelist as Historian'

J. D. B. Miller (Professor of International Relations, Australian National University), 'A Special and Puzzling Relationship: Australia and the United States'

Janet Meisel (UT Associate Professor of History), 'The Domesday Book'

Spring Semester 1987

Miguel Gonzalez-Gerth (UT Liberal Arts), Robert Fernea (UT Anthropology), Joe Horn (UT Psychology), Bruce Hunt (UT History), and Delbert Thiessen (UT Psychology), 'Contemporary Perspectives on Evolution'

Alistair Campbell-Dick (Chief Executive Officer, Research and Development Strategic Technology), 'Scottish Nationalism'

Anthony Mockler (British Freelance Historian and Biographer), 'Graham Greene: The Interweaving of His Life and Fiction'

Michael Crowder (Visiting Professor of African History, Amherst College), 'The Legacy of British Colonialism in Africa'

Carin Green (UT Lecturer in Classics), 'Lovers and Defectors: Autobiography and *The Perfect Spy*'

Lord St. Brides, 'The Modern British Monarchy'

Victor Szebehely (UT Richard B. Curran Professor of Engineering), 'Sir Isaac Newton'

Patrick McCaughey (Visiting Professor of Australian Studies, Harvard University; Director, National Gallery of Victoria, Melbourne), 'The Persistence of Landscape in Australian Art'

Adolf Wood (Deputy Editor of the *Times Literary Supplement*), 'An Informal History of the *TLS*'

Nissan Oren (Visiting Professor of Political Science, The Johns Hopkins University; Kaplan Professor, Hebrew University, Jerusalem), 'Churchill, Truman, and Stalin: The End of the Second World War'

Sir Michael Howard (Regius Professor of History, Oxford University), 'Britain and the First World War'

Sir John Graham (former British Ambassador to NATO), 'NATO: British Origins, American Security, and the Future Outlook'

Daniel Mosser (Virginia Polytechnic Institute and State University), 'The Chaucer Cardigan Manuscript'

Sir Raymond Carr (Warden of St. Antony's College, Oxford), 'British Intellectuals and the Spanish Civil War'

Michael Wilding (Reader in English, University of Sydney), 'The Fatal Shore? The Convict Period in Australian Literature'

Fall Semester 1987

Peter Green (UT Professor of Classics), Winfred Lehmann (UT Temple Professor of Humanities), Roger Louis (UT Kerr Professor), and Paul Woodruff (UT Professor of Philosophy), 'Anthony Burgess: The Autobiography'

Robert Crunden (UT Professor of History and American Studies), 'Ezra Pound in London'

Carol MacKay (UT Associate Professor of English), and John Henry Faulk, 'J. Frank Dobie and Thackeray's Great-Granddaughter: Another Side of *A Texan in England*'

Sarvepalli Gopal (Professor of Contemporary History, Jawaharlal Nehru University, and Fellow of St. Antony's College, Oxford), 'Nehru and the British'

Robert D. King (UT Dean of Liberal Arts), 'T. S. Eliot'

Lord Blake (Visiting Cline Professor of English History and Literature, former Provost of Queen's College, Oxford), 'Disraeli: Problems of the Biographer'

Alain Blayac (Professor of Comparative Literature, University of Montpellier), 'Art as Revelation: Gerard Manley Hopkins's Poetry and James Joyce's *Portrait of the Artist*'

Mary Bull (Oxford University), 'Margery Perham and Africa'

R. J. Moore (Professor of History, Flinders University), 'Paul Scott: The Novelist as Historian, and the *Raj Quartet* as History'

Ian Willison (Head of the Rare Books Division of the British Library), 'New Trends in Humanities Research: The *History of the Book in Britain* Project'

The Duke of Norfolk, 'The Lion and the Unicorn: Ceremonial and the Crown'

Hans Mark (Chancellor, The University of Texas System), 'The Royal Society, the Royal Observatory, and the Development of Modern Research Laboratories'

Henry Dietz (UT Professor of Government), 'Sherlock Holmes: A Centennial Celebration'

Spring Semester 1988

Lord Jenkins (Chancellor of Oxford University), 'Changing Patterns of British Government from Asquith via Baldwin and Attlee to Mrs. Thatcher'

Lord Thomas (author of *The Spanish Civil War* and *Cuba, or the Pursuit of Freedom*), 'Britain, Spain, and Latin America'

Barbara Harlow (UT English), Bernth Lindfors (UT English), Wahneema Lubiano (UT English), and Robert Wren (University of Houston), 'Chinua Achebe: The Man and His Works'

Charles Townshend (Professor of History, Keele University), 'Britain, Ireland, and Palestine, 1918–1947'

Richard Morse (Program Secretary for Latin America, Woodrow Wilson Center), 'T. S. Eliot and Latin America'

Chinua Achebe (Nigerian Novelist), 'Anthills of the Savannah'

Tapan Raychaudhuri (Reader in Indian History, Oxford University), 'The English in Bengali Eyes in the Nineteenth Century'

Lord Chitnis (Chief Executive of the Rowntree Trust and Chairman of the British Refugee Council), 'British Perceptions of US Policy in Central America'

Kurth Sprague (Senior Lecturer in English), 'Constance White: Sex, Womanhood, and Marriage in British India'

George McGhee (former US Ambassador to Turkey and Germany), 'The Turning Point in the Cold War: Britain, the United States, and Turkey's Entry into NATO'

Robert Palter (Professor of the History of Science, Trinity College), 'New Light on Newton's Natural Philosophy'

J. Kenneth McDonald (Chief Historian, CIA), 'The Decline of British Naval Power 1918–1922'

Yvonne Cripps (UT Visiting Professor of Law), '"Peter and the Boys Who Cry Wolf": *Spycatcher*'

Emmanuel Ngara (Professor of English, University of Zimbabwe), 'African Poetry: Nationalism and Cultural Domination'

Kate Frost (UT Assistant Professor of English), 'Frat Rats of the Invisible College: The Wizard Earl of Northumberland and His Pre-Rosicrucian Pals'

B. Ramesh Babu (UT Visiting Professor of Government), 'American Foreign Policy: An Indian Dissent'

Sir Antony Ackland (British Ambassador to the United States), 'From Dubai to Madrid: Adventures in the British Foreign Service'

In the Spring Semester 1988 British Studies helped to sponsor four lectures by Sir Brian Urquhart (former Under-Secretary of the United Nations) on 'World Order in the Era of Decolonization'

Fall Semester 1988

Peter Green (UT Dougherty Professor of Classics), Diana Hobby (Rice University, Editor of the *Yeats Papers*), Roger Louis (UT Kerr Professor), and Elspeth Rostow (UT Stiles Professor of American Studies), Round Table Discussion on Richard Ellman's *Oscar Wilde*

Hugh Cecil (University of Leeds), 'The British First World War Novel of Experience'

Alan Knight (UT Worsham Professor of Mexican History), 'Britain and the Mexican Revolution'

Prosser Gifford (Former Deputy Director, Woodrow Wilson Center, Washington, DC), and Robert Frykenberg (Professor of Indian History, University of Wisconsin at Madison), 'Stability in Post-Colonial British Africa: The Indian Perspective'

Joseph Dobrinski (Université Paul-Valéry), 'The Symbolism of the Artist Theme in *Lord Jim*'

Martin Stannard (University of Leicester), 'Evelyn Waugh and North America'

Lawrence Cranberg (Consulting Physicist and Fellow of the American Physical Society), 'The Engels-Marx Relationship and the Origins of Marxism'

N. G. L. Hammond (Professor of Greek, Bristol University), 'The British Military Mission to Greece, 1943–1944'

Barbara Harlow (UT English), 'A Legacy of the British Era in Egypt: Women, Writing, and Political Detention'

Sidney Monas (UT Professor of Slavic Languages and History), 'Thanks for the Mummery: *Finnegans Wake*, Rabelais, Bakhtin, and Verbal Carnival'

Robert Bowie (Former Director, Harvard Center of International Affairs and Deputy Director, Central Intelligence Agency), 'Britain's Decision to Join the European Community'

Shirley Williams (Co-Founder, Social Democratic Party), 'Labour Weakness and Tory Strength—or, The Strange Death of Labour England'

Bernard Richards (Fellow of Brasenose College, Oxford), 'Ruskin's View of Turner'

John R. Clarke (Art History), 'Australian Art of the 1960s'

Round Table Discussion on Paul Kennedy's *The Rise and Fall of the Great Powers:* Sandy Lipucci (UT Government), Roger Louis (UT Kerr Professor), Jagat Mehta (LBJ School), Sidney Monas (UT Professor of Slavic Languages and History), and Walt Rostow (UT Economics and History)

Spring Semester 1989

Brian Levack (UT Professor of History), 'The English Bill of Rights, 1689'

Hilary Spurling (Critic and Biographer), 'Paul Scott as Novelist: His Sense of History and the British Era in India'

Larry Carver (Director of the Humanities Program), 'Lord Rochester: The Profane Wit and the Restoration's Major Minor Poet'

Atieno Odhiambo (Professor of History, Rice University), 'Re-Interpreting Mau Mau'

Trevor Hartley (Reader in Law, London School of Economics, and Visiting Professor, UT Law School), 'The British Constitution and the European Community'

Archie Brown (Fellow of St. Antony's College, Oxford), 'Political Leadership in Britain, the Soviet Union, and the United States'

Lord Blake (Former Provost of Queen's College, Oxford, and Editor of the *Dictionary of National Biography*), 'Churchill as Historian'

Weirui Hou (Professor of English Literature, Shanghai University), 'British Literature in China'

Norman Daniel (British Council), 'Britain and the Iraqi Revolution of 1958'

Alistair Horne (Fellow of St. Antony's College, Oxford), 'The Writing of the Biography of Harold Macmillan'

M. R. D. Foot (former Professor of History, Manchester University, and Editor of the *Gladstone Diaries*), 'The Open and Secret War, 1939–1945'

Ian Willison (former Head of Rare Books Division of the British Library), 'Editorial Theory and Practice in The History of the Book'

Neville Meaney (Professor of History, University of Sydney), 'The "Yellow Peril": Invasion, Scare Novels, and Australian Political Culture'

Round Table Discussion on *The Satanic Verses:* Kurth Sprague (UT Associate Professor of American Studies), Peter Green (UT Dougherty Professor of Classics), Robert A. Fernea (UT Professor of Anthropology), Roger Louis (UT Kerr Professor), and Gail Minault (UT Associate Professor of History and Asian Studies)

Kate Frost (UT Associate Professor of English), 'John Donne, Sunspots, and the British Empire'

Lee Patterson (Professor of English, Duke University), 'Chaucerian Commerce'

Edmund Weiner and John Simpson (Editors of the new *OED*), 'Return to the Web of Words'

Ray Daum (Curator, HRHRC), 'Noel Coward and Cole Porter'

William B. Todd (UT Emeritus Professor of History), 'Edmund Burke on the French Revolution'

Fall Semester 1989

D. Cameron Watt (Stevenson Professor of International History, LSE), 'Britain and the Origins of the Second World War: Personalities and Politics of Appeasement'

Gary Freeman (UT Associate Professor of Government), 'On the Awfulness of the English: The View from Comparative Studies'

Hans Mark (Chancellor, UT System), 'British Naval Tactics in the Second World War: The Japanese Lessons'

T. B. Millar (Director, Menzies Centre for Australian Studies, London), 'Australia, Britain and the United States in Historical Perspective'

Dudley Fishburn (Member of Parliament and former Editor of *The Economist*), '*The Economist*'

Lord Franks (former Ambassador in Washington), 'The "Special Relationship"'

Herbert L. Jacobson (Drama Critic and friend of Orson Wells), 'Three Score Years of Transatlantic Acting and Staging of Shakespeare'

Roy Macleod (Professor of History, University of Sydney) 'The "Practical Man": Myth and Metaphor in Anglo-Australian Science'

David Murray (Professor of Government, the Open University), 'Hong Kong: The Historical Context for the Transfer of Power'

Susan Napier (UT Assistant Professor of Japanese Language and Literature), 'Japanese Intellectuals Discover the British'

Dr. Karan Singh (Ambassador of India to the United States), 'Four Decades of Indian Democracy'

Paul Woodruff (UT Professor of Philosophy), 'George Grote and the Radical Tradition in British Scholarship'

Herbert J. Spiro (UT Professor of Government), 'Britain, the United States, and the Future of Germany'

Robert Lowe (Wine Columnist for the *Austin American-Statesman*), '"God Rest you Merry, Gentlemen": The Curious British Cult of Sherry'

Spring Semester 1990

Thomas F. Staley (Director, HRHRC), 'Harry Ransom, the Humanities Research Center, and the Development of Twentieth-Century Literary Research Collections'

Thomas Cable (UT Blumberg Professor of English), 'The Rise and Decline of the English Language'

D. J. Wenden (Fellow of All Souls College, Oxford), 'Sir Alexander Korda
and the British Film Industry'

Roger Owen (Fellow of St. Antony's College, Oxford, and UT Visiting Professor of Middle Eastern History), 'Reflections on the First Ten
Years of Thatcherism'

Robert Hardgrave (UT Temple Centennial Professor of Humanities),
'Celebrating Calcutta: The Solvyns Portraits'

Donatus Nwoga (Professor of English, University of Nigeria, Nsukka, and
Fulbright Scholar-in-Residence, University of Kansas), 'The Intellectual Legacy of British Decolonization in Africa'

Francis Sitwell (Etonian, Seaman, and Literary Executor), 'Edith Sitwell:
A Reappraisal'

Robert Vitalis (UT Assistant Professor of Government), 'The "New Deal"
in Egypt: Britain, the United States, and the Egyptian Economy
during World War II'

James Coote (UT Professor and Cass Gilbert Teaching Fellow, School of
Architecture), 'Prince Charles and Architecture'

Harry Eckstein (Distinguished Professor of Political Science, University
of California, Irvine), 'British Politics and the National Health
Service'

Alfred David (Professor of English, Indiana University), 'Chaucer and
King Arthur'

Ola Rotimi (African Playwright and Theater Director), 'African Literature
and the British Tongue'

Derek Brewer (Professor of English and Master of Emmanuel College,
Cambridge), 'An Anthropological Study of Literature'

Neil MacCormick (Regius Professor of Public Law and the Law of Nations,
University of Edinburgh), 'Stands Scotland Where She Should?'

Janice Rossen (Senior Research Fellow, HRHRC), 'Toads and Melancholy:
The Poetry of Philip Larkin'

Ronald Robinson (Beit Professor of the History of the British Commonwealth, Oxford, and Visiting Cline Professor, University of Texas),
'The Decolonization of British Imperialism'

Fall Semester 1990

Round Table Discussion on 'The Crisis in the Persian Gulf': Hafez Far-
mayan (UT Professor of History), Robert Fernea (UT Professor of
Anthropology), Roger Louis (UT Kerr Professor), and Robert
Stookey (United States Foreign Service Officer, Retired, now Research Associate, Center for Middle Eastern Studies)

John Velz (UT Professor of English), 'Shakespeare and Some Surrogates:
An Account of the Anti-Stratfordian Heresy'

Michael H. Codd (Secretary, Department of the Prime Minister and Cabinet, Government of Australia), 'The Future of the Commonwealth: An Australian View'

John Dawick (Senior Lecturer in English, Massey University, New Zealand), 'The Perils of Paula: Young Women and Older Men in Pinero's Plays'

Gloria Fromm (Professor of English, University of Illinios in Chicago), 'New Windows on Modernism: The Letters of Dorothy Richardson'

David Braybrooke (UT Centennial Commission Professor in the Liberal Arts), 'The Canadian Constitutional Crisis'

Sidney Monas (UT Professor of Slavic Languages and History), 'Paul Fussell and World War II'

James Fishkin (UT Darrell Royal Regents Chair in Ethics and American Society), 'Thought Experiments in Recent Oxford Philosophy'

Joseph Hamburger (Pelatiah Perit Professor of Political and Social Science, Yale University), 'How Liberal Was John Stuart Mill?'

Richard W. Clement (Special Collections Librarian, Kenneth Spencer Research Library, University of Kansas), 'Thomas James and the Bodleian Library: The Foundations of Scholarship'

Michael Yeats (Former Chairman of the Irish Senate and only son of the poet William Butler Yeats), 'Ireland and Europe'

Round Table Discussion on 'William H. McNeill's *Arnold J. Toynbee: A Life*': Standish Meacham (UT Dean of Liberal Arts), Peter Green (UT Dougherty Professor of Classics), Roger Louis (UT Kerr Professor), and Sidney Monas (UT Professor of Slavic Languages and History)

Jeffrey Meyers (Biographer and Professor of English, University of Colorado), 'Conrad and Jane Anderson'

Alan Frost (Professor of History, La Trobe University, Melbourne), 'The Explorations of Captain Cook'

Sarvepalli Gopal (Professor of History, Jawaharlal Nehru University, and Fellow of St. Antony's College, Oxford), 'The First Ten Years of Indian Independence'

Round Table Discussion on 'The Best and Worst Books of 1990': Alessandra Lippucci (UT Lecturer in Government), Roger Louis (UT Kerr Professor), Tom Staley (Director, HRHRC), Steve Weinberg (UT Welch Foundation Chair in Science Theory), and Paul Woodruff (UT Thompson Professor in the Humanities)

Spring Semester 1991

David Hollway (Prime Minister's Office, Government of Australia), 'Australia and the Gulf Crisis'

Diane Kunz (Yale University), 'British Post-War Sterling Crises'

Miguel Gonzalez-Gerth (UT Professor of Spanish Literature and HRHRC), 'T. E. Lawrence, Richard Aldington, and the Death of Heroes'

Robert Twombly (UT Professor of English), 'Religious Encounters with the Flesh in English Literature'

Alan Ryan (Princeton University), 'Bertrand Russell's Politics'

Hugh Kenner (Andrew Mellon Professor of the Humanities, The Johns Hopkins University, and Visiting Harry Ransom Professor), 'The State of English Poetry'

Patricia Burnham (UT American Studies), 'Anglo-American Art and the Struggle for Artistic Independence'

Round Table Discussion on 'The Churchill Tradition': Lord Blake (former Provost of Queen's College, Oxford), Lord Jenkins (Chancellor, Oxford University), Field Marshal Lord Carver (former Chief of the Defence Staff), Sir Michael Howard (former Regius Professor, Oxford, present Lovett Professor of Military and Naval History, Yale University), with a concluding comment by Winston S. Churchill, M.P.

Woodruff Smith (Professor of History, UT San Antonio), 'Why Do the British Put Sugar in their Tea?'

Peter Firchow (Professor of English, University of Minnesota), 'Aldous Huxley: The Poet as Centaur'

Irene Gendzier (Professor of History and Political Science, Boston University), 'British and American Middle Eastern Policies in the 1950s: Lebanon and Kuwait. Reflections on Past Experience and the Postwar Crisis in the Gulf'

John Train (*Harvard* Magazine and *Wall Street Journal*), 'Remarkable Catchwords in the City of London and on Wall Street'

Adam Sisman (Independent Writer, London), 'A. J. P. Taylor'

Roger Louis (UT Kerr Professor), 'The Young Winston'

Adrian Mitchell (Professor of English, Melbourne University, and Visiting Professor of English and Australian Studies), 'Claiming a Voice: Recent Non-Fiction Writing in Australia'

Bruce Hevly (Professor of History, University of Washington), 'Stretching Things Out versus Letting Them Slide: The Natural Philosophy of Ice in Edinburgh and Cambridge in the Nineteenth Century'

Henry Dietz (UT Professor of Government), 'Foibles and Follies in Sherlock's Great Game: Some Excesses of Holmesian Research'

Summer 1991

Roger Louis (UT Kerr Professor), and Ronald Robinson (Beit Professor of the History of the British Commonwealth, Oxford University, and Visiting Cline Professor), 'Harold Macmillan and the Dissolution of the British Empire'

Robert Treu (Professor of English, University of Wisconsin, Lacrosse), 'D. H. Lawrence and Graham Greene in Mexico'

Thomas Pinney (Chairman, Department of English, Pomona College), 'Kipling, India, and Imperialism'

Ronald Heiferman (Professor of History, Quinnipiac College), 'The Odd Couple: Winston Churchill and Chiang Kai-shek'

John Harty (Professor of English, Alice Lloyd College, Kentucky), 'The Movie and the Book: J. G. Ballard's *Empire of the Sun*'

A. B. Assensoh (Ghanaian Journalist and Professor of History, Southern University, Baton Rouge), 'Nkrumah'

Victoria Carchidi (Professor of English, Emory and Henry College), 'Lawrence of Arabia on a Camel, Thank God!'

James Gump (Chairman, Department of History, University of California, San Diego), 'The Zulu and the Sioux: The British and American Comparative Experience with the "Noble Savage"'

Fall Semester 1991

Round Table Discussion on Noel Annan's *Our Age:* Peter Green (UT Dougherty Professor of Classics), Robert D. King (UT Dean of Liberal Arts), Roger Louis (UT Kerr Professor), and Thomas F. Staley (Director, HRHRC)

Christopher Heywood (Okayama University, Japan), 'Slavery, Imagination, and the Brontës'

Harold L. Smith (University of Houston, Victoria), 'Winston Churchill and Women'

Krystyna Kujawinska-Courtney (University of Lodz), 'Shakespeare and Poland'

Ewell E. Murphy, Jr. (Baker & Botts, Houston), 'Cecil Rhodes and the Rhodes Scholarships'

I. N. Kimambo (University of Dar-es-Salaam), 'The District Officer in Tanganyika'

Hans Mark (Chancellor, UT System), 'The Pax Britannica and the Inevitable Comparison: Is There a Pax Americana? Conclusions from the Gulf War'

Richard Clutterbuck (Major-General, British Army, Ret.), 'British and American Hostages in the Middle East: Negotiating with Terrorists'

Elizabeth Hedrick (UT Assistant Professor of English), 'Samuel Johnson and Linguistic Propriety'

The Hon. Denis McLean (New Zealand Ambassador to the United States), 'Australia and New Zealand: The Nuisance of Nationalism'

Elizabeth Richmond (UT Assistant Professor of English), 'Submitting a Trifle for a Degree: Dramatic Productions at Oxford and Cambridge in the Age of Shakespeare'

Kenneth Warren, M.D. (Director for Science, Maxwell Macmillan), 'Tropical Medicine: A British Invention'

Adolf Wood (Deputy Editor of the *TLS*), 'The Golden Age of the *Times Literary Supplement*'

Eugene Walter (Poet and Novelist), 'Unofficial Poetry: Literary London in the 1940s and 1950s'

Sidney Monas (UT Professor of Slavic Languages and History), 'Images of Britain in the Poetry of World War II'

The St. Stephen's Madrigal Choir, 'Celebrating an English Christmas'

Spring Semester 1992

Jeremy Treglown (Critic and Author), 'Wartime Censorship and the Novel'

Toyin Falola (UT Professor of History), 'Nigerian Independence 1960'

Donald S. Lamm (President, W.W. Norton and Company), 'Publishing English History in America'

Colin Franklin (Publisher and Historian of the Book), 'The Pleasures of Eighteenth-Century Shakespeare'

Thomas F. Staley (Director, HRHRC), *'Fin de Siècle* Joyce: A Perspective on One Hundred Years'

Sarvepalli Gopal (Jawaharlal Nehru University), '"Drinking Tea with Treason": Halifax and Gandhi'

Michael Winship (UT Associate Professor of English), 'The History of the Book: Britain's Foreign Trade in Books in the Nineteenth Century'

Richard Lariviere (UT Professor of Sanskrit and Director of the Center for Asian Studies), 'British Law and Lawyers in India'

Round Table Discussion on A. S. Byatt's *Possession:* Janice Rossen (Visiting Scholar, HRHRC), John P. Farrell (UT Professor of English), and Roger Louis (UT Kerr Professor)

William H. McNeill (University of Chicago and former President of the American Historical Association), 'Arnold Toynbee's Vision of World History'

Derek Brewer (Master of Emmanuel College, Cambridge), 'The Interpretation of Fairy Tales: The Implications for English Literature, Anthropology, and History'

David Bradshaw (Fellow of Worcester College, Oxford), 'Aldous Huxley: Eugenics and the Rational State'

Steven Weinberg (Josey Regental Professor of Science), 'The British Style in Physics'

Sir David Williams (Vice-Chancellor, Cambridge University), 'Northern Ireland'

Summer 1992

R. A. C. Parker (Fellow of Queen's College, Oxford), 'Neville Chamberlain and Appeasement'

Adrian Wooldridge (Fellow of All Souls College, Oxford, and Staff Writer for *The Economist*), 'Reforming British Education: How It Happened and What America Can Learn'

Chris Wrigley (Professor of Modern British History, Nottingham University), 'A. J. P. Taylor: An English Radical and Modern Europe'

Fall Semester 1992

Round Table Discussion on E. M. Forster's *Howards End:* The Movie and the Book. Robert D. King (UT Liberal Arts), Roger Louis (UT Kerr Professor), Alessandra Lippucci (UT Government), and Thomas F. Staley (HRHRC)

Lord Skidelsky (Warwick University), 'Keynes and the Origins of the "Special Relationship"'

Sir Samuel Falle (former British Ambassador), 'Britain and the Middle East in the 1950s'

Ian MacKillop (University of Sheffield), 'We Were That Cambridge: F. R. Leavis and *Scrutiny*'

Walter Dean Burnham (Frank G. Erwin Centennial Chair in Government), 'The 1992 British Elections: Four-or-Five-More Tory Years?'

Don Graham (UT Professor of English), 'Modern Australian Literature and the Image of America'

Richard Woolcott (former Secretary of the Australian Department of Foreign Affairs), 'Australia and the Question of Cooperation or Contention in the Pacific'

Ian Willison (1992 Wiggins Lecturer, American Antiquarian Society), 'The History of the Book in Twentieth-Century Britain and America'

Iain Sproat, (Member of Parliament), 'P. G. Wodehouse and the War'

Standish Meacham (UT Sheffield Professor of History), 'The Crystal Palace'

Field Marshal Lord Carver (former Chief of the British Defence Staff), 'Wavell: A Reassessment'

Lesley Hall (Wellcome Institute for the History of Medicine, London), 'For Fear of Frightening the Horses: Sexology in Britain since William Acton'

Michael Fry (Director of International Relations, University of Southern California), 'Britain, the United Nations, and the Lebanon Crisis of 1958'

Brian Holden Reid (King's College, London), 'J. F. C. Fuller and the Revolution in British Military Thought'

Neil Parsons (University of London), '"Clicko" or Franz Taaibosch: A Bushman Entertainer in Britain, Jamaica, and the United States *c.* 1919–40'

John Hargreaves (Burnett-Fletcher Professor of History, Aberdeen University), 'God's Advocate: Lewis Namier and the History of Modern Europe'

Round Table Discussion on Robert Harris's *Fatherland:* Henry Dietz (UT Government), Robert D. King (UT Liberal Arts), Roger Louis (UT Kerr Professor), and Walter Wetzels (UT Germanic Languages)

Kevin Tierney (University of California), 'Robert Graves: An Outsider Looking In, or An Insider Who Escaped?'

Spring Semester 1993

Round Table Discussion on 'The Trollope Mystique': Janice Rossen (author of *Philip Larkin* and *The University in Modern Fiction*), Louise Weinberg (UT Angus G. Wynne Professor of Civil Jurisprudence), and Paul Woodruff (UT Director of the Plan II Honors Program and Thompson Professor of Philosophy)

Bruce Hunt (UT Associate Professor of History), 'To Rule the Waves: Cable Telegraphy and British Physics in the Nineteenth Century'

Martin Wiener (Jones Professor of History, Rice University), 'The Unloved State: Contemporary Political Attitudes in the Writing of Modern British History'

Elizabeth Dunn (HRHRC), 'Ralph Waldo Emerson and Ireland'

Jason Thompson (Western Kentucky University), 'Edward William Lane's "Description of Egypt"'

Sir Michael Howard (former Regius Professor of Modern History, Oxford University, present Lovett Professor of Military and Naval History, Yale University), 'Strategic Deception in the Second World War'

Gordon A. Craig (Sterling Professor of Humanities, Stanford University), 'Churchill'

Round Table Discussion on the Indian Mathematician Ramanujan: Robert D. King (UT Rapoport Professor of Liberal Arts), James W. Vick (Vice-President for Student Affairs and Professor of Mathematics), and Steven Weinberg (UT Regental Professor and Josey Chair in Physics)

Martha Merritt (UT Lecturer in Government), 'From Commonwealth to Commonwealth, and from Vauxhall to *Vokzal:* Russian Borrowing from Britain'

Sidney Monas (UT Professor of Slavic Languages and History), 'James Joyce and Russia'

Peter Marshall (Professor of History, King's College, London), 'Imperial Britain and the Question of National Identity'

Michael Wheeler (Professor of English and Director of the Ruskin Programme, Lancaster University), 'Ruskin and Gladstone'

Anthony Low (Smuts Professor of Commonwealth History and President of Clare College, Cambridge University), 'Britain and India in the Early 1930s: The British, American, French, and Dutch Empires Compared'

Summer 1993

Alexander Pettit (University of North Texas), 'Lord Bolingbroke's *Remarks on the History of England*'

Rose Marie Burwell (Northern Illinois University), 'The British Novel and Ernest Hemingway'

Richard Patteson (Mississippi State University), 'New Writing in the West Indies'

Richard Greene (Memorial University, Newfoundland), 'The Moral Authority of Edith Sitwell'

Fall Semester 1993

Round Table Discussion on 'The British and the Shaping of the American Critical Mind: Edmund Wilson, Part II': Roger Louis (UT Kerr

Professor), Elspeth Rostow (UT Stiles Professor in American Studies), Tom Staley (Director, HRHRC), and Robert Crunden (UT Professor of History and American Studies)

Roseanne Camacho (University of Rhode Island), 'Evelyn Scott: Towards an Intellectual Biography'

Christopher Heywood (Okayama University), 'The Brontës and Slavery'

Peter Gay (Sterling Professor of History, Yale University), 'The Cultivation of Hatred in England'

Linda Ferreira-Buckley (UT English) 'England's First English Department: Rhetoric and More Rhetoric'

Janice Rossen (Senior Research Fellow, HRHRC), 'British University Novels'

Ian Hancock (O Yanko Le Redzosko) (UT Professor of Linguistics and English), 'The Gypsy Image in British Literature'

James Davies (University College of Swansea), 'Dylan Thomas'

Jeremy Lewis (London Writer and Editor), 'Who Cares about Cyril Connolly?'

Sam Jamot Brown (British Studies), and Robert D. King (Linguistics), 'Scott and the Antarctic'

Martin Trump (University of South Africa), 'Nadine Gordimer's Social and Political Vision'

Richard Clogg (Professor of Balkan History, University of London), 'Britain and the Origins of the Greek Civil War'

Herbert J. Spiro (United States Ambassador, Ret.), 'The Warburgs: Anglo-American and German-Jewish Bankers'

Colin Franklin (Publisher and Antiquarian Bookseller), 'Lord Chesterfield: Stylist, Connoisseur of Manners, and Specialist in Worldly Advice'

Jeffrey Segall (Charles University, Prague), 'The Making of James Joyce's Reputation'

Rhodri Jeffreys-Jones (University of Edinburgh), 'The Myth of the Iron Lady: Margaret Thatcher and World Stateswomen'

John Rumrich (UT Associate Professor of English), 'Milton and Science: Gravity and the Fall'

J. D. Alsop (McMaster University), 'British Propaganda, Espionage, and Political Intrigue'

Round Table Discussion on 'The Best and the Worst Books of 1993': David Edwards (UT Government), Creekmore Fath (UT Liberal Arts Foundation), Betty Sue Flowers (UT English), and Sidney Monas (UT Professor of Slavic Languages and History)

Spring Semester 1994

Thomas F. Staley (Director, HRHRC), 'John Rodker: Poet and Publisher of Modernism'

Martha Fehsenfeld, and Lois More Overbeck (Emory University), 'The Correspondence of Samuel Beckett'

M. R. D. Foot (Historian and Editor), 'Lessons of War on War: The Influence of 1914–1918 on 1939–1945'

Round Table Discussion on 'Requiem for Canada?': David Braybrooke (UT Centennial Chair in Liberal Arts), Walter Dean Burnham (UT Frank Erwin Chair in Government), and Robert Crunden (UT Professor of American Studies)

Ross Terrill (Harvard University), 'Australia and Asia in Historical Perspective'

Sir Samuel Falle (British Ambassador and High Commissioner), 'The Morning after Independence: The Legacy of the British Empire'

Deborah Lavin (Principal of Trevelyan College, University of Durham), 'Lionel Curtis: Prophet of the British Empire'

Robin W. Doughty (UT Professor of Geography), 'Eucalyptus: And Not a Koala in Sight'

Al Crosby (UT Professor of American Studies and History), 'Captain Cook and the Biological Impact on the Hawaiian Islands'

Gillian Adams (Editor, *Children's Literature Association Quarterly*), 'Beatrix Potter and Her Recent Critics'

Lord Amery, 'Churchill's Legacy'

Christa Jansohn (University of Bonn), and Peter Green (Dougherty Professor of Classics) '*Lady Chatterley's Lover*'

R. A. C. Parker (Fellow of Queen's College, Oxford), 'Neville Chamberlain and the Coming of the Second World War'

John Velz (UT Professor of English), 'King Lear in Iowa: Jane Smiley's *A Thousand Acres*'

Jan Schall (University of Florida), 'British Spirit Photography'

Daniel Woolf (Dalhousie University), 'The Revolution in Historical Consciousness in England'

Fall Semester 1994

Kenneth O. Morgan (Vice-Chancellor, University of Wales), 'Welsh Nationalism'

Round Table Discussion on Michael Shelden's *Graham Greene: The Man Within*: Peter Green (UT Dougherty Professor of Classics), Roger Louis (UT Kerr Professor), and Thomas F. Staley (Director, HRHRC)

Robert D. King (Rapoport Regents Chair in Liberal Arts), 'The Secret War, 1939–1945'

Brian Boyd (Professor of English, University of Auckland), 'The Evolution of Shakespearean Dramatic Structure'

Lord Weatherill (former Speaker of the House of Commons), 'Thirty Years in Parliament'

Hans Mark (UT Professor of Aerospace Engineering), 'Churchill's Scientists'

Steven Weinberg (UT Josey Regental Professor of Science), 'The Test of War: British Strengths and Weaknesses in World War II'

Dennis Welland (Professor of English Literature and American Studies, University of East Anglia), 'Wilfred Owen and the Poetry of War'

Alan Frost (Professor of History, La Trobe University), 'The Bounty Mutiny and the British Romantic Poets'

W. O. S. Sutherland (UT Professor of English), 'Sir Walter Scott'

Hazel Rowley (Lecturer in Literary Studies, Deakin University, Melbourne), 'Christina Stead's "Other Country"'

Herman Bakvis (Professor of Government, Dalhousie University), 'The Future of Democracy in Canada and Australia'

Peter Stansky (Professor of History, Stanford University), 'George Orwell and the Writing of *Nineteen Eighty-Four*'

Henry Dietz (UT Associate Professor of Government), 'Sherlock Homes and Jack the Ripper'

James Coote (UT Professor of Architecture), 'Techniques of Illusion in British Architecture'

Round Table Discussion on 'The Best and Worst Books of 1994': Dean Burnham (UT Government), Alessandra Lippucci (UT Government), Roger Louis (UT Kerr Professor), Sidney Monas (UT Professor of Slavic Languages and History), and Janice Rossen (HRHRC)

Spring Semester 1995

Elizabeth Butler Cullingford (UT Professor of English), 'Anti-Colonial Metaphors in Contemporary Irish Literature'

Thomas M. Hatfield (UT Dean of Continuing Education), 'British and American Deception of the Germans in Normandy'

Gary P. Freeman (UT Associate Professor of Government), 'The Politics of Race and Immigration in Britain'

Donald G. Davis, Jr. (UT Professor in the Graduate School of Library and Information Science), 'The Printed Word in Sunday Schools in Nineteenth-Century England and the United States'

Brian Bremen (UT Assistant Professor of English), Healing Words: The Literature of Medicine and the Medicine of Literature'

Frances Karttunen (Linguistic Research Center), and Alfred W. Crosby (American Studies and History), 'British Imperialism and Creole Languages'

Paul Lovejoy (Professor of History, York University, Canada), 'British Rule in Africa: A Reassessment of Nineteenth-Century Colonialism'

Carol MacKay (UT Associate Professor of English), 'Creative Negativity in the Life and Work of Elizabeth Robins'

John Brokaw (UT Professor of Drama), 'The Changing Stage in London, 1790–1832'

Linda Colley (Richard M. Colgate Professor of History, Yale University), 'The Frontier in British History'

Iwan Morus (University of California, San Diego), 'Manufacturing Nature: Science, Technology, and Victorian Consumer Culture'

Brian Parker (Professor of English, University of Toronto), 'Jacobean Law: The Dueling Code and "A Faire Quarrel" (1617)'

Kate Frost (UT Professor of English), '"Jack Donne the Rake": Fooling around in the 1590s'

Mark Kinkead-Weekes (Professor of English, University of Kent), 'Beyond Gossip: D. H. Lawrence's Writing Life'

Summer 1995

S. P. Rosenbaum (Professor of English, University of Toronto), 'Leonard and Virginia Woolf at the Hogarth Press'

Maria X. Wells (Curator of Italian Collections, HRHRC), 'A Delicate Balance: Trieste 1945'

Kevin Tierney (Professor of Law, University of California at Berkeley), 'Personae in Twentieth Century British Autobiography'

Fall Semester 1995

Brian Levack (UT Professor of History), 'Witchcraft, Possession, and the Law in Jacobean England'

Janice Rossen (Senior Fellow, HRHRC), 'The Home Front: Anglo-American Women Novelists and World War II'

Dorothy Driver (Professor of English, University of Cape Town), 'Olive Schreiner's Novel *From Man to Man*'

Philip Ziegler (London), 'Mountbatten Revisited'

Joanna Hitchcock (Director, UT Press), 'British and American University Presses'

Samuel H. Beer (Eaton Professor of the Science of Government Emeritus, Harvard University), 'The Rise and Fall of Party Government in Britain and the United States, 1945–1995'

Richard Broinowski (Australian Ambassador to Mexico and Central America), 'Australia and Latin America'

John Grigg (London), 'Myths about the Approach to Indian Independence'

Round Table Discussion on *Measuring the Mind* (Adrian Wooldridge) and *The Bell Curve* (Richard J. Herrnstein and Charles Murray): David Edwards (UT Professor of Government), Sheldon Ekland-Olson (UT Dean of Liberal Arts), Joseph Horn (UT Professor of Psychology), and Robert D. King (UT Rapoport Chair in Liberal Arts)

Paul Addison (Professor of History, University of Edinburgh), 'British Politics in the Second World War'

John Sibley Butler (UT Professor of Sociology), 'Emigrants of the British Empire'

Round Table Discussion on the Movie *Carrington*: Peter Green (UT Dougherty Professor of Classics), Robin Kilson (UT Assistant Professor of History), Roger Louis (UT Kerr Professor), Sidney Monas (UT Professor of Slavic Languages and History), and Elizabeth Richmond-Garza (UT Assistant Professor of English)

Spring Semester 1996

Kevin Kenny (UT Assistant Professor of History), 'Making Sense of the Molly Maguires'

Brigadier Michael Harbottle (British Army), 'British and American Security in the Post-Cold War'

Carol MacKay (UT Professor of English), 'The Singular Double Vision of Photographer Julia Margaret Cameron'

John Ramsden (Professor of History, University of London), '"That Will Depend on Who Writes the History": Winston Churchill as His Own Historian'

Jack P. Greene (Andrew W. Mellon Professor in the Humanities, The Johns Hopkins University), 'The *British* Revolution in America'

Walter D. Wetzels (UT Professor of German), 'The Ideological Fallout in Germany of Two British Expeditions to Test Einstein's General Theory of Relativity'

Thomas Pinney (William M. Keck Distinguished Service Professor of English, Pomona College), 'In Praise of Kipling'

Michael Charlesworth (UT Assistant Professor of Art History), 'The English Landscape Garden'

Stephen Gray (South African Novelist), 'The Dilemma of Colonial Writers with Dual Identities'

Jeremy Black (Professor of History, University of Durham), 'Could the British Have Won the War of American Independence?'

Dagmar Hamilton (UT Professor of Public Affairs, LBJ School), 'Justice William O. Douglas and British Colonialism'

Gordon Peacock and Laura Worthen (UT Theater and Dance), 'Not Always a Green and Pleasant Land: Tom Stoppard's *Arcadia*'

Bernard Crick (Professor of Politics, University of London), 'Orwell and the Business of Biography'

Geoffrey Hartman (Sterling Professor of English, Yale University), 'The Sympathy Paradox: Poetry, Feeling, and Modern Cultural Morality'

Dave Oliphant (HRHRC), 'Jazz and Its British Acolytes'

R. W. B. Lewis (Professor of English and American Studies, Yale University), 'Henry James: The Victorian Scene'

Alan Spencer (Vice-President, Ford Motor Company), 'Balliol, Big Business, and Mad Cows'

Peter Quinn: A Discussion of His Novel, *Banished Children of Eve*

Summer 1996

Martin Stannard (Professor of English, Leicester University), 'Biography and Textual Criticism'

Diane Kunz (Associate Professor of History, Yale University), 'British Withdrawal East of Suez'

John Cell (Professor of History, Duke University), 'Who Ran the British Empire?'

Mark Jacobsen (US Marine Corps Command and Staff College), 'The North-West Frontier'

Theodore Vestal (Professor of Political Science, Oklahoma State University), 'Britain and Ethiopia'

Warren F. Kimball (Robert Treat Professor of History, Rutgers University), 'A Victorian Tory: Churchill, the Americans, and Self-Determination'

Louise B. Williams (Assistant Professor of History, Lehman College, The City University of New York), 'British Modernism and Fascism'

Fall Semester 1996

Elizabeth Richmond-Garza (UT Associate Professor of English and Comparative Literature), 'The New Gothic: Decadents for the 1990s'

Robin Kilson (UT Assistant Professor of History), 'The Politics of Captivity: The British State and Prisoners of War in World War I'

Sir Brian Fall (Principal of Lady Margaret Hall, Oxford), 'What does Britain Expect from the European Community, the United States, and the Commonwealth?'

Roger Louis (UT Kerr Professor), 'Harold Macmillan and the Middle East Crisis of 1958'

Ian Willison (former head of the Rare Books Branch, British Museum, and Editor of *The Cambridge History of the Book in Britain*), 'The History of the Book and the Cultural and Literary History of the English-Speaking World'

Walter L. Arnstein (Jubilee Professor of the Liberal Arts and Sciences, University of Illinois), 'Queen Victoria's Other Island'

Noel Annan (London), '*Our Age* Revisited'

Michael Cohen (Lazarus Philips Professor of History, Bar-Ilan University, Tel Aviv), 'The Middle East and the Cold War: Britain, the United States, and the Soviet Union'

Reba Soffer (Professor of History, California State University, Northridge), 'Catholicism in England: Was it Possible to be a Good Catholic, a Good Englishman, and a Good Historian?'

Wilson Harris (Poet and Novelist), 'The Mystery of Consciousness: Cross-Cultural Influences in the Caribbean, Britain, and the United States'

H. S. Barlow (Singapore), 'British Malaya in the late Nineteenth Century'

Donald G. Davis, Jr. (UT Professor of Library and Information Science), 'British Destruction of Chinese Books in the Peking Siege of 1900'

Round Table Discussion on the film *Michael Collins*: Elizabeth Cullingford (UT Professor of English), Kevin Kenny (UT Assistant Professor of History), Robin Kilson (UT Assistant Professor of History), and Roger Louis (UT Kerr Professor)

A. G. Hopkins (Smuts Professor of Commonwealth History, University of Cambridge), 'From Africa to Empire'

The Austin Chapter of the Society for the Preservation and Encouragement of Barber Shop Quartet Singing in America

Spring Semester 1997

Round Table Discussion on 'T. S. Eliot and Anti-Semitism': Robert D. King (UT Rapoport Chair in Jewish Studies), Sidney Monas (UT Professor of Slavic Languages and History), and Thomas F. Staley (Director, HRHRC)

Phillip Herring (Professor Emeritus of English, University of Wisconsin-Madison), 'Djuna Barnes and T. S. Eliot: The Story of a Friendship'

Bryan Roberts (UT Smith Chair in United States-Mexican Relations), 'British Sociology and British Society'

Andrew Roberts (London), 'The Captains and the Kings Depart: Lord Salisbury's Skeptical Imperialism'

Colin Franklin (London), 'In a Golden Age of Publishing, 1950–1970'

Susan Pedersen (Professor of History, Harvard University), 'Virginia Woolf, Eleanor Rathbone, and the Problem of Appeasement'

Andrew Seaman (Saint Mary's University, Halifax, Nova Scotia), 'Thomas Raddall: A Novelist's View of Nova Scotia during the American Revolution'

Gordon Peacock (UT Frank C. Erwin Professor of Drama), 'Noel Coward: A Master Playwright, a Talented Actor, a Novelist and Diarist: Or a Peter Pan for the Twentieth Century?'

Roland Oliver (Professor of African History, School of Oriental and African Studies, University of London), 'The Battle for African History, 1947–1966'

Alistair Horne (St. Antony's College, Oxford), 'Harold Macmillan's Fading Reputation'

Richard Begam (Professor of English, University of Wisconsin, Madison), 'Samuel Beckett and the Debate on Humanism'

Christopher Waters (Associate Professor of History, Williams College), 'Delinquents, Perverts, and the State: Psychiatry and the Homosexual Desire in the 1930s'

Sami Zubaida (University of London), 'Ernest Gellner and Islam'

Walter Dean Burnham (UT Frank C. Erwin Chair in Government), 'Britain Votes: The 1997 General Election and Its Implications'

Fall Semester 1997

Judith Brown (Beit Professor of the History of the British Commonwealth, Oxford University), 'Gandhi—A Victorian Gentleman'

Thomas Cable (UT Blumberg Professor of English), 'Hearing and Revising the History of the English Language'

Round Table Discussion on 'The Death of Princess Diana': Judith Brown (Oxford), David Edwards (UT Professor of Government), Elizabeth Richmond-Garza (UT Associate Professor of English),

Anne Baade (British Studies), Sandy Lippucci (UT Government), and Kevin Kenny (UT Associate Professor of History)

David Hunter (Music Librarian, Fine Arts Library), 'Handel and His Patrons'

Anne Kane (UT Assistant Professor of Sociology), 'The Current Situation in Ireland'

James S. Fishkin (UT Darrell K. Royal Regents Chair in Ethics in American Society), 'Power and the People: The Televised Deliberative Poll in the 1997 British General Election'

Howard D. Weinbrot (Vilas Research Professor of English, University of Wisconsin, Madison), 'Jacobitism in Eighteenth-Century Britain'

J. C. Baldwin, M.D. (Houston), 'The Abdication of King Edward VIII'

Kenneth E. Carpenter (Harvard University), 'Library Revolutions Past and Present'

Akira Iriye (Professor of History, Harvard University), 'Britain, Japan, and the International Order after World War I'

Anthony Hobson (London), 'Reminiscences of British Authors and the Collecting of Contemporary Manuscripts'

David Killingray (Professor of History, University of London), 'The British in the West Indies'

Alan Knight (Professor of Latin American History, Oxford University), 'British Imperialism in Latin America'

Round Table Discussion on King Lear in Iowa: the film '*A Thousand Acres*': Linda Ferreira-Buckley (UT Associate Professor of English), Elizabeth Richmond-Garza (UT Associate Professor of English), Helena Woodard (UT Assistant Professor of English), and John Velz (UT Professor of English)

Timothy Lovelace (UT Assistant Professor of Music) and the Talisman Trio

Spring Semester 1998

Richard Ollard (Biographer and Publisher), 'A. L. Rowse: Epitome of the Twentieth Century'

Round Table Discussion of Arundhati Roy's *The God of Small Things*: Phillip Herring (HRHRC, Professor Emeritus of English, University of Wisconsin), Brian Trinque (UT Economics), Kamala Visweswaran (UT Anthropology), and Robert Hardgrave (UT Government)

Jonathan Schneer (Professor of History, Georgia Institute of Technology), 'London in 1900: The Imperial Metropolis'

Trevor Burnard (Senior Lecturer in History, University of Canterbury, New Zealand), 'Rioting in Goatish Embraces: Marriage and the Failure of White Settlement in British Jamaica'

Felipe Fernández-Armesto (Oxford University), 'British Traditions in Comparative Perspective'

Michael Mann (Professor of Sociology, University of California, Los Angeles), 'The Broader Significance of Labour's Landslide Victory of 1997'

Dane Kennedy (Professor of History, University of Nebraska at Lincoln), 'White Settlers in Colonial Kenya and Rhodesia'

Round Table Discussion on 'Noel Annan, Keynes, and Bloomsbury': Jamie Galbraith (UT LBJ School), Elspeth Rostow (UT LBJ School), and Walt Rostow (UT Professor of Economics and History)

Lisa Moore (UT Associate Professor of English), 'British Studies—Lesbian Studies: A Dangerous Intimacy?'

James Gibbs (University of the West of England), 'Wole Soyinka: The Making of a Playwright'

Marilyn Butler (Rector of Exeter College, Oxford), 'About the House: Jane Austen's Anthropological Eye'

R. J. Q. Adams (Professor of History, Texas A&M University), 'Britain and Ireland, 1912–1922'

John M. Carroll (UT Asian Studies), 'Nationalism and Identity in pre-1949 Hong Kong'

Round Table Discussion on the Irish Referendum: Anne Kane (UT Sociology), Kevin Kenny (UT History), Roger Louis (UT Kerr Professor), and Jennifer O'Conner (UT History)

Fall Semester 1998

Louise Hodgden Thompson (UT Government), 'Origins of the First World War: The Anglo-German Naval Armaments Race'

John P. Farrell (UT Professor of English), 'Thomas Hardy in Love'

Carol MacKay (UT Professor of English), 'The Multiple Conversions of Annie Besant'

Roy Foster (Carroll Professor of Irish History, Oxford University), 'Yeats and Politics, 1898–1921'

Robert Olwell (UT History), 'British Magic Kingdoms: Imagination, Speculation, and Empire in Florida'

Sara H. Sohmer (Lecturer in History, Texas Christian University), 'The British in the South Seas: Exploitation and Trusteeship in Fiji'

Helena Woodard (UT Associate Professor of English), 'Politics of Race in the Eighteenth Century: Pope and the Humanism of the Enlightenment'

D. A. Smith (Grinnell College), 'Impeachment? Parliamentary Government in Britain and France in the Nineteenth Century'

Round Table Discussion on the Irish Insurrection of 1798: Robert Olwell (UT History), Lisa Moore (UT English), and Kevin Kenny (UT History)

Robert D. King (UT Rapoport Regents Chair of Jewish Studies), 'The Accomplishments of Raja Rao: The Triumph of the English Language in India'

Donald G. Davis, Jr. (UT Professor of Library and Information Science and History), 'Religion and Empire'

A. D. Roberts (Professor of History, School of Oriental and African Studies, University of London), 'The Awkward Squad: African Students in American Universities before 1940'

Chaganti Vijayasree (Professor of English, Osmania University, Hyderabad), 'The Empire and Victorian Poetry'

Martha Deatherage (UT Music), 'Christmas Celebration: Vauxhall Gardens'

Spring Semester 1999

Round Table Discussion on *Regeneration,* Pat Barker's Trilogy on the First World War: Betty Sue Flowers (UT Professor of English), Roger Louis (UT Kerr Professor), and Paul Woodruff (UT Professor in the Humanities)

Alistair Campbell-Dick (Founding Member of British Studies and Director of Cybertime Corporation), 'The Immortal Memory of Robert Burns'

Hugh Macrae Richmond (Professor of English and Drama, University of California at Berkeley), 'Why Rebuild Shakespeare's Globe Theatre?'

Ralph Austen (Professor of History, University of Chicago), 'Britain and the Global Economy: A Post-Colonial Perspective'

Jerome Meckier (Professor of English, University of Kentucky), 'Aldous Huxley's American Experience'

Peter Marsh (Professor of History, Syracuse University), 'Joseph Chamberlain as an Entrepreneur in Politics: Writing the Life of a Businessman Turned Statesman'

Roger Adelson (Professor of History, Arizona State University), 'Winston Churchill and the Middle East'

Margot Finn (Associate Professor of History, Emory University), 'Law, Debt and Empire: The Calcutta Court of Conscience'

Fred M. Leventhal (Professor of History, Boston University), 'The Projection of Britain in America before the Second World War'

Larry Siedentop (Fellow of Keble College, Oxford University), 'Reassessing the Life of Isaiah Berlin'

Ross Terrill (Research Associate in Government, Harvard University), 'R. H. Tawney's Vision of Fellowship'

Juliet Fleming (University Lecturer of English, Cambridge University), 'The Ladies' Shakespeare'

Elizabeth Fernea (UT English and Middle Eastern Studies), 'The Victorian Lady Abroad: In Egypt with Sophia Poole and in Texas with Mrs. E. M. Houstoun'

Richard Schoch (University of London), 'The Respectable and the Vulgar: British Theater in the Mid-Nineteenth Century'

Ferdinand Mount (Editor, *TLS*), 'Politics and the *Times Literary Supplement*'

Fall Semester 1999

Round Table Discussion on the Boer War, 1899–1902: Barbara Harlow (UT Professor of English), John Lamphear (UT History), and Roger Louis (UT Kerr Professor)

Sharon Arnoult (Assistant Professor of History, Southwest Texas State University), 'Charles I: His Life after Death'

Kenneth O. Morgan (Fellow of The Queen's College, Oxford and former Vice Chancellor, University of Wales), 'Lloyd George, Keir Hardie and the Importance of the "Pro-Boers"'

Richard Cleary (UT Architecture), 'Walking the Walk to Talk the Talk: The Promenade in Eighteenth-Century France and England'

Keith Kyle (Journalist and Historian), 'From Suez to Kenya as Journalist and as Historian'

Malcolm Hacksley (Director of the National English Literary Museum, Grahamstown, South Africa), 'Planting a Museum, Cultivating a Literature'

Ben Pimlott (Warden of Goldsmiths College, University of London), 'The Art of Writing Political Biography'

Geraldine Heng (UT Associate Professor of English), 'Cannibalism, the First Crusade, and the Genesis of Medieval Romance'

A. P. Martinich (UT Philosophy), 'Thomas Hobbes: Lifelong and Enduring Controversies'

Round Table Discussion on Lyndall Gordon's *T. S. Eliot: An Imperfect Life*: Brian Bremen (UT Associate Professor of English), Thomas Cable (UT Blumberg Professor of English), Elizabeth Richmond-Garza (UT Professor of Comparative Literature), and Thomas F. Staley (Director, HRHRC)

Shula Marks (Professor of History, School of Oriental and African Studies, University of London), 'Smuts, Race, and the Boer War'

Henry Dietz (UT Professor of Government), '*The Hound of the Baskervilles*'

Spring Semester 2000

Susan Napier (UT Associate Professor of Asian Studies), 'The Cultural Phenomenon of the Harry Potter Fantasy Novels'

Round Table Discussion on *Dutch: A Memoir of Ronald Reagan:* A Chapter in the 'Special Relationship'?: Roger Louis (UT Kerr Professor), Harry Middleton (Director of the LBJ Library), and Elspeth Rostow (LBJ School)

Norman Rose (Chaim Weizmann Chair of International Relations, Hebrew University, Jerusalem), 'Harold Nicolson: A Curious and Colorful Life'

Charlotte Canning (UT Theater History and Theory), 'Feminists Perform Their Past'

John Ripley (Greenshields Emeritus Professor of English, McGill University), 'The Sound of Sociology: H. B. Tree's *Merchant of Venice*'

Sergei Horuji (Russian Academy of Sciences), 'James Joyce in Russia'

Janice Rossen (Biographer and Independent Scholar), 'Philip Toynbee'

Max Egremont (Novelist and Biographer), 'Siegfried Sassoon's War'

Paul Taylor (Professor of International Relations, London School of Economics and Political Science), 'Britain and Europe'

Lord Selborne (President, Royal Geographical Society), 'The Royal Geographical Society: Exploration since 1830'

Craig MacKenzie (Department of English, Rand Afrikaans University, Johannesburg), 'The Mythology of the Boer War: Herman Charles Bosman and the Challenge to Afrikaner Romanticism'

Peter Catterall (Director, Institute of Contemporary British History, London), 'Reform of the House of Lords'

Bernard Porter (Professor of Modern History, University of Newcastle), 'Pompous and Circumstantial: Sir Edward Elgar and the British Empire'

Craufurd D. Goodwin (James B. Duke Professor of Economics, Duke University), 'Roger Fry and the Debate on "Myth" in the Bloomsbury Group'

Jamie Belich (Chair in History, University of Auckland), 'Neo-Britains? The "West" in Nineteenth-Century Australia, New Zealand, and America'

Round Table Discussion on Norman Davies, *The Isles*: Sharon Arnoult (Midwestern State University, Wichita Falls), Raymond Douglas (Colgate University), Walter Johnson (Northwestern Oklahoma State University), David Leaver (Raymond Walters College, Cincinnati), and John Cell (Duke University)

Fall Semester 2000

Round Table discussion on Paul Scott, the Raj Quartet, and the Beginning of British Studies at UT—Peter Green (UT Dougherty Professor of Classics), Robert Hardgrave (UT Professor of Government and Asian Studies), and Roger Louis (UT Kerr Professor)

Suman Gupta (The Open University), 'T. S. Eliot as Publisher'

Jeffrey Cox (University of Iowa), 'Going Native: Missionaries in India'

Kevin Kenny (Boston College), 'Irish Nationalism: The American Dimension'

Joseph Kestner (University of Tulsa), 'Victorian Battle Art'

James E. Cronin (Boston College), 'From Old to New Labour: Politics and Society in the Forging of the "Third" Way'

Gerald Moore (Mellon Visiting Research Fellow, HRHRC), 'When Caliban Crossed the Atlantic'

Richard Howard (Shakespearean Actor, London) '"Health and Long Life to You": A Program of Irish Poetry and Prose Presented by an Englishman, with Anecdotes'

Stephen Foster (Northern Illinois University), 'Prognosis Guarded: The Probable Decolonization of the British Era in American History'

Frank Prochaska (University of London), 'Of Crowned and Uncrowned Republics: George V and the Socialists'

Robert H. Abzug (UT History and American Studies), 'Britain, South Africa, and the American Civil Rights Movement'

Paula Bartley (Visiting Research Fellow, HRHRC), 'Emmeline Pankhurst'

Thomas Jesus Garza (UT Associate Professor of Slavic Languages), 'A British Vampire's Christmas'

Spring Semester 2001

Betty Sue Flowers (UT Distinguished Teaching Professor), 'From Robert Browning to James Bond'

Larry Carver (UT Professor of English), 'Feliks Topolski at the Ransom Center'

Oscar Brockett (UT Distinguished Teaching Professor), 'Lilian Baylis and England's National Theatres'

Linda Levy Peck (George Washington University), 'Luxury and War'

R. James Coote (UT Architecture), 'Architectural Revival in Britain'

Adam Roberts (Oxford University), 'Britain and the Creation of the United Nations'

Mark Southern (UT Professor of Germanic Studies), 'Words over Swords: Language and Tradition in Celtic Civilization'

Round Table discussion on Ben Rogers *A Life of A. J. Ayer*: David Braybrooke (UT Government and Philosophy), Al Martinich (UT History and Philosophy), David Sosa (UT Philosophy), and Paul Woodruff (UT Plan II and Philosophy)

Bartholomew Sparrow (UT Government), 'British and American Expansion: The Political Foundations'

Jose Harris (Oxford University), 'Writing History during the Second World War'

Charles Loft (Westminster College), 'Off the Rails? The Historic Junctions in Britain's Railway Problem'

Dan Jacobson (University of London), 'David Irving and Holocaust Denial'—Special Lecture

Dan Jacobson (University of London), 'Self-Redemption in the Victorian Novel'

George S. Christian (UT British Studies), 'The Comic Basis of the Victorian Novel'

Paul Taylor (London *Independent*), 'Rediscovering a Master Dramatist: J. B. Priestley'

Fall Semester 2001

Round Table Discussion on Ray Monk's Biography of Bertrand Russell, *The Ghost of Madness*: Al Martinich (UT History and Philosophy), David Sosa (UT Philosophy and British Studies), and Paul Woodruff (UT Plan II and Philosophy)

Alex Danchev (Keele University), 'The Alanbrooke Diaries'

Robert M. Worcester (LSE and Market Opinion Research International), 'Britain and the European Union'

Martha Ann Selby (UT Associate Professor of Asian Studies), 'The Cultural Legacy of British Clubs: Manners, Memory, and Identity among the New Club-Wallahs in Madras'

Roger Owen (Harvard University), 'Lord Cromer and Wilfrid Blunt in Egypt'

James Loehlin (UT Associate Professor of English), 'A Midsummer Night's Dream'

Jeffrey Meyers (Biographer), 'Somerset Maugham'

Elspeth Rostow (UT LBJ School), 'From American Studies to British Studies—And Beyond'

Nicholas Westcott (British Embassy), 'The Groundnut Scheme: Socialist Imperialism at Work in Africa'

Round Table Discussion on 'The Anglo-American Special Relationship': Gary Freeman (UT Government), Roger Louis (UT Kerr Professor), Elspeth Rostow (UT American Studies), and Michael Stoff (UT History)

Christopher Heywood (Sheffield University), 'The Brontës: A Personal History of Discovery and Interpretation'

James Bolger (New Zealand Ambassador and former Prime Minister), 'Whither New Zealand? Constitutional, Political, and International Quandaries'

R. J. Q. Adams (Texas A&M University), 'Arthur James Balfour and Andrew Bonar Law: A Study in Contrasts'

Ferdinand Mount (Editor, *Times Literary Supplement*), 'British Culture since the Eighteenth Century: An Open Society?'

James Loehlin (UT English), 'A Child's Christmas in Wales'

Spring Semester 2002

Round Table Discussion on Adam Sisman, *Boswell's Presumptuous Task*: Samuel Baker (UT English), Linda Ferreira-Buckley (UT English), Julie Hardwick (UT History), and Helena Woodward (UT English)

A. G. Hopkins (UT History), 'Globalization: The British Case'

Susan Napier (UT Professor of Asian Studies), 'J. R. R. Tolkein and the Lord of the Rings: Fantasy as Retreat or Fantasy as Engagement?'

Wilfrid Prest (Adelaide University), 'South Australia's Paradise of Dissent'

Tom Palaima (UT Professor of Classics), 'Terence Rattigan's *Browning Version*'

Alan H. Nelson (University of California at Berkeley), 'Thoughts on Elizabethan Authorship'

Penelope Lively (London), 'Changing Perceptions of British and English Identity'

Hans Mark (UT Professor of Aerospace Engineering), 'The Falklands War'

David Butler (Oxford University), 'Psephology—or, the Study of British Elections'

Robert L. Hardgrave (UT Professor of Government), 'From West Texas to South India and British Studies'

Geoffrey Wheatcroft (London), 'The Englishness of English Sport'

Eileen Cleere (Southwestern University), 'Dirty Pictures: John Ruskin and the Victorian Sanitation of Fine Art'

Jamie Belich (Auckland University), 'A Comparison of Empire Cities: New York and London, Chicago and Melbourne'

Churchill Conference—Geoffrey Best (Oxford), Sir Michael Howard (Oxford), Warren Kimball (Rutgers), Philip Ziegler (London), Roger Louis (UT Kerr Professor)

Catherine Maxwell (University of London), 'Swinburne's Poetry and Criticism'

Round Table Discussion on Churchill and the Churchill Conference: Rodrigo Gutierrez (UT History), Adrian Howkins (UT History), Heidi Juel (UT English), David McCoy (UT Government), Joe Moser (UT English), Jeff Rutherford (UT History), Bill Livingston (UT Senior Vice-President), and Roger Louis (UT Kerr Professor)

Fall Semester 2002

James K. Galbraith (UT LBJ School of Public Affairs), 'The Enduring Importance of John Maynard Keynes'

Michael Green (University of Natal), 'Agatha Christie in South Africa'

Sumit Ganguly (UT Asian Studies), 'Kashmir: Origins and Consequences of Conflict'

Margaret MacMillan (University of Toronto), 'At the Height of His Power: Lloyd George in 1919'

Douglas Bruster (UT English), 'Why We Fight: *Much Ado About Nothing* and the West'

John Darwin (Oxford University), 'The Decline and Rise of the British Empire: John Gallagher as an Historian of Imperialism'

Kevin Kenny (Boston College), 'The Irish in the British Empire'

David Wallace (University of Pennsylvania), 'A Chaucerian's Tale of Surinam'

Peter Bowler (Queen's University, Belfast), 'Scientists and the Popularization of Science in Early Twentieth-Century Britain'

Bernardine Evaristo (London), "A Feisty, Funky Girl in Roman England'

Frank Moorhouse (Australia), 'Dark Places and Grand Days'

David Cannadine (University of London), 'C. P. Snow and the Two Cultures'

Round Table Discussion on 'Edmund S. Morgan's Biography of Benjamin Franklin'—Carolyn Eastman (UT History), Bruce Hunt (UT History), Roger Louis (UT Kerr Professor), Alan Tully (UT History)

Mark Lawrence (UT History), 'The Strange Silence of Cold War England: Britain and the Vietnam War'

Tom Cable (UT English), 'The Pleasures of Remembering Poetry'

Spring Semester 2003

Round Table Discussion on 'W. G. Sebald—*Rings of Saturn*': Brigitte Bauer (UT French and Italian), Sidney Monas (UT History and Slavic

Languages), Elizabeth Richmond-Garza (UT English and Comparative Literature), Walter Wetzels (UT Germanic Studies)

Diana Davis (UT Geography), 'Brutes, Beasts, and Empire: A Comparative Study of the British and French Experience'

Colin Franklin (Publisher), 'Rosalind Franklin—Variously Described as "The Dark Lady of DNA" and "The Sylvia Plath of Molecular Biology"'

Sidney Monas (History and Slavic Languages), 'A Life of Irish Literature and Russian Poetry, Soviet Politics and International History'

Neville Hoad (UT English), 'Oscar Wilde in America'

Selina Hastings (London), 'Rosamond Lehman: Eternal Exile'

Bernard Wasserstein (Glasgow University), 'The British in Palestine: Reconsiderations'

Anne Chisholm (London), 'Frances Partridge: Last of the Bloomsberries'

Philip Morgan (The Johns Hopkins University), 'The Black Experience and the British Empire'

Jeremy duQuesnay Adams (Southern Methodist University), 'Joan of Arc and the English'

Didier Lancien (University of Toulouse), 'Churchill and de Gaulle'

Avi Shlaim (Oxford University), 'The Balfour Declaration and its Consequences'

Martin J. Wiener (Rice University), 'Murder and the Modern British Historian'

Winthrop Wetherbee (Cornell University), 'The Jewish Impact on Medieval Literature: Chaucer, Boccaccio, and Dante'

Philippa Levine (University of Southern California), 'Sex and the British Empire'

Summer 2003

Donald G. Davis, Jr. (UT History and School of Information), 'Life without British Studies is Like . . .'

Kurth Sprague (UT English and American Studies), 'Literature, Horses, and Scandal at UT'

David Evans (UT Astronomy), 'An Astronomer's Life in South Africa and Texas'

Tom Hatfield (UT Continuing Education), 'Not Long Enough! Half a Century at UT'

Fall Semester 2003

Richard Oram (HRHRC), 'Evelyn Waugh: Collector and Annotator'

Round Table Discussion on 'Booker Prize Winner James Kelman: Adapting a Glasgow Novel for the Texas Stage': James Kelman (Glasgow), Mia Carter (UT English), Kirk Lynn, and Dikran Utidjian

Simon Green (All Souls College, Oxford University), 'The Strange Death of Puritan England, 1914–1945'

Elizabeth Richmond-Garza (UT English and Comparative Literature), '*Measure for Measure*'

Lewis Hoffacker (US Ambassador), 'From the Congo to British Studies'

A. P. Thornton (University of Toronto), 'Wars Remembered, Revisited, and Reinvented'

Deryck Schreuder (University of Western Australia), 'The Burden of the British Past in Australia'

Robert Mettlen (Lamar Centennial Professor), 'From Birmingham to British Studies'

Paul Schroeder (University of Illinois), 'The Pax Britannica and the Pax Americana: Empire, Hegemony, and the International System'

Ferdinand Mount (London), 'A Time to Dance: Anthony Powell's *Dance to the Music of Time* and the Twentieth Century in Britain'

Brian Bond (University of London), '*Oh! What a Lovely War*: History and Popular Myth in Late-Twentieth Century Britain'

Wendy Frith (Bradford College, England), 'The Speckled Monster: Lady Mary Wortley Montagu and the Battle against Smallpox'

Harry Middleton (UT LBJ Library), 'The Road to the White House'

Jeremy Lewis (London), 'Tobias Smollett'

Christian Smith (Austin, Texas), 'Christmas Readings'

Spring Semester 2004

Round Table Discussion on 'The Pleasures of Reading Thackeray': Carol Mackay (UT English), Judith Fisher (Trinity University), George Christian (British Studies)

Thomas F. Staley (HRHRC), '"Corso e Recorso:" A Journey through Academe'

Patrick O'Brien (London School of Economics), 'The Pax Britanica, American Hegemony, and the International Order, 1793–2004'

Michael Wheeler (former Director of Chawton House Library), 'England Drawn and Quartered: Cultural Crisis in the Mid-Nineteenth Century'

Walter Wetzels (UT Germanic Studies), 'Growing Up in Nazi Germany, and later American Adventures'

Kathleen Wilson (State University of New York, Stony Brook), 'The Colonial State and Governance in the Eighteenth Century'

Elizabeth Fernea (UT English and Middle Eastern Studies), 'Encounters with Imperialism'

Chris Dunton (National University of Lesotho), 'Newspapers and Colonial Rule in Africa'

Miguel Gonzalez-Gerth (UT Spanish and Portuguese), 'Crossing Geographical and Cultural Borders—and Finally Arriving at British Studies'

Peter Stansky (Stanford University), 'Bloomsbury in Ceylon'

Round Table Discussion on 'The Crimson Petal and the White': John Farrell (UT English), Betty Sue Flowers (LBJ Library), Roger Louis (UT Kerr Professor), Paul Neimann (UT English)

Ann Curthoys (Australian National University), 'The Australian History Wars'

Martha Ann Selby (UT Asian Studies), 'Against the Grain: On Finding My
    Voice in India'
Steven Isenberg (UT Visiting Professor of Humanities), 'A Life in Our
    Times'

Summer 2004

Carol Mackay (UT English), 'My Own Velvet Revolution'
Erez Manela (Harvard University), 'The "Wilsonian Moment" in India and
    the Crisis of Empire in 1919'
Scott Lucas (Birmingham University), '"A Bright Shining Mecca": British
    Culture and Political Warfare in the Cold War and Beyond'
Monica Belmonte (US Department of State), 'Before Things Fell Apart:
    The British Design for the Nigerian State'
Dan Jacobson (London), 'Philip Larkin's "Elements"'
Bernard Porter (University of Newcastle), '"'Oo Let 'Em In?" Asylum
    Seekers and Terrorists in Britan, 1850-1914'

Fall Semester 2004

Richard Drayton (Cambridge University), 'Anglo-American "Liberal"
    Imperialism, British Guiana, 1953–64, and the World Since
    September 11'
David Washbrook (Oxford University), 'Living on the Edge: Anxiety and
    Identity in "British" Calcutta, 1780–1930'
Joanna Hitchcock (University of Texas Press), 'An Accidental Publisher'
Alan Friedman (UT English), '*A Midsummer Night's Dream*'
Antony Best (London School of Economics), 'British Intellectuals and
    East Asia in the Inter-war Years'
John Farrell (UT English), 'Beating a Path from Brooklyn to Austin'
Christopher Middleton (UT Liberal Arts), 'Relevant to England—A
    Reading of Poems'
Gail Minault (UT History and Asian Studies), 'Growing Up Bilingual and
    Other (Mis)adventures in Negotiating Cultures'
Roger Louis (Kerr Professor of English History and Cultures), 'Escape
    from Oklahoma'
John Trimble (UT English), 'Writing with Style'
Niall Ferguson (Harvard University), 'Origins of the First World War'
James Hopkins (Southern Methodist University), 'George Orwell and the
    Spanish Civil War: The Case of Nikos Kazantzakis'
James Currey (London), 'Africa Writes Back: Publishing the African
    Writers Series at Heinemann'
Sidney Monas (UT History and Slavic Languages), 'A Jew's Christmas'
Geoffrey Wheatcroft (London), '"In the Advance Guard": Evelyn Waugh's
    Reputation'

Spring Semsester 2005

Katharine Whitehorn (London), 'It Didn't *All* Start in the Sixties'

Gertrude Himmelfarb (Graduate School of the City University of New York), 'The Whig Interpretation of History'

Kurt Heinzelman (UT English and HRHRC), 'Lord Byron and the Invention of Celebrity'

Brian Levack (UT History), 'Jesuits, Lawyers, and Witches'

Richard Cleary (UT Architecture), 'British Influences on UT Architecture'

Edward I. Steinhart (Texas Tech University), 'White Hunters in British East Africa, 1895–1914'

Don Graham (UT English), 'The Drover's Wife: An Australian Archetype'

Anthony Smith (London), 'The Craftsmanship of Tom Stoppard'

Paul Woodruff (UT Philosophy and Plan II), 'A Case of Anglophilia—and Partial Recovery—Being an Account of My Life, with Special Attention to the Influence of England upon My Education'

Toyin Falola (UT History), 'Footprints of the Ancestors'

Robert Abzug (UT History), 'The History of British Psychiatry'

Deirdre McMahon (Mary Immaculate College, University of Limerick), 'Ireland and the Empire-Commonwealth 1918–1972'

James Coote (UT Architecture), 'Sir Edwin Lutyens and the Viceroy's House'

Jay Clayton (Vanderbilt University), 'The Dickens Tape: Lost and Found Sound before Recording'

A. G. Hopkins (UT History), '"Crooked Like a Stick in Water": A Fractured Autobiography'

Christopher Ricks (Oxford University), 'The Force of Poetry'